HOTEL MARKETING

S.M. JHA *Ph.D., D.Lit.*
Professor,
Department of Commerce and Business Administration,
L.N. Mithila University,
Darbhanga - 846008.
India.

AF520027

Third Revised & Enlarged Edition : 2012

MUMBAI • NEW DELHI • NAGPUR • BENGALURU • HYDERABAD • CHENNAI • PUNE
• LUCKNOW • AHMEDABAD • ERNAKULAM • BHUBANESWAR • INDORE • KOLKATA • GUWAHATI

© Author

No part of this publication may be reproduced, stored in a retrieval system, or transmitted in any form or by any means, electronic, mechanical, photocopying, recording and/or otherwise without the prior written permission of the publishers.

First Edition : 1998
Second Edition : 2008
Third Revised and Enlarged Edition : 2012

Published by : Mrs. Meena Pandey for **Himalaya Publishing House Pvt. Ltd.,** "Ramdoot", Dr. Bhalerao Marg, Girgaon, **Mumbai - 400 004.** Phone: 022-23860170/23863863, Fax: 022-23877178 **E-mail: himpub@vsnl.com; Website: www.himpub.com**

Branch Offices :

New Delhi : "Pooja Apartments", 4-B, Murari Lal Street, Ansari Road, Darya Ganj, New Delhi - 110 002. Phone: 011-23270392, 23278631; Fax: 011-23256286

Nagpur : Kundanlal Chandak Industrial Estate, Ghat Road, Nagpur - 440 018. Phone: 0712-2738731, 3296733; Telefax: 0712-2721215

Bengaluru : No. 16/1 (Old 12/1), 1st Floor, Next to Hotel Highlands, Madhava Nagar, Race Course Road, Bengaluru - 560 001. Phone: 080-32919385; Telefax: 080-22286611

Hyderabad : No. 3-4-184, Lingampally, Besides Raghavendra Swamy Matham, Kachiguda, Hyderabad - 500 027. Phone: 040-27560041, 27550139; Mobile: 09390905282

Chennai : No. 8/2, Modley 2nd Street, Ground Floor, T. Nagar, Chennai - 600 017. Phone: 044-28144004/28144005; Mobile: 09345345051

Pune : First Floor, "Laksha" Apartment, No. 527, Mehunpura, Shaniwarpeth (Near Prabhat Theatre), Pune - 411 030. Phone: 020-24496323/24496333; Mobile: 09370579333

Lucknow : Jai Baba Bhavan, Church Road, Near Manas Complex and Dr. Awasthi Clinic, Aliganj, Lucknow - 226 024 (U.P.). Phone: 0522-2339329, 4068914; Mobile: 09307501550

Ahmedabad : 114, "SHAIL", 1st Floor, Opp. Madhu Sudan House, C.G. Road, Navrang Pura, Ahmedabad - 380 009. Phone: 079-26560126; Mobile: 09377088847

Ernakulam : 39/104 A, Lakshmi Apartment, Karikkamuri Cross Rd., Ernakulam, Cochin - 622011, Kerala. Phone: 0484-2378012, 2378016; Mobile: 09344199799

Bhubaneswar : 5 Station Square, Bhubaneswar - 751 001 (Odisha). Phone: 0674-2532129, Mobile: 09338746007

Indore : Kesardeep Avenue Extension, 73, Narayan Bagh, Flat No. 302, IIIrd Floor, Near Humpty Dumpty School, Indore - 452 007 (M.P.). Mobile: 09301386468

Kolkata : 108/4, Beliaghata Main Road, Near ID Hospital, Opp. SBI Bank, Kolkata - 700 010, Phone: 033-32449649, Mobile: 09883055590, 07439040301

Guwahati : House No. 15, Behind Pragjyotish College, Near Sharma Printing Press, P.O. Bharalumukh, Guwahati - 781009, (Assam). Mobile: 09883055590, 09883055536

DTP by : HPH, Editorial Office, Bhandup (Rupali)

Printed at : A to Z Printers, New Delhi. On behalf of HPH.

PREFACE

Optimism paves the ways for development. If we continue to be optimistic, our efforts are found proactive. We succeed in identifying our potentials and our strategies for capitalising on the same, are found result-oriented. We need to make use of our world-class professional excellence in identifying and creating the opportunities and to tap them in a right fashion. A shoe manufacturing company decided to export to an African country. They divided the country into two halves and sent two sales executives to the country to sell shoes. A week passed and the head office received two separate messages. One executive sent the message that he is coming back because no opportunities are here as everyone walks around barefooted. Another executive sent another telex on the same day that send 10,000 pair of shoes because incredible potentials are here as everyone walks around wearing shoes. If your eyes and minds have a positive vision you get a success even in an adverse condition.

In the Indian hospitality industry, we need a vision like the second executive which would help us in identifying the potentials that we find in the Indian markets. The outlook for the Indian hospitality business is extremely positive because the potentials and the reach of the Indian tourism are enormous. We have incredible opportunities to satisfy almost all the segments of domestic and foreign tourists. We need to promote new dimensions of tourism such as adventure tourism, rural tourism, sports tourism, medical or health tourism, convention tourism, cultural tourism, heritage tourism etc. The creative promotional measures would help professionals in sensitising and persuading the domestic as well as the global tourists.

We cannot deny that hospitality business in India is shining and the root and branch cause for the same is corporatisation which has accelerated the pace of economic transformation. Sky-rocketing economic activities, both at domestic and global levels, have opened new vistas for a significant increase in the GDP leading to a rapid increase in the demands considerably outweighing the supply. The increase in the income level in all sectors has resulted into a better purchasing power and the influx of tourists both at national and global levels. We cannot deny that the hospitality sector is witnessing a robust, growth in both leisure and business travel. According to a CRISIL's report, this trend will continue for the next five years and even after this, the hospitality business would continue to witness steady growth.

On the flip or reverse side, the robust growth in traffic has not met with adequate supply because almost in all the leading cities of the country we find a stage of mismatch between demand and supply both in qualitative and quantitative terms. This focuses our attention on the development of hospitality industry in the face of changing requirements and emerging trends. We need governmental support for developing world-class infrastructural facilities.

The PPP mode needs priority attention. The budget hotels need to be promoted. With the beginning of electronic revolution, the contours of development have undergone radical changes. The emergence of techniculture has injected new life and strength to the corporate culture which has been found paving avenues for the development of hotel culture. New segments are found emerging everyday. New features are found incorporated with more frequency. The penetration of new generation of information and communication technology has been found defining and redefining service quality.

For quite a long time, the western world perceived India as the land of snake charmers and elephants. They were forced to change their perception with the surge of Indian IT firms on the global map. It is against this backdrop that we find biggest rub-off effect benefiting the hospitality industry in a big way. The sudden burst of tourist traffic has spurred hospitality industry players to get into action. It is in this context that we find a host of global biggies having well established brands entering the Indian markets. The international brands like Amanda, Satinwoods, Banana Tree, Hampton Inns, Hilton, Mandarin Oriental, Accor, Marriott, Starwood and many others have been evincing keen interests in tapping the opportunities found in the Indian hospitality industry. On the other hand, we also find domestic players like the Oberoi, Taj, ITC, The Park Hotels, Leela and Bharat establishing independent benchmarks — on their own in terms of world class services and facilities provided by them. This has been found increasing the intensity of competition in the Indian hotel industry.

We consider brand loyalty a fragile idea specially in a cost transparent business world. The professional excellence of a marketer crosses through the stage of acid test in which innovative ideas, product uniqueness and the creative promotional measures may help them in simplifying the process of customer satisfaction and retention. Competition in any field and particularly in the hospitality industry stimulates and spurs all the players in the industry large or small to continually endeavour to activate the process of value addition by upgrading their product mix. The small players may prefer mergers, acquisitions and consolidations to stay competitive.

The development of hospitality industry is considerably influenced by the development of a host of constituents such as tourism, convention, transportation, communication and information, global partnership, cultural exchange programmes positive attitude of government and the incentives offered in different forms etc. We cannot deny that we have tremendous potentials for the development of tourism industry. Carefully and colorfully displayed paintings of the different regions, the Ajanta, the Ellora, the Taj, decorated sacred shrines of God, Buddhist places of worship, coast line, back water, rich cultural heritage, world class medical services, surroundings of the Himalayas if optimally and professionally tapped would keep on moving the demand side. The marketing professionals are here required to make use of their world-class professional excellence.

Formulation of an innovative marketing strategy requires due attention of hotel professionals. This necessitates designing of a sound marketing mix in tune with the changing taste preferences of customers which may simplify the task of excelling competition. We can not deny that a sound product mix would be instrumental in luring customers. Sooner or later, we are rewarded for our world-class services and facilities. Development of popular tourism destinations, innovative tourism products such as medical well-being, golf courses, adventure, wildlife, rural, cultural, heritage tourism are some of the areas where we can attract both domestic as well as the foreign tourists. The hotel professionals need to develop a package which may act as a motivational tool. Even our quality services fail in attracting the customers, if the promotional measures are not found to be creative. This makes it essential that we make use of the different components of promotion in such a way that our efforts are creative, cost-effective and proactive. Informing, sensing, sensitising, persuading and transforming the potential customers into actual customers need a sound promotion mix. Pricing strategy in the hospitality sector is essentially a manifestation of the supply and demand phenomena. A sustainable tariff policy in the hospitality industry not only in India but around the globe is found based on the demand and supply mechanism. The hotel professionals need to make use of pricing as a motivational tool so that they succeed in increasing the occupancy rate. On the other hand, they have also to increase the average room rate as and when the market conditions are favourable. The pricing strategy thus would help hoteliers in many ways. Keeping in view the frequent use of new generation of information and communication technology, the hotel professionals need to penetrate the use of techno-driven channels.

Further, it is also imperative that hotel professionals assign due weightage to the processing of services with the help of a sound mix of manually supported and techno-driven operations so that even the situational or occasional barriers are not to create a gap. The hotel professionals cannot undermine the role of service ambience or servicescapes in the hospitality industry because this would activise the value addition process. The hotel employees would find the ambient conditions helpful in increasing their operational efficiency and in addition, the hotel customers would gain new experiences found distinct to the rivals. The interiors, exteriors, furnishing, lighting, music, ventilation, parking are some of the dimensions of servicescapes activating the tangibilisation process. The hoteliers cannot under rate the role of quality human resources in the value addition process. They have to develop them in such a fashion that their services have a personal touch. In a true sense, world-class human resources may be helpful in improving the quality of services.

It is, of course, party time for the hospitality industry provided the hoteliers succeed in changing the perception of high spending world tourists that services, facilities and tariffs in hotels in India are comparable and competitive with the hotels in competing destination countries.

The author acknowledges with sincere gratitude the co-operation to him by his colleagues and friends in revising and enlarging this volume.

S.M. Jha

CONTENTS

Ch. No.	*Particulars*	*Page No.*
1.	The Foundation of Hotel Marketing	1– 23
2.	Behavioural Profile of Hotel Customers	24 – 47
3.	Hotel Market Segmentation	48 – 67
4.	Marketing Information System for Hotels	68 – 92
5.	Service Quality in Hotel	93 – 114
6.	Hotel Product Strategy	115 – 140
7.	Hotel Promotion Strategy	141 – 185
8.	Hotel Pricing Strategy	186 – 215
9.	Hotel Placement Strategy	216 – 250
10.	Strategies for Expanded Marketing Mix in Hotel	251 – 270
11.	Overall Marketing Strategy for Hotel	271 – 301
12.	Emerging Challenges Before Hospitality Industry	302 – 319
13.	Hotel Planning for 21st Century	320 – 334
(✍)	Bibliography	335 – 339
(✍)	Subject Index	340 – 344

DETAILED CONTENTS

Ch. No. Particulars *Pg. No.*

1. THE FOUNDATION OF HOTEL MARKETING .... 1—23

Introduction – Hotel: The Concept – Motel: The Concept – Hotel and Its Typology – Hotel Marketing: The Concept – Marketing vs. Selling of Hotel Services – Marketing Hotel Services – Customers of Hotel Industry – Significance of Hotel Marketing – Third Wave Civilisation and Hotel Industry – Hotel Marketing in Indian Perspective – Summary – Key Terms – Review Questions – Application Exercises – End Notes.

2. BEHAVIOURAL PROFILE OF HOTEL CUSTOMERS .... 24 — 47

Introduction – Hotel Customer: A General Description – Behaviour of Hotel Customers – Behavioural Influences – Insight from Sociology – Insight from Economics – Customers' Behaviour and Lifestyle – Why Lifestyle Studies from Hotel Services? – Motivational Factors Making People Buy or Spend Money – Understanding the Behaviour of Hotel Customers – Influencing the Aggressive Hotel Customers – Transformation of Attitude into Behaviour and Action – A Buyer Behaviour Model for Hotel – Behavioural Profile of Hotel Users in Indian Perspective – Summary – Key Terms – Review Questions – Application Exercises – End Notes.

3. HOTEL MARKET SEGMENTATION .... 48 — 67

Introduction – Market Segmentation: The Concept – Why Market Segmentation? – Bases for Segmentation – Importance of Market Segmentation – Decision Process for Market Segmentation – Menu Fatigue: An Important Decision-making Area – Know the Changing Drinking Habits – Effective Market Segmentation – Emerging New Segments for Hotel Industry in Indian Perspective – Summary – Key Terms – Review Questions – Application Exercises – End Notes.

4. MARKETING INFORMATION SYSTEM FOR HOTELS .... 68 — 92

Introduction – Marketing Information System: The Concept – MIS: The Sub-systems – MIS: Salient Features – MIS: Functions – Managing Information for Hotel Industry – Marketing Information for Restaurants – Marketing Information System for Function rooms – Key Sources of Information for Hotel – Significance of MIS to Hotel Marketing – Marketing Research: The Concept – Methods of Research – Marketing Research in the Hotel Industry – Managing Information for Quality Decisions in the Hotel Industry – Summary – Key Terms – Review Questions – Application Exercises – End Notes.

5. SERVICE QUALITY IN HOTEL .... 93 — 114

Introduction – Service Quality: The Concept – Importance of Service Quality – Service Quality Management – Service Quality Factors in Hotels – SERVQUAL in Hotel – SERVPERF in Hotel – Service Environment for Hotel Industry – Service Quality Gap – Service Leadership – Quality in Totality in Hotel Industry – Summary – Key Terms – Review Questions – Application Exercises – End Notes.

6. HOTEL PRODUCT STRATEGY .... 115— 140

Introduction – Hotel Product: The Concept – Hotel Product: Salient Features – Product Strategy – Product Life Cycles – Modifying and Revitalising the Services – Failure of Product – Launching a New Product – Stages of Product Screening – Branding – Why Ascribing a Brand Name? – Incredible India Brand – Formulating the Hotel Product Mix – Formulating a Sound Product Strategy – Summary – Key Terms – Review Questions – Application Exercises – End Notes.

7. HOTEL PROMOTION STRATEGY .... 141 — 185

Introduction – Promotion: The Concept – Components of Promotion – Why do We Promote? – Word-of-mouth Promotion – Personal Selling – Why face-to-face Selling is of Greater Importance? – Non-verbal communication – How to Make Possible Face-to-face Selling? – Expression Techniques – Skill Needed to Personal Selling – Sales Sequence – Advertising – Importance of Advertising to Hotel Industry – Advertisement Planning – Media Decision – Selection of Message – Advertising Agencies – The Communication Process and Its Barriers – Testing Advertising Effectiveness – Advertising Campaign – Advertising Strategy – Advertising Plays a Relatively Small Role in Hotel – Public Relations – Sales Promotion – Telemarketing – Cause-related and Sponsorship Marketing – Hotel Promotion Strategy in Indian Perspective – Summary – Key Terms – Review Questions – Application Exercises – End Notes.

8. HOTEL PRICING STRATEGY .... 186 — 215

Introduction – Pricing Decisions: The Influencing Variables – Strategic and Tactical Role of Pricing – Pricing for Room Tariffs – League Tables – Pricing for Food and Beverages – Pricing for Function – Packaging up in Pricing – Hubbert Formula for Hotel Pricing – Different Types of Room Tariffs – Pricing Objectives – Pricing Strategy – Hotel Pricing Strategy in Indian Perspective – Summary – Key Terms – Review Questions – Application Exercises – End Notes.

9. HOTEL PLACEMENT STRATEGY .... 216 — 250

Introduction – Channel: The Concept – Distributions Policy: Influencing Factors – Distribution Chain: The Term – Tour Operators Travel Agents – Importance of Travel Agents to the Hotel Industry – Functions of Travel Agents – In-house Selling and Front-line Staff – Telephone Selling or Tele-marketing – E-CRM Strategy – Strategy for Restaurant Sales – Sales Action

Plans – Balancing Inside and Outside Selling in a Hotel – Sales Letters and Mailing Shots – Other Forms of Distribution of Hotels – Cost of Distribution – Improving Sales Techniques – Distribution Strategy for Hotel – Summary – Key Terms – Review Questions – Application Exercises – End Notes.

10. STRATEGIES FOR EXPANDED MARKETING MIX IN HOTEL .... 251 — 270

Introduction – Expanded Marketing Mix: An Overview – Process – The Front and Back Offices in Service Processing – Physical Evidence and Attractions – Corporate Image – Corporate Identity – Essential Considerations for Physical Evidence – People – Role of Front-line Staff in Hotel – Strategical Decisions for Processing Hotel Services – Strategical Decisions for Physical Evidence and Attractions – Strategical Decisions for People Serving Hotels – Summary – Key Terms – Review Questions – Application Exercises – End Notes.

11. OVERALL MARKETING STRATEGY FOR HOTEL .... 271 — 301

Introduction – Overall Marketing Strategy: Concept and Application – Formulation of an Overall Marketing Strategy – Selecting the Marketing Inputs – Factors in Selecting the Marketing Inputs – Implementation of Overall Marketing Strategy – Strategies for Marketing Inputs – An Optimal Product Mix – An Optimal Promotion Mix – An Optimal Price Mix – An Optimal Place Mix – Smooth, Decent and Time-honoured Processing – Employees and Customer-friendly Service Ambience – Satisfying and Retaining Quality People – Strategic Marketing Tasks – Planning the Business Mix – Deciding the Position or Image – Encouraging and Rewarding Frequent Customers – Integrating Marketing Across Several Units – Evaluation of Overall Marketing Strategy – Systematic Marketing Audit – Understanding the Marketing Mix in Hotel – Summary – Key Terms – Review Questions – Application Exercises – End Notes.

12. EMERGING CHALLENGES BEFORE HOSPITALITY INDUSTRY .... 302— 319

Introduction – Demand Penetration: A Clarion Call – Law and Order Problem: A Challenging Task – Information Technology: Channelising Its Uses – Increasing Volatility in the Business Environment – Inadequate Supply – Long-term Optimism in the Indian Hospitality Industry – Summary – Key Terms – Review Questions – Application Exercises – End Notes.

13. HOTEL PLANNING FOR 21ST CENTURY .... 320 — 334

Introduction – Hotel Location – Hotel Building – Hotel Bedrooms – Hotel Function Rooms – Hotel Restaurants and Bars – Hotel Peripheral Services – Focus on Personal Care Services – Planning for Hotel People – Strategical and Tactical Marketing Planning – Summary – Key Terms – Review Questions – Application Exercises – End Notes.

(✍) BIBLIOGRAPHY .... 335 — 339

(✍) SUBJECT INDEX .... 340 — 344

CHAPTER - 1

THE FOUNDATION OF HOTEL MARKETING

Corporatisation has made ways for the development of hotel culture. The future of hotel industry is bright provided we conceptualise modern marketing and professionalise our strategic decisions.

CHAPTER OBJECTIVES

Introduction – Hotel the Concept – Motel: The Concept – Hotel and Its Typology – Hotel Marketing: The Concept – Marketing Vs Selling of Hotel Services – Marketing Hotel Services – Customers of Hotel Industry – Significance of Hotel Marketing – Third Wave Civilisation and Hotel Industry – Hotel Marketing in Indian Perspective – Summary – Key Terms – Review Questions – Application Exercises – End notes.

LEARNING OBJECTIVES

This chapter of the book aims at studying the various dimensions related to the fundamentals of marketing hotel services. The readers develop their awareness of the terminologies, concept and percept of hotel marketing. The motive is to engineer a foundation for the application of modern marketing principles in the Indian perspective where we find tremendous opportunities for the development of hotel industry. The readers will find it easier to perceive the concept of hotel marketing in a right fashion.

INTRODUCTION

Roman Empire, Roman civilisation, Roman might; we find these words stored in global memory even till date. In a true sense, they significantly contributed to the development of social order. It was in this context that till the downfall of Roman Empire, i.e., 500 AD, the inns and taverns were found well developed. The churches, monasteries, cathedrals and temples made suitable arrangements for the visiting pilgrims. But, the downfall of Roman empire made ways for multi-faceted problems and for several hundred years, the travelers inns were lost to civilisation. Inn-keeping could not flourish because travel was rare and trade at a stand still. The crusade in Europe which started in 1095 AD lasted for over two hundred years. This provided for elbow rooms laying the foundation of a social revolution resulting into the emergence of a new class, i.e., Middle Class. The impact of renaissance was initially visible in Italy and gradually in several countries of Europe. Inn-keeping thus became a remunerative business. The first tavern was opened in USA in 1634. Hotels emerged from the tavern. By 1920 hotel became an accepted term to describe a place where people stayed for night and took their meals on payment basis. Since then, there have been multi-pronged developments in the types and forms of hotel which has now emerged as a big service industry.

The multi-dimensional developments in the society, an increase in the level of income, the development of corporate sector and emergence of corporate culture, globalisation of fashion, culture and civilisation, disintegration in the traditional concept of a large-sized family, sophisticated developments in the field of transportation and communication, inventions and innovations in the field of information superhighway are some of the recent developments opening new vistas for the development hotel culture. In addition, the development of tourism as an industry injected new life and strength to the hotel business. The officials on deputation, the business executives on trade promotion mission, the foreign representatives on peace mission, the development of convention as an industry paved copious avenues for the hotel industry.

From traditional to the modern age, we find so many turning points in the development of hotel. In the past, the hospitality was due to religious and superstitious fears. Of course, we believed that a stranger was either God or a representative of evil spirits perhaps even the devil himself. Hospitality was extended to be the good and bad souls. The hospitality to strangers was necessary to their religious well-being and to the evil spirits because of our superstitious fears. Thus, we find religion and the supernatural forces as the key factors in the conceptualisation of hospitality. In the modern day thinking, the hospitality appears merely a result of a 'give' and 'take' philosophy. Gradually, the hospitality emerged as an industry as we made use of professional excellence and accepted it a way for making profits.

Of late, in almost all parts of the globe the hotel industry has been playing a significant role as a leisure industry and has been benefiting a number of industries like airlines, cruise ships, motor coaches, railways, information and communication technology, etc. In addition, the travel agents, tour operators and transport operators have also benefited with the development of hotel business. The film industry, professional sports, the restaurant industry are the part and parcel of leisure industry whereas the accommodation and food and beverages operations are the integral part of hotel industry.

With the passage of time, we find innovative supporting infrastructural facilities making ways for qualitative improvements in the hotel industry. The new generation of information and communication technology has been found changing the functional behaviour of hotel industry. The emergence of corporate culture has injected new life and strength to the hotel business. This is due to a change in the behavioural profile and lifestyles of people becoming instrumental in the development of hotel culture. New segments are found emerging everyday. Women are found evincing keen interests in traveling. Kids and teens have developed temptation for traveling. In addition, the population of fifty plus have also been fascinated to traveling. We find these developments a positive sign for the development of hotel industry in the Indian perspective.

The development of hotel industry is considerably influenced by the development of its different constituents such as tourism, convention, trade fair and exhibition, sophisticated mode of transportation, communication, etc. The new forms of tourism such as medical tourism sports tourism have been creating a big potential market for hotel sector. We cannot deny that development of tourism as a brand would pave new avenues for the development of hotel sector. Our rich cultural heritage may add new feathers in the tourism *vis-a-vis* in the hotel. Carefully and colorfully displayed paintings of the different regions the Ajanta, the Ellora, the Taj, decorated sacred shrines of God, Buddhist places of worship, coast line, back water etc. are our special attractions opening new vistas for the development of innovative hotels preferred by the high spending world tourists. Actually, we need to develop our cultural heritage as a brand. Wintenitz, a western critic says if we wish to understand the oldest Indo-European culture; we must go to India where the oldest literature of an Indo-European people is preserved. The need of the hour is to identity innovative areas where we can compete both at national and international levels.

The strategic decisions not only in the hotel industry but in almost all the industries have assumed greater significance since 1970s for three important reasons. The first is related to the uncertainties provoked by the major international energy crises of 1973 and 1979. It is important to mention that these events followed by economic recession disrupted all the forecast made in the 1960s to plan long-term business goals. The second is invention and innovation in the field of information and communication technology which gained rapid momentum since 1990 followed by globalisation and liberalisation. The third is the growth of large hotel groups during 1970s with wide range of products, with a wide range of markets. With the beginning of 21st century we find information, communication and transportation activating the process of economic transformation and changing the taste preferences and lifestyles of people. In addition, we find emergence of a new ultra rich segment and a burgeoning middle class developing a craze for hotel culture. We cannot deny that economic recession that we find in the 21st century has been affecting the hotel business not only in India but the world over. However, we find good auguries and with the support of our world class professional excellence, we may be efficacious of capitalising on the opportunities.

Optimism paves the ways for development. If we are optimistic, It is very natural that we succeed identifying the opportunities. We find significant developments in the areas of trade and commerce, the process of economic transformation has also been activated, the provincial as well as the central governments are found positive to the development of travel and tourism as an industry, the supporting infrastructural facilities are available and these developments make India potentially sound for the qualitative and quantitative improvements both in tourism and hotel. We need world class hotels and we need hotels in a good number. It is estimated that 2,00,000 approved quality accommodation rooms would be required in 2011 against the current level of about 100000 rooms.

Non-availability of land is found to be an important bottleneck in the creation of hotel infrastructure. The policy decision makers need to design a Master Plan of major cities identifying commercial sites for construction of hotels, convention and exhibition centers. The hotel sites should be allotted on long-term lease basis or could be allotted under (PPP) Public-Private-Partnership mode through joint venture, revenging sharing, etc. Higher Floor Area Ratio/Floor Space Index (FAR/FSI) should be higher so that more rooms and commercial spaces are created out of the same space for generating additional revenues. The land should also be allotted for building of guest houses in all major cities and tourist destinations. Home stay Programme under the Govt. of India Scheme of 'Incredible India Bed & Breakfast' needs to be promoted by all the state Governments by allowing such establishments to be treated as non-commercial. The possibilities for constructing hotels on the surplus land with Airport Authority of India near international airports needs to be considered. The surplus railway land at specified railway stations may also be utilised for constructing budget hotels.

The hotel sector would also require quality people, and for that, Institute of Hotel Management and Food Craft Institutions need to develop people in tune with our changing requirements.

HOTEL – THE CONCEPT

The common law says that hotel is a place where all who conduct themselves properly and who being able and ready to pay for their entertainment, accommodation and other services including the boarding thus making it a temporary home. It is a home away from where all amenities facilities are available but chargeable. Thus we consider it a public place where all facilities are made available to a person or persons staying in hotels. The facilities like entertainment meals, accommodation, etc. thus become the service products of a hotel. The American concept regarding the hotel considers it a place for business to gather.[1] Further, it is also supposed to be a place where tourists stop, cease to be travellers and become customers.[2]

The definition presented by hotel operators to authorities of the National Recovery Administration in Washington is found to be a more comprehensive definition, formulated by Stuart Mc Namara. The definition says, 'Primarily and fundamentally a hotel is an establishment which supplies boarding and lodging, not engaged in inter-state commerce, or in any intra-state commerce, competitive with or affecting inter-state commerce (or so related there to that the regulation of one involves the control of other). It is a quasi-domestic institution retaining from its ancient and origin certain traditions and acquiring in its modern development, certain statutory rights and obligations to the public where all persons not disqualified by condition or conduct are prepared to pay for their accommodation are to be received and furnished with a room or place to sleep or occupy if such accommodations are available, and with such services and attention as are incident to their use of the hotel as a home, and/or with food at stipulated prices, and with or without contract as to duration of visit and which conducts within the confines of its physical locations the business of supplying personal services of individuals for profit. Incidental to such fundamental and principal business, the hotel may furnish quarters and facilities for assemblage of people for social business or entertainment purposes and may engage in retaining a portion of its premises for shops and businesses whose continuity (i.e., proximity) is deemed appropriate to a hotel.[3]

We can't deny the fact that the definition formulated by Sturt Mc Namara expanded the functional areas for modern hotels. The assemblage of people for social, business and entertainment purposes make it essential that hotels are also furnished with a big conference hall where the maximum possible accommodation is available. We also call it the "Function room".

MOTEL – THE CONCEPT

Initially, the term *'motel'* was meant for local travelers and foreign tourists traveling by road. The concept, primarily, was originated in the USA Basically, motels serve the needs and requirements of these travelers and meeting the demand for transit accommodation. Or, we can also call motel a *transit overnight stay.* Some of the important services offered by the motels are parking, garage facilities. accommodation. restaurant facilities, public catering and recreational facilities. Here, it is essential that the motels be equipped with filling stations, accessories service of elevator to the automobile entrance restaurants etc.

The motels also make available to the guests equipment and tools, if tourists like to repair their vehicles. Motels are mostly located outside the city, preferable highways and important road junctions where tourists may relax. Motels are of different types some motels provide bare minimum services whereas some of them provide all the facilities as provided by modern hotels. The accommodation in a motel is more than in the category of 'chalet facility' which has a dining hall with fixed menu. In USA, the motel accommodation is at par with hotel accommodation.

HOTEL AND ITS TYPOLOGY

Since time immemorial, there have been multi-dimensional changes in the concept and format of hotels. It is quite natural that we find variation in the nature, types and quality of services offered by different types of hotels. The variation in architectural features, the size, the facade, the facilities and amenities cannot be overlooked. The recent changes in the perception of hotel business make possible a large-scale variation in the quality of services.

Here we classify hotel into three main categories, viz., classification on the basis of nature. classification on the basis of standard and control and classification on the basis of star. In Fig. 1.1, we find different types of hotels.

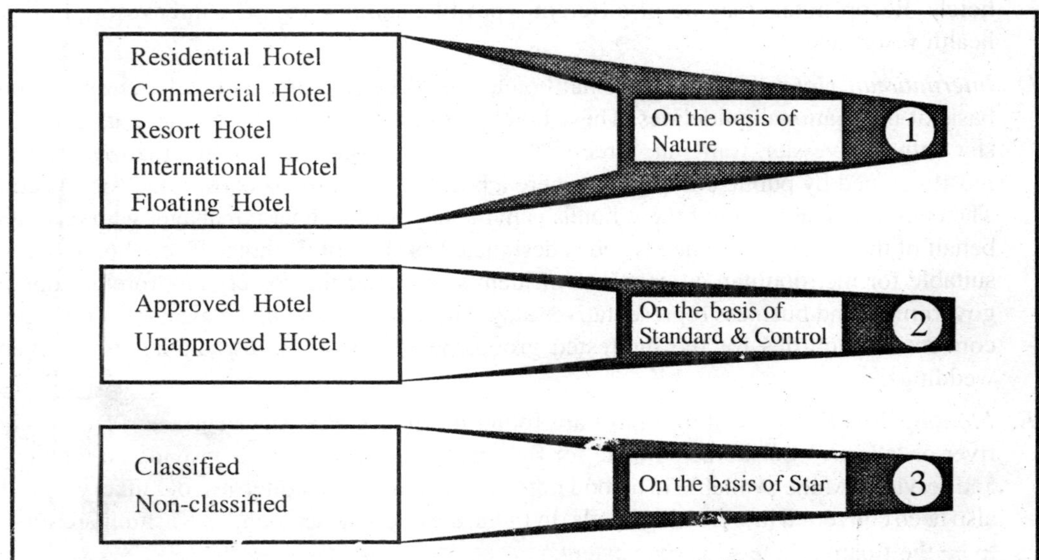

FIG. 1.1: TYPES OF HOTEL

I. Classification on the basis of nature: In this category, we find five types of hotels such as Residential Hotel, Commercial Hotel, Resort Hotel, International Hotel and Floating Hotel.

A. *Residential Hotel:* The residential hotels extend hospitality services as apartment houses. We also call them apartment hotels. They may charge rent on monthly, half-yearly or yearly basis. The accommodation may be furnished or unfurnished. These hotels are found located in big cities where no meals are served to the guests. Initially, the residential hotels were developed in the USA. The services in residential hotels are comparable to an average well-managed home. The guests staying in residential hotels are made available all the facilities for cooling. The rate varies in tune with the services offered. If you have furnished accommodation, the charge is high. Conversely, if you have unfurnished accommodation, the charge will comparatively be low. The location point for residential hotels or apartment houses may also be in the hilly areas or coastal areas where the tourists stay for long time. Since we find duration of stay in the residential hotels long, the guests find it, economic. The beach tourism, eco-tourism or health tourism find this accommodation convenient.

B. *Commercial Hotel:* The commercial hotels are meant for the people who visit a place for trade or business purposes and so these hotels are found located at the big industrial and commercial centers. These hotels concentrate their attention on individual travellers on a business trip or a group of businessmen and are generally run by the owners. A number of commercial hotels receive the guests who are on business tour. No doubt, some of them have also the permanent customers on their registers.

C. *Resort Hotel:* The resort hotels are meant for climate holiday makers, tourists and for those who need a change in the atmosphere mainly on health grounds. These hotels are found located near the sea, mountain and other areas having a natural beauty and healthy atmosphere. The tourists visit these hotels mainly to relax. The tourists or guests expect a special welcome. The entertainment are recreation facilities like swimming pool, tennis courts, boating, golf course, self riding and other indoor sports in addition to restaurant and cafeterias, conference rooms, lounge, shopping arcades, entertainment etc. have gained significance in the resort hotels. Resort hotels may be of different types like summer resort, winter resort, hill resort, health resort, etc.

D. *International Hotel:* The international hotels are modem luxurious hotels, classified on the basis of international guidelines. These hotels are placed in various star categories, e.g., five-star deluxe, five-star, four-star, three-star, two-star, one-star etc. The international hotels are mostly owned by public companies, where a board of directors is constituted for "its control. The overall management of these hotels is in the hands of a general manager who manages on behalf of the departmental heads and is designated as chief of the hotel. These hotels are found suitable for metropolitan cities where affluent sections of the society and foreign tourists or government and business representatives stay. These hotels also make available conference or convention facilities for the interested groups/persons institutions/companies, or even for weddings.

E. *Floating Hotel:* The floating hotels are found located on the water surface. Places like sea, river or lake are considered suitable for floating hotels. These hotels provide all the facilities and services. Made available in a good hotel. In the developed countries, old luxury ships have also been converted into floating hotels. In India, the house boats found in Kashmir are supposed to be the floating hotels to some extent.

II. Classification on the basis of standard and control: On the basis of standard and control, the hotels are of two types, e.g., approved and unapproved, as shown in the Figure 1.2.

- *Approved and Unapproved Hotels:* The approved hotels are of international standards where the accommodations are available as per certain criteria laid down by the Department of Tourism, Ministry of Tourism and Civil Aviation and Government. They have been given social recognition and so, the magnitude of reliance is immense and praiseworthy. Contrary to it, the unapproved hotels lack the official recognition enjoyed by the former. However, it is not meant that unapproved hotels do not maintain international standards. Even the foreign tourists have been found staying in these hotels. Hence, the point of difference between an approved and unapproved hotel is the official stamp or recognition. The unapproved hotels are clean and those who spend money from their own pockets, naturally prefer unapproved hotels as the accommodations are inexpensive.[4] Hence, it is not proper to say that only approved hotels keep up to international standards. No doubt, the users or guests accommodating themselves in the hotels may not be the same. Generally, the approved hotels are attended by foreign or domestic tourists not bearing the expenses on their own account but the unapproved hotels are generally attended by the low and middle income groups bearing their individual expenses.

III: Classification on the basis of star: One more basis is found for classification in which star-wise classification is made on the basis of criterion framed by the Department of Tourism and includes everything from the size of the room to qualifications of staff.[5] On the basis of the star category, there are two important types, viz., classified and non-classified.[6] The star group of hotels are included in the classified group. Hotels having no star categories are deemed non-classified. The four major classification of American hotels are: the commercial, the resort, the residential and the motel.[7]

HOTEL MARKETING – THE CONCEPT

The major difference in hotel marketing as against other consumer products is that once customer has spent money in hotels, he/she has nothing substantial to show for his/her money except the bills, as compared with buying a television or a refrigerator. Effective marketing and dynamic selling become significant in the context of hotel marketing because once you have not sold a seat in a restaurant or a room, in a hotel, the income is lost forever. A hotel bedroom or a restaurant seat has no *'shelf life'*. Generally, the hoteliers explain their marketing by showing their computer booking service or the advertising campaign for the coming season.

No doubt, these things are part and parcel of hotel marketing but only one aspect of the continuous circle of marketing. For marketing hotel services, it is essential that marketing be understood fully by the executive at the top of a hotel or hotel group with total commitment on his part to the continuous need to market. A number of experts have expressed their views relevant to hotels and food services as quoted below:

Gerry Draper[8]

"Ascertaining customer needs, tailoring the product as *closely* as possible *to meet those needs, persuading the customer to satisfy his needs and, finally, ensuring that the product is easily accessible when the customer wishes to purchase it."*

The definition of hotel marketing consists almost all aspects — right from ascertaining customer needs to getting the customers satisfied.

Melvyn Greene[9]

"The ultimate in marketing is to establish brand loyalty so that, eventually, the consumer does not only purchase the goods / services once, but continuously. This is achieved only by the producer following the complete process of marketing."

The definition given by Melvyn Greene concentrates on the transformation process. Actually, the marketing practices in the hotel or other organisations concentrate on transforming light customers into heavy customers. This process is also known as transforming the occasional customers into habitual customers.

Melvyn Greene added that[10]

"Marketing is basically seeking out a demand and then making the product or supplying the service to satisfy that demand. Selling is rather the other way round — creating a product or service and then trying to find a market for it."

In another definition, the author clarifies the difference between marketing hotel services and selling these services.

Anerson & Lembke[11]

"We believe that the real meaning of marketing is listening to the demands of the market and satisfying those demands at a profit; from that it follows that superior marketing is listening to the market more intently than your competitors and satisfying the demands more effectively."

This definition concentrates on creating the demand and satisfying the customers. Further, it emphasizes on the formulation of competitive strategies for excelling the competitors.

Thomas F. Powers[12]

"Marketing is so basic that it cannot be considered a separate function (i.e., a separate skill or work) within the business, on a par with others such as manufacturing or personnel. Marketing requires separate work and a distinct group of activities. But it is first a central dimension of the entire business. It is the whole business seen from its final results, that is from customer's point of view. Concern and responsibility for marketing must, therefore, permeate all areas of the enterprise."

We cannot deny the fact that the definition of Thomas F. Powers is the most suitable definition in which marketing is considered to be the focal point of the entire business. Since it is a central point, the other dimensions are naturally required to be included, specially while formulating appropriate marketing strategic decisions.

MARKETING VS. SELLING OF HOTEL SERVICES

As per the concept of hotel marketing, it is right to mention that marketing and selling of hotel services cannot be tantamount. The definition given by Melvyn Greene clarifies it. The continuous circle[13] of marketing as shown in Figure 1.2 removes the doubts over the perception.

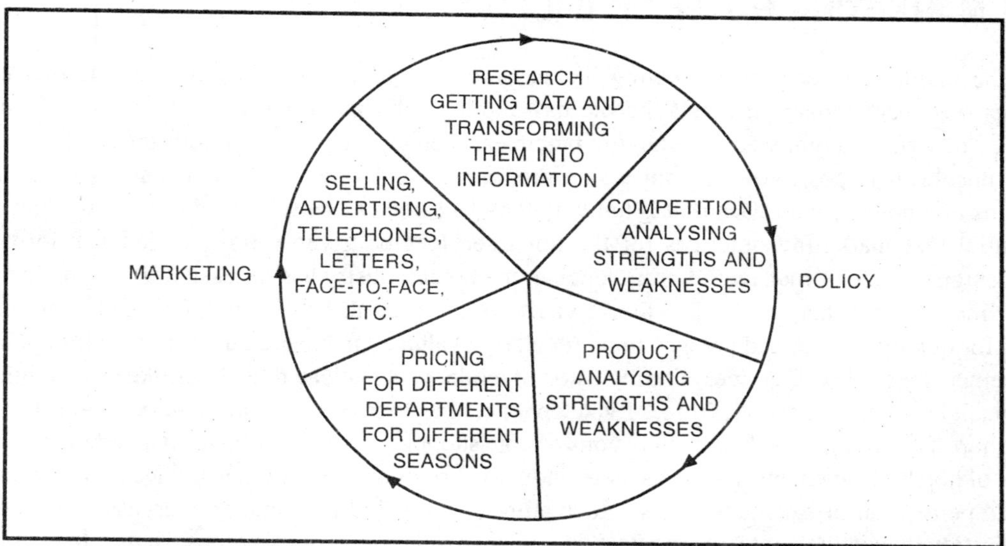

FIG. 1.2: CONTINUOUS CIRCLE OF MARKETING

(Modified from Melvyn Greene; Marketing Hotels and Restaurants into the 90s; Heinemann Professional Publishing Ltd. England) 1989

In Figure 1.2, the continuous circle of marketing clarifies the difference between marketing the hotel services and selling the hotel services. In selling, the key areas are advertising, including other aspects of communication like telephones, letters and face-to-face communication. Often, the hoteliers explain their marketing strategies by showing computer booking service and the advertising campaigns planned for the coming tourist. The fact be refuted that these aspects are important but we consider it as the only aspect of marketing. As per the continuous circle, it is essential to keep into consideration the research required for data collections and on the basis of a sound information system to transform the data into information for making the right decision. In addition, it is also essential that the strategies adopted by the competitors are given due weightage, specially while taking and implementing the strategic decisions. The threats and weaknesses in the markets are identified well and on right time, if we have complete information regarding the competitors in the hotel business. The pricing decisions are also significant, keeping in view the seasonal fluctuations which play a significant role in the hotel industry.

What is really needed is the sound management of information which makes possible creativity in the marketing decisions. It is significant to have detailed information required for an economic and marketing feasibility study for a new hotel or a new bedroom extension. An analysis of the facts makes it clear that marketing involves a lot of thinking in identifying the existing and new sources of business. It cannot be refuted that selling involves no thinking time or it requires less intellectual input. It is against this background that a lot of people like it and rush into it without going through the full process of strategic marketing. If we carry out the full process of marketing, it is very natural that our efforts would be selective. To be more specific, when we talk about the hotel industry, our emphasis here is on studying the changing business conditions. Hotels and restaurants are built and designed on a fixed basis for a specific market opportunity. The creativity in the marketing decisions makes possible enriching the efficacy of individual hoteliers to identify and capitalise on potential opportunities.

MARKETING HOTEL SERVICES

The major difference in marketing hotels as against other consumer products is that after a customer has spent money in hotels, he/she has nothing substantial to show except bills for his/her money as benefits as compared with buying tangibles, such as television or a refrigerator. If the goods remain unsold, it is possible to go for a sale program as and when the circumstances favor. But if the rooms of a hotel remain vacant, it is unlikely that the same can be sold even tomorrow. This makes it essential that marketing practices for the hotel services be given a transcendental priority. The growing significance of managerial proficiency in the hotel industry has necessitated the application of modern marketing principles. Today, the services are required to be planned, controlled, automated, audited for quality control and are also to be regularly evaluated to ensure quantitative-cum-qualitative improvements in the hotel services. The inclusion of modern sophisticated facilities like air-conditioning, four-channel music, cold drinks, fridge, TV, telephone, luxurious beds, round-the-clock room servicing, coffee shop, swimming pool, health club, comfortable shopping arcade etc. have changed the traditional concept of hotel management. Today, the hotel industry thrives on the customer services and satisfaction. And, the perception of satisfaction is so fluctuating that we find it changing everyday. This calls for improvisation in existing strategies to retain customers by particular hotel groups. Hence, the marketing practices become significant to bring about the effectiveness and success of managerial decisions. It is very natural that in an institution of commercial hospitality, the managerial proficiency is assigned due weightage as it determines the intensity of business success.

Significant developments in the transportation facilities, inventions and innovations in the field of communication, laying of strong foundations for industrialisation and urbanisation, emergence of tourism as a potential industry and changing lifestyles have opened up avenues for the development of hotels and motels. Besides, the growing significance of foreign trade is also found to be an important factor contributing a lot to the development of hotels as a facility on an organised basis. The officials on deputation, the business dons on trade promotion missions, the foreign representatives on peace missions, the domestic or foreign tourists interested in visiting a place for pleasure or gaining knowledge cannot perform or enjoy, if well-developed hotels are not available for their accommodation. Restaurants, cafeterias and hotels offer food and lodging facilities to those customers who gradually develop the habit of eating or living out of home. Modern hotels provide refined services to their customers, often termed as respected guests. The customers or guests are considered always right, this business principle in the hotel industry has raised the significance of applying modern marketing principles to sustain the hotel industry.

The industrial transformation has also made possible multi-faceted changes in the socio-economic set-up. As a result, we find a large scale migration of rural people to the metropolis, industrial towns and big cities. The new emerging urban society has provided a fillip to the development of modern hotels following frequent visits to tourist resorts or native places. Travelling for religious purposes is an established custom and tradition, specially in the Indian society. The pilgrims are often found visiting the sacred or holy places. Prospects or potential customer are opening doors for the development of hotel industry. Thus, it is right to mention that even on the domestic front, a favourable milieu for the development of hotel industry is fast emerging. No doubt, the hotel industry has been taken to be an economic bonanza, but the success rate is substantially influenced by the cost-effective application of marketing principles.

The emerging trends in the world tourism industry indicates that the hotel industry has emerged as a major source of foreign exchange inflows. This naturally draws our attention on hotel marketing. If the marketing principles are implemented in a right way, a fair mix of profitability and customer satisfaction is possible. It is time that organisations engaged in the hotel business bid a good-bye to the traditional principles and apply modern principles, assigning an overriding priority to satisfaction, expansion and innovation.

In the hotel industry, the formulation of product-mix becomes significant as new, sophisticated and refined services bear the efficacy of wooing the customers. Not only the lodging and boarding services but even other amenities like provision of amusement centers, shopping complexes, swimming pool, garden, facilities for car parking, conference hall, advanced communication facilities, etc. are also found instrumental in turning the potential customers into long-term customers. Besides, the sound behavioral management helps in excelling competition. To make the managerial decisions sensitive, it is essential to assign due weightage to the behavioural management.

How to behave?

How to offer?

How to respond?

How to convince?

The aforesaid questions will be suitably answered, if the behavioural management is assigned due place in the formulation of a marketing mix for hotels. "Right Sir, I am at your service, Sir," the communication with a sweet smile may be helpful in having a fair match of expectations and realities. Image and atmosphere, two magic words occupy a place of significance, particularly in the hotel industry. To be more specific, in the five star hotels where the customers do not mind the price but the quality, the marketing practices need emphasis.

The promotional strategies are found effective in raising the magnitude of sensitivity. Hotel industry is no exception. In the hotel industry, the expectations of customers are based on intangible qualities like atmosphere and image. Before buying, the customers have high expectations. Here, it is impact generating that customers' expectations are identified and efforts are made to fulfil the same. Failing it, the image problem aggravates and the marketing decisions become irrelevant and insensitive. The promotional tools like folders, cards, price list and list of general and special items to be served, published in attractive form throw a positive impact on customers. The prime motive of publicity is to enrich market information. Here, it is important that publicity and other promotional methods are innovated in the face of changing lifestyles and environmental conditions. The selection of a suitable strategy for advertising, the composition of advertisement slogans, the messages to be communicated etc. are found helpful in transforming the potential customers into heavy customers.

No doubt, the pricing strategies become insensitive for affluent sections of the society but due to worldwide economic depression, we find a significant increase in the number of price sensitive customers. Particularly in the developing countries like India, this aspect is found important and needs transcendental priority. Here, an optimal point between the services-offered and services-charged may be helpful in having a suitable pricing strategy.

In view of the above, it is right to mention that formulation of a marketing-mix for the hotel services is significant to make possible right decisions. Here, it is also important that marketing practices are innovated in the face of changing environmental conditions. In the yesteryears, large-scale movement of human resources, maximum emphasis on foreign trade, cultural exchange, organisation of business conferences, seminars, frequent visits of business executives, medical representatives, pilgrims, domestic and foreign tourists etc. were seen. These developments have necessitated the development of hotels as potential service facilities. The changes in the lifestyles and incomes are also found important for innovating the marketing decisions and giving customers good benefits for the costs incurred in putting up at hotels. The creative decisions are based on innovations which require professional excellence and sound information of management. Of late, a change in the attitude of customers has been seen and this attitudinal change has enlarged the functional areas of hotels. The marketers have to keep into consideration those aspects which would simplify their task of making possible sensitivity in the marketing decisions.

The hotel industry, particularly in the Indian context, has often considered marketing a potential source of generating revenue from sales. Marketing plants the seeds and sales harvests the crops. Is harvesting possible without sowing or besprinkling the seeds? The decline in the growth of the hotel industry is also due to the delayed application of marketing principles. Hotel marketing studies and highlights in its purview, almost all the components — directly or indirectly influencing the commercial viability of hotels. The task before the hotel marketers is to make the industry profitable and at the same time to satisfy the customers, of course in the face of their expectations. We cannot deny the fact that the hotel industry in India is growing gradually, which necessitates handling of the problems in the right perspective. This will be helpful in preparing a sound foundation for its development. Of late, we find an emergence of corporate culture, which would expand avenues for the development of the hotel industry. In this context, the application of marketing principles in the right fashion is the need of hour.

CUSTOMERS OF HOTEL INDUSTRY

In marketing hotel services, it is important to know about the different types or categories of customers visiting hotels with diverse aims and objectives. This will ease the task of marketers, specially while studying the behavioural profile. The classification presented in Exhibit 1.1 summarises a clear picture of different categories of domestic and foreign customers. It is very natural that we find a clear cut difference in the intensity of expectations by domestic and foreign customers.

EXHIBIT 1.1: CUSTOMERS OF HOTEL INDUSTRY

Domestic	*Foreign*
Pilgrims	Political Representatives
Students	Trade Representatives
Officials	Educationists
Trade Representatives	Sportsmen
Political Representatives	Cultural Representatives
Film Stars	Film Stars
Educationists	Pilgrims
Sportsmen	Business Executives
Medical Representatives	Tourists
Business Executives	
Tourists	

Domestic Customers: In the domestic users, the different categories are pilgrims visiting the sacred places, students on educational tour, officials on deputation, political representatives, film stars on location shooting, knowledge-seekers on developing their credentials, sportsmen playing national games etc.

We find different categories of customers in the domestic group who stay in hotels with different motives. It is very natural that we find a change in the level of their expectations. The main thing in studying their expectations is to make efforts to fulfil the same so that the occasional customers are transformed into habitual customers. Generally, the domestic customers pay less emphasis in expectations of benefits from the hotel management. But this is not true to a certain extent. Today, customers have become aware of these expectations while staying in a hotel.

An in-depth study of the behavioural profile helps marketers in understanding the potential customers. To be more specific, when the market has now become more competitive, it is essential that we assign due weightage to the amenities and facilities to be made available by the competitors. This simplifies the task of product innovation, a pre-requisite for excelling competition, expanding market and tapping the market potentials.

Foreign Customers: In the group of foreign customers, we find political representatives, trade representatives, educationists, sportsmen, cultural representatives, film stars, pilgrims etc. These categories of foreign tourists visit hotels with diverse aims, expectations and objectives. They normally prefer to stay in classified hotels. It is very natural that the level of expectations of foreign customers is comparatively high which, necessitates an in-depth study of their behavioral profile. This is essential to understand the customers as unless we succeed in identifying their expectations, the hotel organisations would not be in a position to deliver goods to the customers. With the passage of time, a multi-dimensional development in the transportation and communication facilities to be made available to the customers has emerged. This makes it essential that hoteliers be well aware of the efforts taken in the field of product innovation. To be more specific, when we talk about international hotels, it is imperative that marketing practices are innovated in the face of competitors' strategies.

The foreign customers have also been found staying in unclassified hotels, specially when they are found more sensitive to price. This attitudinal change in the foreign customers is being influenced by worldwide economic depression.

Hence while making marketing decisions, it is impact generating that price-sensitive customers are identified. Thus, important tasks before the marketers are to understand the customers, to identify their expectations and to make efforts to satisfy them. Unless hotel organisations succeed in transforming their customers into heavy customers, the occupancy ratio would not be increased satisfactorily.

SIGNIFICANCE OF HOTEL MARKETING

Together with many other industries, the hotel industry has been facing multi-dimensional problems but the future looks bright for those hotels and hotel companies who implement their marketing strategies in a right fashion. Marketing is a complex attitude of mind. Some people understand marketing in its fullest sense, some others are found too product-oriented and so can miss market opportunities. If we miss opportunities, we miss everything. Hence, the key point is to identify the opportunities and to capitalise on the same in the best interest of your customers/guests. If we continue to deliver goods to the customers, it is very natural that we reach to the stage of perfection and succeed in excelling competition. Against this background, the marketing experts have been found advocating in favor of the application of marketing principles in the hotel industry. Of late, the emphasis has been highly focused upon competition and this necessitates the application of innovative marketing principles. Here, the problem is to point out the importance of hotel marketing.

1. Easy to study the customers' behaviour: Hotel marketing is based on behavioural studies. An in-depth study of the behavioral profile simplifies the task of understanding the potential customers. If we understand the immediate prospects, it is easy to know their needs and requirements, preferences, likes and dislikes and more so their expectations. The sensitivity of managerial decisions rests on our efforts to understand the prospects. It is right to say that expectations and satisfaction move together. The behavioural studies simplify the task of identifying the expectations and so the task of satisfying the customers is simplified substantially.

2. Organisational effectiveness is attained: Considering marketing a perverse approach, a social concept of marketing will be needed to make possible marketing concepts compatible with a social perspective. This holistic approach to management science would also help marketing in proving its instrumentality as a philosophy where an organisation strives to develop an integrating marketing programme, generating long-term wants of the customers. The hotels or hotel companies can be successful in increasing the rate of profitability as by applying the marketing principles, the occasional customers can be transformed into habitual customers. Since the hoteliers know their customers the managerial decisions are found effective. The organisation objectives can be accomplished successfully, if we are well aware of the prospects and their expectations.

3. Sound management of information is possible: For making possible creativity in decisions to give a boost to individual ventures in the hotel industry, it is essential to have information regarding the latest developments in the environmental conditions. In the marketing management, due weightage is given to the Marketing Information System (MIS). To be more specific, when the market is competitive and volatile, it is important to have information related to the different segments directly or indirectly influencing the marketing decisions. Information regarding the local community, local industry, commerce and employment, communications, local events and attractions, catchments area, facilities of the hotel, emerging new trends in competition, profile of customers, activity levels, employees' selling ability, specific selling information, etc. are found instrumental in making the cost effective marketing decisions to hotel industry in terms of growth and substantial revenues. With the help of marketing information system, the strategic marketing decisions are found more creative and effective.

4. The task of setting price is simplified: In managing the market activities for the hotel industry, the decisions regarding a change the hotel tariff is found significant. Pricing menus and drinks in hotel food and beverage areas to obtain maximum possible sales and profits is a very complex subject. This necessitates an in-depth study of cost and competitors' strategies. The competitive restaurant facilities is an important consideration while making the pricing decisions. Availability of regular room occupancy statistics also helps in making the pricing decisions in a major way. Thus, it is right to say that task of hotels and hotel companies for making the right pricing decisions are simplified considerably.

5. Innovation in promotion is possible: The promotional strategies play a fantastic role in making the marketing decisions. For demand stimulation, it is essential that an organisation makes possible. creativity in the promotional decisions. The advertisement and publicity campaigns, advertisement slogans, sales promotion etc. are found effective in transforming the potential guests into heavy guests. The recent developments in the field of electronics have made possible new developments as far as advertisements are concerned. The application of marketing principles in the hotel industry also simplifies the task of innovating the promotional decisions.

The aforesaid facts clarify the significance of hotel marketing in the present competitive and volatile business environment. This makes it essential that hotels and hotel companies make sincere efforts to apply the principles of marketing and to innovate the same in the face of changing business conditions.

THIRD WAVE CIVILISATION AND HOTEL INDUSTRY

The issue of development have undergone radical changes not only in the West but also in the East. Of late, a number of people are better off than the previous decades of the 1950s and 1960s. No doubt, if we talk being better off in terms of material assets, there are a good number of people who own their own homes, possess cars, televisions, video-tape recorders, cameras etc. than one or two decades back, yet, many do not come into this privileged category. There exists considerable social tension, dissension and stress with crime having increased across the globe. A generation gap exists not just between parents and children but even in younger people just five or ten years short. Racial tension appears to be mounting leading to polarisation of views. Despite rapid industrialisation, unemployment is increasing day by day. Employer and employees' relations appear to have worsened in most countries. In the face of these negative developments in the society, the sociologists, economists and writers have been found painting a depressing picture of the future.

Despite numerous negative developments in the society, a number of positive developments, have been seen, though obscured by the technological advancements. The fact cannot be denied that the technological transformation has been triggered off, specially by Americans and Russians and mainly through the space programme. The multi-dimensional developments in the space programme lead to a drive toward miniaturization and the use of machines to assist men in their work, i.e., robots relevant. In this context, it is important to quote the views of great thinkers whose opinions have glorified American management methods and seems to infuriate management of most other countries. One important personality is Jean Jacques Servan-Schreiber who in his book, *The American Challenge,* found the industrialized economies of the West completely exhausted. He frets over the mountains of petrodollars accumulating in Arab hands and paints a terrible portrait of third world countries, often crushed under the weight of famine and illiteracy. He feels that only a dramatically new approach based on enriching human credentials or potentials can bring things on the rail. Servan Schreiber, however, unfolds a fascinating future which at least is optimistic and positive.

Another fascinating contribution is of Alvin Toffler, *The Third Wave,* in which he stresses on sociological problems over the coming years. Toffler finds 3000 years of agricultural revolution (the first wave), followed by 300 years of industrial revolution (the second wave) which in his eyes is turning sour. He describes a Third Wave Civilisation where a large section of the population will work in the electronic cottages. What is the relevance of these new developments to the hotel industry?

The Third Wave of the civilisation is likely to expand new markets and new segments. The technological advances would make possible an increase in the disposable income. On account of the inadequacy of raw materials and cheap human resources, the West has been left with no option but to shift to the East. This is going to increase the development potentials in the third world countries. In developing countries like India, an increase in the disposable income and a simultaneous decrease in the pressure of inflation, clearly indicates that the existing discretionary income will gain a rapid momentum. which in due course is to be instrumental in changing the lifestyles of the general masses. The hotel industry is directly influenced by changing lifestyles and *vice versa*. Thus, the third wave is likely to generate new markets in the third world countries.

In addition to the aforesaid facts, some significant developments in the making of development policies to boost the hotel industry has been seen. The policy makers now have been found viewing the social problems with a different vision. Actually, an attitudinal change in the different sections of the society has emerged. The corporate culture is gaining a momentum. A number of constituents have initiated the recent change. Which has been influencing our life styles *vis-a-vis* the spending behaviour. This paves the ways for the development of hotel industry.

Here, it is important to mention that in this third wave civilisation where the electronic cottages are likely to make substantial contribution to the social transformation processes, the expectations of potential customers being accommodated in hotels would be very high. It is against this background that the urgency of marketing practices for hotels and hotel companies has emerged. It is very natural that multi-dimensional developments in the environmental conditions necessitate frequent innovations in the marketing decisions. Innovative decisions are always based on creativity which is based on the foundations of perfection and professionalism. The inventions and innovations in the field of communication would make possible a qualitative improvement in the marketing information system or say, the decision-assisting Information system is likely to be more sensitive to the decision-makers specially while using it as a problem solving method.

In view of the above, it is right to mention that in the coming decades, an acceleration in the process of socio-economic transformation would strengthen hotel culture which would be considerably supported by the third wave culture. This new culture as a gift of corporate culture has a different identity. The budding and upcoming youths have developed a craze for that culture in which privacy of an individual is not to be invaded. We find them very liberal to live in culture in which unmarried boys and girls prefer to live in the hotels or apartments like a married couple. They prefer a free life, free sex away from home. What to talk of the west when we find this culture gaining popularity even in the Indian context. In the coming years, this culture will spread like a wildfire and this will inject new life to the hotel culture.

The corporate culture has also been making ways for stress and we find a majority of the youths facing the problem of depression. They want to earn more because they need to spend more for leading a luxurious lifestyle. To refresh their minds and diffuse tension, they would be required to visit tourist spots which would also increase demand for hotels. The segment of fifty plus and senior citizens would also demand for budget hotels.

With the emergence of a society where we find concept of marriage as an institution becoming discarded, the concept of apartment hotel, cottage hotel, budget hotel, residential hotel will be much more popular. Here we are not deliberating upon the positive and negative influences of development indeed are focusing on the potential segments to emerge for the hotel sector. Because when social turmoil gains momentum, we find a stage where willingly or unwillingly we find ourselves trapped. Actually we are crossing the same stage of social turmoil.

The migration of rural population to the urban areas and space constraints have been creating a new market for the hotel industry, organisation of marriage and other functions in hotels. A majority of the urban population prefer to celebrate their functions in hotels which is also on account of symbolising the status. Earlier, people residing even in the urban areas were found visiting villages for celebrating these functions but now the scenario is changed.

The above mentioned facts make it clear that emerging disintegration in the social system, increasing temptation for cities and towns, growing problem of time and space constraints, mounting domination of westernised lifestyles, contracting infrastructural facilities in the villages, increasing number of working woman growing influence of third wave and live-in culture are opening new avenues for the development of hotel culture which would require different types of hotels In the days and years to come. The hotel planners and policy decision-makers have to increase the supply position.

HOTEL MARKETING IN INDIAN PERSPECTIVE

The British has the credibility of developing hotel sector in India because till the dawn of independence almost all hotels in India were owned and operated by British or a few of them by Swiss. The Taj Hotel built was Jamshedji Nauroji Tata in Bombay (now Mumbai) in 1903 is the only exception. After the attainment of independence and to be more specific after the adoption of the planned concept of economic development in 1951, a fundamental change in the development concept of national economy was found which injected new life and strength to the hotel sector. The UNESCO conference organised in Delhi paved avenues for the construction of Ashoka Hotel by the Government of India in 1956. The Ashoka chain of hotels is the largest hotel chain in India Which is run by the ITDC, a public sector undertaking. The Ashoka is now known as Ashok. Next chain is Oberoi Group of hotels running hotels even in the foreign countries. The group was founded by M.S. Oberoi, a well-known personality in the development of hotel industry. Another is the The Taj Group of hotels which is managed and Controlled by the Indian Hotels company Ltd. formed in 1903. Currently, the company has a number of hotels in India and abroad. Besides, the Welcome Group is one of the fastest growing hotel chains in India, a division In the ITC. The Hotel Corporation of India, a subsidiary of Air India has also a number hotels. The hotels of HCI were recommended for disinvestment in two hotels, viz., Centaur Hotels at Mumbai airport and Juhu Beach in Mumbai which was completed in 2002-03. The process of disinvestment was however discontinued following a change in the government policy under which it has been decided to run Centaur Hotel at Srinagar and flight Kitchens at Mumbai on a long-term management contract. The two other hotels, viz., Centaur Hotel and Flight Kitchen at Delhi airport will be run by the HCI till the Commonwealth Games.[14] We find it an unvarnished fact that all these hotels need renovation for excelling competition.

Hotel marketing studies almost all the components directly or indirectly influencing the commercial viability of hotels or hotel companies. The task before the hoteliers is to make the industry remunerative and to make available to the guests world class amenities and facilities so that we find this industry globally competitive. This naturally requires world class professional excellence. Particularly after globalisation, we find significant developments in the field of hotel industry which has been immensely promoted by corporatisation and technological sophistication. The increasing domination of information and communication technology helped in redefining the quality of hotel services. The emergence of corporate culture made possible a significant change in our lifestyles and the taste preferences of almost all the segments were found changed. Innovations were visible not only in core services but even in the peripheral services. The intensity of competition and worldwide economic recession necessitated managerial proficiency. It is against this backdrop that we make strong advocacy in favour of conceptualising innovative marketing so that our services have an edge over the rivals.

In the face of world wide economic depression, the guests have now became much more sensitive to price which makes it essential that the pricing decisions are instrumental in motivating the customers and potential customers. A hotel fixes its own tariff but the patrons determine the price at which the services are actually sold. It is also right to mention that hotel tariff is also found to be an indicator of status and therefore the star group of hotels or any luxurious hotel offering services at reduced price structure may adversely affect the image of users. But in a majority of the cases we find customers having an attitudinal change and becoming sensitive to price and therefore the concept of budget hotel or economic hotel has been found gaining popularity. The guests or customers have also been found preferring rural location and instead of multi-storeyed complexes opting for cottages and apartments. We need to keep into consideration the significant changes that we find in the taste preferences and to formulate a product-mix which may get a positive response. The guests expect a number of innovative services as a package. They need playing ground, sports materials, personal care services, eco-friendly environment and peace which cannot be made available to them in the cities precincts. They need more care while designing and constructing the swimming pool, developing gardens and parks, making lighting arrangements, placing signposts, developing parking facilities and tightening safety and security measures to regulate and minimise the unpleasant events. Mounting terrorism around the globe draws our attention on hotel planning and designing not only with the viewpoint of comforts and conveniences but also with the motto of providing much more safety to the guests and working employees.

The emerging trends in the national and global economies and the changing lifestyles *vis-a-vis* the taste preferences of different segments make a strong advocacy in favors of synchronising core and peripheral services so that the concept of product uniqueness helps in excelling competition. Innovative peripheral services need priority attention of hotel planners. Unless we offer something innovative to our guests, it becomes difficult to retain their loyalty. If we have to survive and thrive, this aspect needs an overriding priority.

Innovative services accompanied with creative promotional measures help hotel professionals in informing, sensing, sensitising, persuading and transforming the potential customers into actual and habitual customers. We need to make use of different components of promotion to make the processes cost-effective *vis-a-vis* proactive. The tour operators purchasing in bulk, the travel agents acting as retailer and back and front-line staff helping in right processing plays an incremental role in managing and promoting the services. The channels need due incentives to activate the process. Since the market is becoming much more competitive on the one hand we need luxurious hotels while on the other hand also need to promote budget or economic hotels. The new generation of information and communication technology will help us in the value addition process. The new forms and types of hotels would be a center of attraction for the upcoming generations. The service ambience or service environment would also need due attention of hotel professionals.

The interiors and exteriors, lighting, signposts, ventilation, music, scent, furnishing, curtains, aesthetic management, parking, reception are some of the important aspects helping employees in performing and guests and visitors in gaining new experiences. The service ambience needs to be managed artistically and professionally to be found instrumental in generating service fragrance. The hotel personnel or employees working in different capacities play a decisive role in activating the value addition process. The receptionists, waiters, housekeepers etc. need to be developed in the changing perspective. They must have world-class expertise, personal and human touch and commitment to value system.

In the Indian perspective, we find tremendous opportunities for the development of hotel industry. The Increasing heat of globalisation, mounting domination of corporatisation, galloping impact of corporate culture, increasing influences of western culture, large scale usage of new generation of information and communication technology, attitudinal transformation and increasing level of discretionary income are positive developments for shaping hotel industry in a different way. How and in what way the hotel professionals capitalise on the existent opportunities would determine the magnitude of success. The policy planners, hoteliers and hotel companies, hotel professionals need to make an in depth study of changing markets so that they find themselves in a position to satisfy the customers and further to retain them for developing brand loyalty.

The development of tourism as a national priority becomes significant in the very context. The new areas of tourism such as adventure tourism, rural tourism, medical tourism, eco-tourism, cultural and heritage tourism, beach tourism, sports tourism are potentially sound for attracting high spending world tourists and we have opportunities for their world class development. So far as the economic activities are concerned, we find good auguries which may inject new life and strength to convention tourism. Of late we have witnessed significant developments in the field of shopping malls and shopping plaza. The trade and commerce activities have been gaining momentum and this may be an additional attraction for tourists visiting India. We cannot deny that multi-dimensional developments in all these areas would considerably benefit the hotel industry. We need to innovate strategic marketing decisions for making the hotel industry competitive to the world market. Quality infrastructure is required to be created at strategic points. We need to take the co-operation of experts for having architectural flavors. We need to make use of old havelis and palaces. We need the services of landscape experts. We need right location and professional excellence. We need to increase the occupancy ratio. We need sophisticated technology and at the same time personal touch and humanised leadership. We need sympathy and empathy and the delivery of personalised services.

The conceptualisation of modern marketing principles in the hotel industry would fulfil the desired results. The hotel professionals having world class excellence may provide to us a prescription that is to be much more effective.

Increasing the occupancy ratio appears to be a complicated task before the marketing professionals because the intensity of competition, heterogeneity and diversity found in products aggravate the magnitude of problem. Hotels, lodges, motels, restaurants and bars, dining and beverage services are the different areas where hotel professionals need world class excellence. We cannot negate that hotel industry has witnessed unprecedented growth during the yesteryears. The important variables for a positive result are conducive economic and political environmental conditions. The shifts in lifestyles, travel patterns, technology, demographics, investment patterns have also played an incremental role in the development process. However, the worldwide economic recession has been found obstructing the process and throwing numerous challenges and threats before the hotel industry. How and in what way, the hotel professionals make use of their professional excellence would determine their potentials of countering the adverse conditions.

Business in the hotel industry is unpredictable. This is mainly on account of seasonal fluctuation in the tourism industry on which the development of hotel industry sizeably rests. The political factors also inject life to the problem because as and when we find an invasion on political relations, the tourism industry is adversely affected which considerably affects the hotel business. Inadequacy of supporting infrastructural facilities not only increases the operational costs but also obstructs the value addition process. Today, we find a good number of hotels making use of internet services and due to frequent power breakdowns, the guests *vis-a-vis* the providers face a number of problems.

The increasing fear psychosis due to terrorism and social unrest has been making the task of government policy makers, hotel companies and hotel professionals much more difficult. Whatsoever the odds and constraints that we find before the hotel sector may be removed but the damages to tourism and hotel due to terrorism take much more time for their redressal because the psychophobia aggravates the image problem.

The hotel industry thus faces myriad of problems, challenges and threats which need multi-cornered support. The policy decisions of central as well as the state governments need priority attention so that we find a significant increase in the number and quality of hotels of different types for different segments. The strategic areas are to be identified for locating hotels keeping in view the emerging trends in the tourism and national economy. The problems related to land for the construction of hotels need due support of government. The safety and security measures are required to be tightened. The travel and tourism need priority attention of government. Motivational measures are to be innovated for luring the tourists and improving the demand position badly affected by economic turbulence. In addition, the hotel industry requires world class professionals and well educated and trained back and front-line staff.

The widening gap between demand and supply requires to be bridged. The Food Craft Institutes are required to be strengthened and some new FCIs are to be opened. To enlarge the scope, the hospitality education needs to be imparted through the network of ITIs, Polytechnics and at the + 2 stage as a vocational system of the school education. IHMs which are found engaged in processing the bulk of manpower at managerial and skill level need to be strengthened and capacities to be augmented with international linkages for quality and quantity output of human resources. New IHMs in the states/ regions that have not been covered as yet should be established for better distribution of government resources. Through integrated efforts with states, IHMs under PPP mode should be encouraged. For the young untrained staff who continue to join the industry, the government should build capacities through short-term training programmes. The existing scheme of "Train the Trainer" needs to be strengthened and implemented countrywide for boosting supply of adequate trainers. Capacity building of the service providers through short training courses should be taken up as an integral part for strengthening and enlarging the manpower required by the hospitality industry.

The mounting intensity of competition makes it essential that the motivational schemes are promoted by the government. Provision of Tax Holiday has been made by the Ministry of Finance for 5 years for 2 star, 3 star and 4 star category of hotels in and around the districts of Delhi for the Commonwealth Games.[15] This needs to be extended throughout the country for all categories of hotel. Special incentives may be considered for the hilly areas, rural areas, places of pilgrimage, the NER including Sikkim, J&K, Uttranchal and Himachal Pradesh. We cannot negate that we find acute shortage of particularly the budget or economic hotels and to increase its number the subsidies or incentives should be on the room created basis and should also be applicable to metro towns and the procedure of disbursement of subsidy should be simple. In order to create standard budget accommodation, we may offer incentives to guest houses and accommodation under the Home stay programme of the government.

The above mentioned facts make it clear that for the development of hotel industry, a number of steps are to be initiated. The government as well as the PPP mode may be helpful in creating world-class accommodation for almost all the segments. We cannot negate that professional excellence proves to be ineffective if we find industry experiencing infrastructural constraints. Since we find hotel industry directly related to the tourism industry it is pertinent that governments, provincial and central, initiate and activate measures for the rapid growth of T&T industry which will automatically increase the demand side for the hotel industry.

SUMMARY

Information on the foundation of hotel marketing has been aptly given in this chapter. Before studying other aspects, be sure that the following facts are well versed:

- **Concept of Hotel:** Hotel is a public place where all possible amenities and facilities are made available to a person/persons. It is a large city house of distinction and a public building. It is a place to promote business. It is a home away from home where all facilities are available but chargeable.
- **Concept of Motel:** It is a transit hotel geared to accommodate guests traveling on motors for being accommodated for an overnight stay.
- **Types of Hotel:** On the basis of nature, the different types of hotels are residential hotel, commercial hotel, resort hotel, international hotel and floating hotel. On the basis of official stamp, the different types are approved and unapproved; On the basis of star, the different types are one star, two star, three star, four star, five star. Or, classified and unclassified.
- **Concept of Hotel Marketing:** By the term hotel marketing, we mean application of the marketing principles in the hotel services. Hotel marketing consists almost all aspects right from ascertaining customer needs to getting the customers satisfied.
- **Marketing vs. Selling:** In the selling, the key areas are advertising and other aspects of communication. In marketing, we find studies of information management, formulation of different mixes, study of competition, study of the behavioral profile of guests.
- **Marketing of Hotel Services:** The growing significance of professionalism has necessitated the application of modern marketing principles in the hotel industry. In view of the increasing level of expectations of guests, the hotel marketing simplifies the task understanding the customers and keeping them satisfied and transforming them into heavy customers.
- **Customers of Hotel Industry:** Generally, we find two types of customers domestic and foreign.
- **Significance of Hotel Marketing:** Hotel marketing helps in studying the customers' behaviour, it makes possible organisational effectiveness, simplifies the task of managing the marketing information, helps in setting the hotel tariff and makes possible innovation in promotion.

- **Social Turmoil and The Hotel Industry:** The emerging third wave culture is to pave ways for the development of hotel industry. A change in lifestyles would be helpful in developing hotel culture and vice versa.

KEY TERMS

Roman Empire
Inn-keeping
Hospitality
Supernatural
Evil Spirits
Devil
Hotel Culture
Burgeoning
Motel
Tavern
Residential Hotel
Apartment
Commercial Hotel
Floating Hotel
Classified Hotel
Approved Hotel
Resort Hotel
FCIs
Transcendental
Pilgrims
Marketing Information System
Social Turmoil
Third Wave Culture
Electronic Cottage
Live-in Culture
ITDC
HCI
Terrorism
Service Ambience
Waiters
Housekeepers
Psychophobia
Fear psychosis
IHMs
Home Stay Programme
PPP

REVIEW QUESTIONS

1. What do you mean by Hotel? Discuss its different types.
2. What do you mean by Motel? Distinguish between Hotel and Motel.
3. What do you mean by Hotel Marketing? Focus on the differences between selling the Hotel Services and Marketing the Hotel Services.
4. Throw light on the different types of customers visiting hotels with diverse motives.
5. Discuss the importance of hotel marketing in the present competitive and volatile business environment.
6. Explain the relevance of Third Wave Civilisation to the development of hotel culture.
7. Write a descriptive note on the marketing of hotel services in the Indian perspective.

APPLICATION EXERCISES

1. "Hotel is a home away from home where all, amenities and facilities are available but chargeable." Comment on this statement in the capacity of a hotel professional.
2. In the capacity of a hotel marketer focus on the future of hotel culture in the Indian perspective.
3. Do you find Motel as a transit hotel geared to accommodate guests travelling on motors for being accommodated for their overnight stay? Justify your opinion.
4. "Of late the hotel industry has been facing multi-dimensional problems but the future of hotels and hotel companies practicing marketing would be bright." In the light of this statement, focus on the importance of marketing for hotel business.
5. "The Third Wave Civilisation has been gaining a rapid momentum even in the Indian society." As a marketing professional focus on this new civilisation for the development of hotel culture.
6. As a marketing professional identity profitable opportunities for the development of hotel Industry in the Indian perspective so that the concept of budget hotel lures low-spending tourist both from domestic and overseas markets.

End notes:

1. Daniel J. Boorstem: *The American National Express;* Random House, 1965.
2. Charles K Jr. and Larry E. Halber: *Tourism Planning and Development;* B.B.I Co., 1979, p. 174.
3. Definition presented by Hotel operator to authorities of the National Recovery Administration, 1933.
4. *The Hindu,* May 15, 1983, p. 17.
5. Hotel and Restaurant. Guide India, New Delhi, p. 17.
6. Hotel and Restaurant. Guide India, 1991, General Information.
7. Gerald W. Latten: *The Modern Hotel and Hotel Management;* W.H. Freeman & Co., 1968.
8. Gerry Draper: Quoted from Melvyn Greene, Heinemann Professional Publishing, p. 28.
9. Melvyn Greene: *Marketing Hotels and Restaurants into the 90s;* Heinemann Professional Publishing, Oxford, 1989, p. 29.
10. *Ibid.*
11. Anderson and Lembke: *Advertising Agent of a Swedish Firm.*
12. Thomas F. Powers: *Introduction to Management in the Hospitality Industry.*
13. Melvyn Greene: *Op.cit.,* p. 28.
14. Eleventh Five Year Plan; Planning Commission; Government of India, New Delhi, Vol. III, pp. 245-51.
15. Eleventh Five Year Plan: *Op.cit.,* p. 251.

....ꕥꕥꕥ....

CHAPTER - 2

BEHAVIOURAL PROFILE OF HOTEL CUSTOMERS

The western world considered India as the land of snakes and elephants. The IT revolution initiated and energised by us and increasing heat of corporatisation activised by us changed their perception. The multi-dimensional developments in the national economy and new feathers of tourism developed by us have lured domestic as well as the world tourists. With these innovative developments, the hotel sector has been found getting the biggest rub-off effect. Let's understand the customers and capitalise on the opportunities.

CHAPTER OBJECTIVES

Introduction – Hotel Customer: A General Description – Behaviour of Hotel Customers – Behavioural Influences – Insight from Sociology – Insight from Economics – Customers' Behaviour and Lifestyles – Why Lifestyle Studies from Hotel Services? – Motivational Factors Making People Buy or Spend Money – Understanding the Behaviour of Hotel Customers – Influencing the Aggressive Hotel Customers – Transformation of Attitude into Behaviour and Action – A Buyer Behaviour Model for Hotel – Behavioural Profile of Hotel Users in Indian Perspective – Summary – Key Terms – Review Questions – Application Exercises – End Notes.

LEARNING OBJECTIVES

This chapter of the book aims at studying the different dimensions of behavioural profile of hotel customers. The hotel professionals bear the responsibility of understanding the changing levels of expectations of customers which simplifies formulation of a sound marketing strategy *vis-a-vis* satisfaction and retention of customers. Recently we find an increase in the demand side which makes it essential that we improve the supply position by strengthening the PPP mode. With the increasing heat of globalisation, corporatisation and technological sophistication, the hotel customers have high level of expectations. Gauging the level, innovating the services found to be nationally and globally competitive may help hotel professionals in satisfying and retaining customers and ultimately becoming a brand leader.

INTRODUCTION

Behavioural scientists consider behaviour as a mirror in which everyone sees his/her face/image. Purchase of a product or service and brand is rarely the result of a single motive. The users of hotel services come from different regions or strata or economic categories. Behaviour is not found static as it changes over time and specially in tune with demographic, geographic and socio-economic transformation. Understanding the behaviour of customers coiling diversity and heterogeneity requires world-class professional excellence. Particularly in the hotel services, the lifestyles occupy a place of outstanding significance. From a sociological standpoint, lifestyle is a group phenomenon which pervades many aspects of life and implies a central life interest. Lifestyles vary in the face of sociologically relevant variables. In the context of consumer behaviour, the lifestyles emerge as a system concept.

The emerging trends in the satisfaction index help a marketing professional in evaluating the sensitivity of marketing strategies. If the satisfaction index shows a positive trend, the strategies are supposed to be effective. Conversely, if the satisfaction index shows a negative trend, the marketing professionals need to have a microscopic audit of their strategic decisions. It is against this background that the hotel professionals need to understand the changing behavioural profile of users and potential users. An in-depth study of behaviour is thus found significant to make proactive decisions. The guaranteed or secured way of making profit is customer satisfaction.

It is not enough that hotel professionals just react to the given wants of customers. In a true sense, they are also supposed to play an active role in anticipating the needs and requirements and taste preferences in shaping and designing their desires and aspirations and albeit in helping them in resolving their day-to-day problems. This marketing philosophy should be the way of any business which would dictate activities, operations and policies of an organisation. The customer satisfaction, would, of course, be at its roots. Understanding customers in a right fashion is considered to be an essential dimension for satisfaction and retention.

In the process of studying and understanding customers, the hotel professionals need to study their attitudes, intentions, desires, lifestyles, levels of expectations and taste preferences. Attitude is an emotional predisposition to respond in a positive or in a negative way. The attitude governs their response to a stimulus. It affects both perception and behaviour. An attitudinal change in the customers of a particular hotel is found difficult when they develop brand loyalty. The knowledge of customers' attitude can provide a sound base for initiating qualitative improvements in the services offered by hotels. The hotel professionals thus need to observe the different stages of transformation so that product innovation process simplifies the task of satisfying and retaining the customers.

For the formulation or implementation of marketing strategy, it is essential to have a detailed knowledge of the changing behavioural profile of customers. They come from different segments such as domestic and foreign, literate and illiterate, men and women, rural and urban, corporate executives and government administrators youths and gray visiting hotels with diverse motives. It is imperative that hotel professionals develop their awareness of taste preferences. This simplifies their task of creating and stimulating demand. Customers have individual values, perception, preferences and a behavioural pattern based on the environmental influences. In this context, racial, ethnicity, nationality, leisure habits, health factors and lifestyles have a substantial influence on the behaviour of customers. The customers' age, life-cycle stage, occupation, economic condition and personality influence the way in which they make the buying decisions. Management has been found using new techniques to understand how customers react to marketing. This makes it essential that the hotel professionals analyse their needs and identify to improve marketing products and communication to satisfy them. It is against this background that marketing of goods or services are becoming complex. A study of customers' behaviour helps marketers in diagnosing the levels of their expectations.

In psychological terms, the whole range of the generation of wants and their transformation into buying or using decisions can be explained as behaviour. The core problem of the entire marketing process is to identify strategy bearing the efficacy of activating the transformation process so that a good number of potential customers are transformed into actual customers. In a true sense, the transformation process is the conversion of attitudes into action. The marketers are here required to ensure the potential guests that their attitudes are situational and organisational. The process remains incomplete unless the marketers make a microscopic study of feedback loop as it helps in gauging the levels of expectations and satisfaction. In the face of increasing discretionary income, a change in lifestyles is found inevitable. The lifestyles govern the levels of expectations of customers.

In view of the above, it is right to say that marketing decisions cannot be proactive unless the hotel professionals make an in-depth study of the expectations of users and potential users. The core problem is to satisfy the guests visiting hotels so that they gain new experiences while staying and prefer to visit the same hotel again and again. We cannot negate that satisfaction makes the ways for retention *vis-a-vis* development of brand loyalty. The marketing professionals need to strengthen their realisation that behavioural profile of guests staying in hotels are found much more sensitive.

While marketing hotel services, an experienced receptionist is supposed to know that business guests returning around 6.30 p.m. from a hard daylong schedule tend to be over critical and impatient in waiting just a moment for their key.

He/she is supposed to know that they had a busy schedule and so cannot take it out on their wives and so many blast off as a natural process may be at the hotel staff. Here a few words of "empathy" like Have you had a tough day? may bring positive results. Empathy is the ability to sit in the other person's seat, or wear his shoes and imagine what really makes him tick. What motivates him, what are his worries, his problem? Empathy gives us clues to successful selling, makes us much more successful and helps hotel management in conducting productive business. In hotel marketing, empathy plays an outstanding role. It is a key thought process or ability in successful marketing.

In the behavioural studies related to hotel and hotel companies, it seems appropriate that professionals find it difficult to assess the motivational factors attracting people for buying or spending money. This makes it essential that the hotel professionals assign priority attention on understanding the customers which would provide to them an idea of the motivational factors to be effective in attracting them. In the hotel industry, the key motivational factors are weddings, holidays, launching of product, room for buyers and room for sales people. In weddings, the important factors are status, ego, sentiment, price and security. In holidays, the key factors are the price, value for money, comfort and health. In product launch, the factors are investment, status, value for money. In room for buyer, the factors comfort, status, ego and investment. In room for sales people, the factors are comfort, value for money and status.

In view of the above, it is right to say that arriving at sound marketing decisions cannot be possible unless we conduct an in-depth study of customers' behaviour. Inspite of the individuality and complexity of human behaviour, the marketing professionals are required to continue their research, select a segment likely to reap and exercise the promotional measures expected to be effective to turn the negative into positive. It is in this context that a study of changing behavioural profile is found significant.

The hotel industry has a bright and prosperous future. The outlook for the Indian hospitality business is extremely positive and bright because the scope, the potential and the reach of Indian tourism are enormous. During yesteryears, the PPP mode has been successful in creating world class infrastructure. The rail, road and air connectivity and development of popular tourism destinations have been engineering a sound environment. The innovative tourism has been adding additional attractions and the world class marketing professionals have been making sincere and honest efforts to inform, sense, sensitise, persuade and transform the potential guests into actual and habitual guests. The industry has been found getting a positive response because we have studied and received changing expectations of customers in a right fashion. Despite, worldwide economic recession, the Indian tourism and hotel industry has been flourishing. If we have to remain globally competitive; we need to be innovative.

HOTEL CUSTOMERS: A GENERAL DESCRIPTION

- ***Non-customers:*** Persons not interested in using the services of hotels are known as non-customers or users. They lack willingness, desire to avail the facilities of a hotel. Here, the hotels and hotel companies have to identify them to simplify the task of identifying the potential customers.
- ***Potential Customers:*** We also call them prospects or potential guests. They bear the efficacy to use the hotel services but lack willingness. And so, the hotels and hotel companies have to identify them through effective marketing decisions which would be helpful in transforming them into actual customers.
- ***Actual Customers:*** Persons already using the services of hotels are known as actual customers/ guests.
- ***Light Customers:*** Customers already visiting hotels, but very rarely or occasionally, are known as light customers/guests.
- ***Heavy Customers:*** Customers visiting a particular hotel frequently and forming a habit to visit the same are known as heavy customers/guests.

BEHAVIOUR OF HOTEL CUSTOMERS

We cannot deny the fact that arriving at sound marketing decisions is a difficult task which needs professionalism and excellence. Manifestation of perfection in the purest form is an essential criteria for achieving excellence. All marketing activities concerned with goods/services start and end with marketing. If customers/guests respond positively and heavily, the success rate of hotels or hotel companies are found at peak. Contrary to it, if they are found non-receptive, the game is over and a final departure from the business world is a must. It is against this background that behavioural studies carry an outstanding significance, specially in the literature of hotel marketing. The personality of human beings in general is found enigmatic, the classes are good in number, the motives are diverse and therefore, the task of decision makers is found difficult. The constraints aggravate further when some of the guests are found indifferent or insensitive to hotel tariff whereas some others are found more sensitive to price.

In the hotel industry, the marketers are required to see that guests are unaware or aware, interested or intend to try, or experiment to assess the attitude of light customers or heavy customers. Here, they should not have any confusion regarding the impact of advertisement and the service sensitivity. They may be indifferent or the intensity of sensitivity may be high or low. In all cases, the marketing decisions cannot be uniform. This necessitates an in-depth study of the behavioural profile of hotel customers. In a true sense, we consider behaviour an orderly process where he/she interacts with his/her environment.[1]

To understand marketing, we need to understand customers and to understand customers, we need to understand their behaviour. Marketing success or failure particularly depends on the reactions on target customers expressed in the form of using patterns. The economists as well as the psychologists have studied behaviour in a bit different form which, of course, is a difficult task due to diverse, obscure and enigmatic personality of customers.

BEHAVIOURAL INFLUENCES

An expert says, "*The individual specific behaviour in the market place is affected by internal factors such as needs, motivation, perception and attitudes as well as external or environmental influences such as the family, social groups, culture, economic and business influences*".[2] Regarding the behavioural influences, we find sociological, economic and psychological insights. The economists perceive the problem in a bit different way.

INSIGHT FROM SOCIOLOGY

Sociological Influences: Sociologists view marketing as involving the activities of groups of people motivated by group pressures as well as by individual desires. The sociological studies have emphasised the significance of reference groups, the individual's concepts of a social role, the diffusion process and social class as influences of human behaviour. The reference groups are people with whom an individual regularly or occasionally associates and exerts strong influences on his/her behaviour. The primary groups are people engaged in intimate, face-to-face communication and co-operation. The most influenced primary group is the family. But, after the emergence of the concept of modern family, we find the peer group having more dominance. In the peer group, we find the composition of individuals who spend considerable time together. It is also essential that they are of fairly common age and social background. Knowledge of reference groups and their influences makes it easier to explain why customers behave in a particular way. It is more significant for marketers to know about their behaviour. In the hotel and travelling industries, the customers are generally influenced by individual desires. In addition, the peer group also exerts pressure since all the members of the group are of fairly common age and so, the exchange of views cannot be denied.

Cultural Influences: The culture in which the customers live is an important determinant of their behaviour. It cannot be refuted that customers have values, perception, preferences and behaviour pattern which are the result of environmental influences. An analysis of the different cultural lifestyles help to identify the customers' preferences. The marketers are here required to understand the similarities between customers in the various strata of the society, in particular on economic grounds. Every culture involves unique patterns of social conduct. An analysis of these patterns helps in explaining the behaviour of individuals. This is proved by the cultural variation existing in different countries around the globe, many aspects of American culture and sub-cultures within the US are unique, including the leisure time.[3] This plays a vital role in the hotel industry. The Japanese culture provides for certain patterns of eating, living and behaving. Indian culture is a bit different from other cultures, specially in respect of leisure time and patterns of eating, living and behaviour. There are also nations which have multiple cultures, such as Switzerland and India. In such nations, marketing plans must take into account variations in different cultures.[4] Here, the marketers are supposed to understand not only how the products certify certain needs, but also its adjustments to the modern culture.[5]

The development of the hotel industry should be in such a way which fulfils the needs of different cultures. Particularly while developing hotels and hotel companies, this aspect needs immediate attention. The available leisure time is also an important consideration. Values and lifestyles are vigorously influenced by the availability of leisure time. The hotel services go a long way with increasing leisure time activities to complement the time in a meaningful way. It is very natural that where we find 5-day week, the lifestyles are different as people have more leisure time and the prospects want to visit hotels. In addition, the emerging trends in the discretionary income is also to influence the behavioural dimension of potential customers. In the hotel industry, the buying decisions are influenced by women and children. In a society where women and children are reportedly dominating, the concept of working wives is found gaining momentum and the hotel culture is sure to gain from this momentum. Contrary to it, in a society where we find the concept of housewives, the family members prefer to stay in their homes.

INSIGHT FROM ECONOMICS

Economic Influences: The behavioural pattern is largely influenced by the emerging trends in the discretionary income. Here, it is important to mention that an increase in the disposable income carries no meaning, if the inflationary pressure is showing a positive trend. In addition, the size of family, the income expected and the availability of credit facilities also become instrumental in this very context. To make the perception clear, let's clarify the disposable and discretionary incomes. The disposable income is what people are left with to spend after they have discharged their tax liabilities. The discretionary income is money left in our hands after buying the essential items, such as food, shelter, clothes, education, medicare etc. So far as the hotel services are concerned, the discretionary income plays a decisive role here in making the buying decisions.

The Wharton study[6] disclosed that in urban families with low incomes, average personal consumption spending exceeded the income. The study also revealed that the average propensity to consume declined rather than rapidly as income rose above the poverty level. Similarly, the income expectations and liquid assets available to the customers were found impact generating. If customers expect additional income, they make hotel visiting decisions and behave in a different way.

Insight from Psychology: It is right to mention that no single theory of psychology of consumer motivation is complete enough to explain the behaviour of customers. We find three approaches to the development of psychological theory of customer's behaviour, e.g., the experimental, clinical and Gestalt. The experimental psychology concentrates on psychological tensions whereas in the clinical psychology, the basic psychological drives are examined.

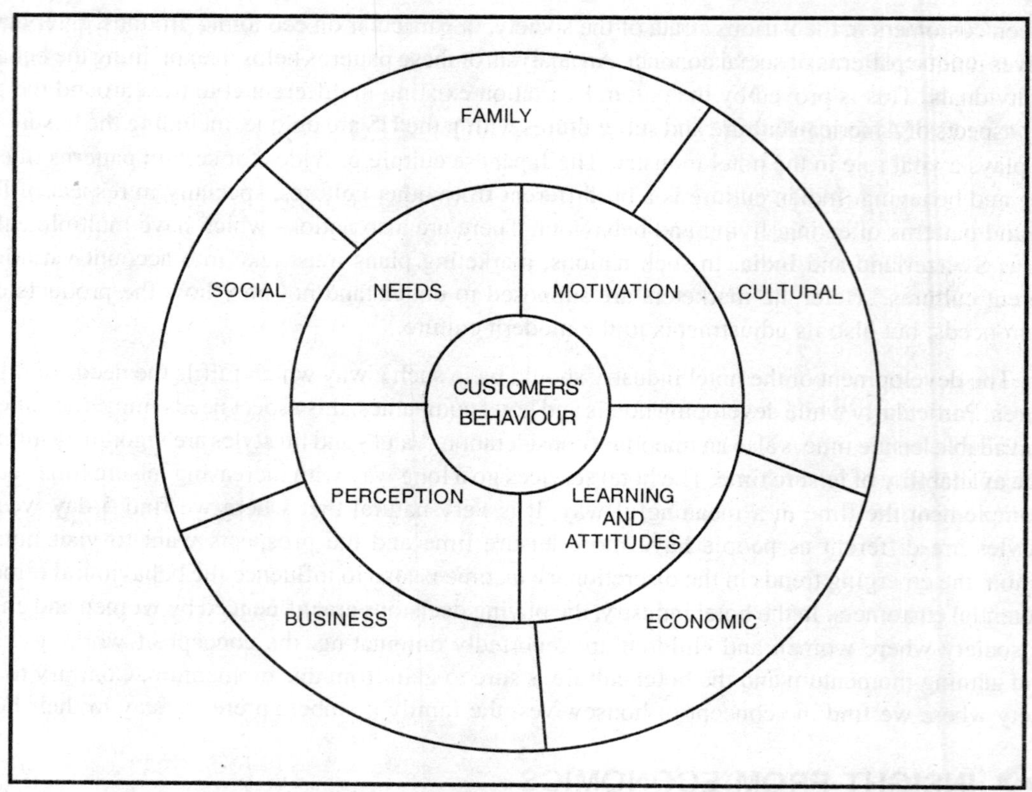

FIG. 2.1: BEHAVIOURAL INFLUENCES

Adapted from: C. Glenn Walters, Consumer Behaviour, Homewood III, Richard D. Irwin Inc., 1978, p. 1.

Attitudes and learning: This concept helps marketers in answering some of the important questions, such as

How do customers learn about products or services offered?

How do they learn to recognise and recall these services?

By what process do they develop using habits?

In a true sense, we consider learning a process in which total functions are altered and rearranged to make them more useful. It is important to clarify that the external stimuli is not the only factor to influence the customers. Here, the external stimuli is in the form of promotional activities. The internal factors[7] have a far reaching impact. Regarding the basic factors, an expert opines[8] repetition, motivation, conditioning, relationship and organisation are helpful in studying the consumer behaviour.

Repetition: It is essential to modify the psychological functions which are required to be accompanied by attention, interest and a goal. Here repetition does not promote learning since the advertisers who depend on repetition alone waste both the money and effects.

Motivation: It is an important factor found instrumental in governing his/her condition or activities. Human motivation is supposed to be the subject of considerable interest.

Conditioning: It is a way of learning. The conditioned response establishes a behaviour pattern but, of course, of temporary nature. It may even disappear, if the reinforcement is not right.

CUSTOMERS' BEHAVIOUR AND LIFESTYLES

The term 'lifestyle' was originally coined by Mex Weber. The term encompasses many of the sociological, cultural and psychological variables. William Lazer defines lifestyles as referring to a *distinctive or characteristic' mode of living in the aggregate and broadest sense of a whole society or segment thereof.* [9]

From a sociological standpoint, Fieldman and Thielber[10] define lifestyle in terms of four characteristics, viz., lifestyle is a group phenomenon, it pervades many aspects of life, it implies a central life interest and it varies according to sociologically relevant variables. It is right to mention that the lifestyle concept is neither a model nor a theory of consumer behaviour. Indeed, it is an organisational concept for understanding many of the determinants and process of behaviour. In the present context, the lifestyle may be defined as unified patterns of behaviour which determine both and are determined by consumption.[11]

WHY LIFESTYLE STUDIES FOR HOTEL SERVICES?

Lifestyle studies are found significant to the hotel industry. We find two cogent reasons for using the concept.

1. Lifestyle draws a variety of analysis together: It is to transform findings into meaningful information about people which provide a portrait of how people are individualised and how do they identify themselves as members of the reference groups, found collectively forming the living patterns. This leads to understand and predict customers' behaviour. The data concerned with incomes, age groups and spending patterns simplify the task.

In visiting hotels, the income is an important consideration. In a society, where, the emerging trends in the discretionary income are positive, it is very natural that prospects prefer to visit hotels. Against this background, it is right to say that in a society where discretionary income is very low, the market potentials would automatically be contracted. In addition, the age groups are also to influence the behaviour. The children and teens are found fascinated to the hotel culture. And therefore, they also influence the decisions. The spending patterns are influenced by the family structure. In a family, where women and children are found dominating, the decisions are reportedly found in favour of visiting hotels.

2. Lifestyle draws a variety of disciplines together: It determines and reflects so many aspects of life and therefore, we consider it a point of convergence between marketing disciplines, such as anthropology, psychology, sociology and economics. Thus, lifestyle emerges as a system concept in the field of consumer behaviour. To be more specific in the hotel business, it is essential that we know everything about our potential customers. A multi-disciplinary approach helps marketers to know the details about the prospects.

The aforesaid facts make it clear that the lifestyles help marketers in studying the behaviour of customers. The sociological studies made in this field clarify the following aspects:

1. *Lifestyle is a group phenomenon:* An individual's lifestyle bears the efficacy of participating in the special groups on the basis of facts obtained from demographic and sociological studies.
2. *Lifestyle pervades many aspects of life:* A person's lifestyle commits him into a certain consistency of behaviour. This helps in predicting the behaviour.
3. *Lifestyle implies a central life interest:* Central interests are family work, leisure and religion and other personal interests like drugs etc. It varies according to sociologically relevant variables like age, sex, ethnicity, social class, religion and others.

An optimal insight into human behaviour cannot be possible unless we study lifestyle patterns. It is a distinctive mode of living in dynamic society which adds richness and dimensionality. Here, people's actions are measured in terms of their activities, interests, opinions and demographic characteristics.[12] The researches made in this field answer some of the questions like

What do women think of the job of housekeeping?

Do they participate in common activities?

Are they interested in the future?

This is concerned with people rather than products. It classifies them into different lifestyle groups, each with a unique style of living.

EXHIBIT 2.1: IMPORTANT ELEMENTS FOUR MAJOR DIMENSIONS OF LIFESTYLE

Activities	*Interests*	*Opinions*	*Demographics*
Work	Family	Themselves	Age
Hobbies	Home	Social Issues	Education
Social events	Job	Politics	Income
Vacation	Community	Business	Occupation
Entertainment	Recreation	Economics	Family size
Club membership	Fashion	Education	Dwelling
Shopping	Food	Products	Geography
Sports	Media	Future	City size
Community	Achievements	Culture	Stage in life cycle

Adapted from: Joseph T. Plummer, *Journal of Marketing*, January 1974, pp. 33-37.

MOTIVATIONAL FACTORS MAKING PEOPLE BUY OR SPEND MONEY

What motivates people to use hotels and restaurants. It is an important question, which is yet to be answered suitably. Actually, we do not know the motivational factors leading people for particular hotels and hotel companies.

There are a number of motivational factors as shown in Exhibit 2.2.

EXHIBIT 2.2: MOTIVATIONAL FACTORS THAT BUY OR SPEND MONEY

Motivational factors that make people buy or spend money		
1.	Fear	Suitable arrangement for insurance
2.	Security	Arrangements like burglar alarms, spy holes, new door
3.	Loneliness	Entertainment facilities like TV, Music System
4.	Status	Luxurious cars
5.	Ego	Luxurious cars
6.	Curiosity	TV, Historical buildings
7.	Professional Envy	Related to status
8.	Basic need	Water, salt, bread and a blanket for warmth
9.	Religion	Money spent on religious functions
10.	Mental relaxation and physical health	Hobbies, sports, relaxation
11.	Price	Buying something at reduced price
12.	Value for money	Not necessarily related only to price
13.	Investment	Shares, stocks, cost of a product launch
14.	Personal comfort	Central heating, AC
15.	Guilt	Present for wife
16.	Shortages	In a regulated economy
17.	Educational/research	Correspondence courses, evening classes
18.	Sentiment	Photographs

In Exhibit 2.2, a list of motivational factors helping the prospects in making the decisions for visiting a particular hotel have been mentioned. The first element is *safety* and for this, it is essential that suitable insurance facilities are extended to the guests. The second aspect is *security* and for this some of the aspects are burglar alarms, spy holes, new doors which would make sure the prospects' that in the hotels they are secured even if accidents take place, they would get signals on time. The third element is *loneliness* and for the same, it is essential that entertainment facilities are made available to the guests. The fourth aspect is *status* and the fifth is *ego.* In a true sense, both aspects are by and large the same. It is quite natural that items related to luxury would be effective in the very context. The sixth item is *curiosity,* which is substantially influenced by the historical buildings or other things having historic importance. The seventh is *profes*sion/*envy* which is related to status. The eighth is giving basic needs in which we include general items of basic consumption like water, salt, food and bedding. The next is *religion,* which should focus on the religious functions. The tenth is *mental relaxation* and *physical health* which include hobbies, sports and relaxation. The next is *price* where it is essential that in the shopping complex of the hotels, the guests are made available goods at reduced price. The next is *value for money* which is not essentially related to price but to the values. The facilities for investment are also found effective in motivating the prospects. The personal comforts are also found instrumental in the very context as the facilities like central heating and air-conditioning would play a positive role. The guilt is related to the availability of items which can be presented to wife. The shortages are very much related to the artificial scarcity or scarcity of goods which we often find in a regulated economy. The educational and research incentives are related to correspondence courses and evening classes. And finally, the sentiment is related to photographs.

In view of the above, it is right to say that motivational factors play a positive role in turning the potential guests into actual guests. And if the guests are found satisfied with the services made available to them, the task of transforming them into heavy guests is simplified. In addition to the factors as mentioned in Exhibit 2.2, there are some more motivational factors influencing the decisions of the guests to use hotels. Here, we talk about the wedding facilities and facilities for a conference/marriage hall. This is found impact-generating, specially in the present day world, where mainly due to space-constraint, people have been found organising marriages in hotels.

UNDERSTANDING THE BEHAVIOUR OF HOTEL CUSTOMERS

Arriving at right marketing decisions cannot be possible unless we develop sound marketing plans. It is natural that before implementing strategies for marketing planning, an organisation identifies its target customers and the decisions process they propose to go through. This necessitates an in-depth study of the behaviour of customers like cultural, social, economic, psychological and personal characteristics. Understanding the behaviour of consumers is vital to the success of any marketing programme. In spite of the individuality and complexities of human behaviour, marketers are required to continue their search for behaviour patterns found reasonably identical and thereafter select a segment expected to be sensitive to their promotional efforts. The fact cannot be that users denied behaviour is dynamic since it changes over time in response to the demographic, geographic and socio-economic factors in a society. In a free enterprise competitive system, the traditional methods are found least effective in predicting which goods/services would be bought/used on the basis of choice preference. The question regarding the frequency is found significant here which is directly related to the transformation process. In the hotel industry, it is not only significant that a particular guest visits a particular hotel. Here, it is also significant that a particular guest visits a particular hotel frequently and ultimately, and thus forms a habit of visiting the same hotel. This helps in increasing the occupancy ratio of hotel rooms in addition to its positive impact on restaurants, bars and cafeterias. This makes it clear that understanding the behaviour of these customers is an important task undertaken by the hotels and hoteliers.

In the hotel industry, the projection of a fair image is found important. If the image is fair, the guests prefer to come to a particular hotel. This makes it essential that hotels and hotel companies make concerted efforts to project a fair image so that word-of-mouth recommendations simplify the task of promotion. The main task before the marketers is to satisfy the customers by offering them the services as per their expectations. Of course, no concept of marketing is more fundamental and pervasive than customers' satisfaction. It is against this background that we consider marketing a customer-satisfaction -engineering strategy. However, the customer satisfaction has been in crisis in service generating organisations in general and in hotel organisation in particular. In an era where marketing searching for a measure of operating effectiveness and business seeks indicators demonstrating in social performance, the customer satisfaction is the single concept to serve the dual role.

In the economic system, satisfaction is equated with utility or the consumers' ability to enjoy goods/services[14] and utility is never measured directly but inferred from the actions of the marketplace through the theory of revealed preference.[15] In the buyers' behaviour model, consumer satisfaction is defined as the point at which expectation and reality coincide.[16] We also say that satisfaction is a generalised positive attitude or a measurable attitude.

The problem faced by the hotel industry is to establish a fair match between services expected and services offered. If the hotels and hotel companies make sincere efforts to understand the behavioural profile of customers, the task of identifying their expectations will be simplified substantially. In studying the behaviour of customers, lifestyle plays a dominating role.

The behavioural studies also make it clear that for studying the behaviour of hotel customers, the attitude of potential guests is found impact-generating. If the attitude is negative and the guests are found overburdened with personal problems, the empathy is found effective. Attitudinal change also necessitates innovative promotional efforts. Generating attraction is the focal point which is possible when we innovate or make possible qualitative improvements in the services offered. It has been mentioned that customers have different attitudes towards service facilities like hotels. Unless the providers have a detailed knowledge of the potential guests, their attitudes cannot be activated to generate substantial revenues.

In the behavioural studies of hotel customers, the important research areas are:

- Collecting and analysing data informing habits, attitudes and needs of the customer. This would help in sorting out customers into homogeneous groups, differentiated by their lifestyles and using behaviour.
- Collecting and analysing data relating to the hotel products/services offered by the competitive hotels and hotel companies. This will help to focus on how these are perceived by the users.
- The data collection will also help focus on actual and potential markets. The marketing strategies for potential markets would be liberal to the promotional efforts. Innovative promotional decisions would simplify the task of transforming the potential into actual.

INFLUENCING THE AGGRESSIVE HOTEL CUSTOMERS

It is not difficult to influence regular customers as experienced receptionists, housekeepers, waiters know the way to tackle them. But the task is really more complicated when the customers are abnormal or are found aggressive. It is not possible that you are going to check the entry of crude persons, *unpolished customers* or aggressive customers etc. All categories of customers are welcome and appreciated by hotel choice. Some of the customers visiting the restaurant, cafeterias create disturbance and generate inconvenience. To be more specific the front line staff bear the responsibility of managing them properly.

Ultimately, this responsibility goes on to the sales executive. Here as a sales executive you have been watching everything. It is found that one guest is not in a mood to pay the bill of your restaurant.:

- Is it practical to ring the police station?
- Is it judicious to check the entry of such customers?
- Is it proper to create a scene?
- Is it commercially viable to take it for granted and to generate the financial losses?
- Is it right to create an image problem?

Of course, a plain answer to all these questions would be 'No'. Then how to understand the behaviour of aggressive customers accessing hotel services to succeed in gaining influence over them? In any case, it is not proper to create a scene as it would create a dent on the hotel's image. The psychologists believe that even the behaviour of abnormal persons can be made normal, if the related personnel understand them and tackle the situation gently and patiently. This is the process of diffusion. In the world of psychology, the word 'Empathy' is found very much sensitive to the diffusion process. This is to share the burden. Here, it is not related to the financial burden. Our emphasis is here on sharing the burden of mental agony by using suitable words and appropriate tactics to solve the problem. Can we deny that words used by us bear the efficacy of generating/diffusing tension? In this case, we have a number of alternatives:

- Let them go, you would not face any problem in identifying them.
- When they disperse, make a request to make payment of bills at your convenience. Here, the use of word 'convenience' may be effective.
- You may get payment the very next day.
- If not, you have to ring/approach to their friends/leaders/ prophets.
- You may get the payment.
- Again if you fail, you should ring/approach their spouses.
- Suppose, you have failed in getting payment, you should now prefer legal actions.

These approaches may see the payment coming through.

We call it phase-wise treatment which provides an opportunity or sufficient time for activating the diffusion process. In a true sense, the image problem needs immediate attention, specially in the hotel industry where the behaviour of hotel personnel and image building of hotels are found to be significant. The money lost can be compensated but the image lost aggravates problems and complicates the business agenda of the hotel industry. We find a number of occasions where guests are found tensed, over pressed with personal official problems. To identify them and to diffuse their tension or to make them normal is essential to retain guests on a long-term basis. This is possible when the hotel personnel in general and the front line staff in particular are well aware of the importance of psychotreatment. We do not find a particular time/occasion for the entry of aggressive customers. They are expected any time and any day.

Of course, the first responsibility is to identify such customers. We consider face an index which conveys us something about customers visiting hotels. The experienced receptionists, waiters, doormen, housekeepers would not face any problem in differentiating normal and abnormal personalities. Your half work is done, if the identification is in a right fashion. If the problem is related to restaurant, the waiters are supposed to deal with them. They have to watch their orders. The style of placing orders would confirm their observation regarding the guests. They have to watch their style, way and dialogues. It will reconfirm the observation of customers being done by the staff/management personnel. Meanwhile, the observation should be transmitted to the sales executive who will make necessary arrangements outside the gate, if circumstances necessitate so. Even if the problem is related to a room where your guests are found creating nuisance and making it inconvenient to others to stay comfortably, the treatment is by and large the same. We call it preventive measure to avoid unexpected complications.

In view of the above, it is right to say that particularly in today's world where the hotel industry is found to be more competitive, a minor lapse on the part of the hotel management staff may result in a major loss to the business. The potential guests outside the hotels are not going to accept the faults of customers. It is really a difficult task for you to convince them. Hence, the most effective solution is to tackle the problem patiently, of course, at the initial stage. This will also simplify the task of projecting a fair image and minimising the problems created by abnormal aggressive customers.

TRANSFORMATION OF ATTITUDE INTO BEHAVIOUR AND ACTION

The *psycholocomotion* of hotel customers is an important aspect of their behavioural profile. The whole process of marketing is the transformation of attitude into behaviour and action. This is presented in Figure 2.2. The model makes it clear that conversion of wants into demands is not automatic. There are a number of processes and the decision-making process is vigorously influenced by the stimuli. Regarding the flow of stimuli, it is right that a man is exposed to a good number of stimuli daily which is due to viewing of messages. The flow of stimuli is shown in the model S1, S2 ...S7. All messages do not reach the level of perception which is meant that a person sees or views or hears what he/she wants to hear or see or view. Needs keep ahead of perceptions. It is the need pattern which plays the vital role in determining where one shall look to.[17] The transformation process acts like a gatekeeper. The opinion leaders play a vital role in activating the transformation process. The opinion and attitude of friends and family members who have already visited a particular hotel is more sensitive than the printed messages. The potential guests endeavour to keep up with the opinion leaders and visit hotels that other members of the group have visited with the motive that it is prestigious to do so.[18] The communications/recommendations made by the opinion leaders are checked by them. This is clear in the figure as S4 is denied entry. The selector system integrates the various stimuli. The predispositional structure is the sum total of attitudes, beliefs, values, goals, personality traits, self-image and group influence which is substantially determined by cultural, sociological and psychological backgrounds. The psychologists believe that since the cognitive structure of an individual is relatively stable, he/she accepts all those messages which are consistent with his/her psychological world. Thus, we find here attitude active and impact generating.

The transformation process is the conversion of attitude into action. For this, it is essential that attitude does not get destroyed. Once a potential guest takes a decision regarding a particular hotel, he/she requires the help of an organisation, specially to ensure that attitude is not destroyed. In the transformation process, we find two important forces, e.g., situational and organisational. So far as the situational aspect is concerned, the decision to visit a particular hotel may arrive at the demand stage unprocessed. So far as the organisational aspect is concerned, the potential guests may seek the co-operation of travel agents, tour operators who transmit to them the required information regarding a particular hotel. This process of conversion of attitude into behaviour is known as 'psycholocomotion' where situations and organisations play an effective role. The last process is 'feedback' which carries valuable information about satisfaction/dissatisfaction reported by customers.

In the feedback process, the word-of-mouth communication is found impact-generating. Here, the visitors act as opinion leaders. If they are satisfied with the services offered to them in a hotel, future communications would definitely be effective. Contrary to it, if they are found dissatisfied, all the promotional efforts put in by the hotel management would be ineffective. If the potential guests,

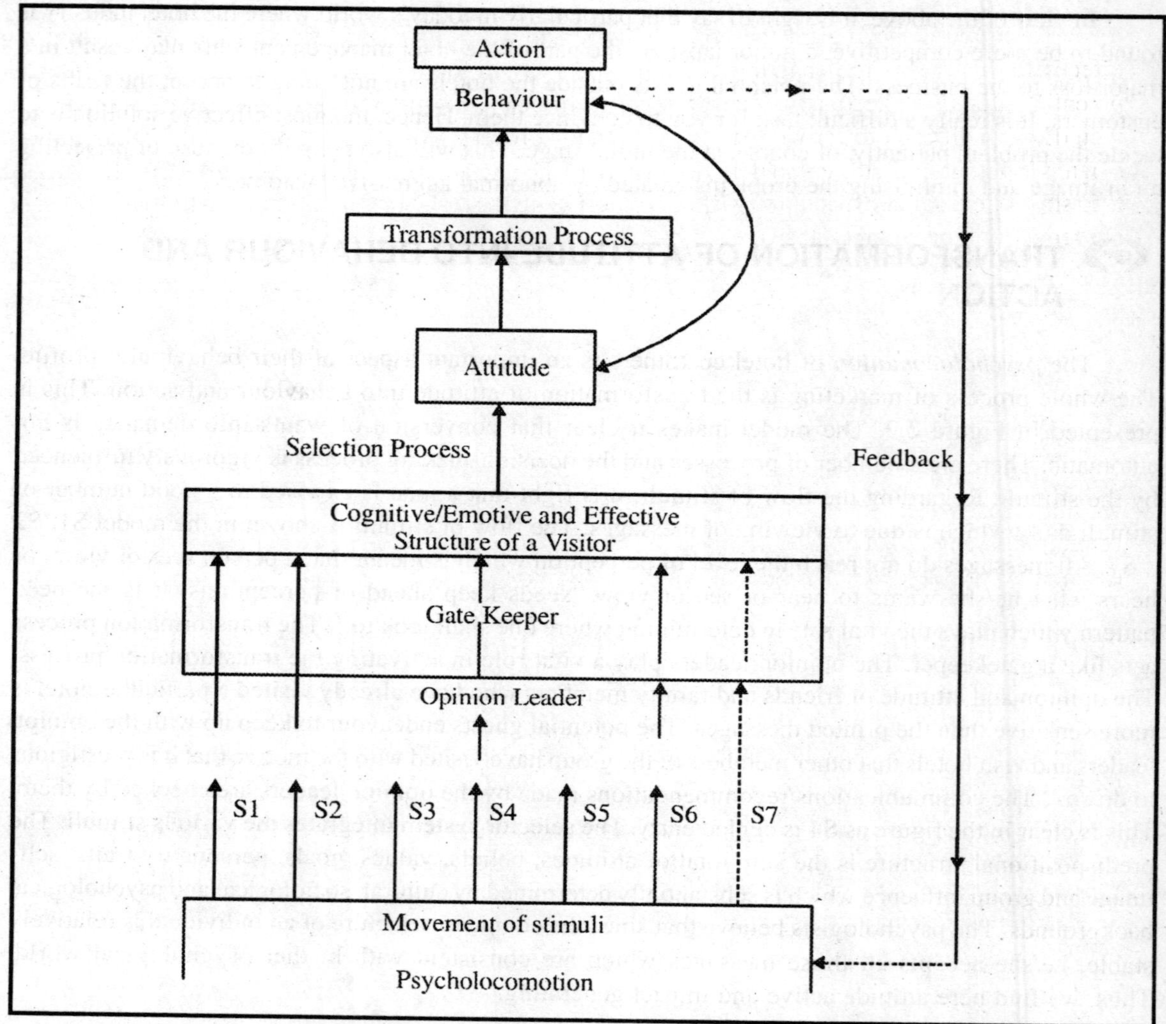

FIG 2.2: PSYCHOLOCOMOTION OF HOTEL CUSTOMERS

Modified from: Anand, M.M.: Tourism and Hotel Industry in India (Prentice-Hall of India)

specially the tourists come to a particular place, a series of steps are traversed before them. Here, the two critical factors influence them, e.g., the pre-dispositional setup of tourists and the instrumentality of tourist organisations. We cannot deny the fact that efficiency of an organisation plays a significant role, particularly in the hotel industry. If an organisation creates messages to cope with demand of the potential guests, the rapid transformation is a must.

The aforesaid facts are effective testimonies to the proposition that the whole drama of demand generation or creation is found well acted, if the *psycholomotion* is processed properly. In a true sense, the demands are ultimately want, processed into behaviour and action (Fig. 2.2). The core problem is the efficiency of hoteliers. If they cater well to their customers, the potential guests are conveniently transformed into heavy guests. If they succeed in satisfying the actual guests, the word-of-mouth recommendations would further activate the process.

To be more specific, in the hotel industry, the word-of-mouth recommendation is found more effective. This makes it essential that the hoteliers assign top most priority to the satisfaction of their potential guests. The feedback, if negative, or word-of-mouth communication, if negative, the hoteliers would find it difficult to activate the transformation process. Thus, it is right to mention that messages, slogans, photographs etc. are no doubt, sensitive to the demand generation process but the chief problem is to study the level of expectations asked by the potential guests. In this context, the following questions are required to be suitably answered.

What do they want?

What are their habits?

What are their lifestyles?

What are their preferences?

Moving from tradition to modern and *vice versa* is a natural movement of styles of living. Of late, we find a fascination for sophisticated comforts and amenities. Tomorrow, the trend may be reversed. Here, it is essential that our marketing strategies are innovated in the face of changing lifestyles. This is essential to raise the effectiveness of our decisions.

A BUYER BEHAVIOUR MODEL FOR HOTEL

For persons trying to understand buyers' behaviour for the first time, it is felt that consumers' minds work like microcomputers. Every computer has a given range of functions determined by its designed features; every buyer similarly has a personality which is partly inherited at birth and partly developed by experience. No doubt, the computers can perform certain tasks quickly through built-in-programmes when other tasks require additional programming to get the desired results. Buyers perform certain decisions by habit and with hardly any conscious thought whereas other buying decisions need careful consideration and extensive gathering of information. Marketing is substantially concerned with supplying prospects with factual and persuasive inputs of information.

The stimulus response concept is shown in Figure 2.3.

In the figure, we find four interactive components with the central component identified as buyer characteristics and decision process which incorporates motivation. The first two components are inputs most of which can be manipulated by the marketing manager whereas the final component represents the purchase outputs of a hotel decision process. The communication filters shown in the shaded part of the figure magnify the obstructions.

Product inputs: Here, we find the whole range of services made available by the hotels to the prospects. In this context, we also find the competitive services and product mix.

***Communication channels*:** In this context, we find two parts, the formal communication channels or media aimed at persuading prospects through advertisement and public relations activities. We also find here information accessible to individuals through the hidden sales force, such as their family, friends and the groups of people with whom they interact at work and socially. We also call them informal channels of information as shown in the figure as friends and reference groups.

***Buyer characteristics and decision process*:** We find three main interacting elements, such as needs, wants and goals, which determine as individual buyer's disposition to act in the defined ways.

We find these elements acting as constraints upon purchase decisions or in some cases even to reinforce motivation to customers to take a decision.

Purchase choices/decisions/outputs: At the final stage we find outputs of the decision process, of course, of direct concern to producers, including which type of product, what brand, at which price and at what time and through what distribution outlet. We find these decisions related to the individual's personal circumstances, which would be systematically monitored by large companies with the help of marketing research activities. The main point here is that action on purchases is linked directly to motivations, which we find are linked to the characteristics of buyers.

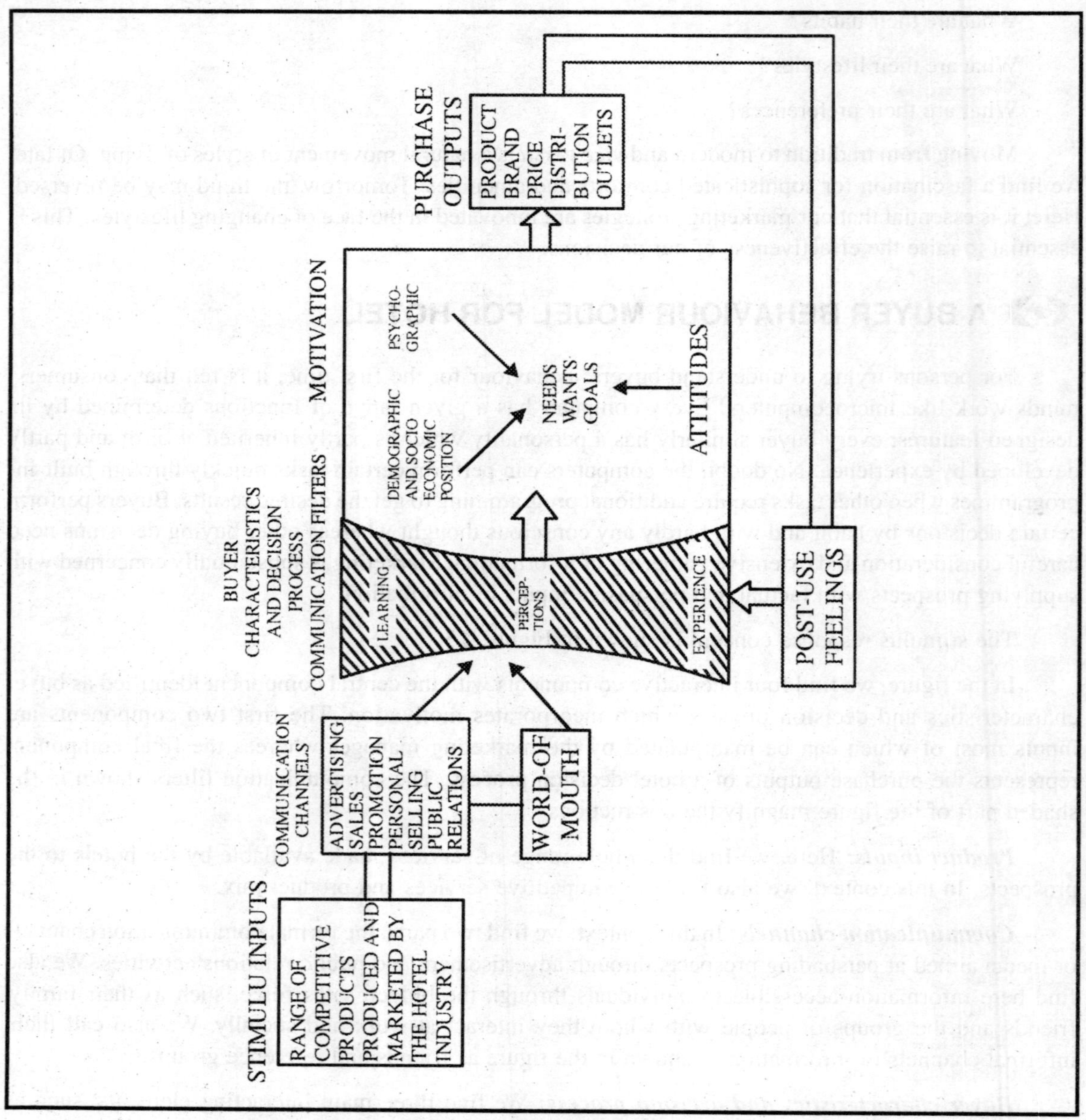

FIG. 2.3: A STIMULUS RESPONSE MODEL

BEHAVIOURAL PROFILE OF HOTEL USERS IN INDIAN PERSPECTIVE

During Post 1990, we find multi-dimensional developments in the Indian economy and credibility for the same goes to globalisation which made ways for corporatisation, emergence of corporate culture and development of hotel culture. Economic transformation engineers a sound foundation for socio-cultural transformation which brings a radical change in our behavioural profile. Since the beginning of 21st century, the techniculture started gaining a rapid momentum which considerably influenced our perception of service quality because we started thinking globally. We got an opportunity to prove our excellence and a few of us established their superiority as a global power house. The techniculture and managerial proficiency helped some of the Indian companies to be listed as large global players. The transformation of Indian companies from domestic to global players is the outcome of third phase of our development which could be activated from the very beginning of 21st century. The Taj Group of hotels is an Indian brand with international recognition.[19] The acquiring of prestigious hotels such as Ritch Carlton in Boston and Blue Sydney in Australia by the Taj group testifies our potentials of going abroad, proving our excellence and gaining and retaining the business. Until the late 1990s, before the IT outsourcing boom, the image of India was detrimental to Indian business but things changed dramatically and even big global players started strengthening their realisation that Indian companies have potentials to throw a challenge and establish an edge.

Willingly or unwillingly, we have to accept that ultimately level of discretionary income plays a decisive role in shaping the level of our expectations. A significant increase in the level of discretionary income of a majority of urban society made possible an attitudinal change which affected the life-styles, cultural patterns *vis-a-vis* the taste preferences. We started earning more and required searching avenues for spending more. The travel and tourism industry also showed a positive trend. The new areas of tourism gained popularity and its imprint was found on the hotel industry. The increasing influence of western culture on the Indian culture or emergence of a cross-cultural society opened new vistas for the development of hotel industry. The medical tourism gained global popularity and based on cost and quality considerations, we find inflow of people from the overseas countries. This also made rooms for hotel business in the Indian perspective. The pilgrim tourism also witnessed a positive trend. The adventure tourism, sports tourism, convention tourism, cultural and heritage tourism started gaining international responses.

The above mentioned facts make it clear that the hotel services were used by domestic or world tourists with diverse motives. The guests started expecting much more from the hotels where they stay. World class restaurants, housekeeping, swimming pool, shopping complexes, personal care services, playing ground, eco-friendly environment, quality service ambience etc. were found getting due place in the taste preferences of guests *vis-a-vis* in the product-mix of hotels.

The different categories of users visiting a place with diverse motives have different hierarchy of needs. Since they visit a place either for enjoying or for attending a conference or convention or for getting medical aid or for recovery of their health, it is pertinent that hotel professionals have an in-depth idea of their taste preferences. They come from different countries, different regions and belong to cross-cultural segments. The multi-faceted services in hotels are required to be delivered to them so that they are found satisfied and get an opportunity to gain new experiences which they have not received in other hotels. This is possible when we find hotel professionals studying and understanding them in a right perspective. The restaurants, bars, cafetarias prove to be the sensitive points of a hotel where even minor lapses may cause major losses. The professionals need much more care while managing the different points of service delivery. The motive is to understand the levels of their expectations and to, make professionalised efforts to fulfil them.

The guests staying in budget or economic hotels have relatively low level of expectations. The packages of services designed for different categories of guests become significant. The guests staying in residential hotels or apartments stay for a long duration. It is to be made sure that they are delivered the promised services. Some of them may have furnished accommodation whereas some others may have unfurnished accommodation. Some of them are provided kitchen facilities whereas some of them may not be provided the same. The guests living in star group of hotels have high level of expectations. The quality of services would vary in tune with the number of stars. The commercial hotels are mostly used by the trade or business representatives. It is significant that professionals keep themselves aware of their schedule. If they need the convention or conference hall, the professionals need to make necessary arrangements for event management. The resort hotels are mainly visited by tourists who stay to relax and enjoy. They need a number of facilities and it is to be ensured that promised services are delivered to them. The professionals managing international hotels are required to be much more sincere to the visiting guests. Since we find them coming with a high level of expectations, the professionals need to watch each and every point of service delivery.

Thus, the hotel professionals bear the responsibility of gauging the levels of expectations of different categories of tourists. With the development of corporate culture, we find a significant increase in the levels of expectations and therefore an attitudinal change while designing the product-mix is imperative. It is not only important that they are sincere to the core services. It is much more pertinent that they are innovative to the peripheral services. The hotels assigning due weightage.to innovative peripheral services would have an edge over others who have delayed or have ignored the innovation process.

During yesteryears, there have been multi-pronged attitudinal transformation in almost all the segments but we find its intensity of high magnitude specially amongst teens and upcoming youths developing a craze for lifestyles influenced by western culture. The credibility for the same goes to the corporate culture. The hotel professionals need to study and understand their behaviour. They earn more and therefore are found in a mood to spend more. The food and drink habits, the communicative style, the body language of such a new generation are found different to their counterparts working or serving the public sector. We find this segment to be profitable for the hotel sector. Earning more is not the only thing influencing our spending behaviour. The most effective variable throwing a major imprint on our spending behaviour is cultural transformation which considerably rests on profession that we opt for. Youths of the same age group, with the same qualification and identical metro character where they have been nurtured and educated cannot develop the same behavioural patterns if they work in the public sector. The hotel professionals need to study the behavioural patterns of different segments. The behavioural intentions need to be studied by the hoteliers which would simplify their task of satisfying and retaining the guests.

The experiences of customers regarding the services delivered to them prove to be an important factor for their repurchase or reuse decisions. The more positive the customers experience, the more likely he/she is willing to reuse the service.[20] How and in what way their experiences are to be made positive depend on the professional excellence of hotel managers. The hotel management should establish a system to monitor the changing needs of customers or guests. The perception of customers regarding the service quality is also to be studied because the service quality perception cannot remain static. The hotel professionals need to be sincere not only while developing a package but they need much more precaution while delivering the same. A number of back- and front-line staff and technology are used for delivery of promised quality of services. The people as well as the technology need to perform as per the desired norms. Even a minor slip may cause a major injury. This is not to be possible unless we find service culture.

In the Indian perspective, the hotel professionals need to assign due weightage to service culture to be efficacious of generating service fragrance where the hotel employees feel pleasure in delivering and the customers or guests feel pleasure in using and gaining new experiences. The service ambience or service environment significantly contributes to tangibalisation process. The professionals need not to forget that what promotional measures fail to convey are smoothly conveyed by the ambient conditions. The interiors, exteriors, furnishing, signposts, lighting, ventilation, music, scent, aesthetic management, etiquette management of people performing there, etc. are some of the aspects to be instrumental in developing service culture. By developing that culture, we simplify our task of marketing the hotel services. Attractions open doors for satisfaction which makes the ways for retention. Creating new customers is expensive as well as a time consuming process but retaining old customers is not only cost effective but even proactive.

The emerging trends in the hotel industry indicate that strategic decisions of hotel professionals would play a decisive role in the development of hotel industry. Though we find a spurt in tourist inflows which has been successful in increasing the occupancy ratio but maintaining the trend specially when we find sluggish behaviour in the global economy would make it essential that hotel professionals keep on moving the process of studying and understanding the customers in general and the international guests in particular. The country is going to witness a surge in demand because of the increased business activity and spurt in leisure travel by the country's rapidly increasing middle class and international tourists. These factors have enticed various hotel chains in the US and Europe to enter the Indian hospitality sector. The launch of the "Incredible India" campaign have supported India to enter into a global platform. More than 142 luxury hotel projects are coming India's way with gross investment of over ₹ 7,300 crores.[20] New brands such as Amanda, Satinwoods, Banana Tree, Hampton Inns, Hil ton and Mandarian Oriental are entering Indian hotel industry collaborating with key local players. The leading Indian players such as ITC, EIH, Bharat Hotels, Viceroy, DLF, Unitech and Royal Palms have also been evincing their keen interests to associate themselves with global brands. Mumbai-based Royal Palms has been negotiating with Anando, Starwoods and Singapore-based Banyan Tree for its three new hotel projects in India. Besides, we find Dubai-based, Holland-based hotel groups have also been negotiating with leading hotel companies in India.

The developments found during the yesteryears, of course, are positive signs for the development of hotel industry in India. But at the same time, the hotel professionals would be required to satisfy the international guests coming from overseas countries which would be easier if they with the help of a sound marketing information system succeed in understanding the guests in a right fashion. Expectations never may remain static and more so in an age of new generation of ICT, we cannot even imagine a situation ensuring our survival if our efforts for satisfying the customers are not of world class. New international brands, of course, would make the business environment much more competitive. This is a stage where only those hotels would survive and thrive who prove their world class excellence while satisfying and retaining the customers.

The hotel professionals also need to focus on a distinct segment significantly contributing to the development of medical tourism. We find India as a health tourist destination. The Healthcare Tourism alone can earn over US$ 2 bn additional revenues by 2012. India is expecting a steady flow of patients from the developed countries as well as from Africa and West Asia. They prefer to come to New Delhi and Bangalore for Cardiac Care, Chennai for Eye Care and Karnataka and Kerala for state-of-the-art Ayurvedic Healing. We need to identify their requirements and to offer to them the best we can.

Thus the hotel professionals need to identify the emerging new opportunities and to capitalise on the same by making use of their world class excellence which would provide to us an exotic environment where we can nurture the service culture.

SUMMARY

You have studied in this chapter the behavioural profile of hotel customers. Before studying other aspects, be sure that the following facts are well versed:

- **Hotel Customers:** The non-customers lack willingness, desire and ability. The potential customers have the efficacy to use the services. The actual customers already use the services. The light customers use the services occasionally. The heavy customers use the services frequently and form a habit to visit the same hotel.
- **Behavioural Influences:** Sociological, economic and psychological are the three dimensions of behavioural influences. The sociological influences are based on the study of reference group, the individual's concept of social role, the diffusion process and social class. The cultural influence insist on studying different cultural lifestyles. Economic influences study emerging trends in income, inflationary pressure and the availability of credit facilities. The psychological influences cover attitude and learning, repetition, motivation and conditioning.
- **Lifestyles:** Lifestyles influence hotel industry substantially. It draws a variety of analysis and discipline together. Lifestyle is a group phenomenon, it pervades many aspects of life and implies a central life interest.
- **Motivational Factors:** Fear, security, loneliness, status, ego, curiosity, profession, basic need, religion, mental relaxation and physical health, price, value for money, investment and credit facilities, personal comfort, guilt, shortages, education and research facilities and sentiment are the motivational factors influencing the potential guests.
- **Understanding the Behaviour:** In understanding behaviour, the personal characteristics of potential guests are found important. The age, life-cycle-stage, occupation, economic condition and personality are found important.
- **Influencing the Aggressive Customers:** Diffusion of tension is an important aspect to normalise the aggressive customers. Phase-wise diffusion is found important. Empathy helps in minimising the intensity of tension.
- **Transformation of Attitude into Behaviour and Action:** We call the transformation process *psycholocomotion*. Situational and organisational factors are found important in activating the process. The task of demand generation is simplified substantially, if the psycholocomotion is processed in a right fashion.

- **A Buyer Behaviour Model for Hotel:** In this model we find the stimulus response concept where product inputs, communication channels, buyer characteristics and decision process and purchase outputs have been shown.
- **Behavioural Profile of Hotel Users in Indian Perspective:** In the Indian perspective, we find significant changes in the behavioural profile of hotel users. The levels of expectations are found high.

KEY TERMS

Ego
Empathy
Sociological Influences
Cultural Influences
Discretionary Income
Motivation
Attitude
Lifestyle
Expectation
Perception
Learning
Anthropology
Guilt
Housekeepers
Waiters
Stimuli
Opinion Leader
Feedback
Psycholocomotion
Cognitive
Hoteliers
Product Inputs
Stimulus
Demographic
Purchase Outputs
Stimulus Response Model
Cultural Patterns
Behavioural Patterns
Cross-cultural
Sluggish

REVIEW QUESTIONS

1. Explain the following categories of users:
   (a) Non-users
   (b) Potential Users
   (c) Actual Users
   (d) Light Users
   (e) Heavy Users
2. Discuss the factors influencing the behaviour of guests in hotel.
3. Explain lifestyle as a variable influencing the behaviour of hotel users.
4. Do you find Psycholocomotion a process for transforming the attitude into behaviour? Justify your stand.

5. Focus on the motivational factors influencing the decisions of buyers.
6. Throw light on the internal and external influences affecting the behaviour.
7. Focus on the personal characteristics of potential guests helping in understanding the behaviour of potential guests in the hotel industry.

APPLICATION EXERCISES

1. "The individual specific behaviour at the market place is considerably influenced by the internal and external influences."

   Throw light on this statement in the capacity of a hotel professional
2. You have been working as a manager in a reputed hotel. Explain the important factors you will go through for understanding the behaviour of guests?
3. Do you find lifestyle an important dimension influencing the behaviour of hotel customers? Justify your stand as a marketer.
4. In the capacity of a hotel manager focus on the motivational factors helping you in influencing the guests so that the problem of poor occupancy ratio is resolved.
5. "Diffusion of tension is an important consideration for managing the aggressive customers." As a sales executive of a hotel, explain your role in the very context.
6. Do you find Psycholocomotion an effective process for transforming the attitude into behaviour? Defend your arguments as a hotel professional.
7. In the capacity of a hotel manager, focus on the personal characteristics of potential guests helping you in understanding the behaviour of potential guests.

End Notes:

1. Cundiff, Still and Govoni: *Fundamentals of Modern Marketing;* Prentice-Hall of India, New Delhi, p. 128.
2. Walter, C. Glenn: *Consumer Behaviour;* Homewood III, RD Irwin Inc., 1978.
3. Walter A. Henry: Cultural Values Do Correlate with Consumer Behaviour; *Journal of Marketing;* 1976, pp. 121-27.
4. Michman Ronald D.: Culture as a Marketing Tool; *Marquette Business Review,* Winter, 1975, pp. 179-83.
5. Thomas S. Robertson: *Consumer Behaviour;* Glenview III Scott, Foresman & Co. 1970, pp. 116-29.
6. Wharton: *Study of Consumer Expenditure, Income and Savings;* Pensylvania, 1958, Vol. 18.
7. Steuart R. Britt: Applying Learning Principles to Marketing; *Business Topics,* Spring 1975, pp. 5-12.
8. Mowerer O. : *Learning Theory and Symbolic Processes,* New York, 1963, p. 225.
9. Lazer William: *Life Cycle Concepts and Marketing,* p. 130.
10. Fieldman, Saul D. and Thiebar, G.W.: *Lifestyles; Diversity in American Society;* Brekeley, California Little Brown & Co., 1972, pp. 1-3.
11. Harold W. Berkman and Christopher C. Gilson: *Consumer Life Cycle and Market Segmentation;* Himalaya Publishing House, Bombay, 1987, p. 136.

12. Joseph T. Plummer: The Concept and Application of Lifestyle Segmentation; *Journal of Marketing;* January, 1974, pp. 33-37.
13. Melvyn Greene: *Marketing Hotels and Restaurants into the 1990s;* Heinemann Professional Publishing, Oxford, 1989, p. 113.
14. Benett, Peter D. and Kassarjian, Harold: *Consumer Behaviour;* Englewood Cliffs, NJ Prentice Hall, 1972.
15. Samuelson, Paul A.: *Foundations of Economic Analysis;* Cambridge, Harvard University Press, 1947.
16. John A. Czopiel, Larry J. Rosenberg: *Consumer Satisfaction: Concept and Measurement;* Ed. Bellur and Berkman; Himalaya Publishing House, Bombay, p. 128.
17. Murphy Gardner: *Personality — A Biosocial Approach to Origins and Structure;* Harper E. Row, NY, 1947, pp. 377-78.
18. Anand M.M.: *Tourism and Hotel Industry in India;* Prentice Hall of India, New Delhi, 1976, pp. 37-45.
19. Global Powerhouses made in India; Vol. 5/4, 2009.
20. Journal of Marketing and Communication; Vol. 3/3, 2009, pp. 14-26.
21. The ICFAIAN Journal of Management Research; Vol. VII/5, 2008, pp. 64-78.

....ꕥꕥꕥ....

CHAPTER - 3

HOTEL MARKET SEGMENTATION

Hospitality business in India is shining and even after worldwide economic recession, there are no signs of burnout. Our contributions to the IT sector, high growth rate, world class infrastructural facilities changed the perception of developed countries of the globe who earlier considered India as a country of snakes and elephants. We need world-class professional excellence to capitalise on the opportunities in the hotel sector.

CHAPTER OBJECTIVES

Introduction – Market Segmentation: The Concept – Why Market Segmentation? – Bases for Segmentation – Importance of Market Segmentation – Decision Process for Market Segmentation – Menu Fatigue: An Important Decision-Making Area – Know the changing Drinking Habits – Effective Market Segmentation – Emerging New Segments for Hotel Industry in Indian Perspective – Summary – Key Terms – Review Questions – Application Exercises – End Notes.

LEARNING OBJECTIVES

This chapter aims at studying the different dimensions of market segmentation in the context of hotel services. The motive is to sensitise the readers to the process and significance of segmentation for studying and understanding the customers. The emerging new segments are to be studied and their changing taste preferences are to be received in a right fashion so that the hotel professionals find it convenient to satisfy and retain the customers. With the increasing heat of globalisation, we find a host of changes in the lifestyles of customers.

INTRODUCTION

The behavioural scientists feel that appeal, strategy and tact vary from segment to segment which in a natural way bring a change in the market behaviour and response. The modern marketing theory prefers the formulation of policies and techniques for each segment which an organisation plans to solicit. The task of winning the game is considerably simplified if we find hotel professionals working as a team leader developing their awareness of changing behavioural profile of customers. Studying, identifying and understanding a small segment is found easier. If you divide; you make it small. And if you make it small; you understand. Winning and ruling become easier; if you understand. Market segmentation is a process for subdividing the markets into different groups and sub-groups. It is based on the principle of divide-and-rule. Segmentation makes possible tailoring of product and marketing programmes uniquely suitable for each segment. In the hotel industry, the segmentation makes possible an optimal combination of different hotel services and the marketing appeal to effectively cater to the changing needs of the potential guests. The marketing opportunities are effectively compared to simplify the task of hoteliers specially while formulating a sensitive marketing programme for target customers.

Markets rather than being homogeneous tend to be more heterogeneous in nature. No two buyers may be one hundred per cent identical. All customers have likes and dislikes of their own. Despite a number of variations, we find some common characteristics which may help hotel professionals in the identification process. The market segmentation is an effort to achieve the most efficient and productive use of marketing resources to extend maximum benefits to customers and generate adequate profits to hotel or the concerned organisation where the segmentation is done. The identification of potential customers is the most important marketing decisions. It is not logical that we waste our excellence in influencing the impulse of non-users.

Spotting the opportunities in the markets is the real identification of your professional excellence. If you develop the art and tact of identifying the markets, the task of formulating a sound marketing strategy is considerably simplified. An organisation found to be strategically sound succeeds in commanding and ruling the markets. Like other industries, the market segmentation is found important even in the hotel industry specially with the goal of making effective marketing decisions. The hotel professionals have been found assigning due weightage to market segmentation showing a far reaching impact on transforming the potential guests into actual and habitual guests.

With the increasing heat of globalisation and corporatisation, we find significant changes in the social order considerably influencing the cultural order. The multi-dimensional changes in the taste preferences and lifestyles need priority attention of hoteliers. Since we find new opportunities, the hotel professionals need to capitalise on the same. The ultimate motto of segmentation is to cater to the changing needs of the potential guests. It is done with the motive of grouping the individual prospects so that their responses to marketing inputs are similar. The success in marketing lies in anatomizing the wants and needs of diverse segments. This allows the strategic marketing planner to prioritise segments and consequently opportunities. It also allows the planner to be in a better position to spot opportunities, provide an orientation whereby service offering can be turned to satisfy the guests. It also simplifies the budgeting task through which marketing tasks are identified and monitored. The marketers need to go through the different variables both at micro and macro levels.

Normally, hotels come up at places of demand. This makes the task of equal distribution difficult. The Federation of Hotel and Restaurant Association India has divided the country into four geographic regions viz., Northern Region, Calcutta Region, Western Region and Southern Region. With a view to monitoring standards and enforcing control, the MoT has developed a system of categorizing the available accommodation as per certain criteria, e.g. approved and unapproved. Such type of segmentation in the hotel industry helps in maintaining standards and control. This is found effective even in studying the taste preferences and identifying the levels of expectations. The main theme of market segmentation is to simplify the task of identifying the potential customers so that professionals initiate marketing efforts to match the services to their expectations.

During the yesteryears, we have witnessed a significant increase in the level of expectation of a new segment which is due to the emergence of third wave culture in which a number of persons prefer to work in electronic cottages. The concept of third wave culture paves avenues for much more sophistication in the lifestyle of people. Since we find major impact of western world and culture on the population loyal to third wave culture, it is natural that their expectations are a bit different to others. From the very beginning of 21st century, we find a change in the spending behaviour of people which has injected new life to the hotel culture. The increasing trade and commerce activities have also opened new avenues for the development of hotel sector.

The globalisation has opened doors for a significant increase in the number of women. The lifestyles of housewives and working married or unmarried women cannot be identical. The emergence of working women segment makes it essential that the hotel professionals have an in-depth knowledge of the taste preferences of this segment. Like this, we also find youths of new generation or upcoming youths developing a distinct behaviour. The towns and cities sizeably influenced by IT hub has different cultural patterns *vis-a-vis* the behavioural patterns.

Thus much more frequency in the transformation of society, economy and culture make it essential that hotel professionals enrich their awareness of the guests coming from different segments so that they find their marketing decisions proactive to the customers.

MARKET SEGMENTATION: THE CONCEPT

The following are the viewpoints of marketing experts on segmentation.

'Segmentation is the act of dividing a market into distinct group of buyers who might require separate products and/or marketing mixes'.[1]

A market segmentation incorporates group of buyers who share qualities that make the segment distinct and which has marketing significance. Existence of a group of individuals with common characteristics does not itself constitute a market segment. Only when they have common characteristics as buyers, do they form a market segment'.[2]

'Market segmentation consists of taking the total heterogeneous market for a product and divide it into several sub-markets or segments — each of which tends to be homogeneous significantly.[3]

In view of the above viewpoints, it is right to mention that market segmentation is the grouping or division of markets.

When we talk about hotel market segmentation, emphasis is laid on grouping the hotel market in different ways. The market segmentation is supposed to be a device to concentrate on a particular segment or group and to design the marketing mix accordingly. With the passage of time, we find multi-dimensional developments in the society. The emerging new trends have been found paving ways for the new segments in the hotel industry. Working hours of the hotel industry will change with more shift work to operate and supervise expensive capital-intensive equipment. We also expect a change in the flexi-hours. A considerable number of people may work at home if not all the time at least part time, communicating with a central or head office by audiovisual telephones. A number of executives will have less need to visit their offices and could connect small briefcase size computers from most countries in the world directly to their major computer at head office by telephone to receive latest prices, output figures, stock delivery dates, latest management accounts, technical data etc. We also expect a change in the traditional family unit.

In view of the above, it is right to say that the market segmentation, particularly in the hotel industry, has been substantially influenced by multi-dimensional changes in the society. A study of different bases for segmenting the market would make it clear.

WHY MARKET SEGMENTATION?

An important question is raised regarding the justification for segmenting the hotel market. We agree with this view that small is beautiful, since it is easily identifiable and even effectively commondable. Against this background, the hotel market segmenting will be appreciated at all levels. The process of segmentation simplifies the task of hotels and hotel companies. The hoteliers find it convenient to identify the level of expectations with the task of reaching to the target customers getting simplified. The following points are a mute testimony to this proposition that by segmenting the market, the marketing strategies would prove effective.

1. Designing of sensitive marketing strategy: Segmentation makes possible the formulation of a sound marketing strategy. The grouping/division/subdivision of the market simplifies the task of hoteliers. They find it convenient to study the behaviour of different groups of customers and marketing activities are programmed in an effective way. This subsequently increases the sensitivity and the economics of marketing decisions.

2. Knowing the lifestyles: Segmentation is found effective even in knowing the lifestyles. When the segment is small, it is convenient to know the lifestyles and the task of satisfying the customers is simplified considerably. We also use lifestyle as an important base for segmenting the market.

3. Identifying the potential customers: A segmentwise study of potential guests is needed for transforming short-term customers into long-term customers. The main thing is to identify the potential guests and tap the market potentials considerably.

This makes it essential for the marketers to know that different guests visit hotels with different motives and expectations. By segmenting, we know their motives, identify their habits and preferences and make concerted efforts to satisfy them.

BASES FOR SEGMENTATION

No doubt, it is difficult to get even two potential guests of identical nature and character. However based on some general characteristics, we group, divide and segment them. Recently, some new trends in the process of social transformation have been paving ways for the emergence of new markets and new segments. To be more specific, in the hotel industry, we need to study different segments as the decision-making practices are vigorously influenced by a change in the attitudes of the society.[4]

***1. Socio-economic considerations*:** Of course, the socio-economic grouping is likely to be of little help for future marketing but most of the marketers and researchers have been time and again advocating for socio-economic grouping, and to some extent, they appear to be right. In this context, there are a number of traditional groups as shown below:

Grade A	Households	Upper Middle Class
Grade B	Households	Middle Class
Grade Cl	Households	Lower Middle Class
Grade C2	Households	Skilled Working Class
Grade D	Households	Semi-skilled and Unskilled Working Class
Grade E	Households	People at lowest level of subsistence.

The justification for grouping on the basis of socio-economic considerations is based on the fact that we find this base most sensitive to consumer spending. Though we also find cases where some lower groups had much more discretionary spending ability than other groups. Here, the family background, culture and profession influence the spending behaviour. When we find directors of companies staying in hotels, the impulse buying is influenced by income, status and ego. On the other hand, when we find. butchers, hair dressers, jewellers, caterers, owners of car showrooms and big shops/super markets staying in the same hotel, the discretionary spending is not substantially influenced by the discretionary income as the guests/customers are staying in the hotel with a different motive, i.e., getting more businesses; attending casino or capitalizing on opportunities to expand their area of business. And so, in this case, the impulse buying is influenced by business opportunity.

Despite a few exceptions, socio-economic consideration is an important base for market segmentation.

Some of the marketing experts[5] have been found searching another base, i.e., Surplus Spending Power, e.g.:

— husband and wife both working.

— one or both in businesses profitable where the whole family works and lives at home.

We cannot deny the fact that these factors play a vital role in influencing impulse buying, specially when we talk about the hotel industry. Here, it is also important to mention that in addition to surplus spending power, surplus spending desire is also to influence the impulse buying. We find several cases where an individual avoids to stay in hotels, specially to save money. In this respect, the impulse buying is not influenced as we find lack of willingness mainly due to his frugality.

2. *Women in Focus:* Recently, we find a new trend even in the Indian condition as women have been found staying in hotels or eating in hotel restaurants. There are women executives and women going on holidays in all age groups, albeit without accompanying men. A number of married women have been found taking an extra holiday on their own. Middle-aged, divorced or single women have also been found staying in hotels. In this context, it is also important to mention that a good number of girls have now developed a fascination or a craze for MBA and other professional courses. Against this new development, it is right to opine that even in the Indian condition, the women segment appears to be the fastest growth segment for hotels.

This new dimension of social transformation is an important aspect for making sensitive marketing decisions. We find some important decision-making areas related to this new development. Women often read different media composed to men and therefore, this media should be induced for future advertising in attracting a major share of this new market. It cannot be refuted that at present most bedrooms are designed by men for men. This necessitates redesigning of the bedrooms with both sexes in mind. In addition, it is also pertinent that we train our restaurant and bar staff to pay particular attention to women executives, provided they do not object. Women are not comfortable in hotel bars and prefer lobby bars and lounges that are open, airy and relatively quiet. Generally, they want a clean room which should be attractive and spacious with good lighting.

The aforesaid aspects are found important to capitalise on opportunities. This new emerging segment for hotel marketing makes it essential that services are innovated, keeping in view the changes in the lifestyles.

3. Short Break Market: This is related to short break holiday. In most countries, we find 4-day/5-day week — also call it four-sevenths or five-sevenths. This has made possible development of a new market, i.e., the weekend market. To improve future marketing, this is an emerging trend in the burgeoning hotel industry. In the hotel industry, activities/service facilities to enjoy the leisure time is an important consideration which would send the cash registers of hotels ringing. Hotels and hotel companies have been found successfully promoting weekend breaks. It is also important to note that for this segment, the catchment area is found very limited. The main factor here is the availability of transportation facilities to the hotels. The catchment area can be defined on the basis of road network or other facilities which may be helpful for future promotion. In this context, it is also significant to mention that in most of the cases, decisions are made by women. This makes it essential that promotional decisions are made keeping in view the taste and the level of enjoyment preferred by women to make the most of weekends. The weekend occupancy rate of rooms can be increased considerably, if the promotional campaigns concentrate on aggressive promotional strategies. In addition to the occupancy ratio of hotel rooms, this would also increase the number of guests coming into the restaurants.

4. Single-parent Market: The experts believe that for future hotel marketing, it is pertinent that we think about single-parent market. Of course, this will create sales and profit opportunities. In this category, we find unmarried mothers with very little money including separated and divorced men/women. It is also important to note that in this category, the single-parent concept is also included; This segment is found suitable to the hotel industry as a good number of single-parents have been found spending more than they can afford. We also find a number of single-parents holding executive jobs with paid holiday. The main thing here is to identify the new emerging segment and to tap the opportunities. It is right to say that hoteliers or restaurants who identify this segment and attempt sincerely to market with empathy get a lot of repeat business or heavy customers, A lucrative growth market is emerging, let the hotels and hotel companies change their literature, their own attitude, the attitude of their staff and the whole sales approach. This will give due weightage to the new segment.

5. Active Leisure: With the passage of time, we find a change in the lifestyles. Of late, we find people more conscious of health or they are found more conscious of their ill health. A good number of people are now found to appreciate physical fitness. Both sexes are now found playing tennis or jogging. This health consciousness has resulted in the emergence of a new segment, i.e., *'active leisure'*. It is pertinent that hotels recognize the importance of this segment and attempt to provide the essential facilities, e.g., Gym, Sauna, the swimming pools including a circuit of exercise machines. This segment has proved to be a lucrative business for the hotel industry.[6] Today, every hotel offers this facility to its customers. The availability of personal care services close to the hotels or in the hotel complex itself, would attract customers. These services include additional incentive offered by hotels. For future marketing, this appears to be an important consideration.

6. Instant Market: It is known that potential customers expect instant services. They would not appreciate waiting for a long time and therefore, we find development of the concept of fast food restaurants and quick access to service facilities in hotels. Rapid development of credit cards has virtually changed the whole concept of payment. Now customers buy things first and make payment later. This is due to the conveniences which they get from buying right now and not waiting for payment. Against this background, it is right to mention that we find a new trend in the society which is related to quick disposal of services. A number of people are now found buying goods, ordering services, booking holidays on impulse and at a shorter time beforehand than in the past. This was not so a few years ago when a large segment of the society booked their summer holidays just in the beginning of winter. Thus we now find a new trend, i.e., buying at short notice. This makes it essential that hotels should have inbuilt systems to take full advantage of this new trend. Direct sales techniques have been adopted by many of the hotels, specially with aim to making possible bookings for accommodation at short notice. The marketing practices are here required to be innovated and reassessed time and again. Hotels also extend the facility of computerized central reservation which is found more effective. Thus instant services are the need of the hour and hotels and hotel companies have to assign an overriding priority to this segment, specially with emphasis on the strategies of future marketing.

7. Hotel Like Home: Hotels should have something better to serve. The guests should feel that they are getting additional, special comforts in the hotels. Earlier, the hotels had something special to offer which could be exciting, luxurious or say, different. The traditionally built and managed houses were not so comfortable. Of late, we find a new concept of house construction where modern amenities and facilities are available, e.g., central heating, double glazing, showers, extra bathrooms, extensions, playrooms, wet bars, wall-to-wall carpets, tiled bathrooms and kitchens. This clearly indicates that hotels are now in a position to make available to their guests something more than they get in their homes. This trend of renovating and upgrading houses would continue even in the future as the spending power of consumer is showing an upward trend and most of the luxurious expenses are to be regulated. The owning of cars, increasing rates of smoking, personal music centers are all avenues of personal expenses. Hotels and hotel companies need to be aware of this new trend and should ensure that the guests would get something more in hotels than those in their private homes. We cannot deny the fact that even today, we find a number of hotels without modern personal care facilities. Here, it is right to mention that most of the hotels survive and thrive because they are unusual, nostalgic or historic. This makes it clear that if hotels are old with unique attractive features, it is essential that the hotel industry establishes its edge over the guests' private homes and this, of course, will be an additional attraction for visiting a hotel.

8. Geographic Consideration: This is a well-known criterion for the market — where the segmentation is based on consideration. In the national perspective, we find four zones on the bases of which market segmentation is made, e.g., North Zone, South Zone, East Zone and West Zone. In the international perspective, we classify like the East and West. The segmentation is done on the basis of an apparent variations in the taste and preferences of the two zones.

9. Psychographic: This is also an important consideration for market segmentation. Psychographic variables refer to lifestyle, buying motives and product knowledge of potential guests. It is very natural that psychographic variables vary from segment to segment. The marketers find it easier to plan, if they are aware of the needs, staying motives, food habits and lifestyles of potential guests coming from different segments and different regions.

10. Lifestyle: No doubt, a number of variables influence the segmentation of hotel market but lifestyle is found to be the most sensitive base.[7] This is due to the fact that buying decisions for the hotel services are directly linked to the emerging trends in the lifestyles. For visiting a hotel, it is not only sufficient that we have the spending power. Here, it is more impact-generating that we are interested in enjoying the leisure time and we prefer to stay in hotels. This is substantially influenced by lifestyle patterns.

The word 'Lifestyle' was first used by Max Webber. Currently, the markets are segmented on the basis of social class (Myers 1971) ethnic (Baur Cunningham 1970) and life Cycle (Rich and Jain 1968). In addition, the traditional variables are also found partially effective. William Lazer (1971) defined lifestyle in terms of four characteristics, e.g., a group phenomenon pervading many aspects of life, a central life interest and sociologically relevant variables. Joseph T. Plummer (1974) advocated that lifestyles of different segments of the society cannot be uniform such as Swingers, home-family types, social or political activists, all have different lifestyles. A. Richard and Elizabeth and Sturman Stephen (1977) opine that the Swinger wears different clothing, buys different recreation equipments, even eats differently. The Swinger buys a speed boat while the home-family type buys a recreation camping vehicle instead. Thus, the lifestyle influences the requirements and therefore, the level of expectations. Generally, it is found significant to categorise people on the basis of their status as users of products. This simplifies the task of identifying their requirements and the level of expectations.

The lifestyle pattern also determines buying decisions. A young single divorce lawyer views himself as something of a swinger. His attitudes and interests are translated into purchases such as yellow porsche, a custom-fitted wardrobe, a pent house apartment in a single complex. His monthly credit card statements list an expensive array of nightspots as well as several plane tickets. He is supposed to be an ideal potential guest for vacation packages augmenting his lifestyle and therefore, he is important as a source of revenue generation for the hotel industry. Another tax lawyer (family man) living in a small suburb and his house and station wagon reflect an orientation towards the home and children. Family vacations tend to be camping trips several times a year and an occasional trip abroad. Entertainment expenses include food and liquor and dinner at home with friends. Thus he is found to be a suitable prospect for life insurance companies first and then to the hotel industry.

To be more specific, in the hotel industry, the lifestyle segment becomes more effective. This is found to be an internationally acceptable variable for targeting customers. In UK, A Classification of Regional Neighborhood (ACORN) has been developed as a system for targeting customers. It has proved its instrumentality in determining the characteristics of different customer groups on the basis of their own records, the high spending tourists or habitual or heavy tourists. In addition, ACORN studies also simplify the task of profitable site locations to attract tourists.

In the hotel industry, the buying decisions are substantially influenced by lifestyle of an individual or a family. The size of a family or the number of children in a family is found to be an important component, specially while taking a decision. The nature of one profession also becomes a dominating factor as it influences the activities offered for the leisure time which is directly related to the hotel industry. It is quite natural that lifestyle of a technocrat differs from the lifestyle of bureaucrat. The lifestyle of an individual engaged in white collar job differs from the lifestyle of an individual engaged in blue collar job.

IMPORTANCE OF MARKET SEGMENTATION

Bernard M. Baruch says, "Never follow the crowd." Of course, this is based on the philosophy that small is beautiful. We experience conveniences in identifying and controlling the small. The segmentation is a process to divide and classify market into different groups and sub-segments which simplifies the task of studying the changing likes and dislikes or preferences of customers. The segmentation has a far reaching positive effect. The following facts strengthen our hypothesis that market segmentation is an effective device to aggravate effectiveness of marketing principles:

1. Making possible a fair blending of market opportunities (demand) to the resources of hotels: A balance between demand and supply is found significant for the development of an organisation. Since the hotels and hotel companies are in a position to estimate the requirements of different groups of customers, the supply position can be optimised by managing the available resources with hotels. It is quite natural that the demand of all users cannot be uniform. One group or segment is found interested in staying in the star group of hotels while another group is found interested in unclassified hotels. This is related to *'price sensitivity'* which plays a significant role in making the buying decisions. The segmentation makes possible an optimal relationship between demand and supply.

2. Effective utilisation of marketing resources: The segmentation simplifies the task of making possible an effective utilisation of marketing resources. This is meant that services offered to the guests, the promotional devices meant for the potential guests and offering of services by the hotel personnel and the travel agents are planned on the basis of changing individual requirements by customers. The tailoring of marketing programmes exactly in tune with the marketing objectives ensures effective utilisation of the marketing resources. The designing of advertisement campaigns, slogans, the nature and type of sales promotion, the instrumentality of front line staff and the Public Relations Officer, the innovative services etc. are required to be fairly matched with the changing behaviour of potential guests. And the market segmentation makes it possible.

3. Marketing strategies can be tailored to the competitors' strategies: Strategies simplify the task of achieving the target to satisfy potential customers successfully. Of late, the market has become more competitive. Most of the hotels are now found innovating their marketing strategies. A successful hotel always thinks of innovative strategies much in advance than its competitive organisations. Any change in the product, pricing and promotion can be made possible by market segmentation. This would ensure the effectiveness of marketing decisions. In addition, the unproductive expenses can be minimised considerably.

4. Creativity in the marketing decisions is made possible: In addition to other aspects, an important aspect is related to creative marketing decisions. It is natural that an indepth knowledge of potential guests received by segmenting the market helps in making creative decisions. The marketing decisions for different group of guests are made in tune with their changing behavioural profile. Creativity is made possible by innovating the decisions. The marketers are well aware of the changing needs and requirements of the high income group, couples, the unmarried category, in job and retired persons, cultural tourists, business tourists etc. They are supposed to be well informed, specially regarding the multi-dimensional changes in the different segments. This simplifies the task of making creative decisions.

5. ***Future marketing is easier:*** The emerging new trends in the socio-economic and technological environmental conditions make it essential that marketing decisions to boost the hotel industry are well planned. Of late, multi-dimensional changes in the society, the spending power of consumers in general are increasingly fast and the technological innovations are very frequent. This in a very natural way affects the process of formulating marketing plans for the hotels and hotel companies. If plans are formulated based on the emerging trends, the decisions are supposed to be effective. The potential guests prefer to stay in hotels where they get more comforts, basic amenities and facilities. To be more specific when the hotel market is found more competitive, it is essential that we make sincere efforts to innovate our decisions, specially related to services and promotion. This is not only a time taking process but also involves substantial financial investment. The hotels and hotel companies have to make plans, keeping in view the changes pointed out earlier. In addition, they are also required to generate financial resources to implement the plans. This is possible when they have an indepth knowledge about their potential guests. And the segmentation makes it possible.

In view of the aforesaid facts, it is right to observe that market segmentation plays a vital role in making possible an optimal utilization of marketing resources. A fair blending of demand and supply is found essential and market segmentation paves ways for the same. It is pertinent that hotels and hotel companies assign due weightage to the segmentation process and make sincere efforts to establish their image in the market. The segmentation helps in many ways. The main aspect of market segmentation is its correlation with the emerging new trends.

DECISION PROCESS FOR MARKET SEGMENTATION

An optimal marketing strategy is found significant for the development of hotel companies. Segmenting the hotel market in an effective way, would definitely bring success to the hotels and hotel companies. They should follow the right process for market segmentation as shown in Figure 3.1. The main purpose of market segmentation is to identify potential guests, to know their expectations and lifestyles. The first task before them is to identify a suitable base for segmentation. After selecting a suitable base, it is pertinent that a behavioural profile of the potential guests is recorded. This move would help hotel marketers in knowing or in understanding the liking and expectations of the potential guests. When the process of designing a profile is over, the next task is to forecast the market potentials. This provides marketers an idea regarding the potential customers likely to be transformed. When we have a detailed idea of market potentials, a suitable strategy can be formulated to tap the potentials and capitalise on the opportunities. After this, we find two important stages, e.g., diagnosing the marketing mix of competitors and formulating the marketing-mix accordingly. For reaching to the target guests, it is significant that the hotels and hotel companies are well informed about their competitors and strategies used by the latter. The next process after knowing the strategies of competitors is to forecast the market share and to estimate the cost to be entailed. Forecasting the market share is essential to make necessary arrangements. If we find a change in the needs and requirements of potential guests, the necessary preparations can be made accordingly. Now the goal is to be set and the target market is to be selected. If hotels and hotel companies succeed in identifying the target market, the marketing activities will be promoted cost effectively.

Against this background, we find market segmentation an important decision-making process. A close study of Figure 3.1 makes it clear that selection of a target market is a prerequisite for raising the effectiveness of marketing decisions. The new markets and new segments have emerged and would continue to emerge. The segmentation thus would be important even for future marketing. If the hotel companies are really interested in establishing their edge over the competitors, the decision of going for a segmentation should be given some time. It is essential that they follow the right process and link their future marketing plans with the new segments emerging or likely to emerge, This would help them in many ways. The marketing-mix would be innovated in time and the marketing decisions would be made proactive. Let's go through the Figure 3.1.

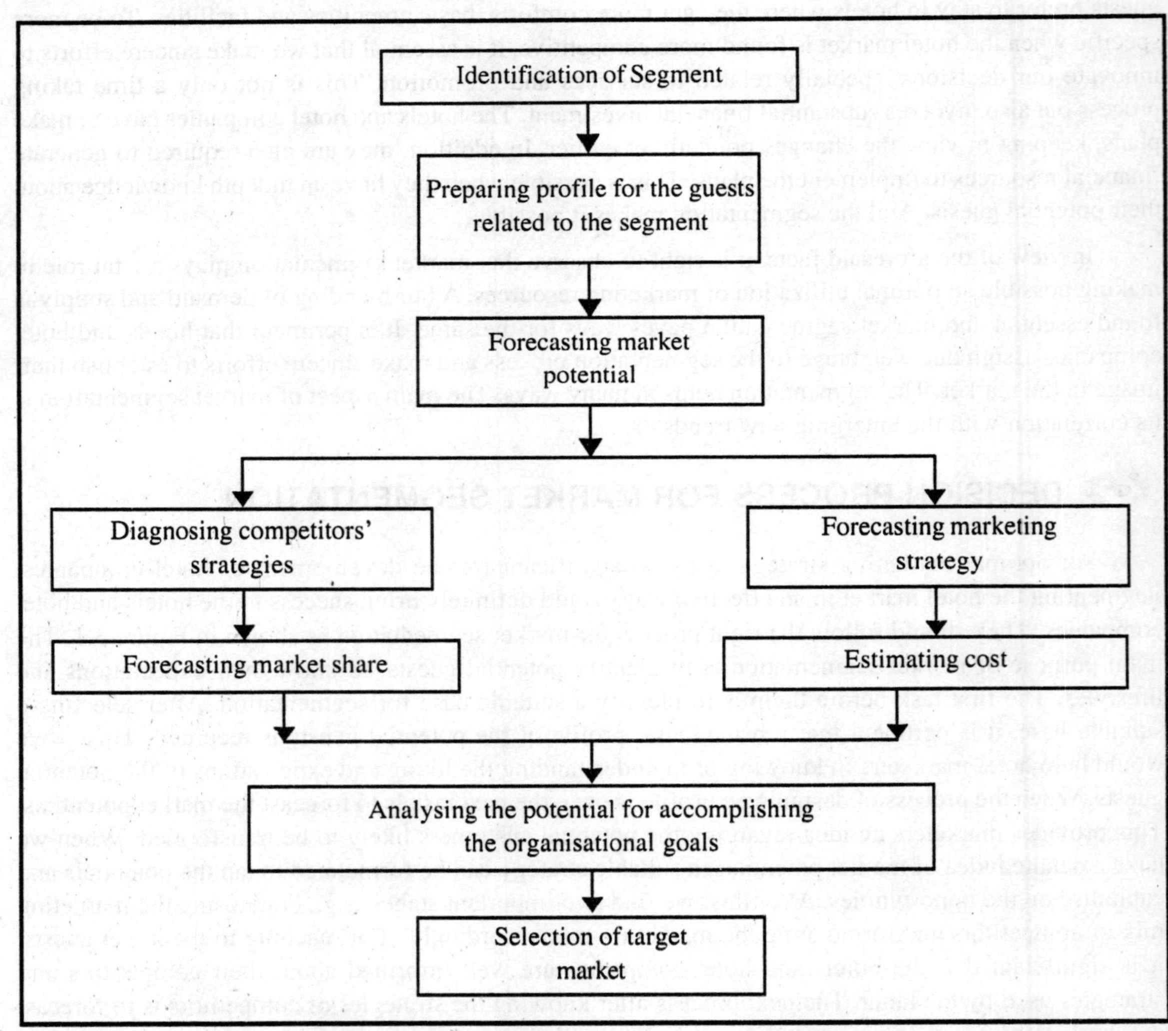

FIG. 3.1: DECISION PROCESS FOR MARKET SEGMENTATION

MENU FATIGUE: AN IMPORTANT DECISION-MAKING AREA

Restaurant is an important part of a hotel. We find a number of people who stay in hotels but prefer to eat outside. Business executives generally stay in hotels and are found eating in the restaurants of hotel. The guests found staying in hotels regularly often claim that they suffer from illness or the problem of indigestion. We call it *'Menu Fatigue'*. This is to be checked with immediate effect. While managing the restaurants, it is not only essential that we take care of the menu served but in addition, the time is also an important aspect. Most of the business executives usually do not get time to eat during usual meal hours — normally between 1 pm and 2 pm. Many more people are going to work flexi-hours. It is very natural that those who work odd hours would prefer to eat at odd hours and hotel restaurants who fail in catering for this will suffer financial loss. Here, it is not meant that we introduce a series of different restaurants to cater to the different markets — indeed our emphasis is here on making possible flexibility in designing the hotels and a varied menu situation. Restaurants would be designed to change. We find various social and technological changes destroying the usual meal hours. We also find guests who go out for a visit or come late after watching movies or theatres. It is to quote the example of Lord Forte's superb Cafe Royal, in the heart of theatreland in London. At the Cafe Royal, they have *'split'* meal if they wanted it. They had the starter and the main course before the theatre and then returned to the restaurant afterward for dessert, coffee and brandy. The main issue here is to understand the guests and making provisions accordingly.

Recently we see a new trend in the food habits around the globe. Of late, more and more people are now found eating Chinese and Indian food. Many more are going for fast foods. In America, consumption of hot and spicy food is increasing at a fast pace. The same trend is found even in the European countries. We call it a significant swing in national eating habits and taste patterns. We should not forget that hotels fall into different market segments, of course, depending on the time and place. We find a well-dressed top executive with open-ended expenses going outside with his family for a Kentucky Fried Chicken.

It is important to mention here that we should reduce incidence of menu fatigue. Here, it is also pertinent to mention that hotels should ensure that a lower proportion of our overnight guests eat out in competitive restaurants and we attract more outside visitors into the hotel's restaurant(s). Of course, we should promote *'chance trade.'* This is meant that the guests come to restaurants by chance. Steady systematic marketing would pave ways for chance guests. Though it is reportedly based on word-of-mouth recommendation or other promotional efforts, generally persons think twice before going to a new restaurant. Essentially, we have to make things happen. If you find in your restaurant guests coming from outside, either they have been recommended or heard of you. May be it is the exterior, menu display, paid and unpaid publicity, mailing shots etc., which have influenced them to come to your hotel restaurant.

A case of menu fatigue should be taken as a warning by hotel managers and their restaurants. Therefore, such cases should be removed. To be more specific in the Indian conditions, we find several cases of menu fatigue which is the result of poor restaurant management. Selection of food items; cooking arrangements, storing provisions are important dimensions. If you eat in the restaurant of a five star hotel, and just after taking food, you get victimized to indigestion, food poisoning, upset of stomach, the ultimate responsibility lies on the management. And, if we find frequent cases; this is ultimately going to question the image of the hotel. This calls for emphasis on menu management, time management and place management. A decision regarding menu, hygiene in food preparation, keeping in view the changing food habits would make available to the guests food of their choice. A decision regarding time, keeping in view the nature and behaviour or engagement of guests would minimize the cases of menu fatigue. A decision regarding place, keeping in view the design of your hotel and its restaurants would serve a better choice of food preparations to the flexi-hour guests.

We are supposed to manage hotels and restaurants in a right fashion. This is mainly related to restaurant management which is a part of your hotel. Here, it is pertinent that hoteliers have an idea of the changing national and international food habits. If change is related to fashion; it is equally applicable to food habits. Americans are now fascinated to spicy food. In the last ten years, the US consumption of hotspices, e.g., red pepper, black and white pepper and ginger, hot flavored items, e.g., mustard seed, canned green chillies, bottled hot sauces and fresh ginger have shown an increase of more than 50%. Even in the European countries, by and large we find the same trend. People in general now prefer spicy foods.

In view of the above, it is right to say that we find a swing in the food habits almost in all parts of the globe. The craze for Indian spicy foods is growing and will continue even in the coming years. Here, it is a challenging task to manage the restaurants as spicy food items are found heavy which take a long time for proper digestion. Any way, the *'menu fatigue'* is to be checked. This makes it an important decision-making area.

KNOW THE CHANGING DRINKING HABITS

The Japanese who initially abstained from drinking, are today heavy consumers of whisky. The British were found satisfied with traditional beer. Today, they prefer large and real ale. The Indian culture did not appreciate drinks. Today, a large section of the population has opted to make 'drinks' a part of their dietary habits. In many ways, drinking habits have now changed substantially. The demand is increasing in almost all parts of the globe. We find a galloping increase in the demand of whisky, brandy, beer etc. The cocktails are now preferred by the new generation. We also find a change in the place of drinking. Of late, they are not satisfied with old pubs. They prefer to go to new style restaurants. In view of these considerable changes in the drinking habits, it is pertinent that hotel bars, restaurant-wine lists and function-wine lists accept these changes and attempt to spot new trends. This highlights the fact that whatsoever the habits we find today will not remain existent tomorrow. Unless we know or forecast about the future, it is difficult for us to make a plan for future marketing. Against this background, it is important for the hoteliers to know about the recent trends in the global drinking culture.

After an analysis of the emerging trends in the drinking culture, it is apparent that people in general now prefer more volume of alcoholic content in their drinks. In place of red wine, they now prefer white wine. In place of pubs, they now prefer to go to new restaurants. In place of slow drinking, they are now found replacing water in the various brands of drink. A change in style, type, place and content makes it essential that before serving drinks, we know everything about the same. You are not supposed to change the way of drinking but making available to your guests the drinks of their choice. Here, it is essential that your guests maintain decorum while going to restaurants for a drink.

The size of bottle is an important factor in influencing the sale of liquor. A number of executives like to have wine, specially with their dinner. They do not want a full bottle but a little. There are a number of restaurants which do not appreciate and promote half bottles on their wine list. Larger bottles or magnum bottles are now found more popular. The Evergreen restaurant in Convent Garden, London reportedly sells champagne by the magnum bottle. We find an increase even in the size of magnum, e.g., two magnum, four, eight, 12, 18 to 24 magnum size. They very often sell the largest sized bottle of champagne. The main thing here is to know and appreciate the drinking habits of your potential guests.

EFFECTIVE MARKET SEGMENTATION

To make marketing decisions, cost-effective, it is essential that market segmentation be effective. This will help hotels and hotel companies in formulating a sound marketing strategy. Davis and Sternquist (1987) mention that for the market segmentation to be effective, the segments must be :

1. Measurable : A distinct group must be identified.
2. Assessable : Promotional efforts must elicit the desired response from customers
3. Substantial : Segment must be large enough to warrant the expenditure of time money effort to attract it.
4. Reliable : Consumer characteristics must be stable indicators.

E.R. Reidenbach and R.E. Pitts (1986) included one new dimension, i.e., *defensibility.* Critics have opined that one cannot control competition and competitors without effective marketing strategies. It is very natural that the competitors like to make a dent in the competitive market whereas the concerned organisations cultivating a segment like to keep it and nurse it. Oppendijk van Veen and Verhallen (1986) have identified three basic approaches to market segmentation, e.g., analysis of consumer characteristics, analysis of consumer response and the simultaneous analysis of both. In the first approach, the customers are grouped on the basis of some set of attributes with different groups being subsequently related to behavioural differences which is also called *forward segmentation.* Initially, we find emphasis on standard socio-economic variables. But this variable could not discriminate effectively between groups which shifted attention to psychographic segmentation which considers less tangible factors, such as attitudes, interests, opinions and lifestyles — Hawes, (1977), Perreault, Darden and Darden (1977) and Shih (1986).

A survey of potential New Zealand travellers to Australia identified four major segments, the older relaxation-comfort seekers, young excitement seekers, the nature, culture group and unadventurous sightseer (Burfitt, 1983). In the second approach, the consumers are assigned to group on the basis of their similarity in behavioural response to the supply of goods and services, such as the chosen type of vacation. Segmentation of consumer responses has been undertaken in a variety of ways including destination activities (Graham and Wall 1978), benefits (Mazan ed. 1984), frequency of visit (Kaynak Odabasi and Kavas, 1986), distance travelled (Etzel and Woodside, 1982), travel patterns (Pearce and Johnston 1986), seasonality (Calantone and Johar 1984), types of tour packages (Thomson and Pearce 1980), time share ownership (Woodside. *et. al.*, 1986) and Taylor (1986) reports on a multi-dimensional segmentation.

The third approach identified by Oppendijk van Veen and Verhallen is *simultaneous analysis* of consumer characteristics and response. This approach is found less common. Assigning consumers to groups on the basis of the relationships between their characteristics and their behavioural response to the supply of goods and services is much more complex. They employed canonical analysis to establish their relationships directly and subsequently identified seven overlapping vacation segments, e.g., the organised vacation, the beach vacation, the domestic vacation, vacation with children, the one-to-two person vacation, the long camping vacation and the short vacation. We find relevance of this segmentation for the growing leisure industry as well as the hotel industry.

The main thing here is to make the marketing decisions sensitive and subsequently make the segmentation process effective. *How to make market segmentation more effective?* Like other industries, the hotel industry has also to answer this question suitably. While segmenting, it is pertinent that due weightage is given to different emerging new markets. In the face of multi-dimensional changes in the socio-economic fabrics, the need of the hour is to identify the new markets, new customers and new segments. Change in the lifestyles, in the leisure hours and changes in the spending power are found significant while segmenting the market. Expectations are closely linked with change, of late, the hotel industry has been benefiting from the electronic wave. This has made possible an overall change in the behavioural profile of potential guests. In view of the same, the future marketing for hotel services has become more competitive. Women and children are found emerging as the most sensitive segment for the hotel industry. This is supported by the fact that they have been found dominating the traveling decisions, visiting hotels, attending restaurants and other related services. In addition, we also find a new development related to the involvement of women as business executives. Not only in the West but even in the East, We find this new development which is likely to influence the segmentation process. The food habits are now changing. Currently, in almost all countries of the globe, we find a fascination for the spicy food. This is going to influence the management of restaurant. Besides, we also find increasing consumption of different types of liquor. This is also to influence the management of restaurants and bars who will have to offer these services.

In view of the above, it is right to observe that hoteliers' strategies make sincere efforts to identify new emerging segments and to active future marketing strategies accordingly. Raising the effectiveness of segmentation is closely associated with increasing the sensitivity and authenticity of the marketing decisions.

EMERGING NEW SEGMENTS FOR HOTEL INDUSTRY IN INDIAN PERSPECTIVE

Hospitality business in India is shining and even after worldwide economic recession, there are no signs of burnout. During the yesteryears, we have found emergence of new segments with new taste preferences and high spending behaviour. This is due to the fact that Indian economy has changed the perception of leading developed countries of the globe regarding our potentials. Earlier the western world considered us as the land of snake charmers and elephants. Today they find us as a country strategically and potentially sound. A host of factors are responsible for such an attitudinal change such as growing IT, ITES and manufacturing sectors, rising level of discretionary income, consistency in the national growth rate, mounting managerial proficiency, increasing craze for professional and technical education, world class excellence in medicare etc. These positive developments have spurred the growth of India's hospitality business. "Incredible India" campaign has also been instrumental in activating the process of attitudinal transformation. It is against this backdrop that we find emergence of new segments for the hotel industry. The innovative tourism, creative promotional measures, world class infrastructural facilities, growing PPP mode are some of the key factors injecting new life to the hospitality business in the Indian perspective. Not only the affluents segment but we find albeit middle and low income segments considerably motivated due to the conceptualisation of budget hotel. We find emergence of women segment emerging as the profitable segment for the hospitality industry.

Prior to 1990, the hotel industry was not in a goad position. A majority of the hotels were facing the problem of law occupancy ratio. The discretionary income was low and the spending behaviour was found very conservative. Credit goes to corporatisation that reverberated the process of development which made possible an increase in the level *vis-a-vis* the attitudinal change in behavioural profile, spending behaviour, lifestyles made ways for the development of various segments which helped a significant increase in the hotel business.

The outlook for the Indian hotel industry is found bright[8] due to the innovative areas of tourism which are not to be affected by the market slump and worldwide economic recession. Medical Tourism, Well-being Tourism, Adventure Tourism, Golf Tourism, Cruise Tourism, Wildlife Tourism, Rural Tourism, Cultural and Heritage Tourism are the areas where we expect tourists in a very good number not only from India but sizeably from overseas countries. The positive results received from Medical Tourism make it clear that even in the years to come, the medical tourism segment would have productive results. The more recession in the developed countries; we expect much more arrival of medical tourists from there because we provide to them world class services at less than half price in addition to the natural fragrance, cultural heritage and quality environment. Like this, we expect arrival of tourists even from other segments.

It is upon the hotel professionals to promote India as a health tourist destination. A study by Mckinsey and Confederation of Indian Industries (CII) reveal that health tourism alone can earn over US$ 2 bn additional revenues by 2012.[9] A steady flow of patients from the developed countries as well as from the Asian and African countries would be helpful in increasing the hotel business.

A number of tourists specially belonging to high spending segment would like to visit India to witness one of the oldest civilisations of the world to enjoy plurality of cultural enjoyment offered by this country. India is potentially sound in respect of both tangible and intangible cultural heritage.[10] The tangible cultural heritage in its monuments and intangible cultural heritage in the form of architecture, music, dance, drama, local rituals and traditions and other folk arts need to be promoted to project India as a heritage destination. This will also create new markets for the hotel sector.

A host of tourists are found interested in enjoying adventure. We are well aware of the fact that India offers the best mountain based adventure tourism in the world in the Himalayas. Of course, a lot of work has been initiated in this segment but they are required to be made comparable to or even better than the Alpine countries. This is also an area where hotel professionals need to tap the opportunities.

With the increasing heat of globalisation, we find economic activities gaining a rapid momentum. The business houses, often, organise conventions and conferences where representatives from all over the world attend and get an opportunity to view the tourist sites or spots. The marketing professional need to identify the opportunities and to sensitise the delegates. This will also open new vistas for the hotel industry.

Indian textiles, handlooms and handicrafts, its furniture and jewellery are already popular abroad. Indian designers have been getting international recognition. Shopping has become an integral part of tourist's itinerary. Now we also find world class shopping malls. The marketing professionals need to develop the awareness of tourists or guests staying in hotels.

Domestic tourism in India is mainly pilgrimage related. Pilgrimage centers are required to be identified and to be integrated with new domestic tourism circuits. Destination like Ajanta Ellora, Bodhgaya, Rajgiri, Nalanda, Kurukshetra, Mahabalipuram and a number of temples in the different parts of the country are required to be promoted.

The above mentioned facts make it clear that new areas and new segments are emerging in India and it is upon the hotel professionals to identify and promote them so that they succeed in increasing the ratio. We are potentially sound and we need be strategically sound. Our aggressive and creative promotional measures would considerably benefit the hotel sector.

The most important thing is dividing the markets into different segments and to understand their changing levels of expectations. When the economy moves upward and the discretionary income is found increasing; the markets for hotel sector show a positive trend. A strong economy means more disposable income; an optimal inflationary pressure means more discretionary income. It is an unvarnished fact that there has been a significant increase in the level of discretionary income of a majority of our population. The burgeoning middle class is a staunch testimony to the proposition that future of hotel industry is bright. The increasing occupancy ratio in the Indian hotels makes it clear that professionalized efforts of marketers and the positive attitudes of policy makers have played an incremental role in the development process. We hope the occupancy ratio to exceed 80 per cent.[11] provided the hoteliers formulate a marketing strategy to be efficacious of luring the different types of tourists.

Priya Paul, Chairman Park Hotels opines that Indian tourism and hospitality sectors continue to remain highly' competitive and attractive to foreign tourists since we are passing through the stage of rapid growth, it is pertinent that media continue to support the hotel industry. They need to activate the publicity measures so that image problem on account of wrong perception of world tourists regarding services at hotels in India is corrected, We can not negate that services delivered in the Indian hotels are of world class and tariffs in hotels in India are globally competitive. Influencing the media people is the prime responsibility of hotel professionals which makes it essential that they develop rapport with them and try to convince them regarding the specialties to be offered to the visiting, guests. The academics may also play here an outstanding role.

Developing India as a brand draws priority attention. Our efforts made for the development of tourism industry mainly after globalisation have been considerably benefiting the hotel industry. Global biggies like Hyatt, Hilton, Starwood and Marriott have been evincing keen interest in the huge growth potential of India. Understanding the customers of different segments is found essential which focuses our attention on managing the information. The hotel professionals need to develop a sound marketing information system so that they are successful not only in enriching their knowledge bank regarding, the markets and the potential customers but also updating their working people who may be successful in delivering the promised quality of services to the ultimate users. In a true sense, the modern hotels considerably rest on ICT and the service processing sizeably depends on the equipment and instruments used by them. The expected segments and their expected priorities become a matter of study for which professionals may intensify the search and development activities. Making themselves aware of the changing taste preferences and ensuring and delivering the promised quality are found easier with the right segmentation. It is quite natural that all the segments cannot be identical in behaviour and taste preferences.

SUMMARY

You have studied in this chapter the market segmentation. Here is a reorientation to the important aspects mentioned in this chapter.

- **Market Segmentation: The Concept:** Market segmentation is the grouping or division of markets. It is a game of divide-and-rule. It is a device to identify the potential customers.
- **Why Market Segmentation?:** The market is segmented with the motives of making sensitive marketing strategy, for knowing the changing lifestyles and for identifying the potential customers.
- **Hotel Market Segmentation:** The segmentation for the hotel market is made on the basis of different factors. Socio-economic considerations, Sex, Short Break Markets, Single-parent Market, Active Leisure, Instant Market, Hotel like Home, Geographical Factors, Psychographic Factors and Lifestyles are the different aspects to be taken into consideration for segmenting the hotel market.
- **Importance of Market Segmentation:** Market segmentation makes possible a fair blending of market opportunities and the hotel resources, effective utilisation of marketing resources, tailoring of marketing strategies to the competitors' strategies, creativity is made possible in the marketing decisions and the future marketing is easier.
- **Decision Process for Market Segmentation:** Identification of segment, preparation of profile for the customers, forecasting the market potential, analysing the potentials for accomplishing the organisation goals and selection of target market are the different processes to be followed for market segmentation.
- **Menu Fatigue:** It is an important decision-making area, specially for the hotel industry; Indigestion, heaviness due to food served in the restaurants are known as menu fatigue. In view of a swing found in the food habits, it is important for making future marketing decisions.
- **Drinking Habits:** It is also an important decision-making area, specially to manage the restaurant and bar in a hotel. Of late, we find a change in the global drinking habits.
- **Effective Market Segmentation:** Raising the effectiveness of segmentation is found closely associated with the sensitivity of the marketing decisions. To make the segmentation process effective, it is pertinent that we assign due weightage to the different emerging new markets. We identify them and make the marketing decisions accordingly.
- **Emerging New Segments for Hotel Industry in Indian Perspective:** With the increasing heat of globalisation and mounting effects of national economic transformation, we find a host of new segments emerging in the hotel sector. It is responsibility of hotel professionals to identify the potentials of new segments and to understand their changing behavioural profile so that the marketing professionals find it easier to satisfy and retain them. The women segment, youth segment, middle class segment rich segment need priority attention of hotel professionals. The changing spending behaviour of customers is a positive sign of development particularly for the hotel industry.

KEY TERMS

- Heterogeneous
- Homogeneous
- Segmentation
- Flexi- hours
- Households
- Spending Power
- Discretionary
- Butchers
- Ego
- Impulse Buying
- Short Break Market
- Single-parent Market
- Hoteliers
- Active Leisure
- Gym
- Sauna
- Instant Market
- Hotel Like Home
- Architecture
- Psychographic
- Lifestyle
- A CORN
- Menu Fatigue
- Chance Trade
- Drinking Culture
- Champagne
- Magnum Bottle
- Leisure Industry
- Hospitality
- Forward Segmentation
- Pub
- Swinger
- Nostalgic
- Occupancy Ratio
- Market Slump
- Confederation of Indian Industries
- Tangible Culture
- Intangible Culture

REVIEW QUESTIONS

1. What do you mean by Hotel Market Segmentation?
   Focus an the justifications for marketing hotel services.
2. Explain the reasons for segmenting hotel market.
3. Discuss the importance of segmentation to hotel industry.
4. Do you find lifestyle an important consideration for segmenting hotel markets? Justify your opinion.
5. Explain the decision processes for market segmentation.
6. What is Menu Fatigue? Explain relevance to the restaurant of your hotel.
7. Explain the relevance of managing drinking habits for effective management of restaurant and bar.
8. Discuss the processes you follow for making the market segmentation effective for your hotel.
9. Do you find market segments for hotel assessable, substantial and reliable? Defend your opinion.
10. Write a note on the emerging new segments of hotel in the Indian perspective.

APPLICATION EXERCISES

1. "Small is beautiful, it is easily identifiable and even effectively commandable. "As a marketing professional serving a hotel, comment on this statement.
2. You have been working as a hotel professional and are supposed to manage the bar. Throw light on the role you need to play for satisfying customers projecting a positive image of your hotel.
3. Your customers have been complaining the cases of menu fatigue which make an invasion on the reputation of your hotel. As a hotel professional, focus on the precautions you would adopt for resolving the cases of menu fatigue.
4. "For effective management of restaurant and bar, it is pertinent that you develop your awareness of the changing drinking habits of your customers", Comment on this statement in the capacity of a hotel manager.
5. By segmenting market, we identify the customers. If we identify them, we divide them. If we divided them, we understand and rule them". Throw light on this statement in the capacity of a hotel professional.
6. With the increasing heat of globalisation, we find emergence of new segments. You need to identify them for satisfying and retaining them. As a marketing professional, focus on the emerging new segments to be productive for the hotel industry.
7. In the capacity of a marketing professional, throw light on the lifestyle found to be an important consideration for market segmentation.

End Notes:

1. Kotler, Philip: *Marketing Management;* Prentice Hall of India, New Delhi, 1990, p. 280.
2. Cundiff, Still and Govoni: *Fundamentals of Modern Marketing;* Prentice Hall of India, 1982, p. 111.
3. William J. Stanton: *Fundamentals of Marketing,* p. 76.
4. Melvyn, Greene: *Marketing Hotels and Restaurants into the 90s;* Heinemann Professional Publishing; Oxford, 1989, p. 76.
5. *Ibid.,* p. 91.
6. *Ibid.,* p. 96.
7. Jha, S.M.: *Tourism Marketing*; Himalaya Publishing House, Mumbai, 2009.
8. The Analyst: November, 2006; Interview with Priya Paul President, HAI and Chairman, Park Hotels, p. 21.
9. The Analyst: *Discovering India*; Amit Singh Sisodiya & Kavitha Putta; p. 19.
10. Eleventh Five Year Plan: Planning Commission; Government of India, New Delhi, Vol. III, pp. 245-251.
11. S. Ray & A. Teckchandni: Indian Hotel Industry Strategy Building for Utilizing Unparalleled Growth Potential; The ICFAIAN Journal of Management Research; Vol. VII/5, 2008, pp. 64-78.

....ꙮꙮꙮ....

CHAPTER - 4

MARKETING INFORMATION SYSTEM FOR HOTELS

Don't float a craft on a river about which you are not well versed with. Know the intensity of current, movement of wind, the shallow and deep points; you reach to your destination, safely on time.

CHAPTER OBJECTIVES

Introduction – Marketing Information System: The Concept – MIS: The Sub-systems – MIS: Salient Features – MIS: Functions – Managing Information for Hotel Industry – Marketing Information for Restaurants – Marketing Information System for Function rooms – Key Sources of Information for Hotel – Significance of MIS to Hotel Marketing – Marketing Research: The Concept – Methods of Research – Marketing Research in the Hotel Industry – Managing Information for Quality Decisions in the Hotel Industry – Summary – Key Terms – Review Questions – Application Exercises – End Notes.

LEARNING OBJECTIVES

This chapter aims at studying the different dimensions of Marketing Information System. The significant changes in the business environment both at national and global levels make it essential that the hotel professionals develop their awareness of the emerging trends. Studying and understanding the customers and identifying the strengths and weaknesses of rivals are the key issues before the hotel professionals which would help them in improving the quality of marketing decisions to satisfy and retain the customers. The increasing arrivals of tourists make it essential that world class hotels are constructed.

INTRODUCTION

Lord Kelvin rightly professed that when you can gauge what you are speaking about and express it in number, you know something about it. But when you cannot measure it, when you cannot express it in number; your knowledge is reportedly meager and unsatisfactory. It is against this background that managing information has become an essential part of managing decision. In an age of new generation of information and communication technology (ICT), the task of managing information is considerably simplified. The main thing in making the information-based decision is to quantify our knowledge which increases our capacity to express, to influence and to turn the negative into positive.

We do not find it right to float a craft on a river about which we are not well versed with. The intensity of current of water, the movement of wind, the identification of shallow and deep points etc. are found important for risk-free safe journey. It is soundness of information that simplifies the task of touching the destination. It is soundness of information that minimises the intensity of risk to the destination. Like this, it is pertinent that an organisation enriches its information.

Information and intuition are the two important pillars for making sound managerial decisions. In the modern world, the inventions and innovations in the field of information and communication have instrumentalised the process of technological sophistication and we find organisations building superhighway for communication. However, the task of making world class managerial decisions makes it essential that we enrich our intuition. Unless we find managers making use of their sense of judgment, the decisions cannot be of quality.

Change is a natural phenomenon. With the human minds becoming much more creative and innovative, we find frequency in change increasing very fast and this has been found complicating the task of professionals. Like other organisations, the hotels have also been found witnessing numerous changes and challenges. The increasing heat of globalisation, emergence of a cross-cultural society, galloping level of income of a majority of the population, mounting intensity of competition in the hospitality sector, multi-dimensional changes found in the taste preferences of hotel users are some of the key issues found influencing the managerial decisions.

The Marketing Information System is supposed to be an important tool used by managers for making decisions. Either we need to formulate a plan for future or we require to resolve our day-to-day managerial problems; we need to develop a sound information system. The emerging changes within and outside an organisation make it essential that marketing decisions are based on the emerging trends. The co-ordinated, systematic and continuous information gathering is an important strategy for managing and using the information related to marketing activities. The need of the hour is to be more effective in our marketing and sales efforts and an MIS makes it possible.

A management reporting system whether it is designed for marketing or for control purposes must be designed for the needs and requirements of every individual hotel. We find a hard core of basic information which hotel management requires irrespective of the style and management strategies of the hotel.

In the last decade of 20th century, the contours of development have undergone radical changes. The introduction of new generation of information and communication technology virtually revolutionized the services of hotels. Leading hotel companies have been found making use of new generation of ICT for making managerial decisions and strategy formulation and implementation. However a number of small hotels are not in a position to make use of the same. The instrumentality of information system is coiled in the essence of designing marketing strategies in tune with the changing taste preferences, lifestyles and likes and dislikes of guests and potential guests. We cannot deny that the innovation and value addition processes in absence of a sound information management would adversely be affected. Our steps in the field of collecting, analysing and disseminating the information determine the intensity of positive or negative results. The multi-dimensional information related to the strategies followed by competitors become important while making marketing decisions. The information regarding the latest developments in the field of tourism industry, information concerned with the extent of transformation of industrial economy, global partnership, political relationships with different countries, the development of new groups or chains of hotel, information related to the strategies followed by competitors become important while making marketing decisions for the hotel industry.

Undoubtedly enough, a majority of us do not venture to welcome change which is the only constant thing in our lives. The world is changing with new market segments developing and new market segments emerging. Spotting the opportunities available in the market is essential and this necessitates identifying and understanding the multi-dimensional changes in the society. The multi-faceted changes in the society create opportunities and the professional, excellence of hotel managers determines the magnitude of success. The MIS helps in identifying the opportunities both at micro and macro levels or national and global levels. If we find hotel professionals updating themselves, enriching their knowledge bank and making use of MIS for strategy formulation and implementation, a significant boost to the hotel industry can not be negated.

The multi-faceted sources of hotel business are conference room for business purposes, recreational facilities for business tourists, restaurants, wedding, conventions, exhibitions, seminars, patients for medical care, social reformists for cultural studies, adventurers for taking pleasure of adventure tourism, historians for witnessing the monuments etc. need to be studied in a right way. The hotel professionals need information for making quality decisions because the hotel companies having up-to -date information may be successful in incorporating the changes in their policy decisions as and when the circumstances necessitate so.

MARKETING INFORMATION SYSTEM: THE CONCEPT

Regarding the concept of Marketing Information System (MIS), *the following* viewpoints are presented:

Kotler says,[1]

'MIS is the combination of sub-systems like the internal reporting system, marketing intelligence system, marketing research and analytical marketing system.'

Cundiff, Still and Govoni opine,[2]

'MIS is an organized set of procedures, information handling routines and reporting techniques designed to provide the information required for making marketing decisions.'

Richard H. Brien and Jamen E. Stafford say,[3]

'Marketing Information System is a continuing and interacting structure of people, equipment and procedures to gather, sort and analyze, evaluate and distribute pertinent, timely and accurate information for use of marketing decision makers to improve their marketing planning, implementation' and control.'

Bellur and Berkman say,[4]

'The MIS is an important tool used by management to assist in planning for the future, solving current and potential problems, and making decisions to accomplish a firm's goals.'

In view of the aforesaid opinions of different experts regarding the MIS, the logical conclusion is that MIS is the *collection, storing, analyzing and evaluating the information to meet the organisational goals.* In a true sense, to manage a business is to manage its future and further to manage the future is to manage the information. Hence, it is the management of future and a sound base for planning activities, without which the present business cannot be secured. We also call it a mix of different sub-systems like internal reporting, marketing intelligence, marketing research and analytical marketing report. It is playing with data and transforming the same into information to simplify the task of marketing decision makers for future marketing. The MIS paves ways for programming the marketing activities in the face of multi-dimensional changes found in the environmental conditions. Thus, it is a prime mover which kindles creativity and helps an organisation in turning the negative into positive.

To be more specific, when we talk about the hotel industry, the management of information becomes pertinent as the system makes available to the marketing decision-makers the required information.

MIS: THE SUB-SYSTEMS

In the present changing world, it is significant that we spot the available opportunities. There are different sub-systems of the marketing information system as mentioned below:

1. Internal Reporting: The base of internal marketing information is the accounting system, which helps in gathering data related to sales, inventories, costs, cash flows, accounts, receivables and payables etc. Of course, the data are collected from internal sources. We call it the *result data* which are managed with the purpose of spotting opportunities and problems. We find this sub-system significant to the hotel industry. Most accounting systems are found based on the American Uniform System of Accounts or a subversion of this accounting system. In the hotel industry, to maximise the ratio of room sales, we need information on the room occupancy percentage and room sales by amount. Any management reporting system, whether it is designed for marketing and control purposes, must be designed for the needs and requirements of every individual hotel.[5]

2. Marketing Intelligence System: Another sub-system of the marketing information system is the marketing intelligence system, which keeps marketing executives well informed regarding the current marketing environment. The new emerging trends in the marketing environment simplify the task of a marketing manager, specially while understanding the changing behaviour of potential guests. Census data, market news and reports, journals, magazines, publications of trade association etc. are found important sources of this sub-system. In a true sense, the marketing intelligence acts as a mirror of the marketing environment. It is also found to be an organised feedback process of marketing communications. This sub-system supplies relevant data having a far-reaching impact on the making of economically feasible marketing decisions. The processes used in the system are undesired viewing, conditioned viewing, informal search and formal search. To be more specific, the feedback process of the sub-system is found important to the hotel industry. The advertising slogans, the public relations activities and sales promotion efforts can be made more effective as the reactions of audience and customers are made available to the marketing manager.

3. Marketing Research: The third component or sub-system of the marketing information system is the marketing research. It provides special information on request, when marketing executives encounter complex marketing problems, necessitating unique information for removing the hurdles. The marketing research studies are to a large extent project oriented. Generally, the information related to be behavioural profile, product, brand name preferences, advertising awareness, sales promotion, physical distribution, dealer behaviour, competition are collected through the marketing research. In the hotel industry, this sub-system is found useful as it provides data related to the behavioural profile. To make possible an optimal utilisation of the marketing resources in the hotel industry, it is essential to develop awareness of the changing behavioural profile. This would help us in understanding the customers. On the basis of research reports, the services can be innovated and promotional strategies planned can be made effective. Thus, it is the marketing research report which helps marketers in innovating the decisions in the face of multi-dimensional changes in the socio-economic conditions.

4. Analytical Marketing System: The fourth and last sub-system or component of the marketing information system is the analytical marketing system meant for the collection of statistical procedures

EXHIBIT 4.1: MIS SUB-SYSTEM

Internal Reporting	*Marketing Intelligence*	*Marketing Research*	*Analytical Marketing*
1 IRS	2 MIS	3 MRS	4 AMS
Result data order, Sales, Inventory levels, Receivables, Payables, Spotting Important Opportunities and Problems	Happening data, set of procedures and sources used by executives to obtain everyday information about important developments in the marketing environment through undesired, conditioned viewing, informal search, formal search	Systematic design, collection, analysis and reporting of data and findings relevant to a specific marketing situation facing organisation. Advertisement research, economic research, product research, sales and market research	Collection of statistical procedures for extracting meaningful information from data. Calculating average, measurement of dispersion, cross tabulation of data computer based marketing decision support system

1. IRS = Internal Reporting System
2. MIS = Marketing Intelligence System
3. MRS = Marketing Research System
4. AMS = Analytical Marketing System

for extracting meaningful information from data. It is a computer base marketing decision support system which simplifies the task of a marketer or a decision-maker as he gets the required information without a special effort. Measurement of dispersion, calculating average, cross tabulation of data are the main features of this sub-system. In Exhibit 4.1, we find a complete list of four sub-systems and their functional areas.

 MIS: SALIENT FEATURES

'Recently, the MIS has emerged as a scientific technique for turning the available data into information. This has simplified the task of decision-makers in any industry. The following are the key features of MIS:

1. A scientific technique for the processing of data: The MIS is a scientific technique for processing the data. Here, the system analysts adopt scientific techniques for the management of data. The scientifically managed and controlled electronic devices make possible right information on right time. We use computers for managing the information. This makes it a scientific and authentic business strategy.

2. Operated electronically: Needless to mention that now the system is operated electronically with the help of software packages. The entire activities of processing, analyzing and disseminating the information are done by advanced computers, operated and controlled by the system analysts. If the hotels and hotel companies manage information with the help of computers, the future marketing is found easier.

3. A master plan for information flow: If the flow of information is restricted, the decision-makers find it difficult to take a decision. The MIS maintains and ensures the flow of information. For future marketing ventures, it is essential that hotel companies prepare a master plan for managing the marketing information. The formulation of a master plan is meant for studying the magnitude of problems, exploring avenues for collecting the information, finalising budget for implementing the MIS, developing suitable staff or personnel to manage the information and getting the needed information on time within the limited budget.

4. Operated by system analysts: The MIS is operated by efficient system analysts. They are supposed to be technically trained to design the system. It is an organised ongoing system for making available to the decision-makers the necessary information. The steps taken for collecting the data are found insignificant, if the system analysts are not efficient. This would also question their caliber.

5. It is a future-oriented system: The instrumentality of MIS is involved in the essence of managing the future. We find future marketing an important aspect of decision-making. If we fail in managing the future, we fail in managing the present. The MIS is an order, a process, an arrangement and a purpose, which is based on the system approach marketing and business planning. The emerging new trends in the hotel industry make it essential that hotels and hotel companies are well aware of the strategies planned and followed by their competitors. This would simplify the task of innovating the marketing strategies, much earlier than our competitors.

6. Integration and co-ordination: An outstanding feature of the system is to make possible integration and co-ordination between the executives and specialists. It is well known that system analysts bear the responsibility of managing the information. The marketing executives need different types of information and the specialists and executives co-ordinate and the deliberations simplify the task of executives in case of confusion and misunderstanding. Such a co-ordination is found essential to make possible effectiveness in the MIS. If the information provider and the information receiver communicate and discuss any problem, the information would be managed effectively.

7. Information flow on a regular basis: Consistency in the flow of information is essential to make effective decisions. In the present business world, the changes are so frequent that a decision maker needs information on a regular basis. The continuity in the flow of information simplifies the task of business planners as they come to know the latest developments in the hotel industry and make sincere efforts to innovate their marketing resources. The new services to be offered by the competitors, the advertising and sales promotion efforts are found significant to the decision-makers. The well organised and developed intelligence system makes available day-to-day information.

MIS: FUNCTIONS

The different functions of MIS are explained below:

1. *Assembling of data:* It is the first stage of managing the data which is collected by research scientists — both from internal and external sources and are stored in data banks by system analysts.
2. *Processing of data:* It is the second stage which is referred to as, editing, tabulating and summarizing the data. The system analysts are also engaged for this purpose.
3. *Analysis of data:* It is the third stage of managing the information. Analysis of data is meant for finding out the percentage, ratio and test of statistical significance.
4. *Storage of data*: In the fourth stage of managing the information, we find retrieval of data. It is also known as filing, indexing, relocating of the data analysed by the system analysts.
5. *Evaluation of data:* It is the fifth stage in which evaluation regarding accuracy, adequacy and reliability is found.
6. *Dissemination of data*: It is the last stage, in which we find dissemination or distribution of needed information to the decision-makers.

The functions of MIS are also shown in Figure 4.1.

First stage	:	Assembling of data
Second stage	:	Processing of data
Third stage	:	Analysis of data
Fourth stage	:	Storage of data
Fifth stage	:	Evaluation of data
Sixth stage	:	Dissemination of data

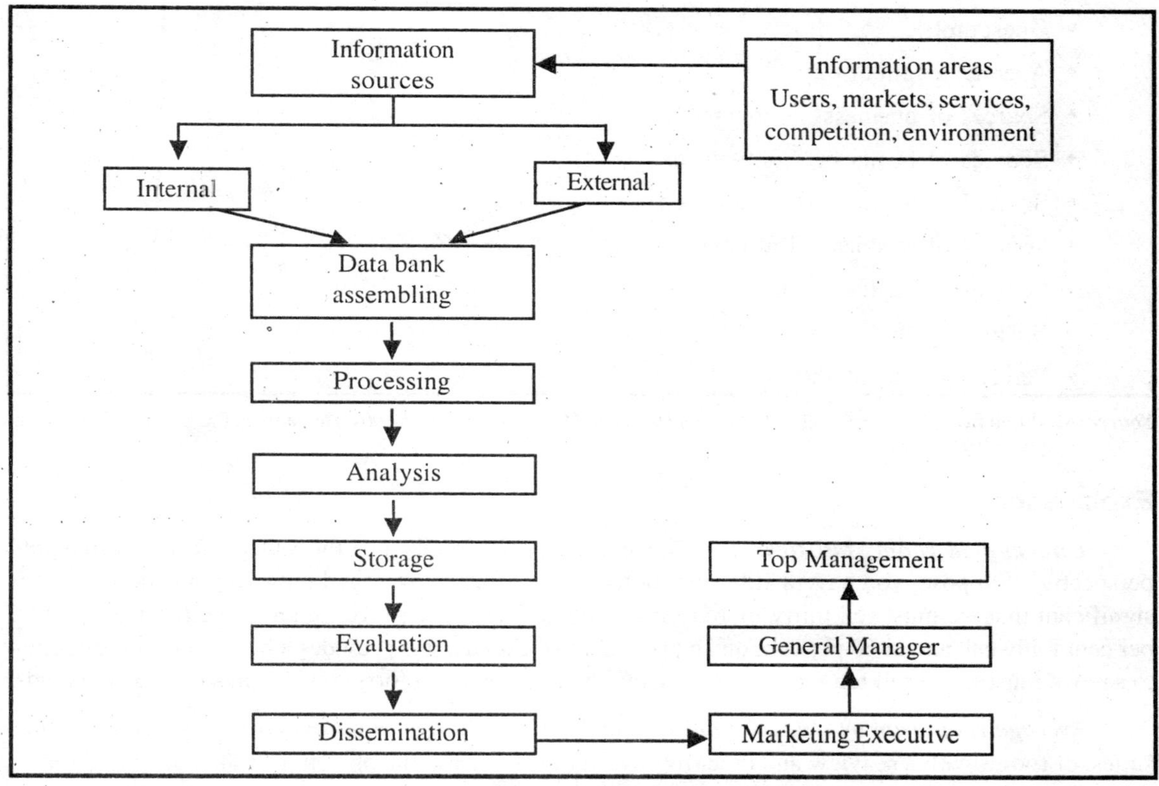

FIG. 4.1: MARKETING INFORMATION SYSTEM

MANAGING INFORMATION FOR HOTEL INDUSTRY

We find three important areas for collecting information for the hotel industry. The hotels are supposed to manage rooms, restaurants and function rooms for generating substantial revenues. These are the sensitive points in the hotel industry, directly related to selling. In Exhibit 4.2 the marketing information for bedrooms are presented. Of course, the table is self-explanatory but explanations are felt necessary to have a clear perception of the concept.

EXHIBIT 4.2: MARKETING INFORMATION FOR BEDROOMS

Marketing Information for Bedrooms

- Unoccupied room statistics by the type of room
- Average room rate by the type of room
- Lost room revenue (number of rooms not sold multiplied by average room rate achieved)
- Occupancy percentage in currency
- Occupancy forecasts
- Occupancy by major sources

- Guest profile
- Average length of stay
- Sources of business by country
- Sources of business (Conferences)
- Sources of business (Businessmen)
- Sources of business (Tourists)
- Sources of business (Others)
- Business turned away
- Percentage of 'no shows'

Source: Modified from: Melvyn Greene; *Marketing Hotels and Restaurants into the 90s*, Heinemann Professional Publishing, 1989, p. 193.

Explanations

Unoccupied room statistics: The unoccupied rooms really put the sales effort required into perspective. Suppose, you have a 100 room hotel and occupancy averaged only 70 per cent. Here, it is significant that we must sell thirty more rooms. Another case, where we find average occupancy at 90 per cent midweek and at 60 per cent on an average at weekends, this provides a better sense of direction to say we must try to sell ten more rooms during the midweek and forty more rooms during weekends.

Average room rate by type of room: In hotels, with different types of rooms like singles, twins, suites, or rooms with a seaview and other rooms over the car park, the objective related to unsold rooms may be specific on types of rooms which require a marketing strategy and a sales team effort. Average rates per room and per guest are important but they have the disadvantage of being average unless all rooms are of standard size.

Lost room revenue: It is a vital issue of concern which should be known on a daily basis as it creates a greater sense of need. The night occupancy statistics is found important to all hotels. Here, it is significant to have a comparative analysis of the target and the actual occupancy. If we find 80 per cent target and the actual is more than 85 per cent, it is very natural that everyone relaxes. Here, it is more pragmatic that the hoteliers use only unoccupied rooms and lost room revenue. This would be helpful in changing the face of the hotel as everyone would be found more conscious, specially to the sales due to non-occupancy of activities.

Lost in revenue clearly indicates the amount of revenue lost. Here, it is significant to mention that revenues are not lost due to non-occupancy of rooms and this should be the aim of all hotels and hotel companies.

***Occupancy percentage in currency*:** Another useful percentage which helps to interpret other information is the Rupees/Dollar/Pound Sterling occupancy percentage. This is Actual Room Sales as a percent of the Total Room Sales, if every room was sold at full occupancy, and full tack (non-discounted) room rate. This is the percentage which should be studied in conjunction with number of unoccupied rooms which discloses the degree of discounting. It is also to clear that the degree of discounting is a stage where the hotel could have full occupancy but show a low currency occupancy percentage if rooms have been sold at a large discount.

Occupancy by forecasts: This is to estimate the occupancy for the coming period (probably, the tourist scam) so that the hotels and hotel companies keep themselves ready and make necessary preparations.

Occupancy by major source: This should disclose whether your major source of business arises from tour operators, local companies, national companies, travel agents or individuals who have pre-booked an accommodation in your hotel.

Guest profile: This is needed to prepare a detailed list of different types of guests visiting the hotels. Here, the important aspects related to the guests are age, sex, mode of cash payment, credit card, charge, business tour, tourists, convention, type of group, employment, place of employment, place of residence, mode of transport, single/double/family, room popularity, new guest, first choice, length of stay and who made the booking in question. This information related to the guests is found useful.

Average length of stay: The average length of stay in a hotel is the average period of stay by the guests. Here, it is also important to mention that lower the average length of stay, the higher the average rate per night. This is supported by the fact when in a hotel, suppose a hotel located near the airport, we find an average length of stay of one night, the rate charged is often higher than where the average length of stay is longer.

Sources of business: We find here four areas, e.g., sources of business by a country, sources of business by conferences, sources of business by businessmen and sources of business by tourists. In addition, there are other potential business areas. This is clearly meant that sources of business deals with income from conferences, businessmen, tourists and others. Occupancy by major source of business should disclose whether your major source of business arises from tour operators, local companies, national companies, travel agents, individuals, who have pre-booked accommodation or individuals who have not made booking.

Business turned away: It is an important statistic not collected by many in the hotel industry. In a year, we find many nights and periods when hotels turn away business because they are fully booked, even though the average annual occupancy may not be too high. This is found helpful in fixing the pricing strategy. Besides, we also find instrumentality of this to know the results during the peak period.

Percentage of 'no shows': It is an important statistic, provided your policy is to overbook. No doubt, overbooking is a controversial subject and in some countries we also find it illegal. Here, it is important to mention that particularly in the top five star hotels, some degree of overbooking is essential due to *'no shows'*. Where we should overbook is really not so important, indeed the important thing is regarding its intensity. How much should we overbook? Of course, it is influenced by a number of factors. Normally, the overbooking should not exceed 5 per cent. This percentage can go up, if we initiate an organisation of some important exhibitions, conferences in town. It is easier to come to a conclusion, specially regarding the intensity of overbooking. Here, we should keep in mind the past record of 'no shows.' A sensible degree of overbooking is essential. But the guests should not be allocated the actual room number till the last moment. To be more specific when we find all rooms identical, we do not find any need for pre-allocation. Besides, basic motivation training and selling are also required for overbooking. As soon as we do not find rooms to be sold, the receptionists would politely tell prospects who telephone or call, saying that they are fully booked. The most effective in filling the *'no shows'* is to have a series of telephone numbers to follow up. The way employees say fully booked requires tact.

 MARKETING INFORMATION FOR RESTAURANTS

Another aspect for managing information is related to the restaurants as shown in Exhibit 4.3.

EXHIBIT 4.3: MARKETING INFORMATION FOR RESTAURANTS

Marketing Information for Restaurants
• Covers per meal period • Covers analysed into residents/chance for each meal period • Average spends per cover (food) • Average spends per cover (drinks) • Total average spends per bill (check) • Average spends analysed into price brackets • Customer profiles • Set turnover ratios per meal period • Table turnover ratios per meal period • Popularity indices per meal period for food, wines and other drinks

Source: Modified from: Melvyn Greene; *Marketing Hotel and Restaurants into the 90s,* Heinemann Professional Publishing, 1989, p. 197.

Explanations

There are various aims and objectives behind the checklist on marketing information on restaurants. These statistics are aimed at assisting in pricing policies, helping to define market opportunities, isolating quiet and busy periods and to assist in menu planning and pricing. These statistics are found helpful to increase sales and profits.

The statistics related to covers sold per day and cumulatively per week, month and year.are found useful in comparing with covers sold in the previous year, the overall target covers for the current year or where we find a change in the menu. This is found important before and after even a minor change in the menus. These statistics are found important in taking immediate corrective action and further for planning the strategies for future marketing, specially when they are analysed into meal schedules and days of the week. It is found more significant to analyse a busy meal into time zones as even a busy period may have quiet periods. The counting of covers in the quarter-hour period, it is possible to draw a graph or chart of the activity pattern in a meal period. It is quite natural that we find variation from day-to-day but here experience shows that restaurants always running busy have a distinct pattern. Some of the restaurants have a great business, from opening time to a peak we find there a steady build-up and then a steady decline at the time of closing. Some of the restaurants have a step-up pattern or a plateau pattern. Here, a restaurant may open at noon, quiet fairly till 12.45 and then again very busy till 2.15 p.m. followed by a quiet period till 3 p.m. Even in the two identical restaurants, we find a different pattern because the pattern of eating in local offices may be different.

Whatever the patterns, the hotels and hotel companies adopt for their restaurants, this can help in setting staff standards and maintaining rotas (ledger books). We also accept the instrumentality of the same in formulating the marketing strategies.

MARKETING INFORMATION SYSTEM FOR FUNCTION ROOMS

It is right to mention here that we find the aims of information for function rooms the same as we find for restaurants and bedrooms. The main thing here is to isolate the real activity of the rooms and to know the quiet periods when they are not sold. Another useful statistic is average per square foot. This helps in knowing the real success of different sizes of function rooms. It helps in comparing one hotel with others. The function business of a hotel is found helpful in producing a lot of business for other areas of the hotel. The marketing information related to the function rooms is shown in Exhibit 4.4.

These statistics are also found helpful in increasing in-house sales. One of the important aspects to monitor on the function side of a hotel is the *'spin-off'* benefit in other areas of the hotel and to actively promote this. It is also found helpful in persuading guests who are attending an evening function that they should not drive when they have been drinking and are tired. The aforesaid management information for making the marketing decisions is found useful to the hotels and hotel companies. Here, it is not only sufficient that hotels have good informational the interpretation if found wrong would turn all efforts in vain. Thus, it is right to say that marketing information system is of no use if the same is just interesting and not sensible. Whatever the information we have gone through earlier are received from the internal sources. The statistics regarding the availability of bedrooms, restaurants and function rooms is, no doubt, important but the management of marketing information would also cover the information received from the external sources. The multi-dimensional changes in the external environmental conditions play a significant role while making the marketing decisions.

EXHIBIT 4.4: MARKETING INFORMATION FOR FUNCTION ROOMS

Marketing Information For Function Rooms

- Utilisation ratio of function rooms
- Type of function-profile of customers
- Number of times the function rooms are fully utilised
- Average size per function
- Numbers attending into groupings related to the total size
- Average spend (food, drinks, total)
- Average spend per square foot or metre (food, liquor, sub-total catering, rental, total)
- Menu popularity (food, wines and other drinks)
- Pattern of utilized days
- Numbers staying overnight
- Estimated benefits for other areas (e.g., bars, coffee shop etc.)

Source: Adapted from: Melvyn Greene; *Marketing Hotel and Restaurants into the 90s*, Heinemann Professional Publishing, 1989, p. 199.

KEY SOURCES OF INFORMATION FOR HOTEL

The management of marketing information is a vital aspect of hotel marketing. The hotels and hotel companies need diverse information related to guests/users, tourism, forthcoming conferences and conventions, level of competition at the market place, emerging trends in society, new trends in economy etc. Since the international hotels are concerned with foreigners, it is also essential that we have the latest information regarding the foreign markets. To capitalise on the opportunities, we need to know the changing lifestyles. The system analysts can help us in many ways. In Exhibit 4.5 we find different types of information required by the decision-makers.

EXHIBIT 4.5: INFORMATION REQUIRED BY THE DECISION MAKERS

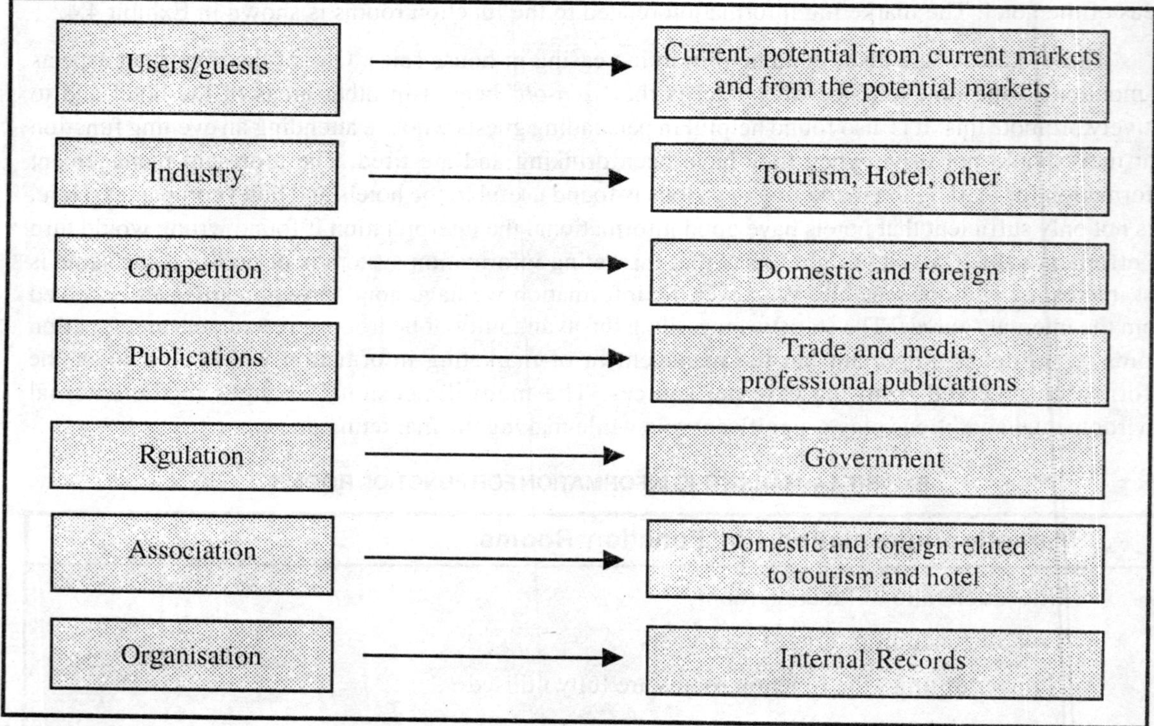

Source: Jha, S.M.: *Tourism Marketing:* Himalaya Publishing House, Bombay, 1995.

SIGNIFICANCE OF MIS TO HOTEL MARKETING

We do not find it right to float a craft on a river about which we are not well versed with. The intensity of currents, the movement of wind, the shallow and deep points etc. are found important for a safe journey. Like this, it is pertinent that an organisation must be well aware of multi-dimensional developments in the business-world. This simplifies the task of taking marketing decisions by decision-makers. An MIS is meant for turning the data into information and to make it available to the decision-makers. The hotels and hotel companies also need diverse information from different sources. The emerging trends in the socio-economic conditions — both at national and international levels, the rules and regulations regarding immigration, the amendments in the foreign exchange regulations, the services to be introduced by the competitors, the multi-dimensional developments in the tourism industry, the modem transportation and communication facilities, the changing law and order situations are some of the important sources of information influencing the marketing decisions pertaining to hotel industry. This makes it clear that if hotels and hotel companies institute and develop MIS, the present and future marketing would be easier. The following points justify the importance of MIS in the hotel industry.

1. Easy access to information: In the age of communications superhighway, it is difficult for an organisation to survive without managing the information. The effectiveness of decisions is substantially influenced by easy accessibility to information. If the hotels are to be well informed, marketing decisions will have to be more sensitive. The MIS makes available to the decision-makers the much needed information without making any effort.

***2. Assisting the planning process for future marketing*:** For time honored development of hotels and the industry on the whole, it is pertinent that they implement a rational business plan. It is not possible to check the flow of development as the wheels of development once activated keep moving unless there are some obstacles or constraints. The recent developments in the areas of communication and fast modes of travelling have made the world a global village where the habits, needs, requirements, lifestyles are to a large extent internationalised. This makes it essential that the formulation process for a plan is in close touch with the latest developments. Unless we make it possible, the plan would not be rational. If we plan well, we act well. If we act well, we get the desired results. It is the crying need of the hour that hotels and hotel companies formulate a scientific and intelligent plan, which would simplify their task of making creative and financially feasible marketing decisions. The task would also involve customer satisfaction.

***3. Co-ordinates, systematic and continuous information*:** The formulation of a sound marketing mix is essential even for the hotel industry.

4. Performance evaluation is possible: The MIS helps in evaluating the performance of different grades of personnel working at different points. If we succeed in quantifying the efficiency, the evaluation process is simplified. The MIS, if instituted and developed scientifically, will pave the way for qualitative improvements. The hotels are supposed to make sincere efforts for improving the quality of their services which would help them in excelling competition. It is right to mention that the system helps decision-makers in getting information regarding the strategies of competitors in the same area of business. The evaluation of performance is also deemed essential to initiate qualitative improvements.

5. Functional co-ordination is possible: For the successful and time honored implementation of a plan, it is essential that superiors and subordinates have a sense of co-ordination. For smooth functioning, it is pertinent that the marketing executives, sales executives, system analysts and research scientists effectively co-ordinate with each other. The data required for transmitting the same into information would be made available to system analysts, to decision-makers, and the instructions would be transmitted to the concerned personnel at the right time and in a right fashion, only if the MIS works satisfactorily.

6. Future orientation is possible: In this changing world, the task of marketing manager tends to get more complicated. This necessitates future orientation as without it, future marketing cannot be effective. Future orientation thus becomes an integral part of the development and expansion of an organisation. By knowing the past levels of performance, we predict the developments in future business ventures. It is possible for hotels and hotel companies to get detailed information regarding the changing needs and requirements of the potential guests the world over. The services, the promotional efforts, the pricing or channel decisions can be innovated as and when the circumstances necessitate so.

7. Helpful in image projection: The projection of a fair image is found essential to get the desired results. The MIS simplifies the task of image projection. With the help of graphic presentation of development results, it is easy to satisfy the target users of services. The impulse using of the potential guests can be influenced if the system (MIS) is working satisfactorily.

In few words, it can said in clear terms that MIS has emerged as an integral part of creative decision-making.

MARKETING RESEARCH: THE CONCEPT

An important component of the Marketing Information System (MIS) or the marketing research is the systematic collection, analysis and reporting of data for the purpose of improved/qualitative decision-making in the marketing of goods and services. The viewpoints of experts are given below:

'Marketing research is the systematic design, collection, analysis and reporting of data and findings relevant to a specific market situation facing a company.'[6]

'Marketing research, broadly defined, is the systematic gathering, recording and analysis of data about marketing problems to facilitate decision-making.'[7]

'Marketing research is *the systematic problem analysis, model building and fact finding for the purpose of improved decision-making and control in the marketing of goods and services.'*[8]

Like other industries, the hotel industry is also required to make sensitive marketing .decisions to match their decisions with the changing needs, preferences, likes and dislikes of the guests/customers. The hotels and hotel companies face a number of problems due to multi-dimensional changes in the socio-economic conditions. In addition, the increasing levels of competition also makes it significant that marketing decisions are based on a scientific research system. Identification of habits, attitudes, and lifestyles is considered to be an important aspect for marketing the hotel services. The new emerging market segments make it essential that the hoteliers be well aware of these changes and to incorporate the same in their future marketing decisions.

METHODS OF RESEARCH

There are two methods for undertaking the marketing research as shown in Figure 4.2.

Desk Research: It is the collection and analysis of data, statistics and published information on emerging trends in markets without any field survey — which is based on secondary source where the published materials are used. The leading hotel associations publish important information on this front from time to time. The Federation of Hotel & Restaurant Association of India (FHRAI) and other important hotel institutes also publish valuable information regarding hotels and management programmes.

Field Research: This is based on the primary source where the sample survey and motivational research are found important. In this method, special research work is carried out. The population of the conglomeration of customers for which information is needed is clearly defined. After this, a statistical valid sample is drawn and the information is collected. All households in a country may be the universe or population under investigation. For field research there are two methods:

Sample Survey: The process of sampling consists of personal interviews of tourists, travel agents, tour operators, hotel personnel etc. The outstanding merit of this method is its economy. Here, the designing of questionnaires is found important. In addition, the selection of a suitable market or segment is also its feature. While circulating the questionnaires, the selection of respondents is also significant.

Motivational Research: In the motivational research, we find emphasis on forecasting the motives behind visiting the hotel. This is supposed to be the most sensitive method of undertaking research. While studying the behavioural profile of guests/customers, we find this method more effective. This helps in identifying the expectations and demands of potential guests. A careful designing of questionnaires governs the magnitude of success of the motivational research. The main thing in the motivational research is to identify potential guests and potential segments. This raises the sensitivity of the research, specially to the hotel industry.

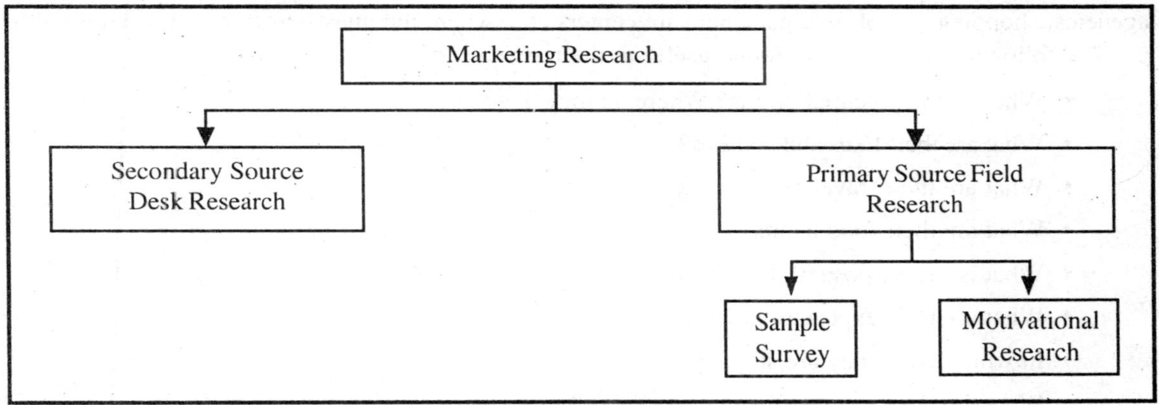

FIG. 4.2: METHODS OF RESEARCH

Thus, it would be apt to mention that the suitability of a particular method of research pertains on the nature of problem.

MARKETING RESEARCH IN THE HOTEL INDUSTRY

We find more weight in the views of Lord Pasteur that chance favours the prepared man. Marketing research is simply not gathering of information but a valuable contribution to an organisation, specially while understanding its services, markets and the overall marketing strategies. But this instrumentality of the marketing research depends upon the efficiency of market researchers. We cannot deny the fact that marketing research plays a unique role in guiding others, but here it is essential that the personnel meant for this purpose have sufficient knowledge based on proper education and training which would enable them to adjust in any adverse situations. The researchers meant for this purpose are expected to be analytical, questioning, adjustable, objectivists and stimulating market personnel. This also makes possible value-added services and the research is found to be effective. Like other industries, the hotel industry also experiences multi-dimensional problems related to product, promotion, place and pricing of the facilities offered by it. It is significant that the hotels and hotel companies try to base their marketing decisions in the face of changing needs and requirements of the customers. The main thrust point here is to identify their preferences and level of expectations. If the researchers design their research plan in the face of emerging changes, the outcome of the marketing research would make available to the guests value-added services. The designing of questionnaires is thus significant in this very context. We have to assign due weightage to the project planning through a systematic research strategy. We accept the fact that time spent on planning the project minimizes the time lag between the beginning and completion of a project. There are different stages in the project planning, e.g., setting the research objectives, planning the required information to accomplish the organisational goals, identifying the sources to be tapped in seeking the information, employing the research design, sampling the procedures and selecting the method for analysing the data. Such a scientific project planning would not only simplify the procedures of research but also make the results effective.

In the hotel industry, we find different categories of customers coming from different sections, regions and economic strata. This in a natural way complicates the task of a researcher, who is supposed to design the questionnaire consisting of places, offices, tourist cities, conventions, conferences, travel agencies, shopping complexes, personal care centers etc., where the guests/customers are expected to go The following questions are found useful to the researchers:

- Who are the potential guests? Where do they live?
- What are their likes and dislikes?
- What are their travel preferences?
- What are their food habits?
- What is the purpose of their visit?
- What are their expectations?
- In which hotel they are staying?
- What are their transportation preferences?
- What are their preferences for entertainment?
- What are their competitors' strategies?

The researchers have to make efforts to include all these issues in their questionnaires and have to collect the opinions of respondents.

Willingly or unwillingly, we have to accept the fact that if there is one thing certain in the world, i.e., change. This necessitates more dynamism in our plans, policies and strategies.

In this context, the additive elements become essential which raise the significance of conducting a systematic and planned research based on changing environmental conditions in the domestic and international perspectives. The lifestyle cannot remain static. The multi-dimensional changes influence the same. The likes and dislikes, preferences are substantially influenced by the emerging trends in lifestyles. The industrial transformation process has recently been accelerated even in the developing countries of the globe. In addition, the electronic revolution is also found impact-generating. The technological sophistication has injected life into the economic transformation programmes.

The leading hotels and hotel companies around the globe are now promoting research activities as the marketing decisions have now undergone frequent changes. The innovative marketing decisions bear the efficacy of creating and expanding markets and we cannot think about innovation unless the research activities are developed in a sophisticated fashion to suit a particular hotel. The need of the hour is to pave ways for the generation of profit which seems involving efforts due to the growing of competition. A developed system of marketing research may be helpful in identifying and capitalising on the opportunities.

Of late, the leading hotel companies have been incorporating the latest developments in their marketing strategies. The MIS has also helped them in forecasting a change to enable them in taking future marketing decisions accordingly. To be more specific, the promotional strategies are now found more innovative and creative. We find a major impact of technological sophistication on the printing media. The credibility for these positive changes goes to the well developed marketing research system (MIS).

Another point of focus is to bridge the widening communication gap with the information technology coming of age globally. The gap between the providers and users of services has been a major constraint in making the effective marketing decisions. This necessitates quick movement of information from one channel to another. A well developed marketing research system attempts to lessen the gap. This move makes possible the emergence of effective marketing decisions which are mostly based on channel-to-channel feedback. The users avail of the world class services and any complaints, grievances, suggestions are immediately forwarded from the desk of the researchers to the decision-makers.

A correct idea of competitors' strategy, well within the time limit, is found essential to excel competition. It is not sufficient that services being extended by a particular hotel are of superior quality. It is more important that the services bear the efficacy of establishing an edge over its competitors. This is possible when the hotel management is aware of their strategies. The marketing research system helps hotel companies in this very context.

So, marketing research is an integral part of the marketing decision-making. The development of a research system in a sophisticated fashion, would make efforts on the part of the hotel industry proactive. Of course, the system is found expensive, but in view of the positive effects, we can call it a productive investment. The main thing is to prepare a research plan which makes possible the transmission of realistic information. This is possible when the information are related to the marketing-mix and the users of services. Thus, the users' centered research is the crying need of the hour, specially to make the future marketing decisions more effective. This is shown in Figure 4.3.

Figure 4.3 also makes it clear that the sub-mixes of the market-mix should essentially be centered to the users. The product decisions need information related to available accommodations in hotels, restaurant and bar services and function room services. In addition, the feedback regarding the transportation and communication services also become significant in the very context. The services to be made available at all points should be in tune with the changing lifestyles. The research activities should also be related to the pricing decisions which are useful in making appropriate decisions. The hotel tariff should have a close relation or link with the emerging trends in the discretionary income. The research activities simplify the identification process. While making the distribution decisions, it is pertinent that the front-line personnel in general and the housekeepers and waiters in particular are given due weightage. These personnel need to change their behaviour in the face of changing behavioural profile of the potential guests. The most sensitive aspect with the viewpoint of marketing research is promotion. The advertisement decisions, the public relations activities, the decisions regarding the tool and duration of sales promotion should also be centered towards the hotel guests.

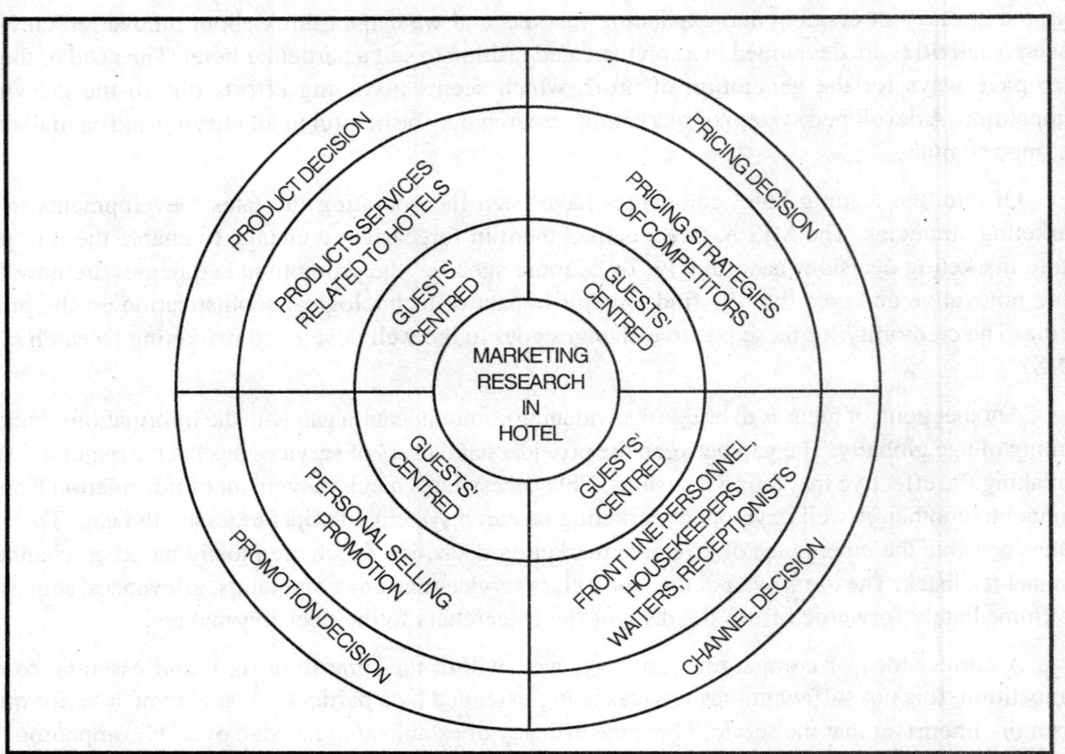

FIG. 4.3: GUESTS' CENTERED MARKETING RESEARCH

Ultimately, the co-ordination between the researchers and the decision-makers is found essential to get the positive results. The information should be centered more to the guests. It is natural that here we make a categorical analysis of domestic and foreign tourists as the preference and the spending power of both the potential customers are not similar.

To manage a business is to manage information in a cost effective manner. The present as well as the future marketing decisions rest on the management of information. This makes it essential that the marketing assign due weightage to the information based decisions. At the outset, the data should be collected from different sources. While managing information, the following questions are required to be suitably answered:

- What is total market potential?
- What would be the market potential in future?
- What is the exact position of competitive hotels?
- What changes in the potential guests are likely to create new opportunities?
- What changes in the government regulations are to motivate the potential guests?
- Who are the experimental guests and who are the heavy guests?
- What are the emerging changes in the lifestyle of properties?

- How and in what way promotional decisions are found influencing the guests?
- What is the role of word-of-mouth communication?

The aforesaid questions are required to be suitably answered and the information system simplifies the task of decision-makers. To strengthen the information system, it is pertinent that the marketing research activities are promoted. Research is found to be an important consideration for raising the sensitivity of the marketing decisions. The decision-making, specially regarding setting of objectives, policies, strategies and programmes is done in a right way provided the researcher has a sound base.

The sub-systems as detailed above are found significant to make the marketing decisions. The internal and external sources are to be used for collecting the data and the MIS bears the responsibility of turning the data into potential information. The sub-systems like internal reporting and analytical marketing are found useful for managing the internal data. The day-to-day activities are managed with the help of intelligence systems and the systematic design, collection, analysis and reporting of data and findings relevant to a specific market situation. Advertisement research, economic research, product research and sales research are done through marketing research.

In the context of marketing information system, it is important to talk about the instrumentality of communicative technologies in turning the data into information. With the introduction of computers, the MIS has now become more effective. All leading hotel companies are found managing information with the help of computers. Not only for future marketing but even for day-to-day marketing, the computers have been providing valuable information. The bulk purchasers like tour operators and transport operators and even the small purchasers like travel agents have been found managing information with the help of computers. The front-line staff also benefits by using computers for providing required information to the system analysts, Thus, at all stages of transmitting information, computers are used in a major way. The different sub-systems contribute a lot to the process of decision-making and the credibility for the same goes to the sophisticated communicative technologies. Not only big hotel companies but even the small hotels are now found using computers for managing the information. This clarifies the growing significance of computerised information in the MIS.

MANAGING INFORMATION FOR QUALITY DECISIONS IN THE HOTEL INDUSTRY

Yesterday your decisions were of world class. Make it sure that your decisions even today are of word class and make it doubly sure that you keep on moving the process tomorrow or a day after tomorrow. The moment we find hotel professionals reaching to the point of satisfaction, the doors for qualitative transformation are closed. We find human minds never inactivate and the moment we find them becoming inactive, the avenues for improvements are contracted. Inventions and innovations keep on moving and the professionals found sensitive in receiving and practicing the new things in their business establish an edge over the rivals. They prove to be a market leader and succeed in developing brand loyalty.

During the yesteryears, we have witnessed much more frequency in the innovation processes and therefore the hotel companies incorporating these new developments in their strategic decisions may prove to be a leader. We cannot negate the outstanding contributions of new generation of ICT in the qualitative improvements of hotel services. Virtually, they have been redefining the service quality.

Mounting frequency in the transformation process makes it essential that hotel professionals update their knowledge bank. This in a natural way draws our attention on managing the marketing information with the help of a techno-driven MIS. It is not only significant that you are aware of your strength and weaknesses. It is equally important that you are well aware of your rivals or competitors. It is not only significant that you are number one in innovating the services. It is much more impact-generating that you keep your customers and potential customers up to date of your distinct services. It is not only significant that you promote your service quality. It is also pertinent that you are very much sincere to the weaknesses or complaints of your customers. The quality information system is to help a hotel professional in all the positive or negative conditions.

The Indian hotel industry has, of course, been sincere to the innovation process but has been found insensitive to the sensitisation process which no doubt increases the cost of using technology but the hotel companies fail in getting the technological advantage. Not only this, we also find an invasion on the value addition process. In managing information, the Marketing Information System plays a decisive role. The quality of computer and the computer professionals and system analysts are the important considerations requiring due attention of hotel professionals. Besides, it is also pertinent that they are sincere to the management of inputs and engage sincere and honest research staff or research scientists who conduct surveys and make available to the system the facts and figures or the inputs for transforming the same into output. We cannot negate that research and development activities act as a lever spring of the information management.

The impact of globalisation on the hotel industry has been found positive. The increasing economic activities around the globe has made possible a significant change in the lifestyles of people. The hotel professionals bear the responsibility of updating their knowledge bank.

The emerging trends in income, the increasing influence of corporatisation, the imprint of western culture, the family background, types of education and profession are some of the important considerations helping a hotel professional in identifying the behavioural profile and taste preferences of domestic and overseas customers. It is quite natural that both at micro and macro levels, all the tourists cannot be identical in nature and behaviour. The food habits, drink habits, fascination to a particular type of tourism, the age group and gender are influenced by our behavioural profile. The prime thing in this process is to know the guests and to observe their taste and temperament. The information management sizeably simplifies our task. The guests and potential guests find themselves in a position to know about the destination with the help of internet. We find tourist generating countries making use of websites for this purpose. The booking of tickets and their cancellation, availability of accommodation services, the details regarding the service quality, food and drink are found available online They find it convenient to design a travelling plan and the required services are found available, online. The climatic condition, seasonal fluctuation, hotel tariffs, provision for shopping everything are found in knowledge of tourists and potential tourists and they are found in a position to make decisions.

The hotel professionals need to make use of call centers where telemarketers may play a significant role. The main task before the hoteliers is to transform the enquiry into booking. The hotel professionals and telemarketers both of them have to play an important role in the transformation process. With the help of new generation of information and communication technology, the professionals may provide all the required information to tourists. If you know about their taste preferences and lifestyles, it is not difficult for you to lure them.

The different sub-systems of Marketing Information System need to play a catalytic role in the identification process. The hotel professionals may use s for developing their awareness of the happening data or day-to-day developments taking place in the industry. The internal reporting helps professionals in the scanning of reports and documents so that they find themselves aware of the developments taking place in the hotel industry. The analytical marketing simplifies the process of searching and identifying the opportunities. And the last one Marketing Research is helpful with the viewpoint of studying and understanding the emerging trends in the hotel markets. The upward or downward trends in the tourist arrivals, the increasing or falling occupancy ratio, the changing taste preferences of customers, the emerging trends in competition, the strengths and weaknesses of rivals, the changing levels of expectations of tourists and the demand supply position are some the areas where marketing research would be found effective.

Increasing sophistication in the Marketing Information System has made it useful both for providers and users. We cannot negate that even in the Indian context, the penetration of e-commerce[9] has been gaining momentum. This is not to be an important impediment in improving the services of hotels in the changing perspective. A good number of hotels have been offering world class services such as The Oberoi, Taj, ITC, The Park Hotels, Leela and Bharat. So far as the process of technological sophistication is concerned, the hotel companies would be required to resolve the problem to make hotels globally competitive.

It is high time that the hotel professionals make use of internet for advertising for greater and wider impact. The e-commerce portals need due attention to extend effective marketing support to SMEs and also offer competitive packages.[10] It is significant to mention that advertising online gives access to global market and can be more cost effective than the traditional media such as newspapers, radio, yellow pages or the direct mail. The hotel professionals need to make use of eye-catching banner ads of generating business. The fastest, easiest and most cost-effective way of advertising need due attention of marketing professionals for promoting the services. They may think in favour of transaction enabled ads. Increased usage of advertising on newspaper websites would considerably benefit the providers and users.

The promotional measures with the support of internet need to focus on safety and security measures so that the psychophobia found amongst the tourists specially on account of terrorism is removed. The MoT and media need to play an incremental role in the very context because the image problem garboils all our efforts for product innovation and creative promotion. During yesteryears, we have witnessed a number of attacks promoted by international terrorists which would sizeably harm the hotel industry if we find government, media and hotel companies not initiating intensive efforts to remove the image problem. The internet may also be used for this purpose where web pages would focus on the safety and security measures of government and in addition the internal conditions.[11]

In view of the above, it is right to mention that hotel companies need to assign due weightage to the management of information for improving the quality of hotel services. High penetration of e-commerce is need of the hour. We have done something but need more to do. Keeping in view the potentials that we have in the travel and tourism sector or the momentum that we find in the national economic activities; we find demand for the hotel sector to exceed the supply position provided the promotional measures need due attention of government and media. Of course, the hoteliers would need priority attention on world-class services but in addition marketing inputs can not be undermined. What to talk of the big hotels when we find new generation of ICT even useful to the budget hotels.

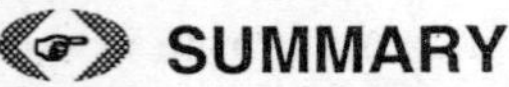

SUMMARY

You have studied in this chapter the Marketing Information System for hotels. A reorientation to important dimensions of the chapter are mentioned below:

- **Marketing information System:** It is the collection, storing, analysis, and dissemination of data and to transform them into information to help the decision-makers in making and innovating their decisions.
- **MIS: the Sub-systems:** There are four sub-systems of the MIS, e.g., Internal Reporting, Marketing Intelligence System, Marketing Research and Analytical Marketing.
- **MIS: The Salient Features:** A scientific technique for the processing of data operated manually or electronically helps an organization in preparing a master plan for maintaining the flow of information. It is a future-oriented system operated by the system analysis.
- **MIS: Functions:** Assembling of data, processing of data, analysis of data, storage of data, evaluation of data, dissemination of data are the functions of the marketing information system.
- **Information for Hotel:** There are three sources for collecting internal data in a hotel. 1. Bedrooms, 2. Restaurant, 3. Function room.
- **Significance of MIS to the Hotel Industry:** MIS is found to be significant to the proper functioning and development of hotel industry. Easy access to information, sensitive future marketing, co-ordinated, systematic and continuous information, performance evaluation, functional co-ordination, future orientation and image projection are the important contributions of MIS to the hotel industry.
- **Marketing Research: The Concept:** It is the systematic problem analysis, model building and fact finding for the purpose of improved decision-making and control in the marketing of goods and services.
- **Methods of Research:** There are two methods of collecting information, e.g., primary and secondary. Desk research is related to the secondary source and sample survey and motivational research are the components of primary source.
- **Marketing Research in the Hotel Industry:** In view of emerging changes in the lifestyles of potential guests, we find development of new segments and new markets. To identify the potential guests and their behavioral profile, it is essential to promote the research activities. The mounting intensity of competition makes it essential that we identify the competitors' strategies and declare our services obsolete much earlier than our competitors. This is possible when the research activities are scientific and well planned.
- **Managing Information for Quality Decisions in the Hotel Industry:** The Hotel industry needs to promote the new generation of ICT for improving the quality managerial decisions so that the providers and users both of them are benefited. The high penetration of e-commerce and use of internet for promoting the services need due attention of hoteliers. New generation of ICT may help Indian hotels in competing global biggies.

KEY TERMS

Intuition
Marketing Information System
Internal Reporting
Analytical Marketing
Marketing Research
e-commerce
Marketing Intelligence System
System Analyst
Dissemination
Occupancy Ratio
Spin off
Communication Superhighway
Motivational Research
Sample Survey
Field Research
Questionnaire
Housekeepers
Waiters
Website
Transaction-enabled ads.
Yellow Pages
Banner Ads.
Informal Search
Formal Search
Physical Distribution
Decision Support System

REVIEW QUESTIONS

1. What do you mean by Marketing Information System? Discuss its salient features.
2. Explain the different features of Marketing Information System.
3. Focus on the different components of Marketing Information System.
4. Explain the different stages for turning the data into information.
5. Hotel companies can successfully capitalise opportunities, if MIS works in a right fashion. Justify your opinion.
6. Discuss the different objectives of Marketing Information System with a special reference to the hotel industry.
7. There are manifold purposes of MIS, the important are making possible scientific and intelligent planning. In line with this statement, focus on the objectives of MIS.
8. Explain the information received from the bedrooms, restaurants and function rooms to make the marketing decisions for your hotel.
9. Describe the key sources of information for managing the marketing decisions in the hotel industry.
10. The hotels and hotel companies are required to manage their information scientifically as the mounting intensity of competition has made the marketing environment more volatile. In the face of this statement, discuss the significance of MIS.
11. Explain the instrumentality of marketing Research as a tool of MIS.
12. Write a descriptive note on the management of information for making the marketing decisions in Indian perspective.

APPLICATION EXERCISES

1. In the capacity of a marketing professional focus on the Marketing Information System helping you in quality of your decisions.
2. You are required to conduct a survey to know behavioural profile of hotel prospects. Focus on the sub-systems to help you in the process
3. As a marketing professional, you are supposed to know the day-to-day developments in the hotel where you are working. Throw light on the sub-system to be effective in the process.
4. As a hotel professional focus on the information that you will like to collect from the restaurant.
5. You are working as a hotel manager. Focus on the information that you find essential for rooms.
6. You as a marketer bear the responsibility of managing the Function Room. Throw light on the information that you need for Function Rooms.
7. You need to identity the emerging trends in hotel markets. As a hotel manager how would you conduct market research to identify the trends ?
8. In the world wide economic recession what measure would help you in increasing the occupancy ratio.
9. As a professional focus on the emerging new segments for hotel industry in the Indian perspective.

End Notes:

1. Kotler, Philip: *Marketing Management;* Prentice Hall of India, New Delhi,1990, p. 102.
2. Cundiff, Still and Govoni: *Fundamentals of Modern Marketing;* Prentice Hall of India, New Delhi, 1982, p. 65.
3. Smith Samuel V., Brien Richard H. and Stafford James E., (Ed.)*: An Introductory Overview in Readings in Marketing Information System,* Boston, 1968, p. 7.
4. Bellur, V.V. and Harold W. Berkman: *Readings in Marketing Management;* Himalaya Publishing House, Bombay, 1987, p. 1.
5. Greene, Melvyn: *Marketing Hotels and Restaurants into the 90s;* Heinemann Professional Publishing, Oxford, 1989, p. 193.
6. Kotler, Philip: *Op. cit.,* p. 107.
7. Cundiff, Still and Govoni: *Op. cit.,* p. 188.
8. Birn, Robin: *The Effective Use of Marketing Research;* Kogan Page, London, 1992, p. 25.
9. Interview with Priya Chairman, Park Hotels, The Analyst, November, 2006. p. 21.
10. Eleventh Five Year Plan; Panning Commission; Government of India, New Delhi, Vol. III, pp. 245-50.
11. Jha, S.M.: Tourism Marketing; Himalaya Publishing House, Mumbai, 2009.

....ꕥꕥꕥ....

CHAPTER - 5

SERVICE QUALITY IN HOTEL

An organisation defining and redefining quality proves to be a service leader whereas others who make a compromise with the quality, perish and ultimately bid a final good-bye to the corporate world.

CHAPTER OBJECTIVES

Introduction – Service Quality: The Concept – Importance of Service Quality – Service Quality Management – Service Quality Factors in Hotels – SERVQUAL in Hotel – SERVPERF in Hotel – Service Environment for Hotel Industry – Service Quality Gap – Service Leadership – Quality in Totality in Hotel Industry – Summary – Key Terms – Review Questions – Application Exercises – End Notes.

LEARNING OBJECTIVES

This chapter aims at studying the different dimensions of service quality in the context of hotel industry. The motive is to sensitise the readers to the factors instrumental in improving the quality of services in the hospitality industry. The readers will also develop their awareness of service quality gap and the concept of quality in totality in the hotel industry. The hospitality industry nas a bright future provided the Indian hotels redefine quality in the global perspective and make their services much more globally competitive.

INTRODUCTION

Sooner or later; today or tomorrow, we are suitably rewarded for defining and redefining quality. Our dedication, commitment, optimism play an incremental role in generating excellence which is the result of our perfection. An individual or an institution succeeds in thriving and excelling competition, if there is no boundary for quality. Innovations make the ways for perfection. If we are innovative, the processes adopted for redefining quality are found proactive. We get an opportunity to develop brand loyalty and become a brand leader. It is in this context that we find almost all the organisations either producing goods or generating services assigning due weightage to quality.

Increasing volatility in the business environment makes it essential that we continue to be innovative. This focuses on continuous research and development activities to enrich our knowledge bank. We live in an age where we have either to compete or to perish. And we cannot excel competition unless we are potentially and strategically number one. Quality in totality, if practised in a right fashion, makes an organisation globally sound. Boom or recession or depression are the words to sensitise our strategists. Actually, we need to keep our feet strongly on the ground particularly to understand the changing market scenario.

Service quality is more a function of attitude than of technology, a majority of us believe but now it appears just a myth. We live in an age of technology and are considerably influenced by techniculture. During the yesteryears, the process of technological sophistication has gained a rapid momentum. The new generation of information and communication technology (ICT) has virtually revolutionised the way of our life. The service generating organisations in particular have considerably been successful in activating the value addition process. Our lifestyles are now completely changed. Our attitudes are now completely transformed. Spending behaviour has been found establishing an edge over the saving behaviour. We are earning more and explore avenues to spend more. The social system, cultural order, economic scenario are found dominated by corporatisation. In a true sense, we are sizeably influenced by corporate culture.

Of course, a host of factors influence the hotel sector but it is an unvarnished fact that increasing level of discretionary income, flow of information and changing lifestyles have significantly contributed to the robust growth in traffic which has created a gap between demand and supply. We can not negate that sudden burst in tourist traffic has spurred hospitality industry players. The Oberoi, Taj, ITC, The Park Hotels, Leela and Bharat have been found attracting high spending tourists. The huge growth potential in Indian markets been has been found attracting global biggies too.

The international brands like Hyatt, Hilton, Starwood and Marriott have evinced keen interests in the Indian hospitality sector. This makes a strong advocacy in favour of service quality. World class services and amenities need priority attention of hoteliers. Actually, we need to change the perception of global customers because in respect of quality our hotels are independent benchmarks on their own. This is not to be possible unless we remove the impediments. Unless we find supporting infrastructural facilities of world class, our efforts would get only luke warm response. The governmental support is needed in the very context. The PPP mode may be preferred to enrich the infrastructural facilities. Low penetration of e-commerce is also standing as a barrier to the process of qualitative transformation. In addition, the quality of people serving the hotel sector also draws our priority attention. Tourism and hotel sectors have been found witnessing a boom which may bring an exponential demand for the workforce at different echelons. While developing world-class infrastructure, we need professional expertise of architects and landscaping experts. The convention centres, golf courses, tourist trains may be created by private initiative where the government will act as a facilitator and catalyst.

An important bottleneck in the development of hotel infrastructure is non-availability of land and for that we need a master plan of major cities for identifying commercial sites for construction of hotels, convention and exhibition centres. For the development of rural tourism, a panel of professionals may be identified for selecting the rural sites, interacting with the community and preparing projects based on the potential of the site.

There are a number of areas where the hoteliers have to be innovative so that the customers visiting India are found satisfied and make use of word-of-mouth promotion for sensitising and persuading others. The hotel services include a number of core and peripheral services and therefore while activating value addition process, the hotel professionals need to be careful. It is not only significant that you create customers. It is much more impact-generating that you satisfy and retain customers. Satisfaction and retention are the results of world class services. The hoteliers considering sky the only limit for quality would be successful in excelling competition.

In today's context, we find safety and security cropping up as important dimensions of service quality. The increasing cases of world terrorism need due attention of hotel planners and designers. Since this is to make an invasion on national brand, the government requires to be much more sincere while networking safety and security measures. Besides, the hotels also need to be careful because this is to affect their existence. The marketing professionals need to brush up the minds of potential users of hotel services. The service quality thus may be an important area where we need multi-cornered support and multi-dimensional efforts.

SERVICE QUALITY: THE CONCEPT

At the outset, we define service quality. A number of authors have defined service quality in different ways. Crosby (1984) finds it conforming to requirements. This focuses our attention on the fact that the concerned organisation at the first requires to clarify its specifications and then makes it sure that mentioned specifications for the promised quality are strictly complied. The complications increase further when we need to answer whose requirements and whose specifications are to be complied. Another definition about quality clarifies that quality is all about fitness for use (Juran 1982)[2]. This definition is primarily based on satisfying the needs of customers. Based on both the definitions, we can say that quality can only be defined by customers and it occurs where an organisation supplies goods or services to a particular specification that satisfies their needs. While defining quality, we find another expert Swan and Combs (1976)[3] who identified two important dimensions of service quality, viz., instrumental and expressive. The instrumental dimension describes the physical aspect whereas the expressive dimension is found concerned with psychological and intangibility aspects. A reputed work by (Gronroos 1984)[4] identified technical and functional quality as the two principal components of quality. The *technical quality* refers to the relatively quantifiable aspects of service which are made available to the customers in the interaction process. We consider it an important base for measuring service quality because it can easily be measured by both the customers and the suppliers. The functional quality cannot be measured as objectively as the elements of technical quality.

The conceptualisation of service quality begins by addressing the abstract expectations that consumers have perceived in respect of quality. It is quite natural that the consumers judge service quality as the extent to which perceived service quality matches up to their expectations about the quality. The conceptual aspect of service quality thus makes it clear that we cannot draw a line between the two as the expectations of users of services and the offerings and delivery by the providers are influenced by a number of developments taking place in the society. It is also to mention that we find service quality influenced by knowledge of users of services, the quality of technology used for offerings and the speed and punctuality followed by the providers in the process of offerings. In addition, attitudes of people, their appearance and atmosphere also influence the quality.

The different authors have opined in different ways. Feizenbaum (1951) finds it as value; Crosby (1979) considers it as conformance to requirements; Jurau (1982) finds it as fitness for use; Parsuraman (1985) has identified it as meeting customers' expectations and the totality of the features and characteristics of product or services that bear on its ability to satisfy stated or implied needs (ANSI/ ASQS 1987). In this context, an instrument was also developed for measuring service quality which is known as SERVQUAL.

IMPORTANCE OF SERVICE QUALITY

Quality assumes a place of outstanding significance in almost all the organisations. It provides to us an opportunity to build and project a positive image. An organisation defining and redefining quality-proves to be a leader whereas others who make a compromise with the quality bid a final goodbye to the business world. The quality concept is significant to both categories of organisations either producing goods or generating services; either working with profit motive or serving with social welfare motive. The following facts testify the importance of service quality to hospitality industry where intensity of competition is found high.

1. Quality for image projection: In the business world of today, we find customers in general and the hotel customers in particular becoming much more quality-sensitive. This makes it significant that they keep themselves engaged in innovating and redefining quality. The Oberoi, Taj, ITC, The Park Hotels, Leela and Bharat are known for quality of world-class and are internationally acclaimed. We are aware of the fact and hotel professionals should not forget that global biggies like Hyatt, Hilton, Starwood and Marriott, Anando, Banyan Tree, Trident Hilton, Golden Tulip Group have been emerging as international brands and the quality factor has been found getting priority attention of policy makers and strategists. If you offer services of world class, you get an opportunity to build and project your image.

2. Service quality makes the ways for service economy: The hotels consistent in their efforts for innovating and redefining quality get an opportunity to make the process cost-effective. Particularly when we find worldwide economic recession, it is significant that hotel professionals promote cost economy. The increasing occupancy ratio makes ways for minimising costs and maximising profits. The hotels in India have been successful in increasing the occupancy ratio and we find its impact on the profits they earn. In a true sense, it moves in a cyclic order and enriches the strengths of a hotel. Quality service makes the ways for high occupancy ratio and this opens doors for promoting service economy and making high profits.

3. Quality makes hotel potentially sound: In an age of corporate culture where we find hotel culture gaining much more popularity, it is pertinent that the hotel chains or hotel groups perceive quality as an essential dimension for their survival. A significant increase in the hotel profits paves avenues for the development of hotel assets, expansion of hotel chains, infusion of new generation of technology, development of a team of quality people and we find hotels potentially sound for excelling competition. Conversely, if hotels start making a compromise with the quality, they have no option but to bid a goodbye.

4. Quality minimises the risk factor: In the marketing of hotel services, we find a number of avenues for the generation of risk. You offer the best and customers visit your hotels for getting the best. This is due to the fact that word-of-mouth communication or promotion brings an attitudinal change in the minds of potential customers. The hotel professionals need to remember that if they keep on moving the process of redefining quality, the word-of-mouth communicators act as a hidden salesforce and their task of promotion is considerably simplified. If you are sure to get the customers, the risk factor is minimised. Actually once you succeed in strengthening the perception of customers regarding the service quality, the satisfied group of customers work for your hotels. Contrary to it, when you invite even a minor case of menu fatigue or delay the service recovery, this is to tarnish your image and the multiplication of negative word-of-mouth promotion is three times more than the positive.

5. Quality helps creation of value system: If we find hotels sincere and honest to the quality, the customers perceive that they would get right or real value for their tariffs. In a true sense, the consistent efforts of hotels for maintaining and improving quality strengthen the realisation of customers about the product of that organisation. Almost all the internationally acclaimed groups or chains of hotels have assigned due weightage to value system while pricing or while delivering the promised quality of services to the customers. It is against this background that they have been successful in establishing an international brand.

The above mentioned facts make it clear that the service quality assumes a place of outstanding significance in the hotel industry and either big players or small players have to make it sure that the promised quality of services reach to the ultimate customers without any delay and distortion. If hoteliers keep on moving the process of maintaining and defining quality and intensify research and development activities for redefining quality, the paths for their success and prosperity are found obstacle free. Conversely, if they fail in delivering the promised quality of services, this is ultimately to tarnish their image. Once your image is tarnished, you find it much more difficult to make it positive. The hoteliers need to make their hotels competitive and attractive. The international players like Amanda, Satinwoods, Banana Tree, Hampton Inns, Hilton and Mandarian Oriental have been throwing multi-dimensional challenges before the Indian hotel industry. The only thing which can protect them is service quality of world class.

In the coming years, the hotel markets in India are expected to be much more competitive. The country is going to witness a surge in demand because of increased business activities, burgeoning middle class, and increasing number of foreign tourists. More than 142 luxury hotel projects are coming India's way with gross investment of around ₹ 8,000/- crore. The hotel chains in the US and Europe have been found showing keen interests in the Indian hotel sector. Key Indian Players like the Oberoi, Taj, ITC, The Park Hotels, EIH, Bharat Hotels, Viceroy, DLF, Unitech, and Royal Palms have to redefine quality so that they succeed in excelling competition. High penetration of e-commerce and development of world-class infrastructural facilities need priority attention for making Indian hotel industry internationally competitive.

SERVICE QUALITY MANAGEMENT

The hotel professionals bear the responsibility of managing service quality which requires managerial excellence while practising the same. They need to concentrate their attention on three important aspects, *viz.*, setting the right standard, implementing the quality service and monitoring service quality.

I. Setting the Right Standard: In the hotel markets where we find intensity of competition very high, it is significant that hoteliers set the standard in the face of benchmarking. We also find some of the organisations forming an association and developing a code of conduct for maintaining service standards. They set the minimum standard to be delivered to the customers. We find quality considerably influenced by the situational factors. We set standards for today and it is not essential that we find it useful even for today. This is due to the fact that we find a change between today and tomorrow. An organisation consistently conducting marketing research succeeds in defining and redefining quality and the standards that we set today become insignificant for tomorrow. Innovators keep their minds always active in defining quality. The hotel professionals in the very context adopt feedback systems for innovating quality. Based on interactions with customers, they set standards. In the hotel sector, we find benchmarking preferred by the hoteliers for setting standards. This is establishment of the base line or benchmarking in which the professionals examine the performance of rival hotels both at national and international levels. The motive of benchmarking is introducing something new in the markets. In the Indian perspective, the Taj, Oberoi, ITC, The Park Hotels, Leela and Bharat are independent "benchmarks" on their own in terms of world class services and amenities provided by them. The "Vilas" properties of the Oberoi Chain, the Taj Luxury Hotels, the ITC, the boutique hotels of the Park collection and Leela Hotels have set exceptionally high service standards[5] which have been recognised by the customers.

II. Implementing the Quality Service: Setting the standards is found easier but its implementation is found difficult .The hotel professionals in the very context need to implement these standards in the service delivery process with the motto of exceeding customer expectations. The hoteliers need not to forget that implementing the set standards requires a team effort where involvement of all echelons of hotel staff is found essential. They need to focus on the internal marketing programme which may help them in the implementation process. The formation of team, proper education and training of the concerned staff, developing communication excellence are found significant in the very context. Quality in totality requires due attention of hotel professionals and it is to made sure that the services are customized in the face of changing taste preferences of customers both at national and international levels. The team spirit, team culture need priority attention. The hotel professionals need to adopt performance-linked compensation and other motivational schemes to make use of the potentials of team. It is in this context that we make a strong advocacy in favour of Total Quality Management (TQM). Our efforts must be customer focussed.

III. Monitoring Service Quality: It is not only significant that we implement the service quality programme. It is much more impact-generating that we monitor the service quality. The professionals may adopt different tools for this purpose. The monitoring helps professionals while incorporating changes based on an interaction with customers. The different monitoring devices are statistical tools, quality function deployment, internal performance analysis, customer satisfaction analysis and customer complaints analysis.

(a) *Statistical tools:* In this method of monitoring, we find use of checklist method or rating method. The customers are required to tick or cross mark or rating on a scale. The professionals find it difficult to rate some of the intangible aspects like courtesy, credibility, security.

(b) *Quality function development:* We consider it a disciplined approach to transform customer requirements, the voice of the customer into service development requirement. In plain words, it focuses on what customers want and how their requirements can be delivered. It translates the customer requirements into technical language for each stage of marketing.

(c) *Internal performance analysis:* This is considered an important tool for monitoring in which we find sales figures, internal reporting data, customer retention levels as the key indicators to quality performance.,

(d) *Customer satisfaction analysis:* This tool is based on customer satisfaction in which we find follow up survey. The customers are asked to rate specific and overall impressions of the service delivery. A questionnaire may be circulated to the customers to get their comments and remarks.

(e) *Customer complaints analysis:* It is natural that we get complaints. It is very unnatural that we do not get complaints from our customers. The professionals need to make suitable arrangements for the redressal of complaints which make ways for customer retention.

While managing quality thus hotel professionals need to make use of a particular method for monitoring service quality. The motive is to develop a fool proof service quality in which we find much more scope for customer satisfaction and retention. With the increasing heat of competition, the hotel professionals need to assign due weightage to the various dimensions of service quality management. They need to benchmark so that they find themselves in a position to compete with the global biggies.

SERVICE QUALITY FACTORS IN HOTELS

Improving service quality is an important functional responsibility before the hotel professionals. This makes it essential they are well aware of the different variables influencing the quality in hotel and make use of their professional excellence so that the desired results are obtained. The Service delivery, Tangibility, Reliability, Assurance, Responsiveness, Empathy, Service product and Social responsibility are the important variables.

1. Service Delivery: Service delivery is of great importance to the customers' overall perception of service quality. Services requiring customers to come to the point of service delivery by the providers make it essential that customers get an opportunity to gain new experiences regarding service quality. In the hotel services, the customers are required to come to the hotels where they get an opportunity to encounter the service delivery process. It is in this context that service delivery dimension draws priority attention of hotel professionals. The customers staying in rooms, visiting restaurants, bars are found present where the services are delivered to them.

2. Tangibility: In the hotel services, we tend tangibalisation significant for creating positive impression. This focuses our attention on the service ambience or servicescapes where the hoteliers need professionalised efforts. The interiors, exteriors, furnishing, lighting, ventilation, music, scent, parking, signposts etc. are some of the important areas where hotel professionals need to make use of their excellence so that prior to the use of services, the customers form a positive opinion. The world class hotels assign due weightage to service environment and make the ambient conditions efficacious of generating service fragrance. Here the customers form an opinion regarding the quality of services delivered to them. All the items or physical facilities require a minute observation. In the age of ICT, we find instruments, equipment, machines used in the process also becoming important areas for the creation of service ambience. The tangibalisation process also includes the dresses and uniforms used by the working employees in the hotels. The hotel professionals need to manage service ambience and to use the services of experts for this purpose.

3. Reliability: This dimension of service quality focuses our attention on the reliability of customers regarding the services to be delivered. The hotels sincere and honest to service quality generate a sense of confidence amongst the potential customers. The word-of-mouth communications may also influence the customers regarding the quality of services to be delivered to them. If we find customers having a frequent repeat visits they in a very natural way rely on the hotels where they have been delivered quality services. This testifies ability of hotels to perform and deliver the promised quality.

4. Responsiveness: This dimension of service quality draws our attention on willingness of providers to help customers and provide prompt services. The hotel professionals need to make it sure that the back and front line staff have been performing excellently and the benefits of use of technology in the service delivery process are made available to the customers. The working staff are required to be responsive to the interests of customers and to resolve their problems.

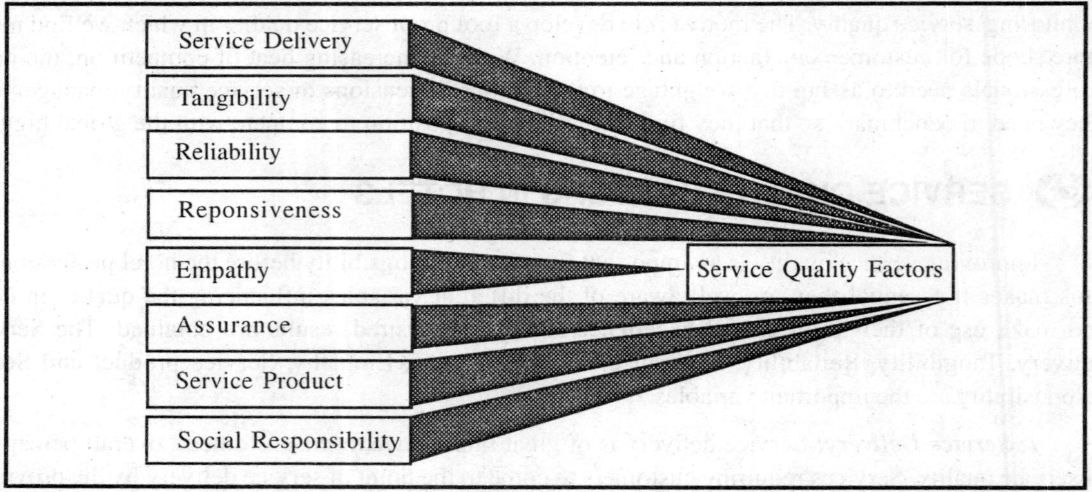

FIG. 5.1: SERVICE QUALITY FACTORS

5. Assurance: This dimension of service quality draws our attention on assurance to be provided to the customers as and when we find dislocation in the service delivery process due to situational barriers. The delay in the process and mistakes committed by people or technology are to be redressed. The customers should not be impatient and hotel professional need to convince them.

6. Empathy: The hotel staff particularly working as receptionists need to show empathy. The contact personnel having face-to-face communication with the customers need to be polite, friendly and helpful. They need to show human touch and personal touch so that diffusion of tension is made possible. They need to watch the facial expression of customers and to show empathy. Flexible communication may diffuse tension.

*7. **Service Product:*** The core as well as the peripheral services need due attention of hotel professionals. The promised services are to be made available to the customers and therefore the marketers are required to be sincere to the service delivery process. It is found to be an essential dimension of service quality and we find different areas for service delivery. The housekeepers, waiters, receptionists need to perform and behave decently. The depth and width need due attention.

*8. **Social Responsibility:*** Like other organisations, the hotels also bear social responsibility. In this context, they are supposed to justify their existence in the society by taking part in the social advertising process. Opening of parks, healthcare centers, child education are the areas where they can participate. The hotels may also think over concessional services to economically backward.

SERVQUAL IN HOTEL

Expectations and satisfaction never remain static. The hotel professionals bear the responsibility of developing their awareness of the changing levels of satisfaction in relation to the different aspects of service quality. Noted marketing experts Parasuraman, Ziethaml and Berry (1988) developed an instrument to measure the level of customer satisfaction and we call this instrument as SERVQUAL. The basic theme that we find in the SERVQUAL model is comparison of perception with expectation. It is found applicable to almost all the service industries. In this model, the dimensions like tangibility, reliability, responsiveness, assurance and empathy need due attention. Strongly agree and strongly disagree are the two sides. We find SERVQUAL a scale involving a survey containing 21 service attributes grouped into five dimensions as mentioned earlier. The data collected from the SERVQUAL scale can be used for a number of purposes as mentioned below:

- For each service attributes determining the average gap between perceptions and expectation of customers.
- Assessing the service quality with the help of five dimensions of SERVQUAL.
- Tracking expectations and perceptions of customers over time.
- Comparing score of SERVQUAL with the score of rivals.
- Identifying and examining the segments of customers found significantly different.
- Assessing internal service quality rendered.

We find application of SERVQUAL for the measurement of quality of service in the multiple contacts, culture and countries. Even in the public sector organisation we find use of this scale which is found applicable all over the world in the services sector. The contexts where we find use of SERVQUAL are real estate brokers, doctors in private practice, the programmes related to public recreation, patient clinic of a dental college, placement centers of a Business School, a tire store, an accounting firm, discount and department stores, gas and electric company, hospitals, banking, dry cleaning, higher education, fast food and even in hotel.

The two different areas where we find SERVQUAL important are consumer service context and Industrial Product Context. The five dimensions of SERVQUAL are the criteria for evaluation. Both the original version of SERVQUAL (Persuraman *et. al.*, 1988) and the revised version (Persuraman *et. al.*, 1991, 1994) focus on five dimensions such as tangibility, reliability, responsiveness, assurance and empathy. Of course, the SERVQUAL has been found one of the leading instruments of measuring service quality, however, it has been subjected with some criticisms where we find focus on SERVPERF which is found to be the measurement of the customers perceptions of the performance of a service provider and adequate assessment for service quality.

SERVPERF IN HOTEL

Though we cannot negate that the model developed by Parsurama *et.al.*, gained popularity as a measure for gauging service quality however it has been subjected with several criticisms. In this context Peter *et. al.,* 1993 Bebko (2000) Andaleep and Basu (1994) focussed on SERVPERF[7] which is the measurement of the customers perceptions of the performance of a service provider and adequate assessment for service quality.

The SERVPERF as a scale represents the performance for measuring the service quality factor which is computed by the mean score of perception service quality variables in each service quality factor (SQF). For exhibiting the perception guests on service quality factors the mean score of SERVPERF scale on each SQF among the guests are computed. In order to analyse the consistency of the perception on SQF, the standard deviation and coefficient of variation of each SQFs are measured separately. The researchers find that the highly perceived SQFs in hotel industry among the guests are service quality delivery and tangibles. The empathy and responsiveness have lesser perceived service quality factors in the hotel industry. In service delivery and tangibles we find higher consistency in the perception. 'The study revealed that the guests' perceptions are moderate in the service delivery and tangibles in the hotel industry whereas it is very poor on empathy and responsiveness factors.

The present study by Peter *et.al.*, has been an attempt to analyse the impact of SERVPERF scale on SQFs on customers satisfaction with the help of multiple regression analysis. The significantly influencing SERVPERF scale on SQFs on customer satisfaction are service delivery, reliability, assurance, responsiveness and empathy.

The above study makes it clear that in the hotel industry the service providers understand the role of service delivery, reliability, assurance and responsiveness in the customers satisfaction. Thus for the successful operation of a hotel, it is significant that hotel managers understand what customers want and how they assess the hotel service quality. The important service quality factors in the hotel industry are service delivery, tangibles, reliability and assurance. It is the responsibility of the hotel managers to assign due weightage to these dimensions. In the context of service delivery, the front line staff play an incremental role. They need to ensure standardised, structured and simplified service delivery process. In respect to tangible dimensions, the hotel authorities need priority attention on the creation of service ambience instrumental in generating service fragrance. This focuses attention on world class physical facilities. In the sphere of reliability dimension, the hotel staff are required to deliver their service right even at the first time itself. For assurance dimensions, the hotel authority need to have quality people to deliver polite, respected, decent and friendly service to the customers.

SERVICE ENVIRONMENT FOR HOTEL INDUSTRY

Merry Jo Bitner in her paper "*Servicescapes*": The Impact of Physical surroundings on customers and Employees", published in journal of Marketing (56/1992) used this terminology for service environment. This focuses our attention on the style and appearance of the physical surroundings and other experimental elements encountered by customers at service delivery sites. We consider service environment an art consuming much more time and excellence. It is designed and built by experts and are not always easy to change. We cannot negate that the studies related to service environment are the areas of environmental psychology. The service marketing academics have conceptualised the theories for developing their understanding and managing customer responses to service environment.

The key dimensions of service environment are ambient conditions which may include music, colours and scents and environmental fragrance throwing a major impact on their behaviour. Besides, the layout, signs, symbols and artifacts also become a part and parcel of service environment. In the lobby of hotels presence or absence of background music, tempo and volume bring an important difference in the perception of satisfaction. Actually, the perception of quality combines or coils in its essence a number of items and the professional need to take care. It is in this context that we find aesthetic management becoming an integral part of corporate culture because we cannot deny its substantial impact on adding additional attractions to environmental fragrance. In almost all the service generating organisations, the service environment has been found throwing a major impact on the feelings and behaviour of customers. Of course, the professionals need to plan everything in the face of nature and types of services and the quality of customers.

The different dimensions of service environment has been displayed in Fig. 5.2. The hotel professionals need to create such a service environment in which we find service fragrance. The ambient conditions (music, scent, colour), spatial layout, signs, symbols and artifacts and particularly public as a part of service environment change our perception of quality. The hotels need to be innovative and creative so that customers visiting hotels gain new experiences and form a positive opinion regarding the quality of services to be delivered to them. The different components of ambience such as the background music, display of colour and environmental fragrance change the perception of quality.

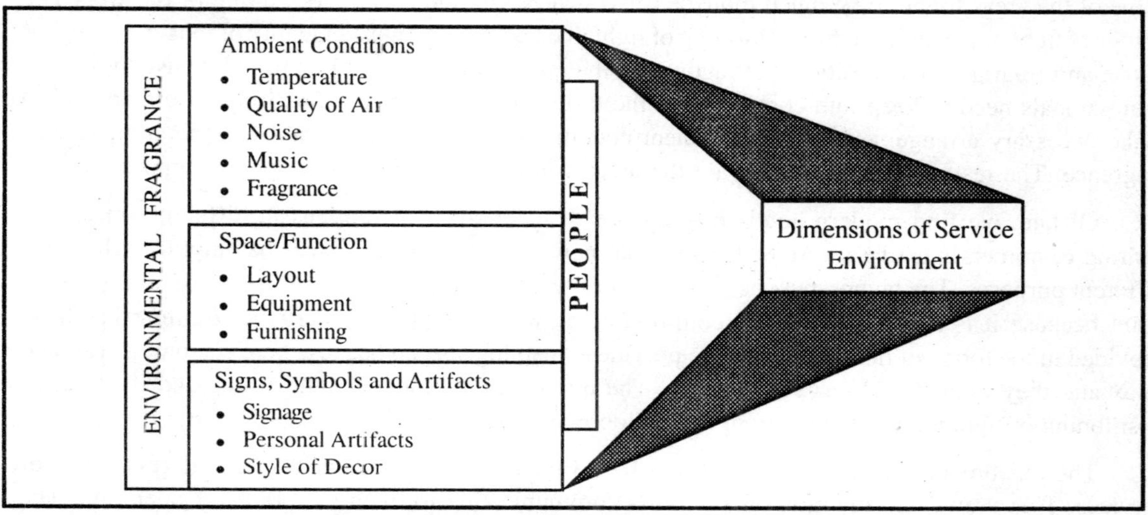

FIG. 5.2: DIMENSION OF SERVICESCAPES OR SERVICE ENVIRONMENT

The hotel professionals need to manage the environmental conditions in such a way that customers coming to the place develop a different perception regarding the quality of services. The quality of air made available to them, the peaceful atmosphere and display of aesthetic management are also considered helpful in changing the perception. The hospitality, banking, insurance, hospital, tourism, food are some of the services in which we find ambience playing an important role.

The availability of space, layout, furniture and equipment are considered important in this context. The counters for office and customers, the designing for convenient offering of services need due attention of professionals. In this context, we make a strong advocacy in favour of spatial layout which refers to the size and shape of furnishing, counters and machines and equipment. Of late, we find almost all the service generating organisations making use of new generation of ICT for improving the quality of their services. The professionals need to make it sure that all the instruments, equipment, machines used in the process are maintained properly.

Explicit or implicit signals are considered most effective ways for communication of organisational image. The queuing system, smoking, no-smoking zones are the rules of behaviour. The signposts, display for different counters or the exist points help customers in forming opinion regarding the services to be offered. The process of delivery would be clear with this display. The star group of hotels, the airports, the big hospitals and educational institutions make the process of delivery much more convenient, if the customers are guided with the help of signposts, symbols and artifacts.

Keeping in view the increasing heat of competition in the hotel industry, it is pertinent that hotel professionals assign due weightage to the development of service ambience so that visiting customers get an opportunity to gain new experiences. It is imperative even with the viewpoint of working people because they get an ambient condition for performing and delivering the quality services to the customers. The servicescapes or development of physical facilities need professional touch. In an age of information and communication technology, the service ambience occupies a place of outstanding significance. In Fig. 5.2, we find focus on three dimensions necessitating priority attention of hotel planners as well as the hotel professionals. The exteriors, interiors, temperature, ventilation, music, fragrance are some of the important areas where the hoteliers need to make use of the services of experts. In hotel, there are some of the areas found to be much more sensitive where we find customers waiting or relaxing. The colour of light, intensity of light, positioning of light, the background music, quality of music, volume of music and fragrance add additional attractions to the quality of services to be used by customers. The professionals need to keep into consideration the taste and temperament of visiting customers and to make necessary arrangements so that ambient conditions become instrumental in generating service fragrance. The restaurants, bars, cafes are the areas where these things carry special importance.

Of late, we find modern hotels making use of techno-driven services in different areas. The visiting customers must be aware of the fact that new generation of ICT will be helpful to them for different purposes. The layout must be convenient as well as attractive. The furnishing becomes a focal point because it is to be ensured that comfortable as well as stylish and artistic furniture has been provided in the lobby of hotels. We need to provide something special because here customers wait and relax and they minutely observe everything. The quality and colour of light, music and its volume, positioning of light are found important for the lobby of hotels.

The customers visiting hotels may not be aware of the different areas for different types of services. This draws our attention on signposts communicating to them the points of operation. The positioning of signposts and positioning of light so that visiting customers are found attracted need due attention of hotel managers. The artistic effects or artifacts are considered to be important for hotels. Since you expect high profile customers visiting your hotels, it is significant that hotel managers make possible artistic touch as and where they find it essential. The Decor must be stylish.

In view of the above, it is right to say that service environment bears the efficacy of adding additional attractions to your hotels. You need to be innovative, creative and imaginative. By giving special and personal touch, you keep your hotels distinct to your rivals.

SERVICES QUALITY GAP

Quality promised makes the ways for shaping of the levels of expectations which if not fulfilled paves avenues for gap. With the mounting competition and increasing domination of new generation of information and communication technology, we find a significant increase in the levels of expectations of hotel customers. The big players as well as the small players have been making professionalised efforts to enrich their strengths and capitalise on the opportunities in the hotel markets. Service quality gap draws our attention on identifying the gap between the service quality promised and service-quality delivered.

Zeithaml, Berry and Parasuraman (1998) identified four potential gaps which may lead to the serious gap between the expectations of customers and offerings of providers. It is also significant to mention that Lovelock (1994) enlarged the gap to seven. All the seven gaps can be grouped into two major parts such as internal and external. The standard gap, delivery gap and internal communication gap are known as internal gap whereas the knowledge gap, perception gap, interpretation gap and service gap are of external nature. The internal gap occurs between different functions and departments within the organisation and therefore we call them internal gap. Contrary to it, the external gap is influenced by the external conditions and therefore we call them external gap.

EXHIBIT 5.1: SERVICE QUALITY GAP

Internal Gap	*Quality Gap*	*External Gap*
Standard Gap Delivery Gap Internal Communication Gap Influenced by Internal Factors		Knowledge Gap Perception Gap Interpretation Gap Service Gap Influenced by External Factors

1. Knowledge Gap: This gap focuses our attention on the difference between the hoteliers believe and the expectations of hotel customers. We may call it a gap between perception and expectation. The hoteliers may fail in identifying the fact that what a particular service has been regarded as number one by the customers and what attributes the services need to meet the expectations of customers. Such a gap is found due to inadequate market research and lack of upward communication from the back and front-line staff to the top management. Inadequate interaction between professionals and customers and lack of market segmentation may also be responsible for knowledge gap. The knowledge gap can be bridged by conducting adequate research programmes for studying and understanding the changing taste preferences and levels of expectations of customers. In addition, enriching the communication system may also help professionals in knowing the customers in a right fashion. Gauging of gap is essential for the professionals and for that purpose, they may use SERVQUAL.

2. The Standard Gap: In this gap, we find focus on difference between management perception of customers and expectations of customers and the quality standards for delivery, We also find cases where customers develop high level of expectations but they do not find the services offered to them to their desired level and this creates a gap. The hotel professionals committing mistakes in transmitting real facts to the customers or other marketing professionals creating a conditions for the formation of standard gap may invite dissatisfied group of customers. Lack of goal setting, right leadership and undefined service design may also be responsible for the standard gap. Communication gap between the providers and customers may also be responsible for the standard gap. In addition, managerial deficiency may also be instrumental in the creation of the standard gap. We cannot negate that the shaping of the levels of expectations regarding the standard and quality is influenced by a number of factors. It is also found that some of the hotels are in a position to deliver quality services but the professionals fail in making available to the customers the services of same standard and we find a gap.

This gap can be bridged by professionals by standardising the service delivery process and by setting proper organisational goals. For this, the hotel professionals may also strengthen their realisation that customer service is of prime importance.

The gauging and assessment of this gap may be by circulating questionnaire for setting the standard.

3. The Delivery Gap: This gap draws our attention on the difference between the specified delivery standards and the actual performance of the service providers related to those standards. We also call it Service Performance gap which is found due to managerial deficiency. The back and frontline staff are supposed to perform in the way directed and advised by their leaders. This gap may be due to poor quality of staff or inadequate training to perform and deliver or due to managerial deficiency. It is also found that in some of the cases, this gap is found due to inadequate motivation to the working staff.

This gap can be bridged by improving the quality of leadership, training and lucrative motivational schemes to the staff responsible for performing and delivering. For gauging of this gap, the professionals may circulate questionnaire to know the potentials and to identify the reason for poor service performance.

4. The Communication Gap: This gap is found as the difference between what an organisation thinks about advertising and sales people such as level of service quality, features of product and performance. Of late, we find the communication processes much more effective as the technology governs the operation. The gap is created due to faulty operation and ineffective communication. The promotional measures particularly advertisements and face-to-face communication by the sales people instrumental in shaping the level of expectations of customers create a gap, because in a majority of the cases we find discrepancies due to exaggerated promises or ineffective communication.

This gap can be bridged with the help of effective communication system in which exaggerations are required to be minimised so that the customers do not form high level of expectations.

The feedback received from the employees that what they delivered against the promise help in gauging the gap.

5. The Perception Gap: We find this gap as difference between the service providers' delivery and the customers or users perception of the services delivered. Since we find new generation of information and communication technology instrumental in shaping the high levels of expectations and customers are not getting the services to the desired level, there is a gap. Thus this happens to be a gap between expected quality and perceived quality. This makes it essential that the service providers or marketing professionals make use of marketing research as a tool to identify, quantify and monitor the perception of customers so that the process to bridge the gap is found effective.

6. The Interpretation Gap: This gap is found as the difference between the service providers and service users specially while interpreting. We find this gap in advance of offerings of services. The providers may interpreted in a different way and the customers may not receive in the same way. Or just reverse, the customers interpreted in a different way and the providers do not receive in the same way.

7. The Service Gap: This gap is found between what the customers expect to receive and their perception of the services actually offered to them. The customers expect high level of services but they do not get the services to the desired level and we find a gap.

Sophistication makes the ways for complications. Of course, the new generation of information and communication technology has been successful in redefining the concept of quality but at the same time it is also right to say that the possibilities for a gap are now found increased. The customers have high level of expectations from hotels and if they do not find the services to their desired level, we find a gap. This makes it essential that hotel professionals are careful while promising and much more careful while delivering and recovering. However, if we find a gap, the professionals need to bridge the same without making any delay.

SERVICE LEADERSHIP

Articulating a vision and performing to bring it about is considered to be the most important dimension helping an individual or an organisation in surviving, thriving and establishing a leadership. This task remains unfulfilled if we find an organisation lacking human leaders bearing the efficacy of setting the standards for service quality, initiating important innovations, promoting new generation of technology for getting the competitive advantage, defining and redefining quality which may help excelling competition and establishing leadership. Getting a success when others are crashing testifies your leadership quality. This makes it clear that the most important dimension in attaining and retaining leadership is the quality of people in an organisation. A team of potentially sound leaders bear the potentials of taking the organisation ahead in the right direction, setting the right strategic priorities and ensuring that the strategies formulated will be implemented throughout the organisation..

We consider John Kotter, the best known authority on leadership. He opines that in most successful change-management processes, people need to move through eight complicated, time-consuming stages.

1. Creating a sense of urgency to develop the impetus for change.
2. Putting together a strong enough team to direct the organisation.
3. Creating an appropriate vision of where the organisation needs to go.

4. Communicating the new vision broadly.
5. Empowering employees to act on that vision.
6. Producing sufficient short-term results to create credibility and counter cynicism.
7. Building momentum and using that to tackle the tougher change problems.
8. Anchoring the new behaviours in the organisational culture.

Kotter says, "Leadership works through people and culture. It is soft and hot. Management works through hierarchy and systems. It's harder and cooler.... The fundamental purpose of management is to keep the current system functioning. The fundamental purpose of leadership is to produce useful change, especially non-incremental change. It's possible to have too much or too little of either. Strong leadership with no management risks chaos; the organisation might walk right off a cliff. Strong management with no leadership tends to entrench an organisation in deadly bureaucracy."

Attaining leadership in hotels is becoming much more complicated in the Indian perspective where we find a majority of the hotels facing numerous challenges and threats. The supporting infrastructural facilities are not found of world class and the penetration of e-commerce is yet to gain a rapid momentum. We expect entry of giant brands which may lead to mergers, acquisitions and consolidation of the lesser competitors or simply leave them overshadowed. The global biggies like Amanda, Satinwoods, Banana tree, Hampton Inns, Hilton and Mandarin Oriental would make it difficult for the Indian hotels to think about attaining leadership unless they are innovative, creative and imaginative while offering world class services to the customers.

QUALITY IN TOTALITY FOR HOTEL INDUSTRY

Quality in Totality remains the only prescription to make a successful invasion on the mounting heat of competition in an age where we have either to compete or to make a final goodbye. Sky is the limit for perfection. An individual or an institution perceiving this philosophy of development gets an easy walk over. Innovations make the ways for achieving perfection. Optimism plays an incremental role in generating excellence which is the result of perfection. Sooner or later; today or tomorrow, we are suitably rewarded for our excellence. Quality in totality is not to be possible unless we keep on moving the process of defining and redefining quality which requires to be innovative, creative and imaginative. We find customers and potential customers our prime source and a strong force for getting an easy victory in the business world of today where volatility makes a strong advocacy in favour of Total Quality Management.

The TQM concept draws our attention on people, technology, quality control, research and development activities and world class supporting infrastructural facilities. An optimal aggregation of all of these components in the face of evolving development opens new vistas for defining and redefining quality. Quality can be split into "technical quality" and "functional quality" and for TQM we need focus on both. The technical quality draws our attention on promoting research and development activities so that we are successful in devising innovative technology for offering the best to our customers whereas the functional quality focuses our attention on practising and promoting the devices for redefining the services which keep on moving the process of offering something distinct to our rivals or competitors. Thus TQM is an innovative effort helping an organisation in becoming a leader.

The Indian hotel industry has been found moving in the right direction. It has kept up the growth momentum that started in the second half of 2004 and are coming up with a robust performance albeit during the period of market slump. Increasing GDP, strong ties with the developed world, globalisation and liberalisation, increasing domination of corporatisation and emergence of corporate culture, increasing FDI, BPO hub, continuing price war in airways, increasing world class supporting infrastructural facilities etc. make it clear that the future of Indian hospitality industry is bright. As per the estimate of World Travel and Tourism Council (WTTC), in 2005, Indian tourism demand is expected to grow at a sustained 8.5 per cent over the next ten years. This makes a strong advocacy in favour of redefining quality in the hospitality sector so that we find ourselves successful in capitalising on the opportunities. It is against this backdrop that we need priority attention on practising TQM in the hotel industry so that the quality of services are found globally competitive. The hotel professionals need multi-faceted efforts in the very context.

The first thing that we find essential for quality in totality is availability of word class infrastructural facilities. Of course, the government bears the responsibility of creating world class infrastructural facilities and this focuses our attention on taking support of PPP mode. The hoteliers have also to promote large revenue projects such as setting up of hotels, convention centres, tourist trains, golf courses etc. with substantial gestation period. One of the major impediments in the creation of hotel infrastructure is the non-availability of land for this purpose. The identification of commercial sites for construction of hotels would have a positive impact. The land should also be allotted for building of guest houses in all major cities and tourist destinations. The possibility of constructing hotel on surplus land with Airport Authority of India near international airports needs to be considered. The surplus railway land at specific railway stations may also be utilised for the construction of budget hotels. Effective step for easier and faster connectivity need due attention. The infrastructural facilities at the airports need to be provided at airports for meeting the rising air traffic requirements. Quality of rail services is required to be improved to encourage tourists to travel by train. Identification of 100 sites by Indian Railways for Budget Hotels and 35 sites by the Airport Authority of India may be considered a welcome step.[11] The most important thing that we find in the context of creating infrastructural facilities is the quality which should maintain global standards.

The infusion of new generation of information and communication technology, equipment, instruments, machines for multi-faceted hotel services need priority attention of hotel professionals. The Indian hotels need to promote techno-driven services at par with the global standards. It is also to be made sure that technology used by hotel is instrumental in the value addition process. The low penetration of e-commerce is found to be an important area where the Indian hotel industry needs due attention. The internet has become the largest distribution channel in the hotel industry. For a majority of the hotel customers the hotel website is the first point of contact and therefore the hoteliers should assign due weightage to the development of web pages and specially while promoting the services, they need to prefer hyper banner. The operation and maintenance of technology need due care. The hoteliers may be successful in building relationships with their customers which may help them in increasing the rate of transformation of interaction booking. The creation and retention both the processes would be found productive with the E-CRM strategy. Building online relationships thus needs to be promoted in the Indian hotel industry.

The hotel professional need to assign top priority to the service delivery processes. They need to be innovative while offering world class services. There are a number of areas where they need to concentrate their attention such as quality of rooms and infrastructural facilities inside the rooms, quality of food and drinks served in restaurants and bars. The entertainment services inside the room and in the lobby of hotels. The availability of peripheral services by the hotel such as the world class swimming pools, playground, parking facilities, shopping facilities, personal care services etc. carry significant meaning while developing peripheral services. Actually, they need to establish an edge over their competitors and for that they need to offer something special which are not offered by others.

The quality of people assumes a place of outstanding significance and therefore the hoteliers need to make it sure that different echelons of people serving hotel have a number of properties and traits. The hospitality industry needs quality people having thematical competence, personal-touch, human-touch, commitment to value system, empathy, high communication excellence, attractive personality, sound behavioural profile, aesthetic sense, etiquette, management and professional excellence, The Food Craft Institutes (FCIs) are required to be strengthened and more to be opened. IHMs processing the bulk of manpower at managerial and skill levels need to be strengthened and capacities augmented with international linkages for quality and quantity output of human resources. Capacity building of the service providers through shorter training courses should be taken up as an integral effort to strengthen and enlarge the manpower required by the hospitality industry.

We consider change a natural phenomenon and this makes it essential that hotel companies develop their awareness of the multi-faceted changes in the globe. They need to know about their competitors and the customers and their taste preferences. They need to develop their awareness of the emerging trends in the global and national economies *vis-a-vis* the changing levels of discretionary income. They need to update themselves of the business regulations and their implications. They need to know about their strengths and weaknesses. This makes it essential that hotel professionals assign due weightage to the development of research activities. Forecasting is considered essential and this makes a strong advocacy in favour of developing a techno-driven Marketing Information System.

The Indian hospitality industry requires qualitative as well as quantitative transformation. On the one hand, we need world class hotels while on the other hand, we also realise the importance of budget hotels. The most important thing is customisation of services and therefore the hotel professionals need to know about the changing taste preferences of customers. New generation of ICT, world class hotel professionals and innovative marketing for delivery of quality hospitality services are the key issues before the hospitality sector in the Indian perspective. The increasing intensity of competition makes it essential that hotels endeavour to improve the quality of services. With the entry of giant brands, we can not check mergers, acquisitions and consolidation of the lesser competitors. The hospitality business in India is shining and we do not find any sign of burnout in the near future. The hoteliers need to be innovative and competitive. They have to devise unique ways to retain customers. Quality remains the lone effective prescription to satisfy and retain the customers.

In the Indian perspective, there are a number of positive developments which would keep on moving the process of increasing the demand and outpacing the supply. The development of regional hubs due to the brisk growth rate of China and some of the South East Asian and the Middle East countries would attract tourists into the country. A significant increase in the middle class population would significantly affect the domestic tourism circuit. The upcoming business opportunities such as the development of commercial zones in metro suburbs and secondary markets will increase the accommodation demand. The projects comprising of retail and commercial space have also gained momentum and in future will emerge as an effective option. The world class potentials of India in respect of medical tourism would bring a significant increase in the demand side. We expect patients both from developed and developing countries. The rich cultural heritage of India would attract tourists from different parts of the globe. Incredible India campaign needs priority attention.

With the increasing heat of globalisation, we expert global biggies envincing keen interest in the development of Indian hospitality industry where they have profitable opportunities to capitalise on. The new brands like Amand, Satinwood, Banana tree, Hamton Inns, Hilton, Mandarian Oriental and Indian players like, ITC, ETH, The Oberoi, Taj, ITC, The Park Hotel, Leela and Bharat, Viceroy, DLF, Unitech, Royal Palms find tremendous opportunities in India.

The emerging trends in the Indian hospitality industry make a strong advocacy in favour of liberalisation of the aviation sector, rationalisation in tax rates, processing of tourist-friendly visa, efficient immigration service, availability of land for the constructions of hotels, setting up some guest houses, focus on medical tourism and rural tourism and innovative marketing with the help and co-operation of world class professionals.

Innovative services and creative promotional measures would help significant increase in the hospitality industry. The sensitisation and persuasion processes need due attention of marketers where government, hotel companies and media would be required to assign due weightage to the pricing strategy. We cannot negate that pricing strategy in the hotel industry is a manifestation of the supply and demand phenomenon. A sustainable tariff policy in hotels evolves around average room rates being higher during the peak season and lower during the off-season. The professionals also need to promote e-commerce and E-CRM Strategy.

SUMMARY

You have studied in this chapter different dimensions of service quality in the context of hotel industry. After going through the chapter, be sure that the following facts are well versed.

- **Service Quality: The Concept:** Quality is all about fitness for use. It is conforming to our requirements. It is fitness for use.
- **Importance of Service Quality:** Improving, maintaining, defining and redefining quality are found significant to the development of an organisation. It helps projection of a fair image, makes ways for maintaining economy, makes hotels potentially sound, minimises the risk factor and helps creation of value.
- **Service Quality Factor in Hotels:** The different factors influencing service quality are service are service delivery, tangibility, reliability, responsiveness, assurance, empathy, service product, and social responsibility.
- **Service Quality Management:** The hotel professionals need to draw their attention on three important dimensions while managing services, viz., setting the right standard, implementing the quality service and monitoring service quality. For monitoring service quality, the different tools are statistical tools, quality function deployment, internal performance analysis, customer satisfaction analysis, and customer complaints analysis.

- **SERVQUAL in Hotel:** It is a model for measuring the service quality developed by Parsuraman, Ziethmal and Berry in which we find comparison of perception with expectation. In this model, the dimensions like tangibility, reliability, responsiveness, assurance and empathy.
- **SERVPERF in Hotel:** It is a scale for measuring the services quality developed by Peter, Bebko, Andaleep and Basu in which we find focus on the customers perceptions of the performance of a service provider and adequate assessment for service quality.
- **Service Environment for Hotel Industry:** The development of service ambience focuses our attention on exteriors, interiors, lighting, ventilation, music, scent, furnishing, signposts, parking, aesthetic management and etiquette management. It also throws light on the dresses and uniforms of working employees.
- **Service Quality Gap:** The service quality gaps are known as knowledge gap, the standard gap, delivery gap, communication gap, perception gap, interpretation gap, service gap.
- **Service Leadership:** It is a stage reached by an organisation after establishing its status as a quality gap.
- **Quality in Totality in Hotel Industry:** With the mounting intensity of competition, it is essential that hotels practise TQM in which quality in totality would necessitate hotels to be potentially, strategically and tactically sound to deliver quality services to their customers. They need to keep on moving the process so that they are in a position to redefine the quality and become a quality leader.

KEY TERMS

Service Quality Gap	SERVQUAL
Echelons	SERVPERF
Burgeoning	Service Environment
Hotelier	Servicescapes
Benchmark	Service Ambience
Global biggies	Service Fragrance
Empathy	Layout
Responsiveness	Signage
Tangibility	Explicit
Reliability	Implicit
Standard Gap	Knowledge Gap
Delivery Gap	Perception Gap
Internal Communication Gap	International Gap
Service Leadership	Service Gap
WTTC	TQM

REVIEW QUESTIONS

1. What do you mean by Service Quality? Explain the importance of service quality to the hotel industry.
2. Focus on the different dimensions of Service Quality Management?
3. Explain the different Service Quality Factor?
4. Focus on SERVQUAL and SERVPERF?
5. What do you mean by Service Environment? Explain it in the context of hospitality industry.
6. Throw light on the different gaps found in service quality?
7. Write a note on the concept of TQM and its application in the hotel industry.
8. Setting the right standard, implementing the quality service and monitoring the service quality are the dimensions of service quality management in hotels. Comment on this statement.
9. Improving, maintaining, defining and redefining service quality are found significant to the development of a hotel. In the light of this statement focus on the importance of service quality for Indian hospitality industry.

APPLICATION EXERCISES

1. You are working as a hotel manager. Do you find service quality an essential dimension for the existence and prosperity of your hotel? Defend your arguments.
2. As a marketing professional you have been assigned the responsibility of managing the quality of services in your hotel. Focus on the factors to be taken care while managing service quality.
3. "The different factors influencing service quality are service delivery, tangibility, reliability, responsiveness, assurance, empathy, service product and social responsibility." Comment on this statement in the capacity of a hotel professional.
4. Do you find service ambience instrumental in helping hotel people in performing and hotel customers in gaining new experiences justify your arguments as a marketing professional of a leading hotel.
5. In the capacity of a hotel manager what measures you would like to adopt for bridging the service quality gap.
6. Do you find TQM as an effective prescription to improve the quality of services in hotels? Defend your opinion as a hotel professional.
7. SERVQUAL and SERVPERF are the two scales for measuring the quality of services. Explain the two scales in the context of hospitality industry.

End Notes:

1. Crosby P.B.: Quality without Tears; New American Library, NY, 1984.
2. Juran J.M.: Upper Management and Quality Juran Institute, New York, 1982.
3. Swan J.E. And Combs L.J: Product Performance and Customer Satisfaction: A Concept; *Journal of Marketing*, April 1976.

4. Gronroos C.: A Service Quality Model and its Marketing Implication; European Journal of Marketing, Vol. 18/4, 1984.
5. The Analyst: November, 2006 Interview with Priya Paul Chairman, Park Hotels.
6. Parsuraman, Zeithaml and Berry: Understanding and Improving Service Quality: A Literature Review and Research Agenda.
7. Vijayadurai J.: Service Quality Customer Satisfaction and Behavioural Intention in Hotel Industry Journal of Marketing and Communication; Vol. 3/3, 2008.
8. Zeithaml, Parsuraman and Berry: Delivering Quality Service; The Free Press, New York, 1990.
9. Lovelock Christopher and Writz: Services Marketing, 5th Edition, pp. 411-13.
10 Ray and Teckchandani: Indian Hotel Industry Strategy Building. The Icfaian Journal of Management & Research, Vol. VII/ 5, 2008.
11. Eleventh five year plan: Vol. III, pp. 245-51.

....ꝏꝏꝏ....

CHAPTER - 6

HOTEL PRODUCT STRATEGY

Strategic decisions focus on product helping guests in evoking boredom, providing to the tourists maximum enjoyment and tranquility, offering to them world class services having uniqueness and cost-effectiveness.

CHAPTER OBJECTIVES

Introduction – Hotel Product: The Concept – Hotel Product: Salient Features – Product Strategy – Product Life Cycles – Modifying and Revitalising the Services – Failure of Product – Launching a New Product – Stages of Product Screening – Branding – Why Ascribing a Brand Name? – Incredible India Brand – Formulating the Hotel Product Mix – Formulating a Sound Product Strategy – Summary – Key Terms – Review Questions – Application Exercises – End Notes.

LEARNING OBJECTIVES

This chapter of the study aims at studying the different dimensions of product strategy in the context of hotel industry. The motives to sensitise the readers to multi-dimensional services of hotels known as hotel product. The hotel professionals come to know about the different stages in the development of product which is likely to be launched. Building a strong brand image is significant to the development of hotel industry. The hotel professionals need to formulate a sound product strategy found to be globally competitive.

INTRODUCTION

It is the fitness of your product that makes your marketing resources much more productive. Product innovation in a right fashion is found significant in the present business world where the intensity of competition is found consistently moving upward. We agree with this view that innovation paves the ways for temptation which develops a craze even for those goods and services which are not developed. With the passage of time, it is natural that some of the services are bound to get obsolete. At the same time, some of the new services are also required to be included in the product mix. Inclusion and elimination thus are found moving in a cyclic order. Every product is aimed at some market and its marketing success essentially rests on its 'fit' with the market. The generation of idea, formation of concept, analysis of product cost and testing of services before their inclusion help in anticipating and visualising needs of the target market. Modification in the old services by adding a few new features is a common strategy followed by a majority of the hotels.

There are a number of categories of hotels and therefore a variation in the product is found to be a natural phenomenon. The decisions regarding, primary, ancillary and supportive services are influenced by the nature and category of a particular hotel. The management of rooms for staying the customers, function rooms, restaurants, bars, food sector, beverages, guest telephones, property operations, maintenance of energy and power cannot be identical in all the categories. Innovative strategies for the formulation of a sound product mix become important to enable hotel companies to survive and thrive in the market where the intensity of competition is found at its peak. Particularly when we find a number of global biggies entering the Indian hospitality sector, it is pertinent that Indian hotels are very much sincere and honest to the innovation process.

The emerging positive trends in the hotel industry indicate that the Indian hotels have potentials to compete with the global players provided the government and hotel companies initiate a joint move to change the scenario. The creation of world class infrastructural facilities is found urgent but the hotel companies find themselves helpless because here both the state and central governments are yet to be involved in the process. The PPP mode may be effective for this purpose. Not only the lodging and boarding services but even other services like amusement centres, shopping complex, swimming pool, car parking, garden, function room or conference hall and the latest personal care services are found significant while formulating the product strategy.

In an institution of commercial hospitality, the development of product has a telling effect on the formulation of marketing strategies. The formulation of a sound product mix is found significant because new sophisticated services add attractions to any business and motivate the customers. The customised services influence the customers. The hotel professional need an in depth knowledge of changing taste preferences of customers. Scientific and technological advances, inventions and innovations in the field of information and communication, latest developments in the field of transportation, increasing global partnership, increasing domination of corporate sector and emerging corporate culture, changing spending behaviour and lifestyles are some of the positive developments specially with the view point of hotel sector. Here, it is also significant to mention that these positive developments have attracted global biggies and a number of hotels having international brand have entered and are planning to enter. This in a natural way will increase the intensity of competition. Of course, the best and safest way of excelling competition is defining and redefining quality and offering something special to the customers even not imagined and planned by the rival hotels.

Development process cannot remain static. This necessitates a continuous effort for making possible multi-dimensional changes in the product. Today AC rooms have become common but a few years back, it was rare. Today computerised governance has become common but yesterday it was very rare. Today online services are available in a number of hotels but yesterday, it was simply a matter of discussion. Today, the hotels have been found offering a good number of peripheral services but yesterday they were very selective. This speaks of the fact that innovation is a continuous process which is considerably influenced by competition. The hotel professionals need to develop their awareness of the multi-dimensional changes in the business environment so that they are in a position to offer to the customers innovative services. The quality and price are the two important considerations helping Indian hotels in surviving and thriving.

We find it an unvarnished fact that whatsoever the positive developments we have witnessed in the national economy of India particularly from the very beginning of 21st century has revolutionised the tourism as well as the hotel sector. Actually, we find emergence of a profitable market attracting the international players like Amanda, Satinwood, Banana Tree, Hamptoon Inns, Hilton and Mandarin Oriental. The Indian players like The Oberoi, Taj, ITC, The Park Hotels, Leela and Bharat are found in a commanding position and they can throw serious challenges even to the global biggies. It is in this context that we find priority attention on quality which would remain as a sharpened weapon.

Indian hospitality sector needs a major change. We need to know about the markets, about the customers and about our product. We have enough potentials and we need to capitalise on the same with a professional touch. The adventure tourism, rural tourism, medical tourism, convention tourism, beach tourism, religious tourism heritage tourism would significantly increase the number of tourists. The hotel professional need to study the changing scenario, identify the changing taste preferences and develop a product mix effective in influencing the customers.

The strategy bears the efficacy of turning the negative into positive provided the strategists have shown their professional excellence in the formulation process. The target is to satisfy and retain the customers. Since the intensity of competition between global and national biggies is found of high magnitude, it is pertinent that hotel professionals develop such a package which is found innovative and attractive. The professionals need to keep in their minds that with the increasing heat of globalisation, we find a significant increase in the middle class and therefore the concept of no-frills or budget hotel would be successful in attracting them. The Tata's Indian Hotel Company which owns and operates the Taj brand of hotel chains has already launched the budget hotels across the country and is planning to launch more in the coming years. The foreign hotel chains like Accor, Marriott and Starwood are making efforts to capitalise on the opportunities.

Indian hospitality industry requires to assign priority attention to Medical Tourism for which they have world class potentials. India is now regarded as health tourist destination. The healthcare tourism alone can earn over US$2 bn additional revenues by 2012. We expect a steady flow of patients from the developed countries as well as from countries in Africa and West Asia where we find lack of quality medical aid. Health tourism is now over a US$300 mn industry attracting about 1,50,000 patients every year. It is right to mention that the main driver of boosting health tourism is its cost-effectiveness. The government, media need to promote and hotel companies need to tap the opportunities by developing a package which is to benefit the patients.

While formulating the product mix, the hotel professionals need to study the taste preferences of potential guests expected to stay in hotels. There are a number of points for service delivery and it is to be made sure that customers are delivered the promised quality. The reception, boarding, lodging, entertainment, shopping, communication, function, medical, personal care, sports are the points of attraction where the professionals need to show personal touch. The strategic decisions make it essential that Indian leading hotels benchmark on their own in terms of world class services and amenities. The high penetration of e-commerce is found essential to improve the quality of services.

We find brand loyalty a fragile idea in a cost transparent world. The professionals need to show their excellence while retaining the customers. We find new products on the rise and here professionals need more care while designing tailor-made services to stay competitive in the niche segments. The rising attrition rate and wage bills need due attention of hoteliers. Formulation of a sound product strategy is an important functional responsibility before the hoteliers which requires world class professional excellence. Let's hope that the strategists make it possible and get a success while going through an acid test.

HOTEL PRODUCT – THE CONCEPT

At the outset, we clarify the conceptual aspect of hotel product and thereafter present different services offered by the hotel. Willingly or unwillingly, we accept the fact that ultimately the services offered by hotels play a commanding turning the negative into positive.

A number of experts have expressed their views regarding the product.

"A product is anything that can be offered to a market for attention use or consumption that might satisfy a want or need."[1]

It is important to mention that most products we think are physical products but products also include services and thereafter we call them service product.

"A product is a bundle of utilities consisting of various product features and accompanying services."[2]

So far as the hotel is concerned, the product a buys feeling, pleasure, satisfaction received from available like restaurants, function rooms and other centres as a hotel services.

Types of Hotel Product

In Exhibit 6.1, the different products/services offered by different categories of hotels are presented.

EXHIBIT 6.1: HOTEL PRODUCT

Reception	Welcome Desk, Counter, Equiry
Boarding	Restaurant, Bar, Cafe
Lodging	Bedrooms, Amenities and Facilities

Entertainment	Radio, TV/VCR/VCP/CD/LCD Music, Dance, etc.
Shopping	Shopping Malls, Arcade, Plaza
Communication	Telephone, Fax, Newspapers, Magazines, Internet, Reservation Enquiry, Immigration
Function	Function rooms, Conference hall, Wedding hall
Medical	First Aid /Ambulance
Sports	Playground, Jogging, Gym, Paddle Tennis, Sports Items
Personal Care	Beauty Parlours, Hair dressing, Facial, etc.

HOTEL PRODUCT: THE SALIENT FEATURES

For the formulation of a sound strategy, it is essential that we are well aware of the salient features:

1. Service product: The product sold to customers/guests are service-oriented. This requires high degree of personal commitment, imagination, adaptation and an assessment of the preferences of the customers etc. Its intangibility poses problems as for satisfying customers, the tour operators, travel agents, the front line staff, the waiters, the receptionists find it difficult to transform occasional customers into habitual customers.

2. Perishability: Another important feature is perishability of the product. Rooms in a hotel, a seat in the restaurant, bar and the function rooms, if not sold, would fail to generate revenues. If the products remain unused, it would cost the hotels in a big way. If a room is vacant for a day, the opportunity is lost, leading to financial loss. This will adversely affect the hotel business. The tangible products can be stored, preserved for later sale. This necessitates concerted efforts to ensure that the hotel has high occupancy rates. It is due to perishability that we find a drastic cut in hotel tariffs, specially during the off-season.

3. Users' presence essential: For availing the services of a hotel, it is pertinent that users come to the hotels personally/physically. However, it is feasible for the hotel management to carry the food items of a restaurant but take home provision is found in a very few hotels. All depends on their policy guidelines. This makes it essential to add other attractions. It is against this background that hotels need to assign due weightage to the behavioural management.

4. Instability in demand: The demand for a hotel product is usually fluctuating. We find an increase in the demand during a particular season or on a special occasion. This seasonal fluctuation in demand makes it essential for hotel companies to develop new strategies of sales promotion and even to increase the duration of sales promotion. In almost all the countries attracting tourists, we find seasonal fluctuation an important obstacle in marketing the hotel services.

5. Rigidity in supply: This is also an important feature .of a hotel product. A number of factors are found responsible for the same. The hotel rooms cannot be built in a day. It takes enough time and money. Once the hotel is constructed and the furnishing is complete, renovation becomes more complicated. The supply side needs highly capital intensive items. A hotel which does not meet a viable level of occupancy would fail to generate adequate revenues to make up for the substantial investments made to construct it. An underestimate of demand may create image problem, since it takes years to create additional facilities to improve the supply and demand ratio. Thus instability in demand and rigidity in supply complicates the task of marketers.

6. Services quality influenced by staff: In the hotel industry, the services offered to the guests customers are substantially influenced by the quality of personnel. The housekeepers not managing bedrooms properly, the waiters and related staff failing to maintain good quality services in restaurants and bars, the staff not decorating properly the function rooms, the receptionists not showing empathy would influence the quality and image of a hotel adversely. The image problem further gets aggravated, if the staff are not professionally qualified and trained. This makes the hotel industry different to others.

7. Largely psychological in nature: In addition to other factors, the hotel industry is vigorously influenced by the psychological attributes. If we find receptionists showing empathy to the customers, the result is to be positive. If we find receptionists, waiters and other front line staff misbehaving with the customers, the result would definitely be negative. This is a clear indication that the hotel industry has today become a specialised business sector.

PRODUCT STRATEGY

Strategic decision plays a vital role in making the marketing decisions much more productive. An organisation is supposed to engineer marketing programmes around two essential elements, viz., the product and the market. We cannot ignore the fact that the success of marketing is involved in the essence of tailoring a product to suit the changing market needs. When we talk about the formulation of a sound product strategy, emphasis is on designing the services in tune with the changing environmental conditions and expectations of the potential guests. If the potential guests are sophisticated, it is imperative that the services are tailored to their taste. Hence, the designing of a sound product strategy is the need of the hour, and this necessitates an in-depth study of the existing market conditions and the customers.

A sound product strategy needs an in-depth study of the product life cycle. With the passage of time, it is very natural that traditional services tend to become obsolete and if we continue with the old services in the market, this is going to affect our business adversely. Earlier rooms in a hotel were equipped with nominal facilities. Today, central heating, playroom, wet bars, wall-to-wall carpets, tiled, bathrooms and kitchens are found in a number of hotels. But the potential guests want something more. The attitude of people has changed considerably. It is seen that people prefer to spend on the construction of modern houses, equipped with new amenities and facilities. And therefore, the hoteliers are supposed to innovate their products. They also need to add attractions and offer incentives to their services. This is an important dimension of product strategy which would make future marketing much more effective.

The main thing which hotels and hotel companies have to make possible is to ensure that hotel facilities are to give at least the same comforts as in the private modern homes.

While developing the services, specially the bedrooms; it is essential to have knowledge of the emerging trends in hospitality services. Probably with women entering the corporate world as business executives, it becomes essential for the hotel management to add accessories in a room which would be of use to them. Of course, this strategy will prove beneficial in the long run. What about the personal care services? We find a good number of hotels today lacking in personal care services particularly in the Indian perspective. Gym and swimming pools, sun tanning facilities with a circuit of exercise machines suitably supervised, jogging tracks, small combined exercise machines, paddle tennis, or say exercise and aerobics opportunities to the customers are preferably to be included in the product mix of hotels.[3]

An expert rightly remarks, "Strategically, the core service is the primary benefit that customers seek from the service provider. The core service often becomes a commodity as a service industry matures. Consumers expect the firm to be competent in providing the core services. The result is that the peripheral services often become the way in which the heart of customers is won."[4] This makes it essential that while formulating the product strategy, the strategic decision-makers take into account key dimensions of service quality. This becomes a reliability which is the ability to perform as promised. It is the responsiveness, the willingness to help customers and to provide them prompt service. We also call it the competence or the skill and knowledge necessary to perform. It is security involving freedom from risks. It is even communication which we feel is communicating with customers in ways they can understand and respond positively to the services delivered. And finally, it is understanding of the customers' needs which is important. Thus, the main task before the marketers is to engineer a sound product strategy which would simplify their task of effective promotion. If we do not make it possible, the intelligent competitors would take advantage of the market condition and would be successful in capitalising on the available opportunities.

At the outset, it is essential that the product management process is managed properly so that the pruning and adding operations are optimised. This necessitates an in-depth knowledge of the changing needs and requirements of the potential guests. The hotel companies are required to strike a balance between the two options, viz., modifying the existing services and developing new services. If the commercial viability is not questioned or is not geared in the right direction, this would call for immediate modification of the existing services but at the same time, they should also pave ways for new services. The moment we succeed in finalising the product strategy, the stage is set for developing the product mix.

It is right to mention here that decisions regarding the inclusion and elimination of reported obsolete strategies cannot be made in isolation from those existing in markets and vice versa. Though it is true that product and market situations have to be carried out separately, the decisions on them must be made jointly. A change in marketing mix alters the sale and profit potential of the products. We find the same case with other services also, specially the tourism industry. Here, we need product-market strategy which indicates the course of action to be taken regarding the product mix. Periodically, some new additions to a product must be encouraged, but of course, in the face of emerging new trends in the market conditions. To be more specific, we need to assign due weightage to the strategies adopted by our competitors. Thus competitors' efforts, market demand and the growing mobility of the customers are important considerations while formulating the product strategy.

Hence, a clear understanding of market conditions is essential for managing the product/services effectively. It is also clear that behaviour of customers depends on how well the lifestyle of customers influences the income. An increase in the discretionary income changes the lifestyle and we find enough scope for developing the hotel culture. Here, it is essential that the marketing executives are well aware of the new opportunities in the market. The process of managing the product is shown in Figure 6.1.

In Figure 6.1, it is clear that the product management process virtually starts from setting the market objectives and strategies. After this, the product-market objectives and strategies are finalised. Thus we find two processes, viz., the generation of new ideas and exploration of opportunities for modifying the existing services. The research and development departments help in simplifying the task of new product development or modification of the existing products. The next step is costing and pricing, of course, related to both the modified and existing products. Thus, for new services, we find test marketing strategies and thereafter the formulation of a marketing mix becomes the final stage of product management.

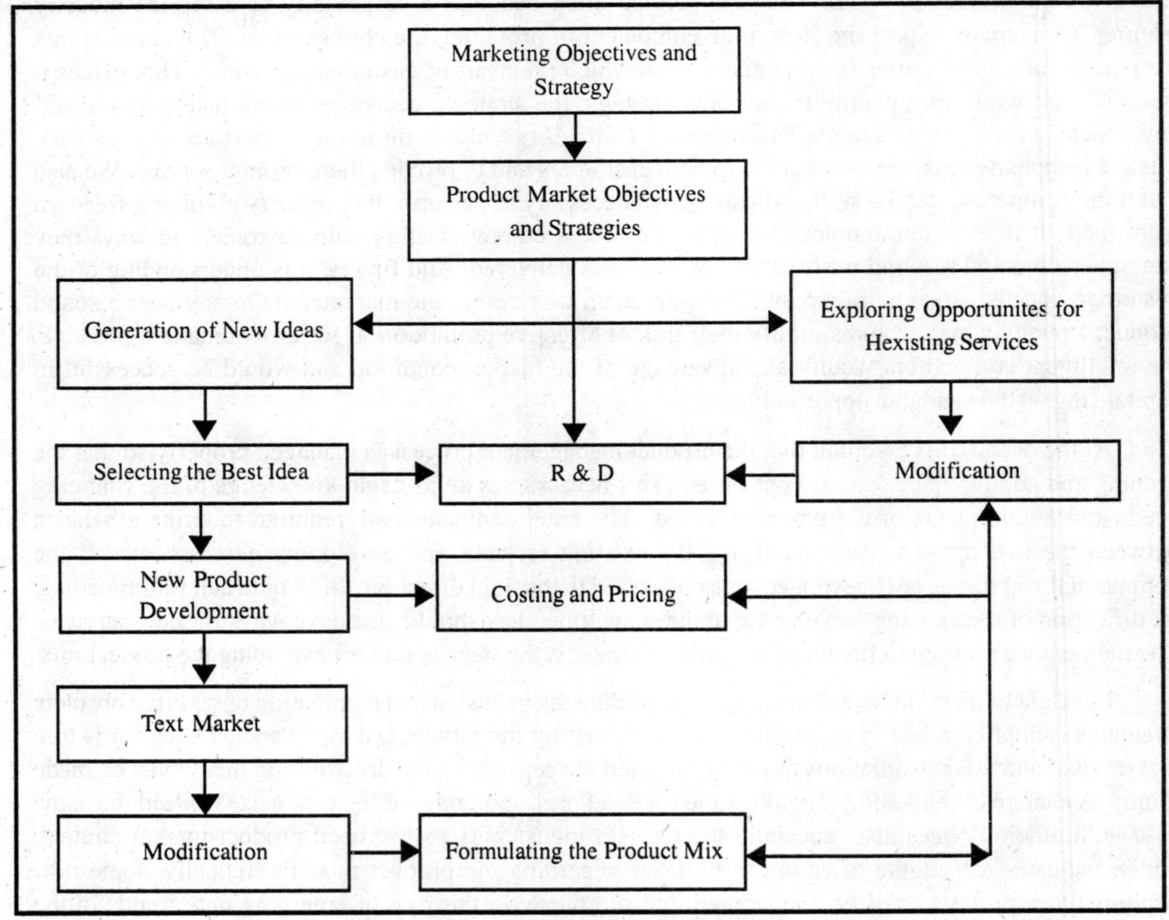

FIG 6.1: PRODUCT MANAGEMENT PROCESS

Modified from: Douglas Foster; Mastering Marketing, Macmillan, London

In the hotel industry, strategic decision are substantially influenced by the emerging new trends in the behavioural profile of customers. The traditional services are either to be eliminated or modified and replaced by new services. The main theme is to promote the product profile found innovative in nature. This adds attractions and paves way for more competition.

PRODUCT LIFE CYCLES

The services delivered by hotels also have a certain length of life during which they pass through different stages which are found identifiable. Beginning with the launching stage almost all products/services reach the stage of maturity and stagnation and finally make a good-bye from the markets. The product life cycle concept has emerged as a major factor in successful and profitable product management — from new product information to old disposable product.[5] We include new services in our product mix and find an increase in the profit.[6] This also hints suitable time for declaring the services traditional and thus replacing them at the earliest indication. In the hotel business, we find several examples to prove the same. The hotels making available to their guests innovative services take advantage of low levels of competition and succeed in capitalising on the opportunities. Contrary to it, the hotels making available traditional services fail in making profits unless they have some unique features. An understanding of the relations between a product and its lifecycle enable marketers to plan their campaigns in a right fashion. We find some new features in the hotel product which calls for better management by the hoteliers. If the services are perishable, the task gets more complicated, which subsequently necessitated a balanced product portfolio.

In today's fast changing society nothing stands still for long. Some of the products are out as fast as they are 'in.' If the products are influenced by ultra-modern trends emerging in the markets, the time span would be very short. If the services included in the hotel products are influenced by lifestyle, the services or products would soon be deemed traditional, old and obsolete. We cannot deny the fact that a number of services offered in the hotel industry are influenced by fashion, cultural transformation and modernisation. This also makes it clear that the services after a gap are termed traditional, become obsolete and turned down by the customers the moment a change is witnessed. And therefore, the services reach the stage of maturity frequently and tend to down.

Personal care services are now getting a proper place in the product mix of hotels and a number of international as well as domestic hotels are found active in including these services in their product mix. The hotel adopting these services receive a positive response and we find them at a good level of acceptance. Recently, almost all the hotels and hotel companies are found innovative and competitive in accommodating personal care services in the product mix.

In Figure 6.3, we find the different stages of product life cycle. It goes without saying that hotel services are very much related to the projection of the hotel's image. If we continue to do business in the markets with traditional services, prospective customers would reject the same and the word-of-mouth communication would drastically affect the image of hotels. This makes it essential that hoteliers identify the existing stage of product in the lifecycle, modify the same, or offer the sales promotion tools and finally declare them obsolete. It is very natural that life spans of all services vary. Almost all the services related to fashion and lifestyles usually have a short span.

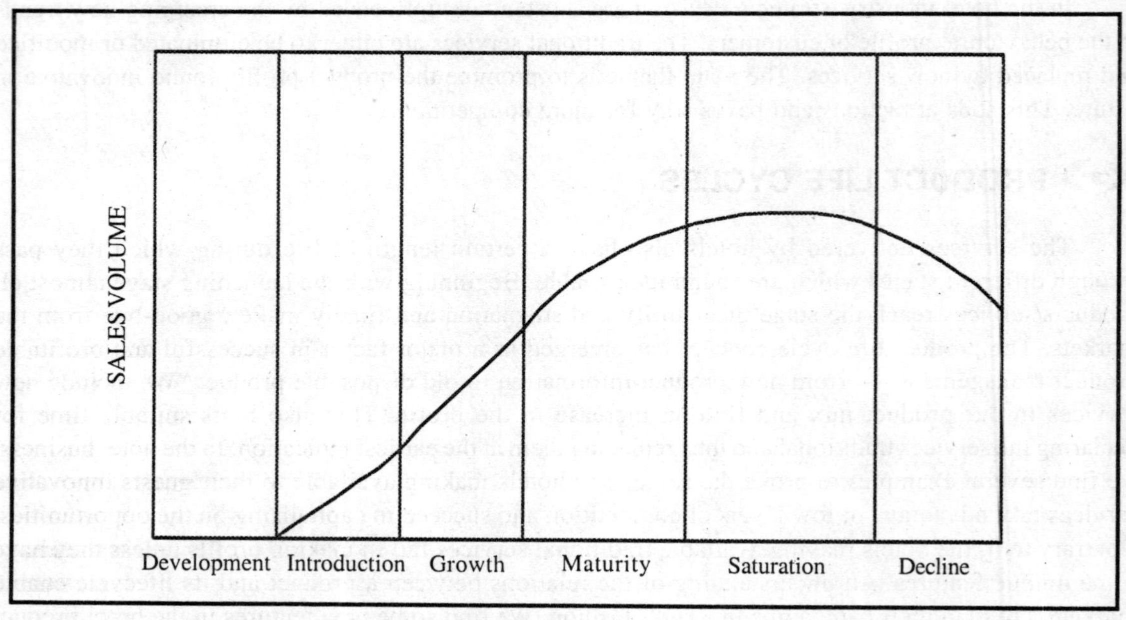

FIG 6.2: STAGES IN THE PRODUCT LIFE CYCLE

Figure 6.2, shows that the sales of a newly launched product service will increase rapidly during the growth period until new competitors enter the market, challenging the very performance of the existing companies. When all potential customers have made maximum use of the available services, the stage of saturation (obsoleteness) starts. Finally, the stage of decline comes when customers reject them for better and more facilities. At this stage, we have no option but to eliminate the same and to launch new product. In the hotel business, a number of services are influenced by fashion and the latest trends in the hospitality business. Therefore we find a different trend in the product life cycle. The moment we find these changes, the stage of saturation starts, making these services outdated. This is shown in Figure 6.3. The electronic revolution has paved way for the development of new products in the hotel business, but how long these services would get a positive response would be determined by a revolutionary change. This is due to the fact that fad products reach to the maturity very fast and tend to become obsolete rapidly.

It is, of course, a difficult task for the hoteliers to include these services as they have to make huge investments in developing these services but the life span is short and so they have to eliminate the same just when the market potentials are tapped. This does not, in anyway, indicate that the hoteliers should not think in favour of these services.

The important thing here is to watch the trend and to make decisions accordingly.

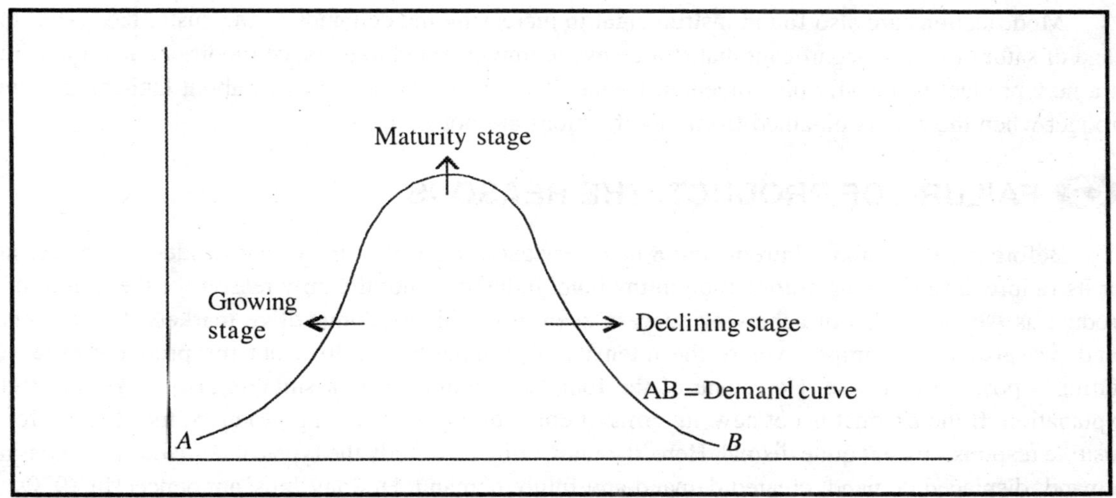

FIG. 6.3: FASHION-ORIENTED SERVICES' LIFE CYCLE

MODIFYING AND REVITALISING THE SERVICES

Rejuvenating and restructuring are the two important decision-making areas in the hospitality industry where it is not possible to develop new services frequently. But it is important that new strategies are planned to enhance these services. Here, the important thing is to watch the efforts made by our competitors. If we find hotels modifying their services just by adding some new features, we have no option but to modify the same. We find swimming pools in almost all the hotels. Of late, some of the hotels have modified the same and now they make available Gym and sun tanning facilities close to the swimming pools. Like this, we also find some of the hotels designing the rooms keeping in view the preferences of women. In addition, we also find cases where hotels have been found redecorating their restaurants. These modifications carry some meaning, specially to get a positive response from potential customers, who are sources of revenue.

A bigger modification may be to add some new features not adopted or offered by close competitors. The provision of a car at the customer's disposal for a few days, specially to the high spending tourists would be an image-building strategy for the hotel. To be more specific, in the Indian condition, it is pertinent that we make sincere efforts to modify the services. We make an advocacy in favour of modification since development of new services would involve more time and money.

Incidentally, it is seldom, that modifications are found in fad or fashion-oriented products as we find them obsolete by subsequent changes. While taking a decision regarding modification, it is also significant that we identify the reasons for getting a negative response for the services delivered.

In view of the above, it is right to mention that a microscopic study of the product life cycle is essential to make the decisions effective. The appropriate alternatives and their suitability are influenced by a change in the stage of the product life cycle. While making decisions for a change, the competitors' strategies would make available to the hoteliers a suitable guideline. Hence, the hotels and hotel companies will have to time and again assess the life cycle of their products.

Modifications are also found instrumental in increasing the demands of the customers. After the stage of saturation, it is significant that strategies are implemented to enhance modifications. Inclusion of a new product is a costly phenomenon. Hence, it is pertinent that we think about launching a new product when the results obtained from modifications are not impressive.

FAILURE OF PRODUCT: THE REASONS

Before we think about introducing a new service/product, it is important to identify the reason for its failure. The growing competition in the hotel industry is not the only reason for the failure of a product as we find cases of achieving success even in the highly competitive markets. On the other hand, we also find examples where the intensity of competition is low, but the products failed in getting a positive response. Here, one of the four Ps is found to be a suitable area to get the right explanation. If the product is not new, in terms of emulation of the existing products, the chances for a positive response appear quite dismal. Here, the main thing is to study the types of demand, viz., existing demand, displaced demand, created demand and future demand. Holiday Inns[7] announced in 1970s to build a new hotel. The city in which the hotel was to be built was already oversupplied with hotel rooms and the occupancy ratio or the occupancy level of the existing hotels was very low. The hotel chain identified its market in a correct way. In a true sense, the hotel guests were dissatisfied with the facilities available but they had no choice. When they were offered a new modern hotel with the desired amenities and facilities, there was a rapid increase in the business of the new hotel whereas some of the traditional hotels were forced to close down their business.

The aforesaid facts are a mute testimony to the proposition that all four types of demand, as pointed out earlier, need to be emphasised upon constantly in the hotel industry with the existing demands resulting from the adequate supply of the product the consumers want; the displaced demand is said to be resulting from the dissatisfaction experienced by the current customers; created demand resulting from wants — latent and unrecognised by customers but the marketers can develop them by effective marketing strategies and the future demand resulting from demographic or changes in lifestyles are found significant, specially with the viewpoint of studying the reasons for the failure of products in the market. Here, it is also essential that products are sold at affordable rates and appreciated by customers. Though no amount of promotion will sell a low quality product, its promotion strategy must be implemented cost-effectively. And finally, the products should have the support of travel agents, the transport operators and tour operators. They can frame out brochures and sell the product through them. An effective briefing by tour operators and travel agents regarding the outstanding features of your products will play a significant role boosting the hotel industry. We find cases where inadequate and unimpressive briefing by retailers or say, the travel agents have played a negative role.

LAUNCHING A NEW PRODUCT

It is an important aspect of the product strategy. In the hotel industry, we find a high level of risks involved. Though we find it difficult to bring down the statistical failure rate of new products, a careful screening of product will definitely be an important tool in the hands of marketers. Before we discuss screening, it is essential to clarify the concept of a new product. An expert says, "By new product, we mean improvement in the existing product which is new in the eyes of prospects. Similarly, if an existing product is launched in an existing new market with a low acceptance level, that product is also at all intents and purposes a new products."[8] In Exhibit 6.2, we find existing and new products in existing and new markets.

EXHIBIT 6.2: EXISTING AND NEW PRODUCT

	Existing	New
New	Introducing new product in the present market	Launching of a new product in a new market
Existing	Modifying the existing product for the present market	Respositioning the present product to attract the new market

It is right to mention here that an organisation which decides to modify the existing product to cater to the demands of the present market and make the product attractive, faces the least possible risk in investments. Here, some outstanding features are also added in the product. If the product is not getting a positive response in the existing market, its repositioning would be a better alternative.

This is meant directing appeal to a different market segments or to prefer a more potentially able overseas market. To make the product highly appealing to prospective customers, it is also advisable to change the concept of the product. Another alternative in this case would be to develop a more authentic product to appeal to the existing consumers. If an organisation succeeds in projecting a fair image, we find all possibilities for getting a trial performance moving existing consumers. Finally, an organisation can choose a genuinely new product to suit a new market segment. Often, the new products are an extension of the present product line. In the hotel industry, if we find an inclusion of some additional facilities in the audio/visual system or in the restaurant, we find that some special spices or the lighting arrangement is changed, in the bathrooms the steam-bath facilities are made available or in the bar of a hotel, some new recreation facilities are made available, etc. We call them 'extended product' or service.

In this context, it is found difficult to determine exactly when a product can be genuinely new, since most of the services we buy are simply modified, extended or advanced. Introduction of the concept of holiday camp, specially designed rooms for women, steam facilities in bathrooms, etc. are on the priority list of service facilities offered by hotel today. The main purpose of launching a product is to find the market-gap which is also a potential product opportunity with a ready market which has not yet been tapped. The market-oriented approach line is found suitable for new product developments where it is essential to see the products desired by customers. It is important here to quote that in the Scandinavian hotels, the high cost of labour was instrumental in raising the price tag of hotel food. Here, the solution was to introduce self-service breakfasts, which was no doubt a break from the traditional service, but was found very popular with hotel guests since it reduced prices and offered an open choice of quantity and quality food.[9]

We have to accept the fact that the launching of a new product in the new market is a risky proposition and therefore, we find other marketing strategies more effective and less risky. Since both the product and the market are totally new to the company so the most careful investigation needs to be done. Any addition, alteration, extension or modification should be environmentally and physically friendly. The hotels and hotel companies are supposed to be mote careful while taking a decision regarding the development of a product. To be more specific, if the development is likely to be more expensive, the steps towards a particular product should not be taken in haste.

 STAGES OF PRODUCT SCREENING

Before we launch a product, it is essential to go through different stages. In Exhibit 6.3, we find four stages for screening the product:

EXHIBIT 6.3: STAGES OF PRODUCT SCREENING

Idea Generation

Idea Evaluation

Business Analysis

Test Marketing

Paradoxically, the idea for anew product is generated by the executives of a company and then we find discussion held amongst them to be responsible for the development of strategies to effectively launch a new product. However, the staff belonging to the low echelon also make a significant contribution to the development of new products. The front line staff in general are found in direct touch with the customers and therefore, they get the right feedback to open avenues for appropriate decision-making. The receptionists, waiters, housekeepers and others at business counters in the hotel, doormen are found in direct touch with the customers. They understand the customers, their expectations, reactions to the basic demand. In a true sense, the hotel services are marketed by the front-line staff at the management level. In addition, the feedback may be in the face of customers 'agencies', discussions, deliberations and dialogues. The feedback, of course, engineers a sound foundation for the generation or ideas regarding the modification, alteration of innovation in the services to make the product competitive. Once the idea is generated, the stage is set for the implementation and evaluation of ideas. The screening process helps in eliminating the irrelevant ideas. In exercising the evaluation process, a number of factors are taken into consideration.

After gathering the data from different sources, the next stage is to evaluate the idea. It is essential that these feasible ideas are carefully evaluated so that the irrelevant ideas are not implemented. This is possible by drawing a checklist of the non-feasible points of each idea. It is also essential to identify the market at which the product is to be aimed at the initial stage. In addition, there should be a listing of the benefits of the product over the existing product and an analytical suggestion on the price factor of the services. After the identification of promising ideas, it is essential to test the same with the viewpoint business viability. In this context, we find it essential to make an estimate of the sales potential based on the target market, the profit potential and the cash inflow. This helps management in getting a clear picture of how long it will take before the new products start to generate major profits. At this stage, it is also essential to undertake research, specially to test the public relations in this case. If the reactions are positive, the service programme can be moved to the final stage. Here, the hotel industry however faces a new problem. In the case of the tourism industry, the test marketing strategy is reportedly found to be easier but the same process in the hotel industry is found complicated. But this fact has been refuted by the former to extent. This is due mainly to the fact that hotels cannot be built with the ability of withdrawing the same, if they are not successful. Some innovative ideas have been used to overcome the problem. As for example, the hotels have been able to test the proposed new room decor by having a few rooms redecorated to retain customers and in the long run we also find here scope for introducing new package tours on a limited scale.

The aforesaid facts thus make it clear that the product screening plays a vital role in getting a suitable product in which the risk element is found very low. If we launch a product without screening, the response will be either negative or partially appreciating. The marketing executives here playa vital role in the generation of new ideas. The executives and even the low level management staff, directly related to the customers have a clear-cut idea of the customers' reactions to services offered has been as mentioned earlier. Thus, to be more specific the front-line staff, may be efficacious in diagnosing the ideas pertaining to alteration, modification, addition and innovation. It is very natural that such generated ideas are found effective in identifying the competitors strategies. This simplifies the task of reformulating the sensitive product policy. The main task is to reach to the target users and this is possible when we follow the processes for effective product screening. In addition, it is also pertinent here to receive a feedback directly from the customers.

BRANDING

Giving a product a brand name is found essential to add perceived values and differentiate the product from its immediate competitors. Branding adds great value to a product. It is an intrinsic aspect of product strategy. It is a name, term, sign, symbol, design or a combination of all which is intended to identify the goods or services of one seller or group of sellers and to differentiate them from its competitors. Branding a product is one of the oldest marketing techniques which, of late, has emerged as a potent marketing tool. Like goods manufacturing industries, the service-generating industries also find this tool significant. Familiar logos of Holiday Inn, Thomas Cook are a proven testimony to the proposition that brand name has been appreciated and opted for the successful marketing of goods and services. Here, it is essential to clarify the term 'Logo'. The name, symbol or combination is referred to as *'logotype'* or in short "logo". The design of the logo may be registered as a trademark. The brand name is that part of the brand which can be vocalised.

WHY ASCRIBING A BRAND NAME?

An organisation ascribes a brand name since it offers a number of advantages — helpful in identifying a particular product and distinguishes a product from those of the immediate competitors. It also acts as a cue to the purchasers in their task of making purchase decisions. It indicates to the buyers the exact level of quality they expect from the specific brand product. This is due to the fact that a range of products marketed under the same brand name carry similar expectations of quality. This makes it essential that hotels branding their products exercise a strong control over their quality. Further, in the hotels where we find most of the products of intangible nature, the purchase of a branded product helps customers in avoiding risks. If they find the services upto their expectations, they go for the services again and become habitual or heavy customers clearly indicating their loyalty to a particular brand. Here, it is important to mention that some of the travel agents/tour operators are committed to acknowledge particular brand. Major tour operators such as Thomas Holidays and owners abroad regularly develop new brand names for their products. In addition, the use of a brand name enables competitors to employ a technique known as *'brand stretching'*, i.e., introduction of new products into an existing range under the same brand name. Well established brand names such as Thomson or Cosmos could go for value addition including a new range of holidays such as seat only flight programmes, e.g., Thomson Airfares and Cosmos Travjet. Thus, it is clear that branding becomes a key tool in formulating the product strategy.

INCREDIBLE INDIA BRAND

The increasing heat of globalisation, mounting sophistication in the development of ICT, popularity of traditional forms of therapy and Yoga, and world class potentials of modern medical aids leading to the rising popularity of medical tourism, increasing temptation of high spending tourists to the cultural heritage of are some of the outstanding features of Destination India which has sizeably benefited the hospitality sector witnessing the highest rub-off effect. It is against this background that even the developed countries of globe have changed their perception about India earlier known as a country of snakes and elephants. Transformation of a snake charmer into an IT hub has made an invasion the image problem which we experienced earlier. The sudden burst in tourist traffic has spurred hospitality industry players to get into action so that qualitative and quantitative improvements in the hotel industry are made possible. We also find cases where tourists have been outnumbering the hotel rooms and demand has been rising far ahead of supply. On the whole we find a significant increase in the occupancy ratio. It is upon high government policymakers, hotel companies, tour operators to initiate and activate joint efforts to promote Incredible India Brand.

The marketers need to identity and tap those segments who have shown interests in visiting India, specially the NRIs and persons of Indian origin may be persuaded to visit the country of their origin and discover their roots. The "Baby-Boomers group in North American and Europe[11] are to be encouraged to visit India by creating in them the desire to discover one of the oldest civilisations of the world to enjoy the plurality of cultural enjoyment offered by this country. We can also develop cultural heritage as our brand because our potentials are sound both in terms of tangible and intangible heritages. The tangible heritage represents the hard culture of a community where as the intangible heritage represents the soft culture such as the people, traditions, folklore, music, dance, traditional games, mythology, rituals, customs, handicrafts, festivals, events, story tellers, local markets and also living human treasures. It is significant to mention that Malaysia could be successful in developing a strong brand image based on Exotic fun and friendly people. China has been successful in developing a strong brand image which is found based on Culture. We have potentials to develop Culture as a strong brand. The professionals in the very context need to link heritage monuments with culturally rich villages which would show multi-dimensional positive results such as the inflow of high spending tourists will gain momentum the occupancy ratio of hotels will be increased and the important of all is the transformation of rural economy, development of rural tourism and showcasing of vast heritage of India which would help in developing a national brand.

For maintaining the positive trends in the development of Indian hospitality industry, it is pertinent that we tap all the avenues that we find in the tourism sector. Building the Brand India is our target and the strategic decisions make it essential that we identify our strengths and with the support of government remove the weaknesses. On the one hand, we need to tap global markets while on the other hand also need to capitalise on the opportunities existent in the domestic markets. Identification of pilgrimage centres and their integration with new domestic tour circuits where transport, accommodation, catering and darshan are all synchronised and packaged need priority attention of MoT. Potentially sound tourist destinations and strategically and tactically sound managerial decisions would considerably benefit the hotel sector.

Building a strong brand image is a result of our consistent and concerted efforts. Destinations without attractions carry no meaning. The image of tourist destination thus proves to be an important dimension for building a strong brand image. In addition to the tour operators, travel agents and MoT; the hotel companies and professionals working there also bear the responsibility of projecting our destinations. We cannot negate that in the Indian context, the tourist destinations need a strong brand image. Developing a positive image for any brand requires unique brand personality, correct positioning, innovative products and creative promotional measures. It is against this background that we find leading tourist destinations in the world having a strong brand image. This is due to the fact that when a tourist wants to take a final decision regarding a particular destination, he/she has a number of options or a number of brands. It is quite natural that destinations with established brand image compete and get a place in the visiting list of a tourist.

The destination image of India lags far behind. We on account of image problem find it difficult to impress upon the potential tourists. The professionals in the very context bear the responsibility of developing a strong brand image and sensitising the potential tourists to develop their awareness. Whatsoever the wrong perceptions that we find in the minds of potential tourists need to be removed. The high level penetration of e-commerce is found to be an effective avenue to sense and persuade the customers. The hotels with the support of Web pages may be successful in sensitising the potential tourists and guests. Developing destination awareness *vis-a-vis* the awareness of accommodation may be preferred through internet.[12]

Strengthening Brand India is thus significant with the viewpoint of developing the hospitality industry. The potential guests or tourists find it difficult to make use of their options unless they have detailed information regarding destination and accommodation. Of course, the tour operators and travel agents considerably simplify the task of hospitality industry but it is not meant that the hotel professionals are not concerned with this problem. The most important thing is activating the sensitisation process and this makes a strong advocacy in favour of highly penetrated e-commerce. A majority of the tourists prefer budget hotels and the professionals need to enrich their knowledge bank related to availability and suitability.

It is found to be an unvarnished fact that the launch of Incredible India tourism campaign and emerging positive trends in the Indian national economy have brought Indian hospitality industry on the global map. The global biggies are found positive and it is in this context that we find that more than 142 luxury hotel projects are now coming to India where we expect an investment of more than ₹ 8,000/- crore.[13] New brands such as Amanda, Satinwoods, Banan Tree, Hampton Inns, Hilton and Mandarin

Oriental are collaborating with key Indian Players and the key Indian players like ITC, ETH, Bharat Hotels, Viveroy DDLF, Unitech and Royal Palms are associating themselves with the global brands.

With the entry of international brands, it is natural that the intensity of competition is found high. The strategic decisions focus on the point that international brands concentrate on metros with big projects whereas the domestic players concentrate on budget hotels along with premium hotels. In the group of Indian players, IHCL is planning to open the budget hotel with "Ginger" brand in Ahmedabad. The Indian Railways Catering and Tourism Corporation (IRCTC) are also setting up budget hotels. The ITC, Taj, Accor hotels Nikko Metropolitan and Crowne Plaza have also been planning to develop budget hotels with the cooperation of IRCTC.

Offer the best; sensitise the potential customers transform them into habitual customers; keep on moving the process of defining and redefining the quality; make your services distinct to your rivals; earn a name and build a strong brand image. Of Course, a host of factors are responsible for the development of hospitality industry in India but the "Incredible India" campaign has been a major one which in a true sense has unveiled Indian tourism to the world and there by creating profitable opportunities for the growth of hospitality sector. Jaishree Anand Dean, National Institute of Tourism and Hospitality Management (NITHM) opines. In addition to other factors, Brand "Incredible India" has significantly contributed to the development of hospitality industry.[14]

The above mentioned facts make it clear that ascribing a brand name is essential for the development of hospitality industry. The hotel professionals need to strengthen the brand image. This focuses our attention on offering to the customers world class services. Besides, it is also pertinent that they keep on moving the process of defining and redefining the service quality. In this context, they have to assign due weightage to product strategy. You need products which helps tourists in evoking boredom. You need product providing to the tourists maximum enjoyment and tranquility. You need products to enrich the knowledge bank of tourists. You need offering pleasure and opportunities to adventurers. And you need product helping patients in getting cost-effective and world class medical aid. You need product of world class having uniqueness and cost-effectiveness. You need to be strategically sound and tactically profound.

FORMULATING THE HOTEL PRODUCT MIX

Offering world class services to the customers/guests is a prerequisite for the development of the hotel industry. This necessitates the formulation of a sound product mix which may be efficacious excelling stiff competition. The main task before the hoteliers is to make a combination of quality services at different stages so that the potential customers/guests are transformed into heavy/habitual guests. This would also help hotels in maximising the occupancy ratio of rooms and function-room. Today, customers expect refined services and decent behaviour. If we prepare a mix which makes available to the customers a package of both, the task of strengthening the business by word-of-mouth recommendation is considerably simplified. In simple words, 'Customer *is king'*.

To make hotel companies internationally competitive, policy makers and decision-makers bear the responsibility of formulating a sound product mix, of course, with the co-operation of their frontline staff. No doubt, all the four Ps are found important to the development of hotels but the first P, i.e., The Product, is considered to be the most important. Right from the generation of a new idea regarding the services to test marketing, the marketers are required to be involved in the process. We should remember it that no policies, strategies, decisions succeed in drawing the desired results unless the organisations/ companies involved in the hotel business (hospitality services) make sincere efforts to prepare a sound product mix. We bear the responsibility of modifying and innovating the services much earlier than our competitors. This will help us in capitalising on the opportunities and tapping the market potentials in this sector.

With the passage of time, the contours of development have undergone radical changes. The concepts and traditions of a family have now entirely changed. We find an apparent change in the lifestyle of almost all sections of the society. It is against this background that we advocate in favour of a change in the product mix. This is essential to survive and thrive in this fast growing business. It is also very natural that customers spending huge money for their comfortable stay would not make any compromise with the quality of services made available to them. Willingly or unwillingly, the hotel companies have to assign an overriding priority to the formulation of a sound product mix to satisfy and retain the customers. With the emerging new concept of spending more on the construction of a modern house and modern amenities, now the customers want something outstanding for the increased accommodation charges being paid by them. If we add attractions to our product, a sound foundation is engineered to process effectively the marketing activities in this sector.

The hoteliers are supposed to keep in mind the services offered by their competitors. The modification, alteration, innovation and elimination are other potential areas where decision-makers need to give immediate attention. In addition to the other factors, it is also important that hotels are located at easy accessible and prime locations. This implies accessibility and comforts to the customers. The place selected should be free from all industrial hazards. Our guests stay in hotels for availing the sophisticated amenities and facilities, i.e., the well furnished rooms, conference hall, restaurant, bar, shopping arcade, swimming pool, transportation facilities, first aid, travel information, and different personal care services keeping in view the emerging trends in the hospitality industry. It is also to be mentioned here that the formulation of the product mix would be in conjunction with the nature and character of a hotel.

In the context of formulating the product mix, it is pertinent that hotel companies assign due weightage to the peripheral services. Here, our emphasis is on the services required for making the stay comfortable and enjoyable. This includes the use of visa cards, currency exchange, shopping arcade, information regarding air tickets, information regarding the availability of transportation facilities, beauty salons for male and female customers, information regarding the tourist spots, information regarding various offices and all other services offered by the competitors. It is pertinent that we make efforts to have a fair blending of both core and peripheral services.

It is not to be forgotten that the product mix bears the efficacy of creating stimuli when we find it socially, culturally, psychologically and commercially tested. This necessitates professionalism. Pruning the non-viable products in the line or optimising the mix is an important task while designing the product mix. In addition to the pruning operation, the decision regarding the inclusion of new services in the mix is also found important.

A deeper product line is found essential for generating a positive response. This is due mainly to the fact that desires, needs, requirements are found divergent. The potential guests come from different regions and segments. If the hotel organisations are found captive and efficient to expand the product line, the services can be matched to the taste preferences of different segments of customers. The extent to which the marketers are successful in expanding and innovating the product line would have a telling impact on the net gains and customer satisfaction.[15] Here, the product line attraction is found important. This is meant locating hotels at such points where the guests can enjoy and gain pleasures, such as natural scenic beauty of historic excellence, and good environmental view, thus enjoying close affinity with nature. We find these underlying factors instrumental in attracting customers to hotels.

FORMULATING A SOUND PRODUCT STRATEGY

The crying need of the hour is to formulate a sound product strategy to give a boost to the hotel industry. Strategies play a vital role while accomplishing organisational goals. Unless we are aware of potential strategies, the set target cannot be achieved. While formulating sound strategy for the development of hotels, it is pertinent that we assign due weightage to the emerging trends in the tourism industry. The reason to do so pertains to the fact that tourists are the potential customers for the hotel industry. In addition, we also need detailed information about the development of corporate culture. Further, it is also significant that we turn our eyes on the growing number of affluent tourists. Recently, fall has been seen in the flow of tourists, specially coming from Japan and USA. Of course, this is due to the worldwide economic recession which has been making potential customers more sensitive to the price factor. Against this background, we find an increase in the low budget tourists. This makes the task of hotel companies more complicated as customers' expectations are gaining a rapid momentum and their spending power has been pruned to a large extent. This necessitates the development of hotels in the face of emerging trends and the economic criteria as far as tourists are concerned.

No doubt, we find a perceptible lack of hygienic and economically feasible or inexpensive hotels to cater to the growing number of low budget customers. In this context, the public sector should bear the responsibility of promoting the accommodation facilities by constructing private guest houses, tourist bungalows, paying guest accommodation, forest lodges, etc. So far as the development of standard hotels/star group of hotels is concerned, the private sector should accept the responsibility and invest in this area of the hospitality industry. The private sector investment needs to be attracted through fiscal and monetary incentives to ease the borrowing and repayment of credit, allotment of suitable sites at concessional rates and other concessions. This is simply to induce domestic or foreign investments in the hotel sector.

In the context of a sound product strategy, it is essential that we assign due weightage to the mix of services expected and desired by the potential customers. We need to make the information system strong enough to initiate suitable guidelines for the strategic decisions. What to offer, what to modify, what to alter, what to eliminate — these areas are found to be important to make our product decisions effective. And this task is suitably done, if hotel companies have a well developed information system. If we find that our competitors have been innovating their strategies, we have no option but to do the same. If we want to project our image as a leader, we have to initiate innovation much earlier than our competitors.

And innovation is to be based on information in this potential business sector. We need broad-based background information related to the local community, the local industry, communications, local events and attractions and the catchment area. In addition, the information regarding the facilities available in the hotel would be related to both — such as areas producing revenue and areas not generating financial returns. The information regarding the details of competition, are also to be collected regarding various facilities made available in a hotel including the prices, profile of potential customers, any planned expansion and information regarding any proposed new competition. Here, the information regarding the profile of the customers would be more important — age bracket, sex, type of group, place of employment, place of residence, mode of transport, room popularity, new guest, first choice, length of stay, any complaints and who made the booking. Besides, we also need information related to hotel activities, such as occupancy statistics, seat turnover percentage, number of empty days, pattern of sales in the restaurant and bar. The information related to the selling ability of the employees also carries some meaning such as analysis, list of staff employed between those who have a lot of contact with guests, some contact with guests and no contact with guests. This information is found significant while innovating the marketing decisions taken to boost the hotel industry.

It is not to be forgotten that needs of the guests are the cornerstone of marketing analysis. An in-depth study of what the competitors are doing, implementation of unique selling propositions to fulfil the needs of customers, determination of objectives and the formulation of strategies, advertise a promise which is genuine and credible and in which the customers can easily discern their own benefits. Keeping the promises simple, continuously managing the information and monitoring of the progress help marketers while formulating and reformulating the strategies. It is pertinent that we view everything from the customers' perspective. The accommodations available in a hotel are found significant, such as reception, uniform services and housekeeping. We need to concentrate on both the core and peripheral services. With a rapid increase in the level of competition in this industry, the competitors have been assigning due weightage to the peripheral services. While formulating marketing strategies, it is essential that we make efforts to include in our product-mix all the new services offered by our competitors. Not only the primary and auxiliary or core and peripheral but supportive services like property operations, maintenance of energy, central heating, air conditioning etc. also need due weightage.

Development process cannot remain static. This necessitates a continuous effort for incorporating the necessary changes in our service mix. The issue of concern here is — how and what to incorporate? Of course, this is significant to formulate a sound strategy. A sound product strategy is found a pre-requisite for establishing a fair or positive image. Image is the way in which a hotel portrays itself. Factors like atmosphere, brand name, the status type of people and corporate institutions patronising a hotel would prospect its fair image. And the most important thing for image projection is the quality of services and the behaviour of front-line personnel.

Here, we are not talking about unusual, nostalgic or historic hotels as these hotels survive and thrive even without modern personal facilities. You will find a seventeenth century hotel which does not have even private bathrooms to each bedroom but the hotel is so unique that we find a craze for a stay in that type of hotel. We also find old Palaces and Havelis transformed into hotels where guests feel fascinated to stay even without getting modern amenities and facilities for a comfortable stay. But these things do not carry any meaning when we think about the business strategies of modern hotels.

One of the visible trends in vogue over the past three decades is that facilities demanded by the public in hotels have increased substantially. Even major tour operators are doing a mass market business nowadays by including in their brochures a list of improved amenities and facilities to be made available to the tourists. The travel agents are also making advocacy in favour of the quality of services to be made available. These facts prove the proposition that marketing strategies should work towards ensuring and retaining customer loyalty.

In the context of formulating product strategy for hotels, it is also pertinent that the hotel management never promise to guests luxury because failing to do so would prove detrimental to the image of the hotel and its business. And therefore, the important thing is to promise potential guests 90 per cent of what we can achieve and offer. If we promise 100 per cent, it is very natural that even a minor shortfall would disappoint them. And if we promise 90 per cent and give them 95 per cent, they would be agreeably surprised. Promise less and offer more is the strategy which would help hotel companies in satisfying the customers. And therefore, what to promise is also an important decision-making area with the viewpoint of formulating a sound product strategy.

In short, hotels have to assign due weightage to the formulation of a sound product strategy which would be governed by a number of factors. Innovation is definitely impact-generating, specially with the growing competition in this potential business sector.

In the hotel services, the innovative decisions are required at almost all the stages. The services related to bedrooms, function room, restaurant, bar or the peripheral and supportive services are also to be improved. The strategic decisions related to different areas are given below:

Let's start from the bedrooms where guests stay and expect the best. Not only in India but around the world, we find designing of rooms keeping in view the taste and requirements of male and female customers. In the case of women, the norms should be equipped with basic amenities to meet their requirements. If rooms are designed keeping in view the needs of both the sexes and we train the management staff to pay special attention to the needs of women executives, this new emerging segment will, of course, stand to benefit. Besides, women tend to stay longer. Women do not feel comfortable in hotel bars and therefore, prefer lobby bars and lounges that are open, airy and relatively quiet. Spacious, clean and attractive rooms are usually a more preferable choice by female customers. Our staff should know it that the restaurant bill for a couple should no longer automatically be presented to the man. If the staff are not sure, they should place the bill in the center of the table. While managing restaurants the related staff should know about the lighting, proper importance of adequate ventilation and music. Besides, they should also offer specialities in the day's menu. While managing bars, it is important that the staff are aware of the changing trends in the quality and quantity of drinks. Of late, we find a change in the drinking habits of customers. In addition, the supportive services are also required to be innovated and upgraded from time to time.

In this context, the personal care service need a special mention. Moreover, hotels need to innovate their business strategies from time-to-time. Of late, jogging is in vogue today. You can include a map or a series of maps in room services with direction to nearby parks. Customers should also be supplied track suits and shoes in case they have not carried the same. The route map of jogging should be made interesting by displaying out-of-town jogging points which would be in close proximity to the hotel. We also find small compact exercise machines which can easily be adjusted in the function room. If you do not have sufficient space for tennis courts or a swimming pools, the options are paddle tennis or jacuzzi to relax in. If your hotels are not close to the golf course, with tennis courts, the option is to make available suitable alternative for exercise. You can also keep swimming pools in close proximity to the gym. The beauty parlours and other personal care services are also required to be made available to the customers. Besides, the first aid facilities and exquisite shopping arcade are now also found in a majority of the hotels.

The strategic decisions related to product make it essential that the hotel professionals have an in depth knowledge of the changing taste preferences of customers and they make their services distinct to their rivals. Frequent innovations in peripheral services may be preferred by them. Customisation is considered an essential dimension for boosting attraction. The Indian hotels in particular need to make their services of world class. They should take lessons from the international biggies. The hotel professionals while designing product strategy should not forget that it is only uniqueness of their competition. This is due to the fact that core services are found by and large of identical nature Innovative peripheral services thus determine the magnitude of your success. They should not forget that with the emergence of a cross-cultural society, we find a basic change in the food culture, lifestyles, taste preferences and levels of expectations. The guest staying in hotels have diverse motives and different time schedule. They come from different cultural background and belong to different regions. They have different style of communication, accent, flow and body language. At all the centres where the services are delivered, the hotel managers need to make it sure that promised quality of services are made available to the customers. The restaurants and bars are the sensitive points where even minor mistakes may result into irreparable losses. Like this, the swimming pools also need due care of hotel professionals. The cases of menu fatigue in restaurants, the cases of supply of poor quality of drinks in the bars and the cases of accident in the swimming pools may considerably tarnish the image of hotel. It is not only significant that you offer them quality services. It is equally important that you make it sure that they are really enjoying and gaining new experiences.

If we serve well, we promote well. Actually our task of promoting the business is considerably simplified; if the strategic decisions related to service quality are successful in satisfying and retaining the customers. Formulation of a sound product strategy, in which we outwit our competitors, is a crying need of the hour which would help Indian hospitality industry in enriching their strengths for becoming a quality leader.

SUMMARY

You have studied in this chapter, the product strategy for hotels. Before studying other aspects, let us have a brief recap of the definitions in the chapter.

- **Product:** A product is a bundle of utilities consisting of various product features and accompanying services. Hotel products are termed to be the service products.
- **Product - salient Features:** We call hotel product, the service product, of perishable nature, where presence of users is essential, demand is instable, supply position is rigid, quality is substantially influenced by the personnel working and is of largely psychological in nature.
- **Product Strategy:** In the hotel industry, the strategic decisions related to products are influenced by the emerging trends in the behavioural profile of users and the discretionary income. The strategy is to make possible innovation much earlier than competitors in the industry.
- **Product Life Cycle:** The life cycle studies of hotel services make it clear that hoteliers should make efforts to modify, alter and innovate the services keeping in view the stage of life cycle.

- **Failure of Product:** For failure of hotel services, there are a number of reasons, of course related to the formulation of four Ps.
- **Launching a New Product:** It is a risky proposition, specially when the services are new to both, the customers and the market. Here, the hoteliers should not take any decision in haste.
- **Stages of Product Screening:** Generation of new ideas, evaluation, business analysis and test marketing are the four important stages for the screening of product.
- **Branding:** It is an intrinsic aspect of the product strategy. It is a name, symbol or combination of the two. Hotels branding their products exercise and maintain a strong control over the quality.
- **The Hotel Product Mix:** An important task before the hoteliers is to formulate a sound product mix. This is meant including and eliminating or altering the services in tune with the changing market conditions. .
- **A Sound Product Strategy:** Formulation process of a sound product strategy for hotels is governed by a number of factors. It is essential that marketers are well aware of recent trends in the market condition, behavioural profile' of the users and the intensity levels of competition.

  We need product of world class having cost-effectiveness and uniqueness. We need product helping tourists in evoking their boredom. We need product offering maximum enjoyment and tranquility to our customers. We need to be strategically sound and tactically profound. We need innovations for enriching our strengths and becoming a quality leader.

KEY TERMS

Primary
Ancillary
Supportive
Peripheral
Fragile
Gym
Paddle Tennis
Product Life Cycle
Steam bath
Product Screening
Branding
Lago
Lagotype
Brand Stretching
Snake Charmer
IT hub
Exotic Fun
Folklore
Baby-boomers Group
Mythology
e-commerce
Boredom
Incredible India
Global biggies
Shopping arcade
Menu Fatigue
Internet
Online
Pilgrimage
Beverages
No-frills
Budget Hotels

REVIEW QUESTIONS

1. What do you mean by Hotel Product?
2. What do you mean by Product Life Cycle? Do you find PLC helpful in formulating the product strategy? Defend your arguments.
3. Discuss the key reasons for the failure of hotel product.
4. Do you find product screening essential for studying the viability of hotel rooms? Justify your opinion.
5. Throw light on the different stages of product screening.
6. Focus on the core and peripheral services in the context of hotel industry.
7. Formulate a sound product mix for hotel.
8. What do you mean by Brand? Explain the "Incredible India" as a brand to promote the hospitality industry.
9. Explain the relevance of studying behavioural profile and taste preferences of customers for the formulation of a sound product mix for hotel business.

APPLICATION EXERCISES

1. Formulate a product strategy for hospitality industry keeping in view the significant changes in the taste preferences and lifestyles of customers in the Indian perspective.
2. You have been working as a hotel manager and in that capacity identify the reasons for the failure of hotel product.
3. An in-depth study of Product Life Cycle simplifies the task of hoteliers, specially while formulating a sound product strategy. Comment on this statement in the capacity of a hotel professional.
4. Right from the generation of idea to the best marketing, the hoteliers need to watch the developments in the different stages of product screening. In the capacity of a hotelier, focus on the role you have to play while screening the product.
5. "Adding perceived values and differentiating the product from others are the two important reasons for giving a product the brand name." Comment on this statement as a hotel manager.
6. "Launching of a new product is a risky proposition." Focus on this statement as a hotel professional.
7. "Behavioural profile of guests, emerging trends in the market conditions, mounting intensity of competition are found important considerations for the formulation of a sound product strategy." Throw light on this statement as a marketing professional.

End Notes:

1. Kotler, P.: *Marketing Management;* Prentice Hall of India, New Delhi, 1990, p. 445.
2. Alderson Z Wroe: *Marketing Behaviour and Executive Action;* Homewood III, 1975, p. 274.

3. Melvyn Greene: *Marketing Hotels, and Restaurant into the 90s;* Heinemann Professional Publishing, 1989, p. 99.
4. Jha, S.M.: *Services Marketing;* Himalaya Publishing House, Bombay, 1994, pp. 240-42.
5. Smallwood, J.E.: *The Product Life Cycle: A Key to Strategic Marketing Planning;* MSU, Business Topics, Winter, 1973, pp. 24-35.
6. Bernard C. and M. Chevalier: *Market Share Strategy and the Product Life Cycle;* Journal of Marketing, October, 1974, pp. 29-31.
7. Holloway J.C. and Plant R.V.: *Marketing for Tourism;* Pitman, UK, 1992, p. 74.
8. *Ibid.*
9. Jha, S.M.: *Tourism Marketing;* Himalaya Publishing House, Bombay, 1995, pp. 160-61.
10. Holloway J.C. & Plant R.V.: *Op. cit.,* p. 66.
11. Eleventh Five Year Plan, Planning Commission, Govt. of India, New Delhi, Vol. III, pp. 245-525.
12. Jha, S.M.: *Tourism Marketing*; Himalaya Publishing House, Mumbai, 2009, Chap. 15.
13. Ray & Teckchandani: Indian Hotel Industry: Strategy Building; The ICFAIAN Journal of Management & Research, Vol. VII/5, 2008.
14. Interview with Jaisres Anand, Dean, NITHM, Hyderabad; *The Analyst*, November, 2006.
15. Jha, S.M.: *Services Marketing*; Himalaya Publishing House, Mumbai, 2009, Chap. 12.

....ꝏꝏꝏ....

CHAPTER - 7

HOTEL PROMOTION STRATEGY

The success rate of a hotel professional is coiled in the essence of converting the inquiries into bookings and transforming the casual visitors into habitual visitors. With the increasing heat of globalisation and competition, the professionals need world class excellence so that sensitisation and persuasion make the ways for transformation.

CHAPTER OBJECTIVES

Introduction – Promotion: The Concept – Components of Promotion – Why do we Promote? – Word-of-mouth Promotion – Personal Selling – Why face-to-face Selling is of Greater importance? – Non-verbal Communication – How to Make Possible Face-to-face Selling? – Expression Techniques – Skill Needed for Personal Selling – Sales Sequence – Advertising – Importance of Advertising to Hotel Industry – Advertisement Planning – Media Decision – Selection of Message – Advertising Agencies – The Communication Process and Its Barriers – Testing Advertising Effectiveness – Advertising Campaign – Advertising Strategy – Advertising in Hotel – Public Relations – Sales Promotion – Telemarketing – Cause – Related and Sponsorship Marketing – Hotel Promotion Strategy in Indian Perspective – Summary – Key Terms – Review Questions – Application Exercises – End Notes.

LEARNING OBJECTIVES

This chapter aims at studying the different dimensions of promotion strategy in the context of hotel industry. The motive is to sensitise the readers to the formulation of a sound promotion strategy which is found proactive but cost-effective. The readers come to know about the application of different components of promotion in the hospitality industry. The components like advertising, publicity, sales promotion, personal selling, telemarketing, cause-related and sponsorship marketing and word-of-mouth promotion need due attention of hotel professionals to inform, sense, sensitise, persuade and transform the potential customers into actual and habitual customers.

INTRODUCTION

Creativity makes the ways for sensitivity which opens doors for acceptability. If you have assigned due weightage to service quality, your task of promoting the business is considerably simplified. The success rate of a hotel professional is coiled in the essence of converting the inquiries into bookings and transforming the casual visitors into habitual visitors. The strategists or the decision-makers are required to play a catalytic role in the entire process. In making the promotional decisions, the hotel professionals have to see that all possible merchandising aids are available. Attractive and well equipped accommodation is made available at the reception desk which is also required to maintain a file of service facilities providing additional information on each room such as location, size, decor, furnishing, etc. Besides, the desk is also required to maintain a file history of its customers both past and present mentioning information like name, home, business address, nationality, credit card rating, likes and dislikes, etc. With the increasing sophistication in ICT, the responsibility of the reception desk has been made easier.

The hotel professionals have a number of options for promoting the business which may be used depending upon the situational requirements and financial provisions. The impersonal or non-promotional strategies also play an effective role in promoting the hotel business. In the group of impersonal promotion, we find advertisement, public relations and sales promotion. Advertisements play an effective role in promoting the hotel business and the hospitality industry. The advertisement measures must be successful in informing, sensing, sensitising, persuading and transforming the potential customers into actual and habitual customers. The print media, broadcast media and telecast media are the options. The sensitive points or strategic points are airports railway stations, bus stops, central place of the city, shopping malls, departmental stores and super markets, offices of the travel agents and office of tourism department.

The publicity or public relations are found influenced by rapport developed by the hotel professionals with the media people, academics, cine artists, mass leaders, celebrities throwing less financial burden on the hotels but providing much more positive results. The professional excellence of hotel managers determines the magnitude of success of publicity.

The sales promotion measures offer a number of incentives to the potential customers and the marketing people engaged in the process of increasing the occupancy ratio. A number of tools or schemes are used for this purpose which help hotel professionals in touching the target.

Particularly in the hotel industry where we find seasonal fluctuation influencing the business, the innovative measures for sales promotion may play an incremental role.

In the hotel industry, personal selling occupies a place of outstanding significance. A hotel receptionist plays an important role not only by selling accommodation but also by generating business for the hotel. The receptionists are thus the nerve center of a hotel. An efficient receptionist is supposed to give due attention to internal selling by encouraging guests to acknowledge the hotel and gain maximum benefits from the service facilities paid for money. A receptionist working in hotel should have attractive personality and he/she must be enthusiastic towards the job, ambitious and respectful to the demands of the guests. He/she is supposed to sell high and to act with the notion that the guests are delivered the promised quality of services. In activating personal promotion, the travel agents also play an effective role. The receptionists also arrange travel services through effective contact with airlines, steamship, railways, companies, rental car organisation, bus companies etc. The travel agents promote the hotel industry in many ways. They help in increasing the occupancy ratio of bedrooms and function rooms. We cannot deny the fact that the hotel business rests on the instrumentality of personal promoters.

In an age of new generation of ICT, we find telemarketing also active in promoting the hotel business. The communication excellence of telemarketers and the sophistication found in the instruments and equipments used by them in the process determine the magnitude of success. They may transform the inquiries into bookings.

Since we find corporate societal responsibility drawing priority attention of boardrooms in almost all the organisations, the hospitality industry cannot be spared from the social responsibility. The cause-related and sponsorship marketing may be used by them for promoting the business where they would be required to get their hotels, chains, groups involved in the social transformation process.

The word-of-mouth promotion is considered the most effective component for promoting the hotel business. The satisfied group of customers convey their feelings and experiences to their friends and relatives which may be found much more effective. Conversely, the dissatisfied customers act in a negative way and the negative effects of word-of-mouth promotion are found three times more than the positive effects. Thus, we find customers acting as a hidden sales force very much instrumental in promoting the business provided the hotels are sincere and honest while fulfilling their promises.

The hotel professionals need to make use of the different components of promotion with the motto of promoting the business and maintaining the cost economy. With the increasing heat of competition, the professionals need to show their world class excellence so that sensitisation and persuasion make the ways for transformation.

PROMOTION: THE CONCEPT

At the outset, we go through the conceptual aspect of promotion. We consider promotion a managerial process to inform, sense, sensitise, persuade and transform the potential customers into actual customers. It is a device to communicate the outstanding properties of different mixes to the customers with the motto of influencing them. It is an effective tool in the hands of a professional to create awareness. The hotel companies offer a number of services to the customers. The promotion proves to be a mix for communicating to the customers the outstanding properties of services, developing their awareness of the pricing as a motivational tool, informing them regarding the channels through which the services may reach to them, impressing upon them by offering a suitable service delivery. Thus promotion is found to be an effective sub-mix of marketing through which the messages reach to the target audience.

COMPONENTS OF PROMOTION

In Figure 7.1, we find different components of promotion. The hotel professionals need to make use of promotional measures in the face of their changing requirements.

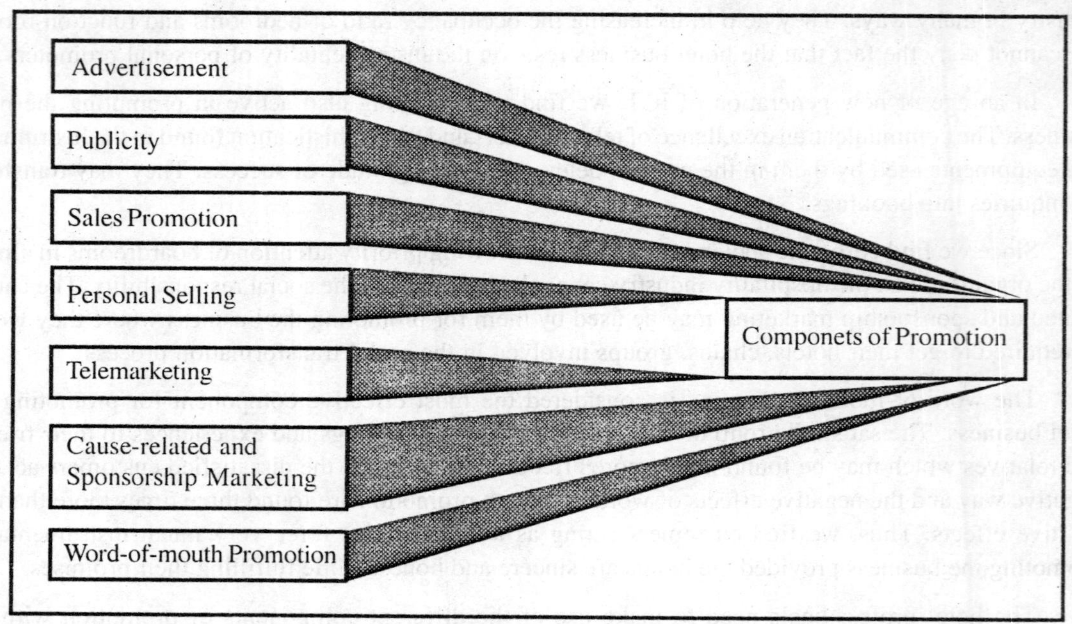

FIG 7.1: COMPONENTS OF PROMOTION

Advertising is a paid form of persuasive communication in which print media, broadcast media and telecast media are the vehicles. The publicity is an unpaid form of persuasive communication in which the professionals develop rapport with the media people, academics, celebrities and other known persons. The sales promotion is a temporary method for achieving the target through hotel people and travel agents. The personal selling is a method used by agents. The telemarketing is used by telemarketers. The cause-related and sponsorship marketing is to meet societal responsibility. The word-of-mouth promotion is a method used by satisfied group of customers.

WHY DO WE PROMOTE?

An important question is raised, here regarding the justifications for promotion through the electronic and the print media as almost all the organisations producing goods or generating services are found using this sub-mix of the marketing mix in a big way. In brief, it can be said that we promote, service facilities/products to persuade, inform, remind and reinforce. The four aspects are discussed here:

1. To Persuade: One of the most important aims of promotion to customers is to act, i.e., to go out and buy. It is also used to encourage customers to adopt a particular attitude towards a product or to improve the image of the products launched by the company. Persuasion is an important aspect even in the hotel business leading to substantial generation of revenues through customers. Unless they come to the hotels, this is not possible. This strategy will be of benefit to a lucrative business like, hotel industry.

2. To Inform: Promotion is found instrumental in conveying information on the product such as the name and price, details about its availability including its outstanding features or specialties. It is very natural that all hotels do not offer uniform services. The potential guests come to know about the specialties only through promotional strategies like advertisements.

3. To Remind: Promotion is also used to remind customers time and again that an old established product is still available in a better format. If customers visit a hotel, it is not essential that they remember. Generally to transform the casual visitors into habitual visitors, this plays an effective role.

4. To Reinforce: Promotion is also used to reinforce customer satisfaction by emphasising that they have made a right decision by accommodating themselves in a particular hotel. This paves way for effective reinforcement. It is not to be forgotten that in the hotel business, this strategy is found playing an outstanding role. This helps in increasing the occupancy ratio of rooms in a hotel.

In this context, it is important to talk about the AIDA model related to the buyer's behaviour as shown in Figure 7.2 This model is important while influencing the foreign tourists.

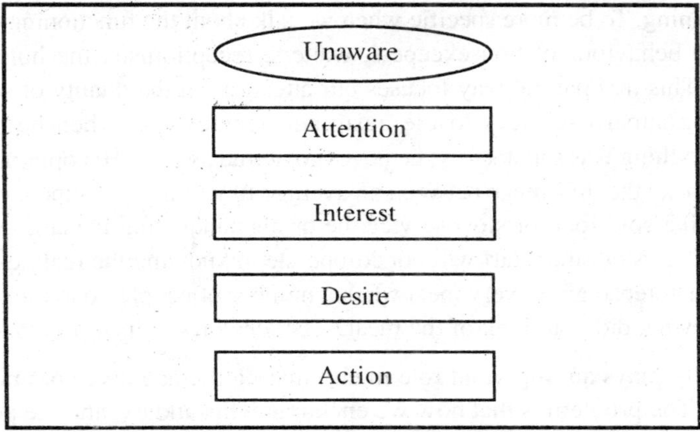

FIG. 7.2: AIDA MODEL

As shown in Figure 7.2, there is a hierarchy of effects as buyers move through each stage. Initially, the potential buyers lack information on important tourist resorts and services made available by the hotels. This tends to become a challenging task for marketers to attract and retain potential customers so that they become aware of the outstanding specialties of a particular hotel. This would considerably ensure customer loyalty. The promotional strategies are found playing a decisive role while generating interest — which then creates a desire to visit that hotel or tourist spot again. If the desire is generated, it is very natural that they would prefer to visit that hotel. It is not to be forgotten that the AIDA model is found effective only when we talk about luxury hotels or hotels giving special services in their product mix plan.

 WORD-OF-MOUTH PROMOTION

We cannot deny that in the hotel industry, the best form of selling is through word-of-mouth promotion. But the problem with this form of oral communication is that it is a time consuming process. According to the principle of Pareto, if a person is satisfied with the product he/she is going to tell six people but if we find them dissatisfied, they tell thirteen people. A satisfied group of customers play an important role in the word-of-mouth communication. At the same time, we find dissatisfied customers more dangerous because the negative word-of-mouth promotion is found very fast with a high multiplier effect. If we find a customer visiting hotel and enjoying quality services and gaining new experiences, he/she communicates to his/her friends and relations as a hidden sales force and positive remarks of satisfied customers help in making new customers. Just reverse to it, if we find a customer dissatisfied with services or behaviour, the transmission process is not delayed. We cannot deny the fact that one bad meal will often do more damage by word-of mouth than fifty good meals.[1] Our guests take a good meal for granted but don't forget to complain to their friends about a bad meal. Of course, they are free to complain to the hotelier or the restaurant owners but often they do not act. We find them close mouthed and stiff-lipped till they make a good-bye and after going back, they think twice before coming to that hotel again. In addition, they do not recommend such a hotel to their friends and relatives. This shows the impact of word-of-mouth promotion specially in the hotel industry.

It is in this context that we find world class services and decent behaviour of hotel personnel carrying important meaning. To be more specific when we talk about the functioning of restaurants, bars, cafes and the role and behaviour of housekeepers, waiters, receptionists; the hotel professionals are required to be careful. This in a natural way focuses our attention on the quality of services of hotels. A hotel manager offering superb services to the customers opines that when he asked the function organisers whether everything was satisfactory, he never got a true answer. His opinion is that it is a series of small points which make the difference between an average function and a superb one. He felt that if it was something major like cold food or slow service, he or his banqueting manager would spot it. After knowing the fact that waiters or other staff will not co-operate in knowing the realities, he started to sit in the toilet with a pen and notepad after every meal when a number of people go to the toilet. He found that many asked each other what did you think of the meal? The feedback helped him in knowing the fact.

Thus oral publicity plays an important role in eliminating the negative comments and improving the quality of services. The problem is that how we encourage this and expand the potential. Almost all the hotels use oral publicity even if we find them engaged in other activities. An important thing here is to put the name of your hotels in the memory of privileged guests so that they remember you and visit your hotel as and when they get an opportunity. It is also pertinent that guests remember your name, address, telephone number etc. You find people always talking about the decent services of a hotel in which they received the best treatment but if you ask them what was the hotel and food like in many cases, they rarely remember. How can one really exploit the potential of the oral publicity, if the hidden sales force or the so called unpaid publicists forget the name of your hotel. We find certain cases where the guests can remember your name. Firstly guests remember a name, if it is the name of a person, e.g., "Joe Allen in Covent Garden." Secondly, they remember a name if it is associated with the theme of the decor of the location, e.g., "The Greenhouse in Mayfair", or the "Swan at Thames Ditton." A much higher proportion of oral publicists remember your name if you give them something to take away with the name on it, or follow them up with some message in the post, e.g., hotel brochure, book matches, sewing kits, shower caps, fringe benefits, gifts on festive occasions or just a follow-up letter, thanking them and hope to see them again. By doing so, we get better results and feedback from oral publicity. We can also use the menu for purposes outside the restaurant by a large print run and giving them away[2]. In addition, we can also offer to them a pen that can be kept by the side of their telephone set.

We can quote David Levin of The Capital Hotel, Street, Knights bridge, as one of the most successful independent British hotel owners and operators. When he opened another restaurant, The Green-house Mayfair, he gave away a packet with a seed and instructions on how to sow and transplant them in a pot. The long lasting plant is a point of memory. People ask about the plant and it promotes the restaurant. You can recommend numerous people to that restaurant by word-of-mouth when people start talking and appreciating the plant.

Thus, it is right to opine that in hotel business, the hidden sales force or oral publicists play an outstanding role in promoting the hotel business for which you have to pay nothing. Hence, it is significant that we get the co-operation of the hidden sales force. For this, well-equipped accommodations, restaurants and bars are required to be improved. You have to be careful that the guests are offered all the promised services and the housekeepers are behaving decently towards the customers. In the restaurants, quality food is served keeping in view the taste of your guests and also keeping in mind that the food served to them is not going to generate *menu fatigue*. In the bars, you have to be careful that they are served quality drinks in a decent way. In addition, you have also to think about the gifts to be offered to your guests so that they can speak words of appreciation for your hotel, restaurant and subsequently promote your business effectively.

If we talk about the effectiveness of this tool of promotion, we find it a two-step communication method in which messages are transmitted to market opinion leaders. We include different persons in the list of opinion leaders, such as major business executives, representatives of the mass media, social workers, leaders of a travelling party etc. An important question regarding the instrumentally of this promotional tool is related to its magnitude of sensitivity and level of acceptability. Why do we find this tool so effective? Of course, a plain answer to this question is the positive opinion of customers who have experienced the quality of your services and are found satisfied with the same. If our friends or relatives communicate to us the positive points regarding the services that they were made available in a hotel or a restaurant, it is very natural that we desire to visit the same again. Against this background, the customers' satisfaction is found to be an integral part of oral publicity. This creates a potential market in a very natural way and helps in planning budget for promotion. Word-of-mouth recommendation is the result of satisfaction. If we scientifically engineer the product mix, we find all possibilities for getting a positive response. Here, you have to be careful that the customers are in a position to appreciate the services offered by the hotel, restaurant when you offer to them a gift as a complement for having stayed in the hotel as a potential customer.

PERSONAL SELLING

Nothing happens unless anyone sells something and nothing is sold unless the buyers are motivated to purchase things of their choice and preference. The oral representation in conversation bears the efficacy of transforming motivation into persuasion, provided the management of sales force is effective in generating substantial revenues by selling the services. Personal selling consists of contracting prospective buyers of products personally.[3] Hence, persuasion is here the main thing in accelerating the pace of marketing. We persuade investors to invest, persuade suppliers to supply the raw materials on reasonable terms and conditions and persuade markets to patronise the product. Of course, this is found to be the most sensitive tool of promotion. We find it a highly distinctive form of promotion — having two-way communication. No doubt, the goods or services are found half sold, if the special features or properties of the product are well told and acknowledged. This art of "selling" or "telling" is more impact-generating, when we talk about the hotel services industry. Every business house — be it insurance, travel and tourism, the hotel industry, the professionally trained sales force with them, an in built creativity, innovation and imagination play an important role in giving a potential boost to business of any category. Persuasion through motivation is the main source for profit generation including customer satisfaction.

The hotel business industry is sizeably influenced by personal selling — which brings substantial momentum in the business. The feedback received from the sales force helps marketers in designing the development plan. Besides transmission of first hand information is also an outstanding contribution of personal selling, helpful in making marketing decisions creative and sensitive.

Personal selling is also found to be a highly distinctive form of promotion which involves social behaviour. The social characteristics of personal selling make it an activity which is found difficult to manage. Foster says, *"Personal selling is the personal persuasion of a tangible product* or *intangible service or idea to the potential customers"*.[4] The products, pricing and markets in particular, determine the nature and form of personal selling required. For holidays, the personal selling is initiated through travel agents and at the sales office which a tour operator may have. In the hotel industry, the sales force are found responsible for dealing with the customers behind the counter, e.g., receptionists, hotel waiters, barstaff, porters, hotel cleaners.[5] All of them play a decisive role in ensuring that the hotel services are satisfying and appreciated by the guests.

Service does not mean servility. The Phrase — 'the customer is right', applies specifically to the hotel industry. The sales personnel are required to be friendly in dealings and cheerful in expression. To put it another way, personnel and services offered by them are found indivisible. However, the phrase has its own limitations. This makes it clear that the hotel business is linked with the performance and behaviour of the sales force. They are required to be helpful and patient and above all, they should appear friendly and work towards customers' satisfaction.

For selling, we find 'empathy' playing a vital role. Here, our emphasis is on projecting yourself in a right way empathy is substantially influenced by projection, i.e., the ability to project yourself. Projection is a combination of technique and psychology. The technique is related to your way of strategic words of promotion and presenting the offer. Psychology is related to one's ability to understand and deal with the people. We find more dynamism in technique as it is found to be always changing. If the circumstances are different, if the characters playing the role are different, it is very natural that the dealings would be subsequently different. As for example, if you are selling an identical product in your hotel, e.g., a four day convention for 400 delegates, you are supposed to sell this directly communicating in the actual function room, in the office of the buyers which might be private and quiet, or in an open office, to a committee, in a foreign country. An important point to be clarified here is that in all circumstances, we find different sales techniques. You may have enough time for making preparation, or you may be called at a moment's notice.

Hence, the sales force cannot refute the fact that they have nothing to learn about selling or claim that they are very good at selling. 'Selling is a continuous learning process'. We find enough scope for improving the sales technique as this is a field of continuous growth where one can never stop learning about peoples psychology. Against this background, one should never stop improving his/her sales ability. Thus, you always find ample scope for improvement — even if you are considered the best. To be more specific in direct face selling, you have to understand the psychology of the people and appreciate their needs. In hotels and fast food service, we often have to face the worst side of the people. It is against this background that we find face-to-face selling difficult but of greater importance and at the same time very interesting. An important question in this very context is as to why direct selling is of greater importance than any other sales technique. The following facts support this proposition in a major way.

WHY FACE-TO-FACE SELLING IS OF GREATER IMPORTANCE

1. Instant communication: The first is regarding the sales situation, where we find direct instant communication, and can also get reactions from the buyers. Here, the buyers are found free to raise questions. You face buyers either in your hotel or in the potential guests' own office.

2. Rapport can be developed: We find it an opportunity to move a prospect forward to achieve the pre-set sales objectives and finally seeing the prospect going for a booking in a particular hotel. This is the point where we find face-to-face communication. Not only this, it also provides the most sensitive condition to establish a personal relationship. A good rapport is thus possible. However large a hotel is, the importance of customers having a relationship with an authority cannot be underestimated. Its importance lies in two negative situations. It is very natural that every hotel has some plus and minus points. There are a few hotels having adequate facilities for every different sources of business or every different category of buyer. It is also very difficult to find a hotel where we find everything okay. Even in a big hotel with more than 150 rooms, if you survey the guests, they would point out a number of drawbacks.

3. Shortcomings can be identified: If we develop a rapport, it is possible to get the true estimate of the reactions of the guests. In a hotel, it was the feeling of a hotel manager that everything is right. The manager asked five of his regular visitors whether this was true. Almost all the five complained about three lapses — inadequately lit rooms (they said the light switches were not immediately inside the bedroom door); bathroom shelf in front of the mirror was too deep so some had to wear their glasses to shave; and they all felt that the two hotel elevators or lifts were not functioning properly, much slower in the morning when they were hurrying out to work. Of course, all of them had good personal relations with the hotel manager and the problems (realities) were identified and rectified immediately.

4. Preventing regular customers trying another hotel: If we have developed good personal relations, it is also possible that our guests narrate their difficulties and we try our best to correct them. Suppose, our guests find it difficult to stay as a series of things have gone wrong. Or, his accommodation budget has been reduced by the head office. If there is a personal relationship, we find a much greater chance that the guests will communicate this to the manager who would ensure appropriate action in this case. But if good personal relationships are lacking, so, he just leaves your hotel.

In view of the above, it is right to say that face-to-face selling is found significant as this will pave way for developing personal relationship and open more avenues for personal selling. To be more specific in the hotel business, this element is found playing an outstanding role. All the personnel directly related to guests are substantially involved in the process. It is against this background that personal promotion becomes an important tool of the promotional decisions. It is not only sufficient that we make provisions for refined services. It also bears an outstanding significance that our personnel meant for selling the right services are exercising their faculties cost-effectively.

NON-VERBAL COMMUNICATION

In addition to the positive effects of face-to-face selling pointed out earlier, this area has one other major advantage — that of non-verbal communication. In the face-to-face selling, we find a situation where it is possible to practice non-verbal communication. It is very natural that a number of potential guests do not like to comment or to speak anything while going through a dialogue with the business executives or other personnel. You can watch here the movement of your potential guests. Suppose, a new customer has come to your office. Generally, you are supposed to follow the practice of not selling too much as soon as he is seated. At the outset, you may ask him whether he wants a coffee/cold drink/ tea and you start selling by giving a patient hearing, if he wants to talk. You are supposed to move gradually, of course, in a logical sequence. Believe it or not, the good clue is to identify the way and style of the future prospects/buyers. When we get an opportunity to sit down in a strange or a new office, we do not sit on the whole chair, we sit on the two-third portion of the chair and do not lean back. The moment you find him on the full chair, he begins to relax. You find his eyes resting on you and his attention on your selling activities. Whatever the messages you are transmitting are now sincerely received by the prospects. This is the high point where you find your communication sensitive and focal receptive.

Besides, we also find other advantage of face-to-face communication — i.e., it is easier to sense the vibrations (outcome) or chemistry of a business meeting. We cannot get it from any audio visual link-up. You find a time when the potential guest is found tired and led up or in the gap of some — possible indication that the meet may not end on good terms, despite putting in the best to attract customers. Here is the acid test of your professionalism. If your are positive, it is possible to change the whole chemistry of the meeting as he is receiving right vibrations from you. Just by watching the attitude of the customers, you can easily identify the mental state of the customers. In a busy restaurant, it is to identify the temperament, the reactions just by watching the drumming of fingers and the swiveling head. This speaks of the fact that the face-to-face selling has a number of positive points.

HOW TO MAKE POSSIBLE SUCCESSFUL FACE-TO-FACE SELLING?

The following aspects are found instrumental in raising the effectiveness of face-to-face selling. Research, planning, communication, consumer-orientation and others are important in this very context.

1. Research: It is an important aspect for raising the effectiveness of your efforts. You are supposed to carry as much research as possible in advance. This will simplify your task of understanding the customers.

2. Planning: It is also considered to be essential for successful face-to-face selling. The detailed planning of sales call/situation including setting of your objective would prove beneficial in many ways.

3. *Communication:* This is related to your communications with the client. You are supposed to watch the attitude of your customers. In any case, you have not to be vocal even if you find something wrong in your customers. You have to use soft words and decent behaviour. It is your communicative ability to be more specific, in the personal selling which would lead to achieving the desired results — that of satisfying and retaining customers.

4. Consumer-orientation: You have to be consumer-oriented. Guests are always right. With this notion, you have to deal with everything. This orientation would simplify your task of dealing with customers. To make it possible, it is pertinent that you are well aware of the profile of guests.

5. ***Close of sales***: It is also found instrumental in raising the effectiveness of your efforts. The whole objective behind any form of selling is to close and obtain some actual business. We should not feel that any comment on closing a sale, obtaining a booking and achieving an objective is a waste of time. You get business after some enquiries. This may be by letter or over the telephone. We also find provisional booking. If you get an enquiry over the telephone, you should try to ask one question, When are you thinking of coming? You should try for at least a provisional booking. We cannot deny the fact that the close is one of the most difficult things to achieve. In this context, we find some important facts as mentioned below:

1. *Set achievable objective*: While setting objectives, be sure that objectives are achievable. It should not be merely be fact gathering and research. It would be better not to display those services which they do not want. If he wants to book his annual dinner dance without seeing your function rooms, you should bypass his more limited objectives and take the booking. It is not to be forgotten here that if you move step by step, the outcome is likely to be positive.
2. *Identify your guests:* There are three types of people, e.g., people who make decisions, people who advice decision-makers and people who carry out the decisions. It is possible to obtain an objective and a booking more easily from the first group of people, e.g., the decision-makers. But they are found very busy. Thus, it is right to sell initially to the second group, i.e., person advising the decision-makers. In every company, we find some persons playing this role. In this context, you need some telephonic research. The third group is the largest, people complicating your task in proving this case successful one.

Situations where the potential guests come to you

The following are the situations where the potential guests come to you. In the context of face-to-face selling, it is essential to be aware of these situations:

1. It is significant that you set your objectives beforehand. Knowledge of the guests before their arrival, such as full name, his/her requirements, his/her employment position and date of arrival are found important here.
2. You are supposed to keep index history at your desk. In case it is a first enquiry, you should get it ready for a meeting.
3. The information should be transmitted to the receptionist and porters that a guest with the details mentioned therein is expected to come on (the date) and at (a particular time). This would help in the hotel management greeting him by name.
4. Try your best to receive the guest at the reception-desk and be punctual about the meetings.
5. Introduce yourself by stating your surname, be friendly rather than familiar. Try to break down the formal barriers — usually seen in first meetings.
6. Select a suitable place which is quiet, specially for the meeting.
7. You should offer to your guest coffee/cold drink/tea/cigarette. You need special care when a guest is coming to your hotel for the first time.
8. Avoid physical or mental barriers, such as a desk between you and your guest, chairs unnecessary papers on the table. This would initiate effective direct talk with the customer.
9. Present the outstanding services to be offered by you in brief.

10. Always ask direct questions so that he is not confused.
11. Avoid interruption by your personnel or telephone.
12. Keep yourself well informed.
13. Avoid interruption when he starts talking, but try to continue the conversation till you come to a conclusion.
14. Allow adequate time for a meeting.
15. During the sales meeting, mention the cost of accommodation in clear terms.
16. What do you feel? Have you achieved your objective?

You cannot be sure that you are not going to lose a sale, even if you have given due weightage to all the points mentioned earlier. Hence, it is pertinent that you try to avoid some personal aspects, such as insincerity, disrespect, distraction, unfriendliness, doubt, unreliability, disproportionate enthusiasm and extending, inadequate knowledge of the product or client/customer and overconfidence. This would help you in projecting a fair image of the hotel.

EXPRESSION TECHNIQUES

While face-to-face selling, you are also supposed to see that you do not lose a sale on account of technique expressions. The expression techniques are:

1. ***Eyes:*** Look straight in the eyes without staring. In a few cases, we find some people looking at you or looking down when they are asked a question. If your eyes are not concentrated, you may lose his attention.
2. ***Voice:*** To the extent it is possible, try to keep your voice varied and interesting. You should avoid talking in a monotone, short delivery after pause and dropping the voice at the end of every sentence.
3. ***Speech:*** Your speech should be clear. Do not change your original accent, otherwise the business communication would be ineffective and confusing. Always maintain natural flair in initiating sales to a large extent.
4. ***Attitude*:** You are supposed to be positive. If you are really interested in seeing the business develop, you should develop enthusiasm.
5. ***Listening*:** Often, the efficient salesmen are found good listeners. We consider it the halfway to be a successful salesman. Against this background, we find it a prerequisite for an efficient salesman. Learning is an art as it generates concentration and creates interest in the people. It also flatters people, if you listen to them patiently. Of course, there is a time when you have to stop listening — you will have to await.

Appraisal of Selling Technique

Before and after a sales call, you should check the points mentioned below. Try to judge your performance on the basis of Exhibit 7.1.

EXHIBIT 7.1

1. Appointment getting and planning	2. Planning pre-call
3. Punctuality	4. Greeting
5. Your appearance	6. Information seeking
7. Yes to questions	8. Listening
9. Not interrupting	10. Control of interview
11. Closing	12. Product knowledge
13. Empathy	14. Business ethics
15. Mannerism	16. Originality
17. Handling	18. Logic
19. Use of alternatives	20. Ask for sale

We cannot deny the fact that selling with integrity is as professional as practising law or accountancy. This requires professionalism, excellence, patience. It is against this background that personal selling plays a vital role, specially in the hotel business where the successful salesmen are found helping generate large revenues to your business in many ways.

SKILL NEEDED FOR PERSONAL SELLING

To be more specific, in the hotel industry, it is difficult to motivate the guests, which, requires both personal and social skill. In both categories, we find verbal and non-verbal communications in initiating cost-effective personal selling.

Personal Skill: At the initial stage, when the hotel receptionists, housekeepers, waiters, travel clerks encounter their clients or guests, the first impression projected by them will have a far-reaching impact. The appearance and proper grooming of the personnel dealing with the guests plays a significant role. We find a number of tourist organisations and hotel companies paying attention to regulating the same. Of course, it is not judicious to invade the privacy of an individual. Presenting a good show by the personnel goes a long way in influencing the image of your hotel. The hotel personnel here should realise that their way of dealing with customers and behaviour are found influencing the business. They should learn to adjust to the constraints (which are usually forced) under the service conditions. In almost all the standard hotels we find that personal grooming of the staff is given importance, and certain provisions are given to the personnel like uniforms — keeping in view of their position. Though we find that USA Continental Airlines were judged to have acted illegally when they dismissed a female employee with an exemplary professional record for refusing to wear make-up.[6] In this context, it is significant to mention that hotel personnel coming into close contact with customers must be fastidious about personal hygiene. This draws our attention on the hygiene criteria — with oral and dental care, restrictions on food may offend clients or guests such as garlic or onions and a pleasing disposition, which matters a lot in any client servicing industry.

Here, we also assign due weightage to deportment since we communicate verbally as well as non-verbally. This needs due care on the way we walk, sit or stand that is, the whole behaviour of the staff is taken into perspective. We cannot deny the fact that these communicate or reflect an attitude of their mind towards the job. The staff is required to have an alert disposition and avoid slouching when they walk and to sit upright instead of first slumping in a chair. Clothes must be clean and neatly pressed. We find a number of hotel companies conveying a corporate image and presenting a uniform appearance. Hotel, airlines, car rental staff, courier services, tourist resort representatives and travel agents are required to assign due weightage to a well written corporate image. We find these non-verbal communications conveying a lot to the guests, the image of hotels and hotel companies. If the hotel personnel succeed in projecting a fair image, it is very natural that verbal and non-verbal communications (a result of personal skill and care) would pave the way for substantial business. This makes it essential that the front-line personnel show commitment on this front.

Social Skill: Direct communication skill may be both verbal and non-verbal. It is significant that the hotel personnel approach customers in a friendly and confident manner. It is meant welcome smile, direct eye-contact (i.e., face-to-face talk), attractive disposition and willingness to listen. While shaking hands, we convey a sense of confidence and responsibility — essential traits for opening negotiations transforming the same into good business. It is against this background that hotel porters are trained to read the labels on incoming guests baggage — so that they are in a position to use the 'surname' as early as possible just to harmonise the host-guest relationship. This trend is yet to catch up in the Indian hospitality industry. Here, the manner of the vocal disposition also matters. Almost all the hotel personnel are required to have a well modulated and soothing voice, categorically while dealing with the guests/ clients in totality. While handling complaints, the voice should convey concern. Some of the clients look for a sounding board to work off their anger, specially when they have a legitimate complaint and expect immediate redressal of it. The clients seek two things, e.g., an apology and a reassurance that the action will be taken to investigate the complaints.

The hotel personnel, need in some cases to pay more attention. For example, the waiters, housekeepers, porters, receptionists work in close association with the guests. They can ask a customer — attitude browsing through the brochures — is there any particular holiday you have in mind? This helps in generating a sales sequence. If they say 'Yes', you may request for their stay in the same hotel. If they say 'No', you may request them to stay in the hotel as and when they get an opportunity. This speaks of the fact that hotel personnel in general and front-line personnel in particular need to show their professionalism. Above all, the attitude of the personnel towards services must change. The use of derisive terms such as punters — is symptomatic of a poor attitude to service which is indefensible, if the hotel industry has truly to be professional in approach. Our concern for guests must improve.

The aforesaid facts are a mute testimony to the proposition that personal and social skills are found impact-generating, specially with the viewpoint of transforming the occasional guests into habitual guests. This also necessitates a rational plan for the recruitment and development of the hotel personnel.

SALES SEQUENCE

It is necessary to analyse and assess the effectiveness of a sales sequence. The sales sequence has two aims, e.g., selling the services and matching the same with the expectations of clients/guests. We accept the fact that general principles for selling apply equally in all situations where clients and staff are in face-to-face contact. In view of the outstanding merits of sales sequence, it is pertinent that the sales personnel follow the different processes, e.g., establishing rapport with the clients, assessing and extending the needs of the clients, offering the product to clients, handling possible objections and showing their level of commitment towards the clients.

1. Rapport: It is the first step of the sales sequence. Developing rapport is possible when the sales personnel are engaged in activating the process of face-to-face selling. If you engage the clients in conversation, it is easier to know about their needs and requirements. We call this process 'rapport building' which would be of benefit to the clients and the hotel management. The Phrase, Can I Help You? is still in vogue in today's hospitality industry. The generation of discussions should be with questions like —

Do you have a particular kind of holiday in mind?

Are you thinking about a particular destination?

What would be your plan for the next year?

We accept the fact that the hotel sales personnel should have the knowledge of the psychology of potential customers so that they succeed in developing a rapport with their guests. Non-verbal communications convey a lot to a great extent. To the extent it is possible, the attitude of the hotel personnel should be appreciated by the customers.

2. Investigation: The second step in the sales sequence is investigation. At this stage, it is better to put open questions before the prospects. If you ask open questions in lieu of closed questions, the replies being 'Yes' or 'No'— would help in identifying their expectations. Some of the questions are: In the case of a prospective conference —

- Who are participating in the conference?
- When do they like to come and for how long?
- What type of function room would be used?
- What category rooms would be booked?
- How much they can pay?
- Would they visit hotel restaurants/bars etc.?

The needs of customers must never be assumed.[7] If you investigate, you get an opportunity to identify and cater to their demands effectively. And if you can identify, you can satisfy.

3. Presentation: It is the third step of the sales sequence. Once the sales personnel feel that they have sufficient information in the demands/needs of the customers, they should move to the next stage, i.e., presentation. It is meant presenting the right product in the right perspective to the guests. The key to success in the very context is not only to mention the features of your services but also to highlight the new services which you have included in your product mix. If you provide to your client an opportunity to view the function room, other forms in general, restaurant, bar, etc., we find scope for immediate booking. Here, you should not forget to focus on the supportive services which you offer to your guests. Your statement should be to the point otherwise the transaction — following satisfaction on the part of customers, booking could be delayed, as too many alternatives pave way for confusion.

4. Handling objections: It is the fourth step which helps in identifying the additional needs of clients. If the product is expensive, it becomes essential to assure clients regarding the additional benefits associated with that service. This is mainly related to justifications regarding the charges for services. If you have been offering to your guests sophisticated services which are yet to be provided by your competitors, it clearly reveals effective management by the hoteliers — including knowledge of the existing trends in the hospitality industry. If they have some questions regarding the services made available in the function room, you are supposed to explain the same.

*5. **Commitment:*** It is the final stage in the sales sequence which is meant getting the clients into action. It is not essential that sales sequence would always bring about effective booking by the clients. They may book, may like to have time, may like to make payment in installments, may like to call later or may leave the office without giving any assurance. No doubt, the motive here is to close the conversation with a positive result. But in all cases, it is not possible and therefore, you should make the best possible effort to get the assurance from the prospects for getting booking done at the earliest.

The aforesaid facts make it clear that in the hotel industry, the role of the sales personnel is found impact generating. If they are efficient, we find much scope for booking and generation of substantial revenues. This responsibility rests with the sales executives. If they are showing professionalism, behaving gently and performing efficiently, the clients will be motivated to ensure and initiate on their part. This calls for effective business talks between the hotel management and the customers. You have also to be very particular regarding the time of conversation. The sales executives are found selling face-to-face, and therefore, they should have an in-depth idea regarding the preferences and attitude of the client. This would, of course, simplify their task of initiating dialogues and closing the same with booking.

ADVERTISING

Advertising is an active business strategy at influencing people to action through reason or emotion to go for a particular product brand service facility. As an important part of the total promotion mix, it influences the sales results. It is a potent tool of marketing and a component of overall promotion activities. We define advertising as a paid form of presentation of a product brand or service by an identified sponsor.[8] It is aimed at selling to potential guests the existence of services and the benefits to accrue from its uses; reminding guests of its continued existence to obtain repeat business and seeking to retain their customers and regain the loyalty of those who may have switched to other hotels. Categorically, for advertising, a hotel, it is aimed at the public to apprise them of the existence of the service mix and develop awareness of the same in a potential manner. The media available for advertising are newspapers, technical press, magazines, TV, radio, poster sites, bill boards, movies and theaters.

Of course, hotel managers find ways of bringing our facilities to the notice of the potential guests, and reminding past and present guests that their preferences are of prime importance and are still interested which would be made available if they give to you an opportunity. We consider advertising a paid form of persuasive communication. Most of the experts feel that advertising is way down the line in cost effectiveness, specially when we compare it with face-to-face selling, telephonic selling, letter writing or so. Some of the experts also opine that half of all paid advertising is ineffective but they find it difficult to identify which half. We spend a lot of money on advertisements. Is it due to the fact that we find it pleasant to see or hear our own advertisement or is it due to the fact that the advertising industry traps you? It is, of course, a difficult task to answer these questions basically.

No doubt, advertising has a number of advantages, such as simplifying your task of informing the mass audience and explaining to them the outstanding merits of your services, creating awareness and persuading them to opt for a particular service or product you favor. However, there are a number of disadvantages — it is expensive and in most cases it is also found ineffective. Despite these facts, hotel companies take to advertising as a potential medium to boost business. In the present day world, we find a changed scenario. This is also likely to affect your advertisement decisions.

The latest inventions and innovations in the field of technologies, significant developments in the field of electronics and printing technologies, the growing influence of communicative technologies for advertising goods or services are some of the issues complicating decision-making regarding this paid form of promotion. In a true sense, the advertising industry is a very concerned industry, not just due to worldwide economic depression but because of technological changes.

Cassettes in motor vehicles, the growth of portable televisions, the impact of breakfast television will cause change and problems. The technological change in producing magazines and newspapers will be revolutionary just by the end of this decade. However, we find a number of situations where advertisement is found most effective. Suppose a hotel or a restaurant is renovated and the most effective and quick way of reaching a large number of audience getting the hotel known is through advertising. Even you have innovated your product mix, the advertising is found more effective in informing your potential and actual guests. As and when we think about reaching a large number of customers who might eat in a restaurant, or drink in a bar, advertising is found the best method with a clearly defined catchment area. In addition, when we find quiet period and produce a specific package to try and fill that quiet period, the advertising is found effective. Hotel groups and in particular restaurant chains with a standardised system or theme find advertising the best device to promote business, by reaching a volume market.

IMPORTANCE OF ADVERTISING TO THE HOTEL INDUSTRY

Advertising plays an important role in enhancing the hotel industry. No doubt, oral communication, direct recommendations and face-to-face play a commanding role, still there are some special circumstances where the hotel companies have to depend much on advertisement. For the hotel industry, advertising is considered as paid public messages designed to enhance the image of a hotel, its services and thus, develop this sector in a great way. In the hotel industry, the products of different core and peripheral services are made available to the guests. We can advertise in newspapers, magazines, specially in the form of posters or bill boards etc. In order to transmit a predetermined message to a predetermined audience, we also advertise on radio and televisions which are through their commercial services or advertising agencies through media.

Of course, the widest coverage to products/services is an outstanding merit of advertising. It is possible to approach a number of prospective guests, offering a uniform sales message. It is not possible for a salesman to cover many customers in number one shot. It is possible for the hotels and hotel companies to repeat and broadcast messages regarding facilities frequently and to pave way for customer loyalty in a big way. Besides, the accessibility is also an outstanding advantage. Advertisement enables approaching to the prospects through different media which act as a vehicle. In addition, the cost economy is also found possible, if we advertise to the mass audience information regarding these services.

Advertisement spreads information amongst the potential guests about the particular hotel. This offers to the prospects preferences and opportunity of making a good choice. The multi-faceted services offered by hotels will leave prospective customers well informed with the help of advertisement. Thus it proves to be a sensitive tool of promotion. The important decision-making areas are planning, budgeting, testing the effectiveness of the 'selected media, composition of messages to enhance the available services, seeking the cooperation of advertising organisations and making it an effective promotional tool. We accept the fact that most hotels and restaurants have one major advantage over their competitors that may persuade people to stay in a hotel or visit a particular restaurant. It could be the chef or the restaurant manager as craftsman or personality, joints on a trolley, special desserts, one special main course, a range of malt whiskies, good parking, a superb view, lovely grounds or landscape, the personal care services etc. all outstanding merits of a hotel are well promoted with the help of advertisement in the electronic and print media and specially through websites. This is due to the fact that advertisement has evolved in a very special and unique manner to literally grab someone's attention.

In view of the above, we find advertisement playing an important role in promoting the hotel business. But here it is essential that we have a cost effective plan, a balanced budget, and outstanding facilities to persuade customers and publicise services in a big way.

ADVERTISEMENT PLANNING

Planning for advertisement is an important dimension for raising its effectiveness. It requires an in-depth study of the services made available by hotels. The advertising agency helps in preparing an intelligent plan for the concerned clients. For the formulation of good advertisement, it is essential to have a detailed knowledge of services offered by the competitive hotels, and an idea of present and emerging segments in the hotel industry. The market research studies are conducted to gather data on who are the guests, when do they visit, why do they stay in a particular hotel, why do they visit a particular restaurant, who are the travel agents, why do they prefer a particular airline, etc. The advertising agency is also expected to analyse and conduct research on the marketing methods and channels used by the guests in the past. In addition, it is also significant to have knowledge of the various media available for image building information related to their character, influence, circulation, extend audience and cost. We accept the fact that each medium has its own impact on a segment of the market and the availability of time and space.

The advertising agency should also give a careful consideration to a cost-effective advertisement in terms of the headline copy, illustration, colour schemes, size, layout and method of printing or reproducing the advertisement should be planned carefully. A careful plan becomes inevitable to gravitate attention of the prospects, to maintain their interests, and to remind them for a repeat purchase/use of a facility etc. The question regarding the periodicity of advertisements or frequency of advertisements being aired is found to be equally important. We generally find that repeated advertisement initiate impact, provided the slogans, contents of the advertisements are interesting.

An advertisement agency plans advertisement in view of the aforesaid facts. Once the plan is okayed, its execution is entrusted to the agency. Thus, the agency writes the advertisement copy, prepares the layout, designs the advertisements, draws the illustrations, produces the commercials and makes them ready for release. After this, we find making contracts for the space and time slot available in the media, be it electronic, print or otherwise, checking and verifying displays, billing for the services, space and preparation of advertisement and co-ordination with the client's sales force and distribution network. Thus, the planning for advertisement is found essential to get the desired result. A careful and intelligent plan, keeping in view the new emerging trends in technological advances and changing lifestyles of the potential guests is found instrumental in raising the effectiveness of an advertisement.

MEDIA DECISION

We consider media as an important vehicle to offer the messages to the target audience in a big way. The advertisement messages are put forth before the prospects with the support of advertisement media. A number of media are available to an advertiser. It is an important decision-making area, which determines the magnitude of success of a particular brand or facility. Conveying a right message, through a wrong medium, at the wrong time is nothing but the waste of time and money. Against this background, the right media selection plays a significant role. Media selection decision refers to the selection of a specific medium of advertising, such as newspaper, magazine, radio, TV, the mail service or outdoor advertising. Media decisions are found related to the following:

- The available media are serving best our advertisement needs.
- The individual medium is supposed to be the best vehicle for a advertisement.
- We find best the combination of different media used for total advertising.
- We find best specific schedules for the release of advertisements in each available medium.

The selection process is influenced by a number of factors, such as area to be covered, type of audience, messages to be made and services and facilities of the particular medium in relation to cost and its effectiveness. Media habits of the target audience, product characteristics and cost of the media are found important for selecting the potential media.

An advertisement may be sound intellectually but that would be a waste if the selected media are not effective. The budgets of local travel agents may run to the needs of local newspapers, local radio and possibly the local or regional publications. In considering what is best, they must weigh not only the price but also the positive and negative effects. Thus even for the hotel industry, TV, radio, newspapers and magazines are found effective but the suitability of a particular medium is governed by a number of factors, specially the cost element and the intensity of competition.

FACTORS GUIDING THE SELECTION OF MEDIA

1. ***Circulation:*** The circulation is audited net sale per issue or the number of copies sold. Advertisement rate varies according to audited net sale. Quality and caliber of the people attending to the circulation are important here.
2. ***Readership:*** It is the total number of people who see or read the publication, which is usually greater than the number of purchase. It is found to be the better figure to work considering the media to use and cost effectiveness.
3. ***People:*** This refers to proportional breakdown of the readership by social or income groups which is found useful when selected media match appropriately to the market segment.
4. ***Primary or support media*:** This refers to an initial powerful impact by reason of its coverage (leading women's magazine, radio, Sunday newspapers, special supplement to added papers).
5. ***Product life cycle*:** Here, we find staircase and leapfrog effects find a reference to established products whose life cycle is extended or takes off from the maturity stage as new markets are found for the same. In the leapfrog effect, the products with a long lifespan may not suffer

any real decline in sales by encountering periodic market challenges which are often met by the product modifications, alterations, and restyling. In this case, it is necessary to leapfrog the new challenges by the emerging new developments. The choice of media will then depend on the nature and scope of the challenges in the markets and how best this can be countered or overcome.

6. ***Penetration:*** The degree of market penetration achieved will depend on a blend of creativity in the designing of advertisements and the effectiveness of the media used with the assumption that the product has the right attributes. How will media assist successful penetration of any market is important to guide the executives to conduct good business and generate substantial revenues.

It is important to mention here that a wise advertiser seeks cooperation of experts and selects a medium in the face of budgetary provision, organisational requirement and the existing intensity of competition.

SELECTION OF MESSAGE

Message is an idea. The quality of audience and the objectives of communication are the two key points for the selection of messages, presented either centrally or peripherally. A central message takes a direct route to persuasion. It is a well documented advertisement. A peripheral message provides pleasant association, scenic background and favorable influences about the product being advertised. The advertisement message consists of this idea presented in an advertisement together with other relevant information. The idea develops and spots the uniqueness of the product being advertised to get a place in the mind of the customer. The following points are essential, specially while selecting the message:

- Nature of the product : Its category
- For whom it is meant : The segment (target group)
- The competitors : The promises
- Outstanding features : Usefulness to consumer
- Product differentiation : Technological breakthrough
- Occasion for using the product : Frequency

The selected message should be efficacious in retaining the interest of the target customers. The customer should maintain interest in the messages and should secure the action desired by the seller. The effective messages should be:

- Informative : Adequate for a decision
- Interesting : Able to catch attention of the target audience
- Authentic : Exaggeration of facts should be avoided
- Persuasive : Capable of creating a favorable conviction in the target audience
- Memory value : Memorable

Stages	AIDA Model	HOE Model	Communication Model
Congnitive (thoughts)	Attention ↓	Awareness Exposure ↓ Knowledge ↓	Exposure ↓ Reception Response ↓
Effect (Feelings)	Interest ↓ Desire ↓	Likes ↓ Preference ↓ Conviction	Attitude ↓ Intention ↓
Behaviour	Action	Purchase	Behaviour

FIG. 7.3: MODELS OF MESSAGE

In raising the effectiveness of advertisement for a product, message is found playing a critical role. This makes it essential that possible efforts are made to raise creativity so that messages are successful in generating a positive impact on the target audience. It is very natural that we find some variations in the designing of message at different stages of the product brand. The messages should be informative and interesting. Besides, the exaggeration of facts should be avoided. The capability of creating a favorable attitude towards the product in the target audience and memory value are also found significant in the very context. In designing, selecting and developing the advertisement messages, the advertisement models simplify the task of researchers, advertisers and agencies. In Figure 7.3, we find AIDA MODEL, HOE MODEL and COMMUNICATION MODEL. From the standpoint of the hotel industry, we find AIDA model helping us in many ways as shown in Exhibit 7.2.

EXHIBIT 7.2: MODELS AND THEIR ROLE

AIDA Model	:	Here we find attention at the cognitive stage and interest and desire at the effective stage and finally we find action.
HOE Model	:	This is a hierarchy of the effect model. Here we find awareness, exposure knowledge (cognitive stage) liking, preference and conviction (effective stage) and purchase at the final stage.
Communication Model	:	In this model, we find exposure, reception and response at cognitive stage, attitude and intention at the effective stage and behaviour at the final stage.

We find AIDA Model[9] suitable for the hotel industry. Here the message should be efficacious in attracting the attention of customers, creating interest and turning their interest into desire. If we succeed in doing so, it is clear that the desire would be transformed into action — which is meant making the decisions in favour of a particular hotel. In the HOE Model[10], we find different stages like awareness which is followed by knowledge, likes which are followed by preference and conviction and finally the purchase. In the Communication Model, the different stages are exposure, followed by reception and response, attitude followed by intention and finally the behaviour of the prospects.

ADVERTISING AGENCIES

No doubt, the travel agents play an outstanding role in promoting the hotel business but we cannot underestimate the instrumentality of advertising agencies in the very context. They create, design, prepare and place the campaign efficiently as they have an access to statistical information from major market research programmes not readily available to the hotel companies. This is an additional incentive which simplifies the task of hotels while advertising. A modern advertising agency offers specialised knowledge, skill and experience which makes the advertising campaign effective. It has a team of experts like writers, artists, media experts, researchers, television producers, account executives, etc. By creating effective advertisements and delivering them with the help of suitable media, the agencies implement advertisement plans and strategies. In a true sense, they represent the core of the advertising profession.

Advertising agencies have evolved over a period of time. Of late, we find studio-based agencies, some industrial and specialised agencies and hot-shops who only plan reactive campaigns by engaging the free lancers. In India, we consider Mumbai the 'Mecca' of advertisements. However, London is considered to be the creative capital of world advertising. Recently we find a shift from the creative mode to marketing mode. The emerging trends in electronics have paved way for multi-dimensional developments in the advertisement world.

In the international perspective, we find a number of hotels and hotel companies having their own advertising agencies, specialists in the field of planning, creating and placing of advertisements. They have artists and copywriters for creative work of developing advertisement designs, photographers and printers for printing, type-setting etc. We also find advertising agencies having their own research departments to undertake consumer studies and advertisement testing. The ideal agencies have media account and art executives. Normally, the advertising agencies get a commission ranging from 15 per cent to 20 per cent.

The selection of a suitable advertising agency is an important task before hotels which is substantially influenced by the size of their advertisement budgets. The hotels and hotel companies not having their own agency for advertisement should consider the following points while selecting a suitable agency:

- Agency must be known to the hotels.
- Agency must have creativity. Secret of creativity is simplicity.
- Agency must have a sound track record and experience.
- Account executives should have the capacity to understand the problem of clients. They should be committed in their profession.
- You should go through the work produced for other clients and assess their calibre and professionalism.

  You should have a good rapport with the agency.

The hotels should select an ideal advertising agency for making possible creativity and economy in advertisements. It is important to advertise and sell oneself — as it carries an outstanding significance to enhance one's business. This is directly related to effectiveness of advertisements. Hence, the hotels and hotel companies are required to select a suitable agency so that they reach to the target audience in a right way and at the right time. This would help them in making possible feasible economy decisions and effectiveness which would simplify the task of image projection. It is unlikely that all hotel companies have their own agency. And we do not find any justification for investing a lot on organising a separate cell for an advertisement since it is not likely to be a commercially viable proposition.

THE COMMUNICATION PROCESS AND ITS BARRIERS

The main problem in the advertisement field is to design and express chosen messages in a form that is most likely to communicate effectively with a target audience. If our messages are not in a position to reach to the target audience, there can be no communication. Even with maximum reach and wide exposure of an advertisement, we do no find any communication unless the message is actually received, understood and is of interest to the receiver. Barriers and filters in our mind influence the ways in which we perceive and understand the messages. Of course, these barriers are the product of our attitude, personalities and experience. We find different perceptions of the same message in a group of people. Thus, a vital skill in advertising communication lies in understanding at least the main filters at work in the minds of the targeted buyers. This necessitates designing messages, symbols and images, likely to be well received by the target audience. The *'reach and communicate'* is represented in Figure 7.4 To clarify the process, we have quoted an example of a hotel group.

In this figure, we find a hotel group with around 10 per cent share of a residential sales conference market. The group uses its own sales team to motivate the important conference buyers amongst clients' companies. It also seeks to communicate the outstanding advantages to the wide target audience of business people, who have attended a residential conference at least once in the last three years. Here, the hotel group has decided to use press advertising to reach its target audience. The figure indicates how the original message passes through different stages to the purchase decision. It shows how in percentage terms the potential impact of advertising is reduced in practice. In the figure, a represents

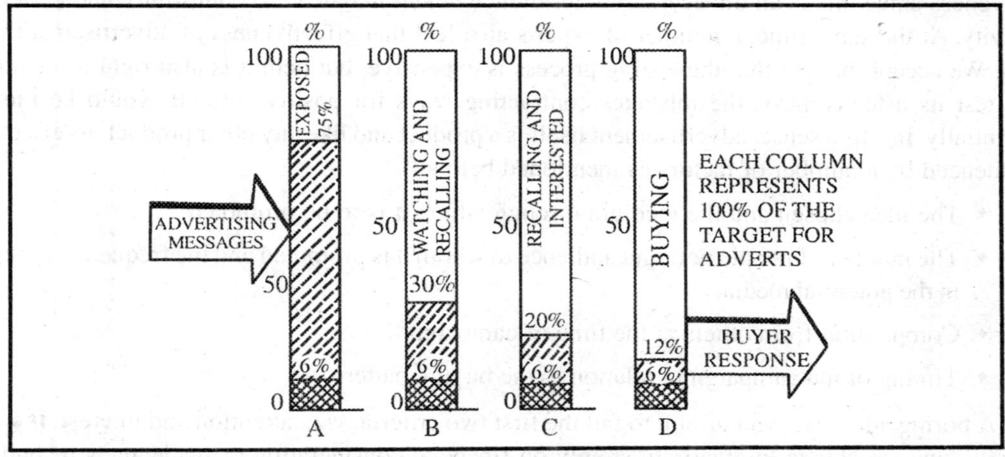

FIG. 7.4: FILTERS IN THE COMMUNICATION PROCESS

100 per cent of the target segment of people who attend sales conferences. We include here the profile of persons attending the conferences, which would be identified in detail as consumers and would be quantified in the hotel's marketing planning. With a realistic budget, the hotel group expects to reach to the target audience and expose its message to about 75 per cent of the hotel target group. This is clearly meant that buying space in magazines, which three fourth of the target are likely to buy and look at during the advertising campaign. It is very natural that the readers do not go through all the pages and pass on very quickly to other pages and even forget what they have seen. Here column B indicates that in this case, 30 per cent of the target audience saw the advertisement of that hotel group and remember at least seeing it, if they are asked to do so. Column C represents the proportion of the target audience who not only remember the advertising they have watched, but are also sufficiently interested in considering the service produce of that hotel group. Column D represents those who .actually attend the sales conference at one of the hotels of that group, in the 12 months during which we find the advertising campaign. The dotted line in all the columns represents the 6 per cent of the existing regular or repeat buyers who buy the product and are committed towards it by the advertisement, though they may be reinforced to opt for the other products in the same category through advertisements.

In the aforesaid example, an additional 6 per cent of target customers use the product as first-time buyers during the period of the marketing campaign. Here, it is possible that during that time, some previous buyers have switched to the competitors' products over the same period — emphasizing the fact that advertising serves to maintain as well as increase share of markets. This is meant that we need great expertise at each stage of the communication process; to purchase the spaces best calculated to reach the target (per cent of A), to arrest and capture attention with appealing messages (per cent of B), to keep attention through interesting information (also a per cent of B), to communicate the key points that matter to buyers (per cent of C) and to turn interest into purchase (per cent of D). At each and every stage, we find losses in the communication process. Thus we find that advertising messages usually *'Wear Out'* so are required to be repeated and improved upon at intervals.

TESTING THE ADVERTISING EFFECTIVENESS

Some of the market experts feel that testing the effectiveness of an advertisement will stifle its creativeness since this is an unnecessary interference which may lead to conformity and deficiency in creativity. At the same time, a number of experts also feel that effectiveness of advertisement must be tested. We accept the fact that the testing process is expensive, but here it is also right to mention that if we test its effectiveness, the mistakes contracting ways for positive effects would be minimized substantially. In a true sense, advertisement itself is a product and like any other product, its effectiveness is influenced by a number of factors as mentioned below:[11]

- The idea chosen and the medium through which it is to be promoted.
- The number of people or target audience to whom it is promoted and the frequency of repetition in the potential media.
- Competition from others at the time of campaign.
- Timing of the campaign in relation to the buying pattern.

A boring advertisement is sure to fail the first two criteria, viz., attention and interest. If we fall in assigning due weightage to creativity simply on financial consideration or inadequacy of budget, the advertisement messages cannot be effective. A series of slide photographs on TV with an end caption *'Surprising Germany'* surprised none. Italy obtained its first appropriation in many years and instead of catching attention by promoting uniqueness of the country, produced, "Italy has everything", but it was hardly believable or attention getting. Contrary to it, the Swedish Tourist Office was awarded for a creative memorable advertisement on TV. They were winners of CIMTIG/TTG award (Chartered Institute of Marketing Travel Industry Group/Travel Trade Gazette.) In the advertisement, a moose puppet told of Sweden's virtues in a sing-song voice that combined clear English and yet a sound of Sweden. Here, is an advertisement which is connected with food and hygiene as an illustration one which although not new is very good. This is one by Saatchi & Saatchi, UK, for the Health and Education Council. It was used as an advertisement and reproduced as posters in Kitchens and where food was used. The advertisement from the beginning to end was found very effective. It is totally true and credible. It takes full advantage of the chosen media without being too verbose and had a maximum impact-generating potential.

> 'This is what happens when a fly lands on your food.
>
> Flies can't eat solid food,
>
> So to soften it up, they vomit on it.
>
> They stamp the vomit in until it's a liquid.
>
> Usually stamping on a few germs for good measure.
>
> Then when it's good and runny, they suck it all back again, probably dropping some excrement at the same time.
>
> And then, when they've finished eating. It's your turn.'[12]

These examples speak of the fact as to what makes for good advertising in the hotel industry. The main thing for effectiveness is creativity. If we make creativity possible, the effectiveness of the advertisement would be great.

The inventions and innovations in the field of communicative technologies have also made it essential that like other organisations, even the hotel companies, industry on the whole, raise their advertisement budgets. An important thing to be kept in mind is whatever you do, try not to be boring. A number of people do not buy newspapers and magazines to read the advertisements. This makes it essential that you should be simple, clear and complete. Try to get your advertisements placed at the top or bottom right-hand corner of a page. You should not forget it that a full-page advertisement does not necessarily attract twice as much business as a half-page advertisement.

What to test?

The problem is what constitutes effectiveness. Here, the effectiveness should be measured in terms of a dependent variable as weight is measured in Kgs., or height is measured in centimeters. Increased sale is the ultimate criterion of advertisement effectiveness. Here, we get psychological response in the form of heart beat, seating, movement of eye balls etc. A verbal response is the answer given to a question, written or spoken.

When to test?

Of course, the testing should be before it is run so that any corrective steps are taken on right time. The effectiveness of an advertisement message should be tested before preparing an advertisement.

Key Methods

In determining the effectiveness of an advertisement, the following methods are practiced:

1. ***Inquiries:*** In this context, we are supposed to answer back coupons incorporated in advertisements. The responses indicate the effectiveness of the concerned advertisement.
2. ***Recall test:*** In this method, the respondents are shown the cover of magazine or any other media in which the advertisements have appeared. The viewers are asked to answer as to which advertisements in that issue are memorable.
3. ***Recognition test*:** In this method, the viewers are shown the advertisements and are asked whether or not they have gone through the advertisements.
4. ***Sales test:*** Here, the actual sales results before and after the advertisements are examined. The sales results in the 'test markets' are compared with the 'control markets.' The test markets are some selected markets where we have advertised and the control markets are the markets where we have not advertised.

In Figure 7.5 the different methods for testing are presented.

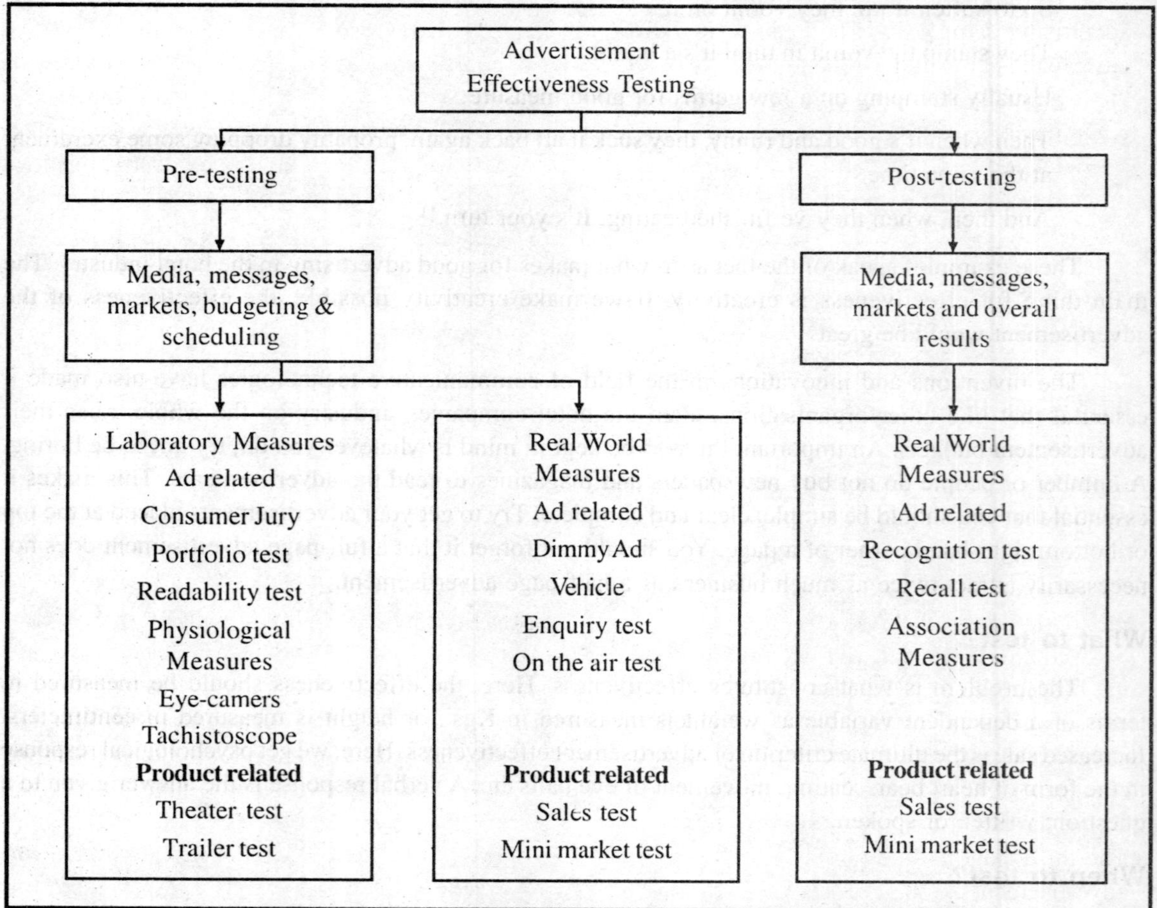

FIG 7.5: ADVERTISING EFFECTIVENESS TEST

In the figure, we find pre-testing and post-testing methods. It is important here to mention that usually we apply laboratory and real world measures to test the effectiveness of an advertisement. Both the methods are either related to advertisement or to the product. The testing methods are used in the face of methods adopted for advertising a product brand. Both the methods have their own merits and demerits. The suitability of a particular method depends on the prevailing circumstances or the effects of advertisement planned. Here, it is important to mention that pre-testing paves the way for effective advertising since it allows an opportunity to detect and eliminate weaknesses or flaws. The post-testing is found elaborate, expensive and realistic since test advertisements in real life setting — lead to non-acceptance of a particular product brand.

Of course we find it difficult to test effective advertisements, but keeping in view the amount to be spent on an advertisement, it is right to test the same. This provides an opportunity to correct the errors usually occurring while planning out advertisements.

ADVERTISING CAMPAIGN

In the present age of growing competition, it is essential that we assign due weightage to the advertising campaigns. The need of the hour is to make the advertising campaigns innovative. If an advertising campaign is robust, the effectiveness will, of course, gain a momentum. It is right to say that the low cost leadership is always vulnerable. Our claim that we are cheapest invites multi-dimensional complications, if especially price war results. We find an inherent belief that cheap products available are an indication of poor quality. And to be more specific when we talk about the hotel industry, this needs immediate attention. Differentiation is supposed to be the path chosen by a number of brand leaders in any industry. We cannot quickly copy a campaign based on a true marketing advantage, such as 'all our villas have private swimming pools' and further 'We have trained our baby patrollers at each of the hotels marked' and 'Every cabin has shower and toilet.' Thus, we find here three important aspects, first low cost leadership, i.e., selling cheaper than our competitors; second, differentiation, i.e., creating a high added value and third focus, i.e., specialisation to a substantial degree that makes copying difficult and time taking.

Advertising campaigns should have a sufficient interval, especially when the hotel management/ industry is facing the problem of budgetary constraint. We are supposed to wait for an opportune moment. The timing of publication of brochures is an important aspect in this case. Persuading customers to commit themselves needs a substantially larger budget and extremely persuasive reasons. Unsold holidays and travel facilities are glaring examples of perishable services, since they have no value once the tourist season is over. They tend to lose their economic feasibility. Anything paid for them must be better than nothing and the way in which late booking opportunities are promoted considerably affect the business fortunes of any company. Offering knock-down prices, a major cut in hotel tariff during off season need tactful advertising. Thus an important problem to be looked into is to campaign advertisements strongly, intelligently and rationally. We find different stages for such a campaign. Advertisement experts feel that at the outset, the product should be defined. This simplifies the task of fixing the target area. The second stage is defining the market segment, which fixes the priority area. The third stage is interpreting the market objectives and the fourth stage is planning for an effective advertisement campaign. It is pertinent that we insist on creative strategies which help in transforming the proposition into the idea. Another aspect is media planning. The fifth stage is implementing the campaign and the sixth and final stage is assessing the impact and value of the campaign. If we follow the aforesaid stages, the advertising campaign is expected to be strong, economically viable and intelligent. It is very natural that advertising effectiveness resulting into such a campaign would be praiseworthy at all levels.

At the first stage, when we talk about defining the product, it is important to clarify the specialties of the services to be offered to the users. If users feel that these services would be instrumental in making their stay in hotels comfortable and pleasant, it is natural that they prefer to stay in that hotel. Hence, the advertisement slogans should explain the outstanding merits or features of the product. If you include care services in your product mix, or if you are introducing new rooms exclusively meant for the women, your advertisement should convey the features.

At the second stage, it is important to define the market segments. The users belong to different categories, they come from different parts of the globe, they are from both sexes and their needs and requirements cannot be identical or uniform. A study of the segmentation of the consumers simplifies the task of identical users and we succeed in identifying their specialties and needs. This helps marketers in identifying the prospects or the potential guests.

At the third stage, the marketing objectives are to be interpreted. It is related to the environmental studies. The moment we succeed in identifying the objectives, the advertising would be effective. The information to be collected are the sales targets for the coming year, or the regional target, the distribution process and the sales promotion activities, the instrumentality of an advertisement in creating new customers, the inhibiting factors preventing from achieving the target, competitive products and their advertising and the attitudes of customers.

At the fourth stage, the advertising campaign is to be planned. We need here the information related to the prospects. It is significant that we create an advertising campaign which is sure to reach the target audience. Here, we need to take a decision on two important aspects, e.g., creative strategies and the media plan. For creativity, we need to transform the proposition into an idea. This necessitates re-channelizing idea through an effective campaign. Besides, we find creativity playing an important role even in the context of media planning. The media planners are required to assign due weightage to the formulation of the media mix, of course, in view of the changing target audience preferences.

At the fifth stage, the campaign is to be implemented. This includes processes right from preparation of the press advertisement to the production of TV, commercial films and advertisement highlighting a product.

At the sixth and last stage, we assess the intensity of the effect by a particular ad, promoting an 'advertisement.' This is related to awareness, creation of attitude, purchase and repurchase. In the hotel industry, it is meant taking a decision in favour of a hotel, staying in that hotel and again forming a habit to stay in that hotel, again and again.

Thus, the aforesaid stages are found helpful in raising the effectiveness of our advertising campaigns and ensuring good business to the hospitality industry.

ADVERTISING STRATEGY

When we talk about the formulation of a sound advertising strategy, it is important that advertising opportunities are optimised keeping in view the changing market trends. The strategies are required to be tailored to fit the market situations. It is also pertinent that these strategies are consistent with the advertising policies. The formulation of a sound advertising strategy deserves immediate attentions and in-depth analysis care. In the context of formulation of a strategy, the pre-testing of an advertisement is found impact-generating. This is due to the fact that pre-testing helps an assessment of the communicative value of media. It simplifies the task of identifying an attitudinal change in the prospects. Here, a set of advertisements are prepared and shown to small groups or the representatives of clients. The effectiveness of the various approaches in transmitting the messages is measured which also helps the policy makers in assessing the idea generated as an advertisement. This paves way for creativity.

Whatever the slogans we adopt should be acceptable to the potential guests. The messages should retain interest in the minds of customers and should be able to catch the attention of the potential target audience. The exaggerated claims should be avoided. This in a natural way necessitates professionalism in this industry. There are various media and while selecting a particular medium to advertise we need to consider a number of factors. The composition of slogans is an important area which requires more precaution and detailed information regarding the lifestyles of prospects. An in-depth information regarding the emerging new trends in the environmental conditions simplifies the task of a marketer to plan out strategies to the business. We find numerous developments in the field of communication technology and the strategies planned earlier can't remain static. While formulating the strategies, we are supposed to keep in mind the recent developments.

The hotels and hotel companies should make advertising consumer oriented. It is also to be seen that concentration is on the most important and persuasive advantages available. It should present a unique and competitive idea. It should involve the consumer and should also be credible and sincere. It should be simple, clear and complete. The strategy should take full advantage of the chosen media and should demand cost effective action, leading to good sales. Not only this, its instrumentality is also involved in the essence of reminding the customers to repeat their decisions. The hotel companies should not forget that the whole face of advertising could well change by the 21st century, because of new generation of information and communication technology. Video tape recorders could revolutionize TV, sponsored industry is to witness a number of changes due to technological changes. In our strategic decisions, this aspect needs a priority attention.

ADVERTISING PLAYS A RELATIVELY SMALL ROLE IN HOTEL

F. Buttle (1986) opines that for hotels and restaurants, hospitality advertising appropriation are very small compared to major fast moving consumer goods manufacturers who may budget over 30 per cent of the annual turnover.[13] To some extent, we accept it as in terms of total sales revenue for tour operators, travel agents and transport operators. If we exclude breweries, only nine travel and tourism firms featured in the top 250 British advertisers spending league in 1984 and only three in the top 100 travel tourism group in 1985. The nine were mostly national transport operators or national tour operators and for all of them advertising was below the 3 per cent of turnover level. Paradoxically, advertising expenditure appears to an average of 1 per cent to 3 per cent of the total turnover for most travel and tourism producers.

Despite the comment made by an individual operators, we find advertising delivering goods to an organisation and contributing a lot to the promotion of hotel business. The hotel companies have a number of options and they should make their own decisions. The distribution channel, the role of the print media, the availability of links with other operators for co-operative promotion, the scope for good sales promotion and merchandising are some of the options. Of course, they are found more effective in influencing the demand for many hotels and hotel companies.

How can we agree with the opinion of Mr. Buttle, when we find advertising helping hotels in promoting the business. Attractive and natural photographs of different types of available accommodation, decor, furnishing, beautifully decorated rooms, swimming pools, electronically operated fountains are all found attracting the guests. Tourist attractions are also considered a focal point, where advertising plays an effective role. It is also right to mention here that in the beginning of 1980s, the communicative technologies were not so sophisticated and advanced. We have witnessed a number of developments since then. Of course, only the leading hotel companies are able to use these devices.

In the 1990s, we find a major change in the environmental conditions, which have made possible significant developments in the advertising industry. The electronic revolution has also thrown a major impact on the functional behaviour of this industry. This has paved ways for innovation in advertising campaigns. The printing technologies are now so advanced that potential guests are now found motivated and influenced. In addition, the information value of an advertisement has also justified its existence for creating interest. We are found innovating our services consistently. Whatever the media we prefer, the positive impact on the potential guests cannot be denied, of course, we may find a change in the intensity of the effect of a particular medium.

PUBLIC RELATIONS

Public relations activities are considered as a major communication function in the wider context of corporate goals, as well as in the marketing. British Institute of Public Relations has defined it as the 'deliberate, planned and sustained effort to establish and maintain mutual understanding between an organisation and the public'. Public Relations may be personal and non-personal, but it does not involve the purchase of media space and therefore, the level of control over what appears in the media is limited. Here, the public has to be interpreted as comprising all target groups an organisation wishes to influence — from ministers to local politicians and residents of an area in which the businesses is located. This segment is found to be more opportunistic in its execution, exploiting events and maintaining good links and good will with the media and the public on the whole.

Public relations covers a wide range of activities. It is the art and science of planning and implementing a two-way communication and understanding between hotel companies and potential customers. It is also known as the reflection of the organisational programmes and activities. Its main function is to inform the public about the activities of an organisation. It's purpose is to create the best public relations.

In the hotel industry, we find public relations more instrumental in informing the clients the outstanding merits of different services offered. The specialties of hotel are presented in such a way that the prospects are motivated to avail of the facilities offered by a particular hotel. It also helps in creating an atmosphere where the users at large are convinced. In addition, it also helps in collecting the information on the preferences of the prospects.

It is right to mention that we find a very few consumer industries to benefit substantially by public relations as the hotel industry. Yet, we find it as one of the most under utilised forms of publicity for many hotels, specially in smaller towns and cities. The print and electronic media make the most of advertising hotels and available facilities during the tourist season. Food is another effective business proposition. All of us are interested in food. All of us read about holidays and leisure. A number of people stay in hotels we find interested events there. The vast majority of hoteliers welcome free press publicity not only because it is free but because they know that most people buy a magazine or newspaper to read the articles, news and editorials, rather than the advertisements, unless they are looking for a product, or are interested in booking a holiday or a restaurant.

In the hotel business, we find a number of events which should be fed to the local press, such as, the appointment of a new chef, list of cocktails, menus for certain functions held at hotel, particulars of certain important conferences or exhibitions to be held, menus for special days of the year, photographs of staff dressed up for special days and well-known people staying in the hotel. We find a number of hotels doing a lot of charitable work and helping in organising charitable, fund-raising events. Of late, the sponsored events start and finish at hotels or are run even in the hotel grounds. Sponsored walks, sponsored car rallies, sponsored fashion designing events, sponsored entertainment programmes, we find all appearing in the newspapers and magazines. Hotels need press coverage for most of their activities — from the largest omelette to the longest sausage.

The aforesaid facts are a staunch testimony to the proposition that for the smooth and successful functioning of hotels, it is important to develop rapport with local journalists on newspapers, local radio and local television. Spending time and money for their entertainment would not be unproductive. Establishing a personal relationship with them is found to be a paying proposition. A hotel manager was able to persuade a television crew to move the cameras six inches, as they featured a story of a robbery at a bank next door to his hotel, so that the shot included the hotel name and sign and the voice mentioned the bank was next to hotel. This appeared at peak viewing time, just for a cold beer or a coke as they were working outside and the temperature was very high.

Journalists always prefer to visit a hotel as they get their full enjoyment even free of cost. You can give journalists a write-up of your story, and preferably a story with a photograph. Of course, photographs cover a lot of space but if they use it, we find this the finest eye catching free publicity. Sometimes a stunt is also thought to obtain a write-up. Here, an example of Crest Hotel next door to Wembly Stadium, London, where they arranged for a horse to check in at reception when 'Horse of the Year' show was on. In the magazine, it appeared as Horse and Hound. This is an example of a right stunt, for the right location and in the right media. Another example is related to Carlton Tower Hotel in London. When this hotel reopened its Rib Room restaurant; renowned for its roast beef, with a new menu and decor, they got a prize Aberdeen Angus bull outside the hotel which received considerable free press publicity. We again find it a right publicity for the right theme.

In view of the above, it is important to mention that press publicity plays a positive role in promoting the hotel business but right creative thinking and planning is essential for the same. An example is here related to the London Tara with 844 rooms who could not get free publicity mainly due to the fact that there were a number of hotels. One day, they introduced a theater show in the function room of the hotel. The show was *'Another Bride, Another Groom'* which the general manager had watched in a show in Australia. The slogan was 'Another Bride, Another Groom brought to London.' In addition to free press publicity, they also got bookings of their function room for a long period.

The aforesaid illustrations make it clear that if you have an interesting story and a good rapport with the pressmen, it is easier for you to get good coverage and that too even free of cost. The main thing is here creative thinking and right planning.

In the public relations, the activities range from a press release to newspapers and magazines, specially to create the interest of prospects in a holiday package in a good resort or a country. The holiday package tours and tips on familiarity with a tours spot, organised by tour operators for the travel agents help them in enriching their knowledge and making the travelling decisions. The wine and cheese parties organised by the British Airways to launch not required Seychelles as a new resort or other such functions with the motto of enriching the knowledge of the prospects testify it.

In view of the above, we feel that public relations activities occupy a significant place in the promotion-mix of hotel companies. If the hotel companies, tour operators, travel agents explore opportunities for educating the masses, the promotional activities are bound to be effective. But, here the media should evince interest in extending their best co-operation. Besides, financier, investors, employees, social bodies etc. should also contribute them best in educating the masses with the help of innovative communicative technologies. Short stories, dialogues, regional songs, dances etc. are found playing here an important role. If we publicise for the development of travel and tourism in a very natural way, we are paving ways for the development of the hotel industry and generating major forex reserves in the Indian exchequer.

There are a number of media sources available for publicity. Illustration, copy and the spoken word are the primary publicity by media which are grouped into the following heads:

- Printed Publicity
- Advertising Publicity
- Projected Publicity
- Structural Publicity
- Personal Publicity

The illustration method of publicity is found helpful in achieving emotional effects specially in the production of landscape and its atmosphere which is universally appreciated. Hence, the publicity effects of illustration is found impressive. The illustrations are employed in different forms like drawing, printing and photographs. If we talk about the copy, its main purpose is to give expression to the publicity idea. Like illustration, the copy is also found effective in creating desires and the urge to go travelling. The spoken word is found important, specially in the case of personal publicity, which acts as a vehicle to reach the imaginative world. Why not, if words are not only conveyors of thoughts and ideas but also of emotional contents, consequently they reach not only the intellect but also the inner thoughts of the recipient developing the desire to go on a good holiday package and are expressed to this end.

SALES PROMOTION

The American Marketing Association (AMA) said about sales promotion that, *'Sales promotion is a part of marketing communications, other than advertising, public relations, personal selling and sales literature. It is primarily designed to stimulate consumer's purchasing activity, and dealer and sales-force effectiveness in the short-term, through temporary incentives and displays.'* One thing is clear that while advertising is described as *'above the line', sales promotion and merchandising are usually referred to as 'below the line.'*

It is also to be clarified that all components of promotion, except advertisement are found *'below the line.'* We do not find a clear cut difference between these two concepts. As for example, the window display is one of the merchandising techniques designed to promote products at the *'point of sale.'* It is also argued that the display windows of travel agencies are used advertise the products like current bargain offers for flights and holidays, the window display is still identified as a form of *below the line promotion'* strategy.

Sales promotion is considered to be a short-term activity, seeking to boost sales during peak demand periods, to ensure that the firm obtains its markets share and help launch a new product or support an ailing or modified service.[14] It is also said that sales promotion activities are attention getters, since the objective is to achieve immediate sales impact. No doubt, the money-off or bargain offers are also found effective, but this can have the effect of demeaning the inherent value of the product. Ronnie Corbett's strategic joke[15] that he remembers an event because it was the week Allied Carpets were not having a sale, carried an important message for the marketer that too much emphasis on 'deals' will degrade the product in the eyes of consumers and at the same time will undermine profit levels.

The aforesaid facts make it clear that sales promotion is complementary to advertising. Sales promotion and advertising objectives do not conflict but reinforce one another. This tool of promotion is designed to appeal particularly to those customers who are found price-sensitive. It is natural that sales promotion tools attract buyers having little brand loyalty. Against this background, this component of promotion is found useful in those 'areas where brand loyalty is a feature, such as certain cruise makers are holiday package operators, but here it is essential that efforts are aimed particularly at present clientele to attract more business from the existing market instead of trying to encourage brand switching and targeting new clients. This will not be a case of value addition to the business of the tour operator, travel agents. It can't be refuted/with less expensive products in hotel and travel or in other businesses, sales promotion using bargain offers may be successful in gaining a number of uncommitted customers. In the hotel business, perishability is a risk and this factor component is also used to offer off-season accommodation at low price tags.

Sales Promotion Techniques

Repeated advertising, and competitive market conditions are the two important reasons for the growing significance of sales promotion in the hotel industry. The techniques may be directed at the hotel staff, tour operators and travel agents including guests/clients. Figure 7.6 summarises the key promotional techniques.

We find three-tier arrangements for sales promotion in the hotel business. First is directed at the hotel staff, or personnel working in the hotels. There are a number of incentives given to them. In addition, some of the hotel companies also provide concessional travelling and accommodation facilities to their staff. They also offer to them function rooms when the wedding is related to the staff. In addition, we also find organisations of competition and contest. The close relations are also allowed a concessional stay.

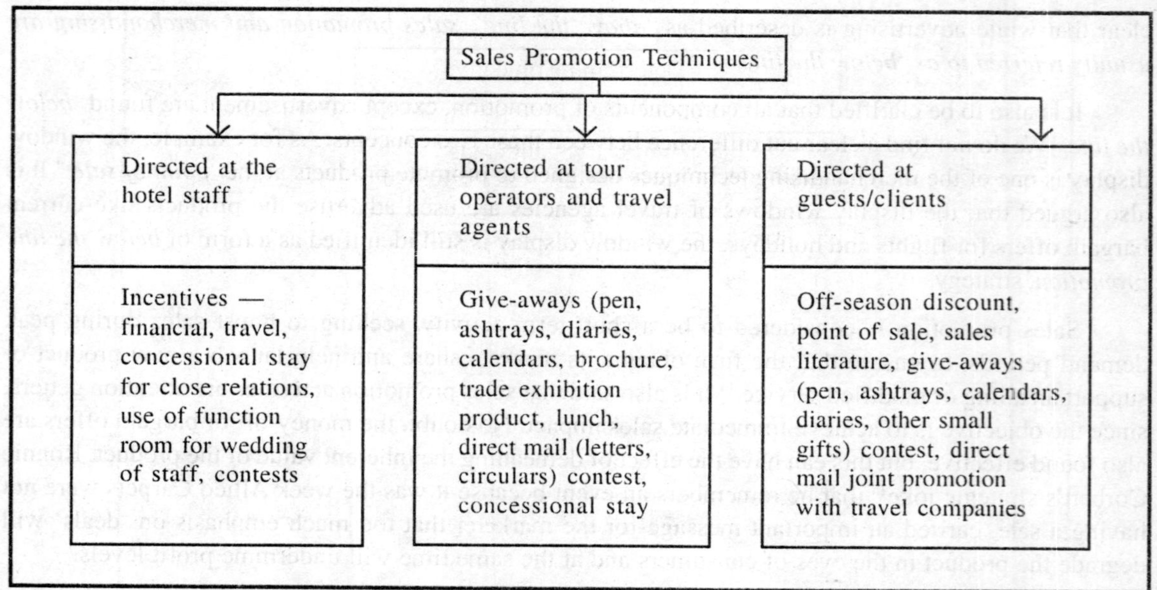

FIG 7.6: SALES PROMOTION TECHNIQUES

The second is related to or directed to the channel or tour operators or travel agents. The fact is clear that tour operators work as a whole seller as they buy rooms in bulk and the travel agents work as the retailers. We also find give-away provisions for them where they are given some small gifts.

The third is directed to the guests or clients. They are also allowed accommodation during the off season at low costs. In addition, they get a number of small gifts, of course, specially which are given to the regular guests and business executives visiting hotels frequently.

Stages in Sales Promotion Decisions

For a successful sales promotion programme, hotel companies need to undertake strategic planning. There are a number of stages through which the planning is undertaken as shown in Figure 7.7. The first stage is related to the determination of objectives. This stage needs to clarify that whether the sales promotion schemes are to attract the new customers or to appreciate the old customers by offering some incentives to the habitual guests who are frequent bar visitors to the hotel. The second stage is to identify the target audience. It is to make clear that whether the sales promotion would be directed at the hotel's staff, or at channel or at guests or clients.

Before we move on to the third stage, the hotel companies should attempt to enrich the information bank. This may be helpful in selecting the best. They would also know the strategies adopted by the competitors. When a final decision is taken regarding the technique to be adopted, we develop the sales promotion and subsequently test the programme to know its effectiveness. After knowing the effect, we implement the programme in tune with the decisions taken regarding duration of the programme. At the last stage, we know the effect of the programme already implemented.

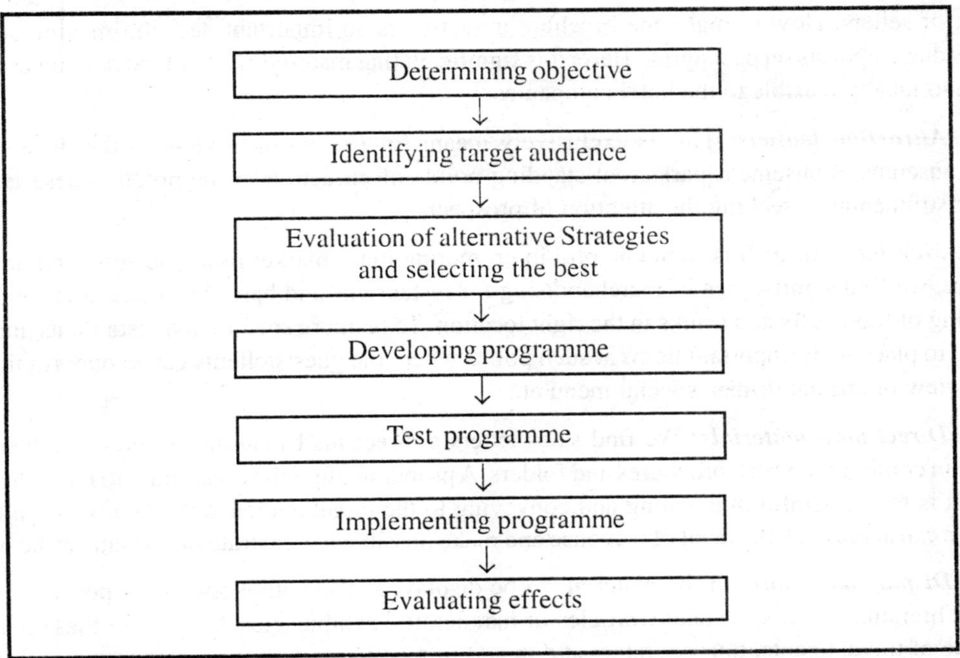

FIG. 7.7: STAGES IN SALES PROMOTION DECISION

Key Tools of Sales Promotion in Hotel

There are a number of sales promotion tools for promoting the hotel business.

1. Brochure: It is a device to stimulate customers and motivate them to visit hotel and avail of the benefits by the management staff of that hotel. It is a detailed publication helping hotel companies in promoting their businesses. We also call it a pamphlet bound in the form of a booklet. It describes and illustrates the services made available by hotels. We find brochure different to folder in size and content as well. It requires careful planning of the layout, colour and paper used for publishing the contents. Normally, the brochures are found bulky and expensive. The brochures are expected to focus on the theme and message of advertising and other promotional areas. The guests/clients get detailed information regarding the core and peripheral services available in a hotel.

2. Folder: We find folder the most commonly used sales promotion tool. In this respect, it is essential that folders have an impressive appearance in totality. The particulars should be in brief but clear. We find it a single piece of illustrated paper which is less voluminous than the brochure. And therefore, it is found less expensive and less time consuming. The folders are usually printed on a single sheet of paper and then folded. The quality of paper and printing used for its publication are found significant to make folders more attractive. The hotels can use folders for promoting their businesses where the prospects get important information regarding the services to be made available to them.

3. Packaging: We call packaging an attractive wrapper of product/services in a hotel, found instrumental in attracting the prospects. When we talk about packaging in the hotel industry, emphasis is on the outer cover and internal layout of brochures and leaflets. We find it a final persuasive move on the part of sellers. How to make the brochure attractive is an important decision-making area which requires due emphasis on packaging: Here, it is significant that materials used for packaging be attractive and economically feasible to the hotel companies.

4. Attraction leaflets: This is exclusively meant for presenting a view of the different theme parks, museums, amusement parks, out-standing points of attraction in the hotels. These leaflets are found instrumental in seeking the attention of prospects.

5. Merchandising: It is found helpful in promoting mass-market like foodstuffs and drinks. And therefore, we find significance of merchandising for restaurants and bars. The merchandising involves displaying of foodstuffs and drinks in the right location. To be more specific the restaurants and bars are required to place their important items at such points where the guests/clients get an opportunity to have a close view of special drinks, special menu etc.

6. Direct mail materials: We find sales letters a direct mail material which can either be used alone or in combination with brochures and folders. A proper mailing list is essential to reach all potential guests. It is found helpful in reaching and conveying to the target audience the facilities available in a hotel. We can also check the level of response and make possible better strategies to satisfy the prospects.

7. Display materials: In the materials to be displayed at sensitive points are posters, dispensers for sales literature, cardboard stand, articles of handicrafts, exhibits etc. We can use these materials in the office of travel agents, tour operators and in addition at places where tourists come, such as tourist resorts, airports, railway and bus stations and major cities with tourist potential. In the preparation of materials, emphasis is called for on selecting the quality material. With the new inventions and innovations in the field of printing technologies, we find enough scope for the publication and preparation of standard posters, or other printed materials.

8. Organising competition: For promoting business, the hotel companies have been investing in organising competitions during particular times. They sponsor even the goods manufacturing companies and provide accommodation facilities to the winners of the competition contest. We find hotels organising competition even for tour operators and travel agents.

9. Exhibition: We see hotels and hotel companies organising exhibitions. These exhibitions are aimed at the public and at the trade. World Travel Market, London gives members an opportunity to see and be seen. The travel agents in particular get an opportunity to know about the emerging new trends in the hotel market.

10. Special offer: We also find provision, of special offer for all categories, such as guests/ clients, travel agents, tour operators, hotel personnel. Price reduction, free gifts, are some of its important components.

11. Maps and hotel group-directories: Some of the hotels also offer to the tourists the city map and the tourist map. These are mostly provided free out of the marketing budgets. In addition, they also provide the directories of the hotel group.

12. Alternative brochure formats: In the present age of technological sophistication, radio cassettes, video films, video text and online between a principal's stock of products and a consumer's home TV set could replace in theory, the role of the brochures. But here it is also right to mention that visual communication cannot be replaced by printed materials, specially when we talk about its application in the hotel industry.

The aforesaid promotional tools are found useful to the hotel industry. No doubt, we have a number of alternatives. It is very natural that all tools are not equally effective for all purposes and in all situations. In this case, strategic planning becomes essential to achieve the maximum benefits from these promotional tools.

TELEMARKETING

With the increasing popularity of information and communication technology, we find telemarketing also emerging as a component for promoting the hotel business.[16] The instrumentality of telemarketing is considerably influenced by the communication excellence of telemarketers *vis-a-vis* the quality of ICT used in the process of transmission and reception. A person with high communicative ability performs as a telemarketer who bears the responsibility of answering to the questions and queries of customers, prospects or potential customers. In the hotel industry, the telemarketing can be successful in promoting the business because the tour operators, travel agents and potential customers want plain answers of their questions and clarification of their queries which can be successfully done by the telemarketers. The questions related to booking, cancellation, confirmation, availability of a package tour, concessions and discounts or a change in hotel tariff require due co-operation of telemarketers. Since we find multi-channel services available, the telemarketers with the help of audio-visual exposure may be successful in influencing the customers. The promotional dimension of telemarketing is coiled in the essence of transforming the inquiries into bookings.

The hotel companies need to make use of the expertise of telemarketers and it is to be ensured that instruments and equipments used in the process are of quality and the telemarketers are aware of the proper operation and maintenance of technology or they are tech-savvy. The rich and uninterrupted communication services are found essential for the proper functioning of telemarketing. With the development of internet, we find the functional responsibility of telemarketers becoming easier. The reception and enquiry, complaints and grievances redressal, booking, confirmation are strategic areas where the hotel professionals require to guide the telemarketers so that they succeed in impressing upon the customers. The potential customers may also enquire about the tools of sales promotion offered by the hotel companies and in addition the information related to the availability of a number of supporting infrastructural facilities to make their trips comfortable and enjoyable.

The aforesaid facts make it clear that in an age of satellite communication, the telemarketers may also tangibilise the outstanding properties of their hotels *vis-a-vis* the tourist sites with the help of audio-visual exposure. The most important thing in the process is sensitising the prospects who have confusions and wrong information or incomplete information. Persuasion and transformation need due attention of telemarketer for which they need to enrich their communication excellence. It is to be made sure that transmission is in tune with the reception capacity of the receiver. The language, flow, volume, pause are the important dimensions for making the communication process result-oriented. The hotels as well as the travel agents are found making use of the services of telemarketing. Selling and promoting are the results that we get from this component of promotion. Patience is a trait that we expect from the telemeters.

 CAUSE-RELATED AND SPONSORSHIP MARKETING

With the changing corporate culture, we find corporate societal responsibility assuming an outstanding place in the policy decision-making practices of almost all the organisations. In a true sense, the cause-related and sponsorship marketing as an important component of promotion focuses our attention on the social responsibility of hotel sector. It is not only significant that hotel professionals ensure high level of occupancy ratio and help hotel companies in making high profits. It is equally important that like other organisations, the hotel companies also justify their existence in the society by promoting social interests in tune with their potentials. It is against this background that we include it in the list of components for promoting the hotel business.

The most important thing in the business promotion is creation of a platform where you get an opportunity to magnify your contribution to the process of social transformation. Particularly in a country like India where we find much more frequency in the natural calamities and problem of refugees or victims of terrorism; the leading national and global hotels may come forward for extending possible support to the victims. By organising such an event, the hotels create a platform which is with the motto of protecting and promoting social interests. The display of banners, literature, incentives, schemes at the place where such an event is organised would help hotels in many ways. On the one hand, they will be successful in building a social image while on the other hand also get a place for promoting the business.

The next in this context is sponsorship marketing which throws light on sponsoring an event and using it as a platform for business promotion. It is natural that the required expenses on the event would be met by the hotels and the amount collected as charity or donation would by used for protecting and promoting the social interest. We find focus on searching a place or making a place where you get an opportunity to build and project a positive image.

The hotels may also think in favour of special reliefs or discount for socially and economically backward segment or for physically challenged people. They may also explore opportunities for developing a park in the cities precincts where a number of people from diverse segments assemble and witness the advertisements of the concerned hotel.

The hotel companies need to realise their societal responsibility. Particularly the international biggies coming to India to earn more should not forget their social responsibility which would simplify their task of promoting the business. Business for society and society for business. The hotel professionals need to make use of this component of promotion which has been found neglected in a country like India where social image of an organisation is yet to draw priority attention of policy decision-makers. Business for profit and profit for society; offer you avenues for much more profits.

HOTEL PROMOTION STRATEGY IN INDIAN PERSPECTIVE

It is not only significant that you serve well. It is equally important that you promote well. In the Indian perspective, we find a good number of hotels offering world class services but so far as their promotional measures are concerned, we do not find their efforts at par with their counterparts coming from the foreign countries. The Oberoi, Taj, The Park Hotels, Leela and Bharat, ITC, ETH, Viceroy, DLF, Unitech, Royal Palms, no doubt, have been providing world class services but they lag behind in terms of promotion when we talk about foreign hotels like Accor, Marriot, Starwood, and new brands such as Amanda, Satinwoods, Banana Tree, Hampton Inns, Hilton and Mandarin Oriental.[18] This makes it essential that Indian hotels assign due weightage to their promotion strategy.

The formulation of a sound promotion strategy makes it essential that a suitable component of promotion is identified in the face of changing situational requirements and financial provisions. It is quite natural that all the components cannot be equally effective in all the conditions. The only way of identifying a suitable tool for a given market is to evaluate the various measures and to test them in light of the predetermined criteria and the objectives to be attained. The target market and the target audience are the two important decision-making areas where the hotel professionals would be required to focus their priority attention. The market status of hotels is also an important aspect to be taken into consideration while finalising the promotional strategy.

Advocating through others cannot be much more effective. It is in this context that we find today customer advocacy found to be a powerful tool for promoting and marketing the hotel business. The customers make a strong advocacy in favour of your products or services if they find them in tune with their taste preferences. Your expensive promotional measures may not be effective or may get only a lukewarm response, if the customers have not found the services to the desired level of their expectations. The word-of-mouth promotion is found even of negative nature[19] when the customers are found dissatisfied with the services and in this case, we find its impact very much instrumental in regulating the behaviour of customers. This makes it essential that hotel professionals assign due weightage to the changing taste preferences of hotel professionals. The product strategy thus throws a major impact on the promotion strategy. The customers being treated first and receiving the additional services are found satisfied. Increasing the number of satisfied group of customers is the prime motive which would make the ways for positive word-of-mouth promotion.

In the hotel industry the personal selling also simplifies the task of business promotion. This is related to direct selling where we find excellence of hotel professionals determining the magnitude of success. The front-line personnel in particular play an incremental role. The communication excellence of hotel personnel need due attentions of hotel professionals.

In the entire process, the sales executives play a decisive role. This makes it essential that hotel professionals brush-up and update marketing people so that they are found successful in performing as front-line staff.

The hotel professionals need to develop rapport with the media people, academics and celebrities so that they with their write ups publicise the services of hotels. The trading partners like tour operators and travel agents play a supporting role. The public relations need due attention of hotel professionals. The focus here is on getting adequate press coverage. The strategic decisions of professionals play here an outstanding role. Impressing upon the media people is essential in the very context. If the media people or academics get an opportunity to witness the service quality of hotels; they will be convinced and may provide coverage in their newspapers.

Though some of the experts feel that advertisement is not so much effective for the hotels but when we find professionals concentrating on creative advertisements, the advertisements may be helpful in the persuasion process. In the early 1980s, the Holiday Inns Inc. had a series of advertisements in the US with the headline "only one hotel chain guarantees, your room will be right". Subsequently extended to Europe, the advertising copy said, "Everything in your Holiday Inn room will be right". Or, "we will make it right". We will refund the cost of your room. "The important aspect of this theme is "guarantee". The Holiday Inn created the proposition, claimed it first and made it effectively their own concept since no other chain in the hotel business could say, we guarantee our room too without appearing to copy the original. Hence the main thing is to make possible creativity in your advertising decisions. About creativity, let's quote Doyle Dane Bernbach, the International Advertising Agency, "...........people can't believe you if they don't know about what you are saying, and they can't know what you are saying, if they don't listen to you and they would not listen to you if you are not interesting. Hence the main thing is creation of interest. For making the advertisements creative, it is pertinent that the advertising professionals have an in-depth idea of the changing behavioural profile of customers.

Regarding sales promotion as a component of promotion, we find it effective in promoting the hotel business. The hotel personnel and customers both of them are found influenced by the schemes of sales promotion. The hotel professionals need to offer innovative tools so that we find them effective in motivating the hotel personnel and the guests or potential guests. The trade partners are also required to be motivated and for that the hotel professionals may have schemes even for them. Keeping in view the intensity of competition, it is significant that tools of sales promotion are found effective in increasing the occupancy ratio.

In the face of increasing sophistication in information and communication technology, the telemarketing may also be used as a component of promotion.

The hotel professionals need to make it sure that telemarketers have excellence in communication and the supporting technology used in the process are of world class. They should have the potentials of turning the enquiries into bookings and further transforming the casual bookings into frequent bookings.

The cause-related and sponsorship marketing as a component of promotion makes it essential that the policy decision-makers assign due weightage to societal responsibility on their development agenda. This will help them in building and projecting a positive image.

The hotel professionals need to have an in-depth analysis of changing emerging trends in the markets, a microscopic audit of the promotional strategy adopted by the rivals, an idea of influencing situational forces and to develop a strategy and tact helping in persuading the customers. It is quite natural that while selecting a particular component your attention is on the motives entailed behind. You need to go through the product life cycle stage and to make it sure that normal or aggressive promotional measures would click. We cannot negate that particularly in the hotel business, the word-of-mouth promotion if of positive nature is found to be proactive. For this, the services must be of innovative nature. If you are sincere and honest to your customers, ensure personal-touch in the service delivery process, show empathy and human touch; the customers start making an advocacy in your favour. While promoting, you need priority attention on the marketing people engaged for this purpose. A team of dedicated and committed back and front-line staff would considerably help you. You need to make it sure that they have developed communication excellence and are efficacious of increasing and retaining the customers. Since we find worldwide economic recession, it is pertinent that you use pricing as a motivational tool. It is in this context that the concept of budget hotel needs priority attention of hotel chains or groups. On the one hand, we need to develop luxury hotels while on the other hand also require to promote budget hotels. We cannot deny that in the changing scenario, pricing as a motivational tool is expected to show the desired results. Developing a package in tune with the changing requirements of customers, if promoted in a right way, would help in increasing the occupancy ratio. The government needs to motivate the hotel companies interested in expansion. Whatsoever the incentives you propose to offer must be conveyed to the parties interested in developing hotels preferably at strategic points.

Thus, the hotel professionals need to formulate such a promotion strategy which succeeds in creating and retaining the business. Creativity, sensitivity and acceptability are found interrelated. With the help of different components of promotion, the hotel companies may develop such a brand which will earn loyalty. The task of satisfying and retaining the customers would gain a rapid momentum.

SUMMARY

You have studied in this chapter different dimensions of hotel promotion strategy. After this chapter, be sure that the following facts are well versed:

- **Promotion the Concept:** We consider promotion a managerial process to inform, sense, sensitize, persuade and transform the potential customers into actual customers.
- **Components of Promotion:** The different components of promotion are advertisement, publicity, sales promotion, personal selling, telemarketing, cause-related and sponsorship marketing and word-of mouth promotion. The hotel professionals need to select a component in the face of their requirements.
- **Why Promotion:** We promote with the motto of persuading customers, informing customers, reminding customers and reinforcing customer satisfaction.
- **Word-of-mouth Communication:** Satisfied group of customers act as a hidden salesforce and they advocate in favour of product to their friends and relatives. This process in known as word-of-mouth communication.
- **Personal Selling:** It is a highly distinctive form of promotion which involves social behaviour. It is the personal persuasion of tangible or intangible product by instrumentalising personal excellence. This is a process of face-to-face selling.
- **Why Face-to-face Selling?:** It is instant communication where rapport can be developed, shortcomings can be identified, and shifting of customers can be checked.
- **Non-verbal Communication:** An important advantage of face-to-face or personal selling is to communicate non-verbally. The movement of different parts of body communicate non-verbally. It is based on personal skill and care.
- **How to Raise the Effectiveness of Face-to face Selling?:** We find personal selling effective in many ways. It helps us promoting research, making possible detailed planning, helping in communicating effectively, paving the way for consumer-orientation and getting mix businesses.
- **Expression Techniques:** The expression techniques in the face-to-face selling are eyes, voice, speech, attitude and effective listening.
- **Skill Needed for Personal Selling:** We find here personal and social skills where both the verbal and non-verbal communications are found.

- **Sales Sequence:** The processes in the sales sequence are development of rapport, investigation, presentation, handling objection, and commitment.
- **Advertising:** It is a paid form of persuasive communication and an important dimension of non-personal promotion.
- **Importance of Advertising to Hotel:** Advertisement spreads information and offers to the prospects an opportunity of making choice. It helps in persuading the customers.
- **Advertisement Planning:** Planning for advertisement necessitates an in-depth study of services to be made available by the hotels in future.
- **Media Decision:** Media are considered to be an important vehicle to travel the messages. You bear the responsibility of selecting an economic but effective medium for advertisement.
- **Factors Guiding the Selection of Media:** Circulation, readership, people, primary or support media, product life cycle, penetration are the different aspects to be taken into consideration.
- **Selection of Message:** Message is an idea. The messages should be informative and interesting. Exaggeration of facts should be avoided. In addition, the messages selected should be capable of creating a favourable conviction.
- **Advertising Agencies:** The agencies meant for developing advertisement must have creativity, simplicity, a sound track record, and experience.
- **The Communication Process and Its Barriers:** It is pertinent that we are well aware of the main filters at work in the minds of target buyers. This is essential to make the communication effective.
- **Testing the Advertisement Effectiveness:** The idea chosen and the number of people or target audience, competition from others at the time of campaign and timing of the campaign in relation to the buying pattern influence the effectiveness of advertisement.
- **Key Methods for Testing:** Inquiries, recall test, recognition test and sales test are the key methods for testing the advertising effectiveness. Pre-testing and post-testing are the two important components.
- **Advertising Campaign:** The crying need of the hour is to make the advertising campaigns more and more effective. There are different stages, such as defining the product, defining the market, interpretation of objectives, planning of advertisement campaign, implementation of campaign and assessing the intensity of effectiveness are found helpful in raising the effectiveness of advertising campaigns.
- **Advertising Strategy:** The whole face of advertising is likely to be changed in the coming years. This makes it essential that our strategic decisions are in the face of emerging trends.
- **Public Relations:** We consider public relations as the deliberate, planned and sustained effort to establish and maintain mutual understanding between an organisation and the public. Publicity is an important aspect which is non-paid form of promotion.
- **Sales Promotion:** It is an important component of promotion or marketing communication. It is a short-term measure to increase the sales results.

- **Sales Promotion Techniques:** Sales promotion techniques are found directed at hotel's staff. Tour operators and travel agents, and guests/clients.
- **Key Tools of Sales Promotion:** The important tools of sales promotion are brochure, folder, packaging, attraction leaflets, merchandising, direct mail materials, display materials, competition, exhibition, special offer, maps and hotel group directories, alternative brochure formats.
- **Hotel Promotion Strategy in Indian Perspective:** In the face of increasing heat of competition when we find a number of international players in the race, it is essential that hotel professional develop such a strategy for promoting their businesses which strengthens the realization of customers that the services they would be delivered would have uniqueness and cost-effectiveness. In addition to other devices, they need to make use of internet for advertising. Creation of attractive web pages would be instrumental in advertising the hotel business. Since we find India potentially sound, a cost-effective measure for promotion needs due attention.

KEY TERMS

Personal Promotion
Impersonal Promotion
Oral Communication
Hidden Sales force
Advertisement
Publicity
Personal Selling
Sales Promotion
Telemarketing
Cause-related Marketing
Sponsorship Marketing
Word-of-mouth Promotion
AIDA Model
Stiff-liped
Greenhouse
Empathy
Instant Communications
Rapport
Non-verbal Communication
Sales Sequence
HOE Model
Brochure
Folder
Celebrities
Brand
Service Ambiance
Privileged Guests
Shower Caps
Fringe Benefits
Expression Techniques
Mannerism
Logic

REVIEW QUESTIONS

1. What do you mean by promotion? Focus on its components.
2. What do you mean by word-of-mouth promotion? Explain its role in promoting the hotel businesses.

3. Define personal selling. Explain its importance to the hotel industry.
4. What do you mean by sales promotion? Focus on the different tools of sales promotion to be effective in the hotel industry.
5. Discuss the different stages of sales sequence and their relevance to the hotel industry.
6. Explain the importance advertisement as a component of promotion in the context of hotel industry.
7. Discuss the different points to be taken into consideration while selecting media for hotel business.
8. Focus on the role of advertising agencies in producing creative advertisements for the hotel industry.
9. What do you mean by advertising effectiveness? How and why you find it essential?
10. Explain the instrumentality of telemarketing and cause-related and sponsorship marketing for promoting the hotel business.
11. Explain the justifications for offering sales promotion schemes to the tour operators and travel agents.
12. Write a note on Hotel Promotion Strategy in Indian perspective.

APPLICATION EXERCISES

1. "The hidden salesforce play an effective role in promoting the hotel business". Comment on this statement as a marketing professional.
2. In the capacity of a hotel manager, you have been assigned the responsibility of promoting the hotel business. Focus on the components to be effective in the process.
3. We promote hotel business to persuade, inform, remind and reinforce. Focus on this statement as a hotel professional.
4. Do you find personal and social skill important while marketing the hotel services? Defend your arguments as a hotel manager.
5. Like an electric current, we find flow of advertisement messages from one and to another. In the light of this statement focus on the points you will take care while selecting media for hotel businesses.
6. A well-planned publicity programme is found instrumental in raising the effectiveness of your hotel business. Comment on this statement as a marketing professional.
7. If the tour operators and travel agents are motivated, the ways are paved for promoting the hotel businesses. In the light of this statement focus on the role of sales promotion.
8. Formulate a promotion strategy for the hospitality industry in the Indian perspective which is found proactive but cost-effective.

End Notes:

1. Greene Melvyn: *Marketing Hotel and Restaurants into the 90s*; Heinemann Professional Publishing, Oxford, 1989, pp. 152-154.
2. *Ibid.*, pp. 153-54.
3. Richard H. Bushirk: *Principle of Marketing*; p. 414.
4. Foster Douglas: *Travel and Tourism Management*; McMillan, London, 1985, p. 256.
5. Holloway J. Christopher: *Marketing for Tourism*; Pitman, London, 1992, p. 105.
6. *Ibid.*, p. 105.
7. *Ibid.*, p. 107
8. Foster Douglas: *Op. cit.*, p. 263.
9. Strong E.K.: *The Psychology of Selling*; McGraw Hill, NY, 1925, p. 9.
10. Lavidge and Stenier: *Journal of Marketing*: October, 1961.
11. Holloway J. Christopher: *Op. cit.*, pp. 139-49.
12. Greene Melvyn: *Op. cit.*, p. 216.
13. Buttle F: *Hotel and Food Service Marketing: A Managerial Approach*, Hotel, Rinehart and Wintson, London, 1989, p. 354.
14. Foster Douglas: *Op. cit.*, p. 261.
15. Holloway J. Christopher: *Op. cit.*, p. 159.
16. Jha, S.M.: *Services Marketing*, HPH, 2009, Chap. 12: Hotel Marketing.
17. Jha, S.M.: *Op. cit.*
18. Ray & Teckchandnani: Indian Hotel Industry; Strategy Building; The Icfain Journal of Management and Research Vol. VII/5, 2008.
19. Pandey, V.K. Sahu & Jaiswal: Customer Satisfaction as Predictor of Customer Advocacy and Negative Word-of-mouth: A Study of Hotel Industries, Abhigyan, Vol. XXVI/3, 2008.

....ജ്ജ....

CHAPTER - 8

HOTEL PRICING STRATEGY

We cannot deny that Indian hospitality industry is reeling under the euphoria or room-boom. Since titans are found foraying into the hospitality sector, the domestic players need to promote pricing as a motivational tool.

CHAPTER OBJECTIVES

Introduction – Pricing Decisions: The Influencing Variables – Strategic and Tactical Role of Pricing – Pricing for Room Tariffs – League Tables – Pricing for Food and Beverages – Pricing for Function – Packaging up in Pricing – Hubbert Formula for Hotel Pricing – Different Types of Room Tariffs – Pricing Objectives – Pricing Strategy – Hotel Pricing Strategy in Indian Perspective – Summary – Key Terms – Review Questions – Application Exercises – End Notes.

LEARNING OBJECTIVES

This chapter aims at studying the different dimensions of pricing strategy in the hospitality industry. The motive is to sensitive readers to the strategical and tactical decisions enabling the hotel professionals in maximising profits and excelling competition. They are required to develop their awareness of pricing for food and beverage, pricing for room and pricing for function. With the increasing heat of competition mainly generated by global biggies, it is essential that hotel professionals adopt pricing as a motivational tool. The domestic players need to promote tactical pricing to increase the occupancy rate.

INTRODUCTION

The pricing decisions are critical, chaotic and challenging where marketing professionals are required to go through an acid test. The survival or prosperity of an organisation considerably rests on the effectiveness of pricing decisions.

The pricing as a tool of marketing is found complicating the decision-making practices due mainly to the increasing heat of competition. Pricing is not only the outcome of the marketing forces. It also conveys something to customers about the quality of a product. How to handle and monitor this tool of marketing depends upon the emerging trends. Modern marketers except in a few cases enjoy considerable freedom in making the pricing decisions. The freedom comes from their success in manipulating other controllables like product, promotion, place, process, physical evidence and people. The pricing decisions are influenced by a number of variables and the hotel professionals need to develop their awareness of the emerging trends in the markets. The formulation of a sound pricing strategy becomes significant in the very context.

The existence and prosperity of hotels or hotel chains or group are considerably influenced by the strategic decisions made for pricing. This makes essential that like other service generating organisations, the hotel companies also assign due weightage to strategical and tactical considerations. If we succeed in having a rational pricing structure and make the same nationally and globally competitive; the avenues are paved for excelling competition. Pricing strategy in the hospitality sector for is essentially a manifestation of the supply and demand phenomena. The seasonal fluctuation in demand plays a commanding role in pricing the services of hotel industry. A sustainable tariff policy in hotels the world over evolves around average room rates found higher during the season and during the off season. The professionals thus need priority attention on hotel average room rates. Increasing the occupancy ratio and increasing average room rate by using effective techniques of marketing are the two instruments available in the hands of marketing professionals. The role of a hotel professional in achieving such an average increase in room rates through effective application of marketing to stimulate demand reflects a number of decisions round the year.

The marketing professionals play an incremental role in the entire process. Use of price mechanism to manage demand is common and a daily concern. The hotel tariff cannot remain uniform throughout the year. During off-season, we find problem of low occupancy. The marketers make use of pricing as a motivational tool to bring down hotel tariffs and increase the occupancy ratio. For example, if a hotel of 150 rooms operate at 70 per cent room occupancy, charges ₹ 1,000/- per room per night, the annual sales revenue will be 150 × 365 nights × 70% × ₹ 1,000/- = ₹ 3,83,25,000/-. If by using more effective techniques of marketing the hotel tariff is increased by 5 per cent, i.e., ₹ 1,050 without loss of volume, the annual sales revenue will be 150 × 365 × 70% × 1050 = ₹ 4,02,41,250. The difference is of ₹ 19,16,250. If fixed costs are found constant, it represents a significant percentage of gross operating profit earned by this hotel. But the main problem before a professional is to increase the average room rate. Of course, the task is found easier during the season but particularly during the off season, the marketing professionals need to make use of their excellence and increase the occupancy ratio by minimising or rationalising the tariff.

Of late, we find worldwide economic recession and this is also to affect the pricing decisions of hotel companies. In the Indian perspective, we find a changed scenario because despite volatility in the global business environment, the Indian hospitality industry has been witnessing positive signs of development as we also find cases where tourists outnumber hotel rooms. During the yesteryears, the hotel industry has been found witnessing a strong growth particularly across some of the segments such as five-star segment, five-star deluxe, four-star and three-star categories. The ratio of foreign tourists along with domestic tourists across the country increased drastically, resulting into a record occupancy ratio of 70.8%, although a marginal growth of 2.6%. Nonetheless, foreign tourist arrivals for the period 2003-05 showed a significant jump of 45.5% with foreign exchange earnings of $5.7 mn in 2005 from $3.5 mn in 2003. In the Indian context we consider Park Hotels, one of the India's leading hotel chains flourishing under the leadership of Priya Paul. A bullish Chairperson Priya remarks that the foreign tourists have been visiting India in a good number and they are also found spending money because the trends indicate that the average spending of a foreign tourist in India has been found establishing an edge even over the France top tourist destination in the world. These facts make it clear that we find good auguries in the Hospitality sector provided the scope, the potentials and the reach of the Indian tourism continue to be enormous.

The pricing decisions rest on the demand and supply position. The increasing heat of globalisation and positive trends in economic transformation engineer a sound foundation for a further increase in the demand position. Since we find new projects to be completed in the years to come and at least one lakh rooms are to be added in the supply side; the demand is not expected to outweigh supply. We cannot negate that the hotel sector would thrive even in the years to come and if we find such a bullish trend continuing in the business environment, it is natural that we find an increase in the average room rate and it is in this context that the biggies have been planning to further increase the rates. The high pricing strategy has been found during the yesteryears; even today, we find the same strategy and we expect that such pricing strategy will be sustainable albeit in the long-run provided the "Incredible Indian Brand" continues to remain popular both in the domestic and global markets. Thus, the marketing professionals would be required to play a catalytic role in capitalising on the opportunities found in the new areas of tourism.

Since we find intensity of competition increasing fast due to the entry of a number of global biggies, it is pertinent that the marketing professionals assign due weightage to the tactical decisions so that the occupancy rate is increased even during the off season. We cannot deny the fact that discount may be a good pricing tactic and the large international players have also been adopting it for increasing the occupancy ratio specially during the off-season. There are many circumstances when there is an opportunity to obtain business albeit in a quiet period or booking for a definite large number of people like a group tour with double occupancy or an overnight convention when a discount on normal quoted tariffs is found raised. In these cases, the discounting up to an agreed maximum percentage is found logical. In a true sense, while obtaining business in a quiet period or developing new markets, such as weekend and short break holidays, pricing strategy should be to make tariff competitive. Though discounts are appreciated by companies or hotels to attract and retain their customers, the offering at the right time and in a right way so that the potential customers are not confused or they claim for more. The strategy related to discount should be cashed on carefully and at an opportune moment. If the marketing professionals while giving a presentation suggest a discount at an early stage where the potential customers have not even received the whole presentation and even may not prefer a discount, the offering at the very beginning of your presentation is likely to complicate your task. It is in this context that the marketing professionals need to offer the same at an opportune moment.

The present chapter studies different dimensions of pricing decisions. Pricing strategies for rooms, restaurants and function room has also been gone through. We find focus also on the different variables influencing the pricing decisions. The emerging problems while formulating the pricing strategy have also been deliberated. Presently when we find the market becoming much more competitive, it is not rational that we invite a stage like price war. Of course, we need to promote the tariffs found to be competitive. It is an unvarnished fact that talking about the pricing strategy is easier but writing about it much more complicated. This is due to the fact that when we start talking about the pricing strategy, someone may interrupt; may also ask a question and we find the ideas cross-fertilised. It is against this background that most of us find writing on a pricing as a time bomb where we find enough scope for committing a mistake. Despite a number of constraints complicating our task, it is right to say that a sound pricing attracting potential customers, maximising the occupancy ratio, increasing function room booking has been deemed necessary because it is to minimise the non-business days and further to help hotel professionals in maximising profits. Thus, the strategical and tactical decisions are the two important areas where marketing professionals need to make use of their world class excellence.

PRICING DECISIONS: THE INFLUENCING VARIABLES

When we talk about pricing decisions, it is pertinent that the different internal and external variables are considered in a larger perspective. The internal variables are also known, as *'controllable factors' as* the hotel companies or hotels can regulate or adjust the same, such as decisions related to product, promotion and distribution. But so far as the external variables are concerned, it is not possible for hotels or hotel companies to adjust or control the same, such as intensity of competition, changing profile of users or guests, emerging trends in society, changing economic scenario, changing political climate and changing lifestyles. Against this background, these factors are termed as uncontrollable. If hoteliers are well aware of both the controllable and uncontrollable variables, the pricing decisions are found to be sensitive.

Internal Factors

Product: This is an important factor influencing the pricing decisions of not only hotels but of all the organisations producing goods or generating services. In the hotel industry; hotel companies tend to make possible a fair blending of core and peripheral services. We accept the fact that not only core services are the point of attraction for the prospects, but the peripheral services also are the point of attraction. The hotel companies bear the responsibility of including new services in their product mix. In addition, they also need to introduce new peripheral services much earlier than their competitors. The pressure of growing inflation has also affected the hotel industry in a big way. This, in a natural way influences the cost structure. On the other hand, the prospects in general are now found more concerned for the services available for the price they pay. Of course, this is due to worldwide economic recession. If we are spending more for inputs, it is natural that we charge more for outputs. Hence, the hotel companies have to formulate such a product-mix which is not obstructing the formulation of a sound pricing strategy. The motive is to make the price structure competitive.

Promotion: We find both aspects of promotion instrumental in the hotel industry. We are supposed to pay handsome incentives to the personnel engaged in selling activities and promoting the growth of this sector. In addition, we have also to make our advertising campaigns successful. The tour operators and travel agents also expect handsome commission. The electronic revolution has paved ways for including advertisement to boost the hotel industry. The public relations activities also need major trends in attention. The customers also appreciate discount. Against this background, the hotel companies need to chalk out a big promotion budget. However, for promotional activities, the costs would go up. To be more specific, in the hotel industry, our strategic decisions should be biased to oral promotion or publicity for which we have to pay nothing. The hidden sales force or oral promoters can publicise business without affecting the budget planned by hotel companies. How to strike a balance between paid and unpaid forms of promotion is an important decision-making area. The motive is to optimise the promotional budget and to stimulate the customers by using pricing as tactical or motivational tool.

Distribution: In this context, the decision-making area is to strike a balance between inside and outside selling. So far as small hotels are concerned, they can work smoothly even with zero level channel. But the big hotels have to depend on tour operators and the travel agents for getting tourists to stay in this hotel. In this case, the hotel management also works out strategies to retain the tourists as habitual clients. The optimal distribution expenses may be helpful in optimising the hotel tariff. This inside selling would make possible a good economic score, and the hotel companies have to minimise their dependence on outside selling. Since the distribution expenses would influence the pricing structure substantially, a well-thought distribution policy becomes inevitable.

The aforesaid facts are a mute testimony to this proposition that the internal factors or controllable factors influence the pricing structure of hotels. The market is highly competitive so the hotels and hotel companies bear the responsibility of optimizing the distribution expenses. Accounting practice dictates that total costs are divided between Variable Costs (VC) varying with the products and Fixed Cost (FC) relatively difficult to change in the short-run. The break-even point is to be identified or the point where the total costs are equal to the total revenue is to be achieved. This would help in establishing how this point will be affected by changing different prices for the product. This also explains that how the quiet period could be minimised and the occupancy ratio maximised to ensure large revenues.

External Factors

In addition to the internal or controllable factors, there are some factors or uncontrollable factors influencing the pricing structure of hotels.

Competition: John Dean[1] identifies three kinds of competitive situations, e.g., lasting distinctiveness, perishable distinctiveness and little distinctiveness. A product has distinctiveness to the extent it can be sold at a price above or below the competitors' price without causing a change in its own price. In the hotel industry, the products are found to be of perishable nature. In this context, the level of competition faced by a hotel and substitutability between competitive products is found significant.[2] Here, it is pertinent that due weightage is assigned to the attitude of competitors. As and when we find a change in the price of our competitors, a hotel company has to bring its structure in line.

Economic health: Depression and slump damage the economic health of a country. It influences the disposable and discretionary incomes which govern the lifestyles and the development of the hotel industry. Pricing decisions directly or indirectly are influenced by a change in the behavioural profile. The hotel pricing decisions are to a certain level, also influenced by emerging trends in lifestyles. If we find a positive change in the discretionary income, avenues are subsequently paved for increased spending power. Contrary to it, if the pressure of inflation is found rising upward, a fall in the discretionary income follows, which contracts the spending power of masses. Recently, we have been witnessing economic depression and this has been making customers more sensitive to the price factor. The hotel companies while making pricing decisions or while fixing hotel tariff cannot underestimate the economic health of a country.

Governmental regulations: The regulations to control the tourism and hotel industry are also important considerations while making pricing decisions for hotels. If the governmental regulations are found liberal to the development of tourism industry, the flow of tourists would increase the demand for hotels. If the regulations are biased to promote a hotel, the customers would get an incentive to travel and stay in hotels. In the hotel industry, information regarding room prices at the reception and that food and drinks prices at the restaurants or money-off offers on original prices etc. carry some meaning. An increase in surcharge or in the slab of services tax would also raise the price (cost) of staying in a hotel. These facts make it clear that governmental regulations influence pricing decisions.

Users' behaviour: This is also an important consideration influencing the pricing decisions of hotel. Special low prices to large or institutional buyers, organisation of functions, overnight conventions and wedding etc. also influence the pricing decisions. In addition, the corporate culture is found gaining a momentum. We find a change in the behavioural profile of users, as prospects are found evincing interests in the hospitality sector for establishing their business through new ventures and deals.

Ethical consideration: In the pricing decisions for a hotel, in addition to other considerations as detailed earlier, we find ethical values significant. In major hotels, the tariff structure is found to be a status symbol. This makes it essential that a standard is maintained. Besides, it is also essential that the scope for profiteering is minimised considerably. This necessitates a fair computation of costs.

Code of conduct: For setting price, different associations regulating hotels are also important. In the Indian context, the Federation of Hotel and Restaurants Association of India (FHRAI) is an important body regulating the pricing structure. The Chartered Institute of Marketing Travel Industry Group (CIMTIG), London has its own code of conduct.

The hotels and hotel companies, while making pricing decisions should assign due weightage to the internal and external factors as detailed earlier. This would help them in making the price structure rational to be appreciated by their customers. What we have to think about and consider carefully in these situations is to study the market. Added to the factors that we have discussed earlier, it is essential that we have customer profiles to inform us about the markets untapped. A much greater degree of segmentation with a pricing policy taking into account the circumstances of different segments is found inevitable. Besides, the research activities are also to be strengthened, specially to ascertain whether the hotel is a first, second or third choice based on different facilities like rooms, restaurants and bars. It has been deemed necessary to undertake the market research activities on a regular basis to see that hotel is not sliding in popularity. Regarding consumer profiles, information related to rooms are age bracket, sex, cash, card, charge, business, tourist, convention, employment, place of employment, place of residence, mode of transport, new guest, first choice, length of stay etc. A well designed guest registration card, guest history records and information from the billing machine can supply this information. Regarding the segmentation, we will have to research different market like businessmen, women, foreign tourists, local tourists and conventions. The research would make available to us much more about them in future. Regarding choice, it is to be ascertained that what choice is your hotel. Market research should be carried out in busy periods because obviously the degree of the first choice will tend to be much higher in the quiet period of the week or year.

The following back-up information would simplify the task of making reasonable pricing decisions

- Maximum and minimum discount,
- Current charges,
- General economic situations affecting the market,
- Estimated inflationary impact on costs for the coming year,
- Intensity of competition, guest and customer profiles,
- Market segments and relevant strategies for each segment,
- Intensity of repeat business,
- Emerging trends in the currency exchange.

The above-mentioned back-up information would simplify the task of formulating, a sound pricing strategy. The motive is to avoid cases of over and undercharging. In the complex (volatile) business environment, strategic decisions related to pricing are prone to frequent changes. As and when the circumstances necessitate, it is essential to increase the structure but in any case this should not create an image of charging more or charging less. The hotel companies the world over, of late, face the urgency of increasing average room rates as well as occupancy. How to make it possible, specially when the intensity of competition is found moving upward. The task is difficult but a well thought strategy can make it possible.

STRATEGIC AND TACTICAL ROLE OF PRICING

Strategic Role: The strategic role of pricing reflects objectives of companies such as maximum growth or maximum profit. It communicates expectations of product quality, status and value to prospects, reflects the stage in the product life cycles and determines long-term revenue flows and good returns on investment. Here, price is found a management tool to achieve strategic business objectives. For hotels, this strategic price is the so called *"rack rate"*. This pricing corresponds broadly with the marketing strategy. It is the structure which an operator is obliged to publish in advance of production in brochures. The strategic decisions are made within an overall strategic framework which gears up the business towards its chosen goals. The hotels and hotel companies are supposed to use this tool here with the motto of achieving their business objectives. In plain words, it is right to say that regular and published prices are found in this category.

In the hotel industry, the strategic role of pricing is related to the development of a hotel. If it communicates quality of services offered by hotels, it is essential that the structure is not so low that prospects develop a wrong notion about the quality. While setting structure here, it is essential that the status of customers visiting the hotels is given due weightage. If in the five star hotels, the tariff is reduced, the customers feel that there is something wrong with the product. Besides, this would put a question mark on the image of the hotel and be a let down for the customers visiting the five star hotels. The strategic value of pricing is also to communicate effectively the stage of product in the life cycle. If we include a new and expensive service in the product mix, it is very natural that price structure would be high. Contrary to it, if the product is at the stage of saturation, it is natural that price structure would be low. The strategic role is also related to the long-term revenue flows. In the hotel business, it is related to the structure that we follow normally to increase the hotel revenues. Return on investments is also found to be an important role of strategic pricing. Capital appreciation on assets is as important as the operating profit. The investment on hotel land for constructing the hotel building is found a paying proposition — a profitable investment, particularly at sensitive points. It is found common specially in the big hotel companies. Here, the hotel companies are expected to measure the profits earned each year as a proportion of the total capital invested. Another objective of strategic pricing is to increase the annual turnover. A hotel is found attracting more customers by including new services but not increasing the structure so that the sales results are found impressive.

Tactical Role

The tactical role of pricing is involved in the essence of using it as a tool to promote the hotel industry. This corresponds to marketing operations or tactics with which an operator is prepared to do business on a weekly, daily or hourly basis. It changes as the date of production approaches in light of bookings and expectations at that time. This may be many weeks or months after the published price decisions. The tactical price is well advertised. It may be a closely guarded commercial secret when tour operators undertake business deals with hoteliers facing cash flow crisis or bankruptcy, unless the additional revenue is generated from the empty rooms. We also call tactical price as *'discounted'* or 'promotional'. Here, the price manipulates the marginal demand through incentives which may be general or restricted to particular segments. It matches competition by the quickest route and promotes trial for the first-time buyers. It provides a short-term tool for crisis management and determines short-run cash flows.

Pricing decisions are found important in both strategic and tactical sense. In the tactical sense, it plays an outstanding role. This is due to the inseparability and perishability of the hotel products. This is also due to the inability of the service generating organisations to carry over unsold stocks as a buffer to cope with future demand as found in the goods manufacturing organisations. Thus, whilst a hotel with 150 rooms in the budget end of the market has a capacity of 54,750 room nights to sell in a year, the marketing requirement is to organise budget level demand in *'blocks'* of 100-150 room buyers per night. To achieve this feat involves managers and in what amounts to a continuous obsession with demand manipulation in which tactical price cuts are usually the most important and often the only available tool decided and appreciated by the management.[3]

Also known as *price deregulation,* tactical pricing is found instrumental in promoting the hotel business. Experiences show that in the hotel industry, it is found to be a major selling tool. It is a matter of grave concern to explain whether such developments are required to be controlled or to be continued. This is also to show negative impact on the development of hotel industry or even decline in this business. There are a number of ways for practicing and benefiting from this tool:

- Special Discounts : Found applicable in the hotel industry. Customary to charge lower prices, specially during the off-season.
- Trade Discounts : Found applicable in the hotel industry as tour operators and travel agents are offered discounts.
- Seasonal Discounts : In the hotel industry, we find special Function room rates for overnight convention.

PRICING FOR ROOM TARIFFS

Here, we go through the guidelines for fixing reasonable room tariffs. Of course, the pricing policy considerations are helpful to establish pricing, maximum discount policies and goals. While fixing room tariffs, it is essential that we assign due weightage to the fact that whatever the price structure is to be adopted, the market will pay. It is not important that you are paying more for newly constructed hotel building as interest and therefore, you charge more. The average room rate should not be much higher than the competitive hotels, otherwise the market will not welcome it. In a few cases, the market is found ready to pay more, but here they expect something outstanding from you. Such as bookings in luxurious hotels, or hotels with attractive location or outstanding facilities. It is significant here to mention that a higher capital cost is not a guarantee to charge higher prices. In a hotel where we find inefficiency at peak, it is very natural that the capital costs would be higher but it is not going to justify the proposed increased tariffs. A far older, less cost-effective design of hotel is also to influence the cost but not the quality and so we do not find any justification for charging higher prices. A hotel may also adopt a policy to give high pay roll to provide a higher standard of services which the customers are ready to pay. In this context, there are a number of factors to be considered while fixing the room tariffs not only the cost.

There are some common factors considered by the hotel management and the public

- Current charges prior to a review,
- The estimated inflationary effect on cost,
- The general economic situation,
- The emerging trends in currency exchange and
- The intensity of competition.

In the last few decades, when the rate of inflation was not so high, most of our customers only looked at the current charges and the inflationary impact on cost. But now the situation is much more complex and against this background, our customers now consider all the aforesaid factors together with league tables. In addition, it is also to be answered as to what tariff increase will the market bear. This is an important consideration which is however, not given due weightage. Of course in some of the consumer industries, we find scope for testing a new product, a price increase in a geographical region which simplifies our task. In the hotel industry, we find a different case. All hotels tend to express apprehension towards some level of price increase, the whole market or that a significant proportion of the market could disappear. This apprehension is genuine to some extent. Here, we quote an example. In many European tourist capitals like Paris and London, the hotel tariffs were increased in 1978 and the value of dollar came down. This resulted in a fall of American tourists in 1979. Of course, the market did not disappear but the spending power was affected adversely which affected the hotel industry here. This could be the situation in any part of the globe.

Right averages and average room rates are the two important aspects to be taken into consideration while fixing these tariffs. The following are the economic criteria on room tariffs:

1. The total amount of net operating costs (after contribution from the food and beverage departments) of the note. Net operating costs, net operating cost plus rent (if payable), net operating cost, plus interest and net operating cost plus a target return on capital.

2. This helps in calculating the total room sales and to achieve various levels of profits with the assumption that room department cost ratios, staff numbers and staff standards are known.
3. On the basis of the above, a schedule should be produced as per the average room rates required in order to break-even and/or to achieve the profits-targets at various occupancy levels.
4. Budgets on room sales are to be planned, based on sales mix taking into account the different sources of business.
5. After this, based on the current quoted tariffs, it is possible to calculate what percentage discounting factors, subdivided between the different sources of business, must/not be exceeded if the average rate required is to be achieved.

Figure 8.1 and Figure 8.2 are based on a quoted room tariff of ₹ 1,800 (single) and ₹ 2,400 (twin) and an average rate requirement per room of ₹ 1,650. It is evident from Figure 8.1 that the policy decision on discounts shown do not allow the average rate requirement to be achieved.

	Business Mix %	Double Occup. %	Average quoted rate ₹	Discount %	Average room rate ₹
Individuals	40	30	1,980	10	1,782
Conferences	10	10	1,860	20	1,488
Groups	50	80	2,280	40	1,368
					1,546

FIG. 8.1: FIRST EXAMPLE FOR ROOM TARIFFS

Adapted from : Melvyn Greene; Marketing Hotels and Restaurants, p. 43.

	Business Mix %	Double Occup. %	Average quoted rate ₹	Discount %	Average room rate ₹
Individuals	40	30	1,980	5	1,881
Conferences	10	10	1,860	20	1,488
Groups	50	80	2,280	30	1,596
					1,655

FIG. 8.2: SECOND EXAMPLE FOR ROOM TARIFFS

Adapted from: Melvyn Greene; Marketing Hotels and Restaurants, p. 43.

In the first figure, the policy decisions on the discount shown do not allow the average rate requirement to be achieved as at the mix shown and discounts allowed, the average room rate required comes out to be more than ₹ 104 less – ₹ 1,546. However, by fixing lower maximum discounts as in Figure 8.2, the average is ₹ 1,655 – ₹ 5 above the average rate required of ₹ 1650.

6. Whatever the information that we find in Figure 8.1 and Figure 8.2 should be compared in the face of your own judgment on business mix and average room rates so that the possibility of achieving the same at various occupancy levels is known.

LEAGUE TABLES

League Tables show a hotel's position relative to the existing competition. Its objective is to put competition into the right perspective and to show that for some sources of business, there is more competition and for others it is less. Thus, it helps in gauging the intensity of the competition. If we know the relative physical advantages and disadvantages of our hotel and identify the intensity of competition, we get answers as to where to put our sales and marketing effort. For league tables, the following information is required:

1. Preparing a list of the hotels found to be competitive in nature. To assess the available facilities, visit and stay in hotels where you have not stayed. This will help you in assessing the real competition *vis-a-vis* narrowing down the sources of business where the intensity of competition is low.
2. Calculate your market share of the total competitive business capacity and share of your competitors. Independent consumer research is found to be significant in this case, which can also provide you clues to your market share.
3. Though all the following league tables are not relevant to all hotels, some examples of league tables required are:
   - Quoted tariffs (single room)
   - Single tariffs plus car parking costs
   - Quoted tariffs (double/twin room)
   - Function charges (food and beverage)
   - Room hire charges (excluding food)
   - Inclusive conference rates-daily-overnight
   - Group rates (tourists, etc.)
4. Some league tables are required which do not lend themselves too easily to exact gradings but to broad groupings, such as marketing muscle, e.g., site, location, car parking facilities, sales and marketing capability, group handling facilities, location convenience to air travellers and train travellers, conference packages, restaurant facilities etc.
5. We also use a popularity score basis to produce tables for businessmen arriving by train, plane or car, individual tourists, group tourists and conference delegates.
6. It is also essential that various potential markets are considered from different points of new, such as discretionary or essential spending, expanding or contracting market, repeat business potential, definite or provisional booking, seasonality etc.

In addition, it is also significant that you examine your own internal information management and take support of any information you can gather on the emerging trends in the market place. Besides, it would be appreciated to use individual experience and judgment to define more sources of business on which hotels should gravitate their marketing efforts. Towards this end established markets and the busy period should be given attention to a great extent. Since we find a variation in the busy and lean periods of business, it is deemed essential to define markets which will help to generate substantial revenues in these periods. You should also try to exercise this on your own hotels. Be careful while listing the advantages and disadvantages over the competition for the diverse sources of business. This is also known as Advantages/Limitations List (A/L List),

 PRICING FOR FOOD AND BEVERAGES

We cannot deny the fact that pricing meals and drinks in hotel industry (food and beverage areas) is a very complicated task, even more complicated than formulating the pricing strategy for rooms. In majority of the hotels, there are three or four types of rooms, e.g., singles, double, suites, front view, back view etc. But so far as the menus are concerned, we can have dozens of dishes with different price tags. While pricing food and beverages, there are some important points to be taken into consideration:

1. Do you find that your guests are eating in the hotel restaurant or coffee shop or where the competitive restaurants are very close to the hotel? In almost all the hotels, we find more or less the same trend. A proportion do eat in but a significant proportion go out. This habit is found developing the world over *'sleep in but eat out.* Our emphasis here is not on the long stay visitor but on the business executives staying in hotels for one or two nights. Of course, the availability of competitive restaurants close to the hotel affect the business adversely. We find here two factors instrumental, in bringing about this situation; first, the guests have experienced the problem of menu fatigue and second, the in-house selling strategies are not very effective.
2. It is also important to mention that where a hotel has two or more restaurants, they compete with each other and help splitting the market down the middle, rather than offering a true price and experience alternative to the overnight visitor, resulting in the outside business coming to the hotel.
3. Quite often, the hotel has only one function per day in the function room but when you ask the food and beverage manager or banqueting manager, he will often say 'very busy.' We cannot deny the fact that the function sector is one of the most exhausting and repetitive aspects in the hotel industry life. This problem is mainly due to the fact that the function room is usually not proportionate to the requirement of the customers.

A number of hoteliers agree that they must maintain regular room occupancy statistics, if they set efficient staff standards, operate and market the hotel professionality. But only a few of the restaurants have occupancy statistics (total covers, seat turnover ratios, table turnover ratios per meal compared against a target) and similar information exists on the availability of function rooms.

Profitability by Area

An important dimension in the food and beverage sector is to know that whether the areas selling food and beverage are making a net profit or loss which is considered a contribution to the total bottom line figure of the hotel as a whole. The hoteliers should know the departmental profit or loss under the Uniform System of Accounts on rooms, food, telephones, shops and other service facilities. But they often fail to have an indication of whether the restaurant, the function rooms, or the bar make a net profit or a loss. The total sales of a restaurant is not disclosed as they are subdivided in the uniform system under the sources of business for control purposes, i.e., food sales, beverage sales and other sources of potential sales.

A uniform accounting system, which is based on the American system is used by the hotel industry in various countries. This system was originally pioneered by large American hotel accounting firms in the 1930s. But basically, it is the control and accounting system and is not found so useful for policy changes or marketing. This makes it essential that accounts should be reanalysed twice a year or at least annually by incoming areas of production. A few years ago, this system was carried out in one major London hotel, where the management was found convinced that the function area with sales of around $ 4 million per year was, of course, the biggest area contributor to annual net profit. Based on past experiences it has been indicated that such information can be important in changing policies, creating a greater sense of sales urgency or in changing the existing pricing strategy.

Economic Aspects of Food Areas

The economic yardsticks for hotel rooms should also be prepared for a restaurant. It is essential to know individual staff standards, food costs and estimate other operating costs also. In addition, an estimate of the area's proportion of energy bills and rates (property taxes) can be included, so that a reasonable estimate of the total sales required for producing a departmental profit, breaking even at a house profit level, at the net profit level and at various net profit levels are calculated.

The following aspects are required to be considered carefully in the pricing strategy of a hotel/ restaurant:

1. Econòmic criteria, target average spends, target covers per meal period.
2. Current menu and drink prices.
3. Estimated inflationary effects on all costs.
4. Popularity indices for meal periods.
5. Average rates of spending.
6. Competition and emerging trends.
7. Customer segment profile – outside visitors to hotel — guests eating in.
8. Total cost of staying in room plus the average meal.

PRICING FOR FUNCTION

Restaurants can get more business because the food, services or atmosphere is unique or just a little better than the competitors. But this aspect is found more complicated for function room services. Most of the functions are fairly routined affairs which makes it difficult to produce a gastronomic experience when you are found engaged in serving the large numbers. In addition, this aspect is also found more competitive, specially on the price front. Of course, a number of points discussed earlier are found applicable even to functions and will be effective in maximising both the number of functions and the number of attendants. Payroll is also found to be a major cost on functions. Unless we move to the self-service (buffet style) functions, the payroll would be an important dimension which would also generate good sales revenue. In most of the countries, the service faculty in function rooms (waiters and waitresses) are casual employees engaged for the only function or a series of functions. Hence, it is not a part of the fixed cost.

Generally, a function organizer is offered a series of sample menus covering a range of prices. It is very natural that these prices vary, depending on the commodity and cost of the dishes. Payroll does not enter into the calculations. A number of hotels are found fixing a staff standard for functions based on their style of hotel or one waiter to a table of ten people or one waiter to two tables. Yet, we find payroll more expensive. In the hotel industry, where we want to stimulate overall growth in the function market, it is essential that we consider waiters as well as food cost an important variable in the pricing strategy.

The changing environmental conditions necessitate a change in the ways of fixing the pricing strategies because they are based on tradition. The world is changing. This makes it essential that the hotel management comes together and reviews the situations. We have to go through the exercise of fixing room tariffs, restaurant, bar and function room prices. We should look at the competition, identify the market needs and think out new strategies. When we complete the exercise, we should compare the results with the prices being currently charged. If we find a variation, we should identify the reason and should come to a conclusion what we should charge. Derek Taylor's excellent book (1979) entitled, *'How to sell Banquets' is* an excellent reading on this problem.

PACKAGING UP IN PRICING

We have gone through the pricing strategy for room tariffs, restaurant and function room prices. In an abnormal condition, the hotel companies have no option but to offer tactical pricing decisions and to allow discount on normal quoted tariffs. But it should not be a regular feature, as we find many circumstances when it is possible to obtain business even at the quoted tariff. We also find a possibility of obtaining a booking for a definite large group a high double occupancy, or an overnight convention or a quiet period, specially when tactical pricing may be practiced to get more businesses. Hence, the important decision-making area is to identify an opportune moment to obtain and expedite this possibility.

Generally, we prefer tactical pricing or offer discounts to obtain business in the lean business period. Here, it is an important question that why is it quiet? What are the important reasons that prevent business in those periods? What motivates the present market to ask for a discount in the lean times? This abnormal business condition requires a pricing package. This pricing package may not be abnormally low.

The manager of an hotel in the Scottish ski resort of Aviemore was interested in attracting more of the honeymooners' market. For that he produced a special brochure and the part of the package price was a bottle of Moet & Chandon on ice in the room on arrival. In fixing the price, he thought of including each bottle at the cost price only. After that he wanted to know the result if he charged the full price for the champagne in the total holiday price and offered both the basic price with no extras and an alternative with the champagne and other extras. Every couple bought the honeymoon package with the extras.

Another example where a client was to enter the weekend break market for the first time. He was ready to invest time and money for promoting and developing the market over a three year period. He was persuaded by an expert to offer two weekend packages, viz., one the standard package including accommodation, breakfasts, two dinners, service charges and taxes and the other was a VIP package, only for that special occasion and a half bottle of champagne on ice on arrival — a box of Elizabeth Shaw mints-fruit and flowers in the room-free cocktail before every meal, breakfast in bed etc. On an average just over a quarter, 27 per cent purchased the higher priced weekend break.

Here, it is important to mention that the total price per delegate of the VIP conference package was nearly twice the price of the lower executive package but it was bought without any hesitation or alteration.

The Executive Package was given on the usual conference rate for an overnight conference reduced *'to the bone'* no hidden extras. The VIP conference package included accommodation, all meals, use of exhibition and conference rooms, fruits and flowers in every room, one bottle of gin, sherry and whisky, opening cocktail party first evening, one evening at the theatre, last dinner special Elizabethan evening and a complete entertainment programme for wives.

Some of the hoteliers and sales executives feel that the only way to get a major deal is to offer discounts or to prefer tactical pricing. Of course, this is an easy way out, but at the same time, it is also right to say that only tactical pricing is unlikely to motivate the customers, in all conditions. This applies to all potential customers. We accept the fact that customers are now more sensitive to the price factor but if they are sensitive to quality and more conscious to the status symbol, even the tactical pricing would not bring any positive result. It is however, unwise to pay too much or pay too little. When you pay too much, you have a little money to lose but when you pay too little, you lose everything because the thing you buy is not going to serve the intended purpose.

The aforesaid facts make it clear that we find an opportune moment for offering discounts, specially on quiet nights but before we offer, the following aspects are to be given due weightages:

- Find out much more about the market, its motivation, price sensitivity etc.
- Isolate quiet periods clearly and try some creative selling first and then think about discounting.
- Try packaging up rather than pricing down.

To the extent it is possible, we should avoid the high levels of discounting schemes which lowers the average rate earned per room to a level which is so low that hotels would not be successful in showing a reasonable profit level even though the occupancy rate is very high. The main problem is that once the customers have used discounting facilities, it becomes difficult to increase them. Your professional excellence is involved in the essence of studying the market, customers and the competition and taking a decision in the face of the changing market conditions. If you prefer to package up, you are not only to sell more but also in a position to project your fair image. Even in the goods manufacturing organisations, we find that some of them are found selling the expensive products. This is also possible in the hotel industry but you need an in-depth knowledge of the market. We cannot deny the fact that the hotel costs are small compared to the overall costs of marketing, in relation to the development costs of a new product and compared to the sales price of that product. Hence, you should prefer to package up rather than pricing down.

HUBBERT FORMULA FOR HOTEL PRICING

The Hotel Review and Survey Committee of India which submitted it's report in August 1969, had recommended that hotel rates should not be allowed to rise unchecked.[4] It is important to mention that hotel pricing is not a simple mechanism of demand and supply. The regulations influence the process substantially. In the Indian context, the Hubbert Formula[5] is used for fixing hotel tariffs. According to the modified Hubbert formula, the hotel rates are computed as under:

- Operating expenses under all headings and a reasonable return of 6% on land and buildings except where leased, unless the lease approximates the sale price of the existing hotels and a return of 10% on the capital employed in hotel-keeping should be allowed in the calculations. In the case of new hotels, built after 1955, the return on land and buildings may be allowed at 8% with the same exceptions. The return in both cases should be the net return after allowing for taxation, insurance and depreciation.
- Less income from other sources such as store rentals, food and beverages and miscellaneous income.
  - Balance : The balance comes to the amount to be realised from room income.
  - Compute : Number of guest rooms multiplied by 365 days and reduced by giving an allowance for average vacancies (the room occupancy ratio to be postulated for arriving at this return should be 60%. In the case of hotels on hill stations and sea resorts, the occupancy or 60% per cent, whichever is lower)
  - Result : c/d average room rate.

The formula mentioned above provides a scientific basis for computing hotel rates by providing a reasonable return on the capital employed in the hotel industry. But at the same time, it provides a premium on the inefficiency of hotels. This is clear from the working results of the two hypothetical five star hotels presented in Figure 8.3.

Number of rooms	Hotel A 300 rooms	Hotel B 300 rooms
Operating expenses	₹ 106 lakhs	₹ 118 lakhs
Less income from other sources	₹ 14 lakhs (Including 10 lakhs from food and beverages)	₹ 44 lakhs (Including 40 lakhs from food and beverages)
Balance to be realised from room	$\frac{60 \times 365 \times 300}{100}$	
Average occupancy × days × rooms		
Average room rate	1,31,400	1,31,400
	₹ 140	₹ 112

FIG. 8.3: HUBBERT FORMULA, A PREMIUM FOR INEFFICIENCY

In Fig. 8.3 Hotel B is shown doing a brisk business in the sale of food and beverages, which is found to be a constraint while fixing hotel rates since the income generated from the food and beverages is to be deducted from the total operating expenses. This is to reduce the balance to be realized from room income and thus resulting in lower room rates. Of course, we find this formula suitable where the food and beverages account for less than 50% of the total sales. This formula should be revised on the following lines:

- Operating expenses under all heads should exclude operating expenses on food and beverages.
- Income from other sources should similarly exclude income from food and beverages.

- While calculating room rates, instead of considering individual operating results, average operating results of hotels of similar size and type should be taken into account to avoid multiplicity of rates. Here, the ideal solution would be to base the calculations on the optimum units of beds for various types of hotels.

With the assumption that fixed expenses of food and beverages are ₹ 2,00,000 and that 40 per cent are variable expenses, the operating expenses of hotel A and hotel B will be as :

$$\text{Hotel A} = ₹\ 2{,}00{,}000 + \frac{40}{100} \text{ of } 10{,}00{,}000 = ₹\ 6{,}00{,}000$$

$$\text{Hotel B} = ₹\ 2{,}00{,}000 + \frac{40}{100} \text{ of } ₹\ 40{,}00{,}000 = ₹\ 18{,}00{,}000.$$

In the above formula, the average room rates in case of Hotel A and Hotel B could be as under:

	Hotel A	**Hotel B**
1. Operating expenses under all heads except food and beverage	₹ 106 – 6 = ₹ 100 lakhs	₹ 118 – 18 = ₹ 100 lakhs
2. Income from other sources other than food and beverage	₹ 14 – 10 = ₹ 4 lakhs	₹ 44 – 40 = ₹ 4 lakhs
Amount to be realised from room income	₹ 96 lakhs	₹ 96 lakhs
4. Guest room days	1,31,400	1,31,400
5. Average room rate	c/d ₹ 146	₹ 146

In the face of the aforesaid analysis, it is right to say that Indian hotels face a number of problems while fixing the rate as they are not at liberty to charge arbitrary rates. In addition, the Hubbert Formula in itself presents a number of difficulties before the hoteliers.

DIFFERENT TYPES OF ROOM TARIFFS

The room tariffs are of different types, e.g., the American Plan, Modified American Plan and European Plan. The American plan includes three full meals and room. The modified American Plan includes the price of the room, breakfast, lunch or dinner. No meals are included in room rates in the European plan. Room rates are quoted as per day. Double room rates quoted are for two persons per day. Some hotels have luxurious departments, the tariff for which is available on application. Some hotels add a servicing charge of 10%. In hotels, where the service charge is added, paying tips is not encouraged by the management.[6] No doubt, these plans are good but it is better to give freedom to the guests to eat outside, if they like so. The American plan and the Modified American Plan give the impression that guests have to accept the tariff included in the room rate and so they have no option but to eat inside. This complicates the problem, specially while scheduling the travel plan.

Here, let's quote an example in the Indian context, regarding the American Plan which complicated the problem of a foreign guest. A lady tourist expressed unhappiness when asked whether she had to curtail her visit to any place in India. She remarked, "I missed the Taj ... I came all the way from United States to see the Taj but could not, because I would not like to waste the cost of meals which is a handsome amount." It is not so much the cost of the meals but the idea of waste and feeling of having been cheated which stops the visitors from moving out. The advice of the Federation of Hotel and Restaurants Association of India in this respect to adopt the European Plan (bed only or with breakfast) has not been heeded.

Not only in the Indian condition but the world over, we find guests preferring to eat outside. Since they do not want to spend much for eating in the restaurant of a hotel, they prefer to eat outside. In addition, if they eat outside, they are not supposed to come back during the fixed lunch and dinner times. It is against this background that the European Plan has been found establishing its edge over the American Plan. As in the European Plan, no meals are included, the charge is low and therefore, it is found more convenient and economic to the tourists or guests.

The inclusion of lunch or dinner in the room rate is also to complicate the working schedule of hotels/restaurants. It is in this face that while rationalising the hotel tariffs, it is pertinent that guests are charged only for rooms. If they prefer to eat in the hotel restaurant, it is okay. If not, they are free to eat outside. While promoting the restaurant business, it is also clarified that hotels should try to motivate customers not staying in the hotels. This would make them long-term customers. This is convenient to both the guests and hotels as well. If we are packaging up pricing, it is an additional incentive, otherwise it is found obstructing the hotel business, and making the task difficult in many ways.

PRICING OBJECTIVES

Pricing is a tool to achieve the marketing objectives. Once we identify the market and take a decision of benefit about the product positioning, it becomes easier to determine the price. While setting price, an organisation can adopt one of the three objectives, e.g., to lead the field by keeping the price down, niche marketing by differentiating its product from the market leaders and using pricing as a part of strategic decision. An Organisation with a substantial hold on the market succeeds in maximising profits by finding ways to reduce costs of increasing its share of the market by cutting prices in line with the reduced costs. In addition, an organisation with a more strong hold in the market may either reduce the price or may differentiate its product range from other market leaders. The multi-faced objectives of pricing are summarised in Fig. 8.4.

The general objectives of pricing help in developing the hotel companies, while the marketing objectives make possible a qualitative improvement in the hotel business. The hoteliers are required to have a detailed idea of the general and marketing objectives of pricing which would make their pricing decisions effective.

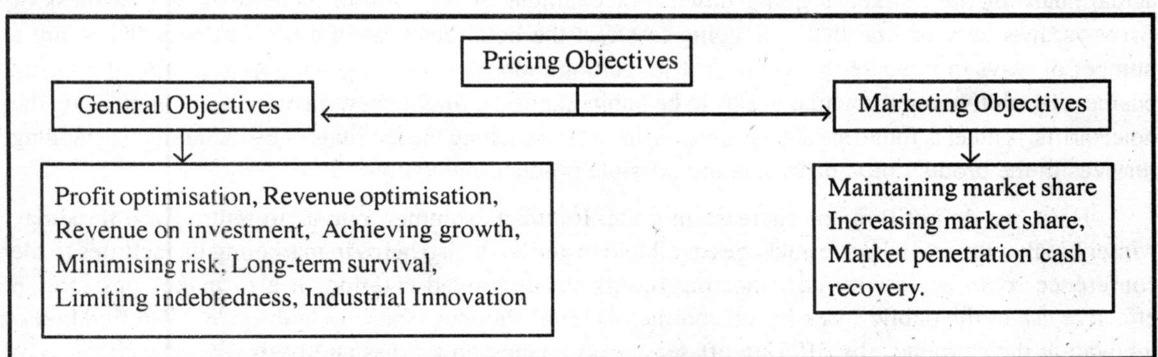

FIG. 8.4: PRICING OBJECTIVES

1. Profit maximisation: This objective is based on what the market will bear. To be more specific for the hotel industry, this pricing objective is found significant as hotels cannot and should not adopt a structure which cannot be paid or which is beyond the capacity of customers. Of course, it is difficult to know the bearing capacity of prospects which is influenced by a number of factors.

This objective paves the way for reducing costs. The hotels and hotel companies in order to fulfill this objective, attempt to bring down the operational costs. A hotel prefers to employ casual staff in peak season when the influx of tourists is found high and closes down during the off-season, specially with the motto of maximising profits. Here, we cannot deny social costs in hiring and firing indiscriminately to be more specific in areas where the intensity of unemployment is found high. When we employ casual staff, it is very natural that they are not dedicated or committed to generate major revenues for the development of hotels, which would ultimately affect the hotel business. The quality of services would deteriorate and the dissatisfied customers would not prefer repeat business. Thus, the long-term result is found negative which would subsequently reduce profit. Against this background, this objective is found elusive and unmeasurable.[7]

2. Return on investment: This is also an important objective for the hotel industry. Here, we identify and assess the profit potentials. If we find investment with the motto of capital appreciation, it becomes essential to get the return on capital invested. The investment in hotel land, or building is considered a paying proposition or a profitable investment, specially in the big cities or at sensitive points. It is more common among big companies than small ones.[8] However, this objective cannot be a sound base for judging the success of hotels or hotel companies. Here, the pricing tool is used to get the return on invested capital, of course, to a limited (percentage) extent annually. One plus point that we find in this objective is related to the capital development, which makes possible development and expansion of the hospitality service industry.

3. Market share objective: This is to achieve a certain share of market. It calls for restraining pricing, specially in the early stages of the product life cycle. At the initial stage, the objective is to penetrate the market, but at the later stage to expand the market. The expansion of leisure time and an increase in discretionary income indicates that holidays and travel would enjoy a long-term growth curve. To be more specific when the companies are found working in a saturating or stagnating market, this objective is found more significant.

4. Increasing turnover: Increasing market share and increasing turnover are the two different objectives. The turnover is a simple base to measure the rate of success. It may disguise that a company's actual share of the market is going down. For example, if we find an increase in the business of Airways, it is very natural that it is going to affect the hotel business in a positive way. There are a number of ways to increase the turnover, e.g., getting more prospects to visit hotels, getting the repeat business by motivating the actual guests to be habitual guests, finding new customers and increasing the hotel tariffs. A hotel is found attracting more business by enriching the facilities or by including outstanding services in the product mix, or by making possible product innovation.

Here, we do not find any increase in price. It attracts summer tourists to return for a three-day winter break with special price packages available to guests. It also helps in marketing its facilities to the conference room users with new meeting rooms and improved catering. It also makes possible an effective use of the public space by subcontracting retail shopping space in lobbies. We also find hotels innovating their products by offering off-season occupancy on a timeshare basis.

5. Meeting competitor's pricing objective: This policy objective reassures customers that they would not find the product by shopping around. This objective helps in attracting customers. It is important to mention that Thomas Cook in their premises regarding price offered to refund the difference in price on package tours if bought more cheaply elsewhere.[9] It is important to mention here that if this is adopted by more than one leading hotel group, a price war is a must. However, this objective is found helpful in the formation of a new market gap for cheaper holidays.

6. Retaining price objective: This objective concentrates on maintaining or lowering price with the motto of retaining the existing market. It helps in heralding a goodwill gesture, specially when the government seeks price restraint to control inflation.

7. Short-term profit maximisation objective: This pricing objective is also known as *'skimming the cream'* objective. It calls for setting up of high prices at the launching stage of the product. As and when new products are offered, we find a craze for these products or services among the customers. The hotel companies offering new services or including personal care services in their product mix attract customers. A theme park with exciting new rides bears the efficacy of attracting the tourists unless other competitors also introduce the same product. This objective provides high inflow of funds. We also find its application in organising the Olympic games, specially to recover the high costs involved in organising the events. We also expect here overpricing, such as when an important world fair is organised, the hotel prices are increased substantially. Or even while organising Olympic games, we find its impact on the business of the hotels.

8. Price leadership objective: This pricing objective is also known as *'going rate policy.'* In this case, the products are distinguishable from the competitors. Here, prices are based on what the competitors charge. A minus point to this objective is that the prices cannot be established or marketed until the competitors publicise their decisions — such as the small seaside hotels and guest-houses do not print their brochures unless they go through the brochures of some of the important hotel groups. They watch the attitude and prices charged by them and publish their brochures accordingly. This also simplifies their task of identifying the competitors' strategies and the amended brochures contribute to increased revenues through effective sales promotional strategies.

9. Cost plus pricing objective: This pricing objective is found very simple. Here, the prices are established for a particular product. The company allocates overhead costs to production plus a percentage of the profit and thereafter reviews the price structure, i.e., the selling price. Here, the concept of marginal costing is found significant since it makes available to marketers a flexible tool for pricing. It takes little into account the market forces and the current and future demand and fails in taking full advantage of the market potential or existing opportunities.

10. Market penetration objective: The objective of pricing helps in penetrating the market. Contrary to the skimming pricing objective, it concentrates on charging lower prices. This policy helps in getting an easy market entry. Here, the prices are set at the bottom of the product penetration range. It helps in gaining maximum exposure and acceptance by the market within the short span of time. The epitome of this objective is free sampling — gives it away.[10] It discourages the rival competitors. The main purpose is here to penetrate the market. We find different hotel companies offering give aways to customers and middlemen to penetrate the market. We accept the fact that is a part of tactical pricing, in which pricing acts as a motivational tool.

11. Cash recovery objective: The cash recovery objective helps in recovering cash, specially when products fail in getting a positive response in the market. In the hotel industry, where we find perishability in the product, it is found more impact-generating. As and when the products tend to become obsolete or the new products are not to be popular, this objective is found helpful. We are well aware of the fact that hotel products (services) are highly perishable. In this objective the motive is to get substantial returns.

In view of the aforesaid pricing objectives, it is right to mention that the setting of the pricing objective is an important task before the hotel companies. The emerging trends in market, the success rate of an organisation, the image of hotel companies, are some of the important aspects to be considered on a priority basis. If the hoteliers assign due weightage to different aspects of the hotel industry and succeed in studying the market, the pricing decisions are to be effective. Here, the important decision-making area is to define the objective in the face of the changing business conditions. The hotel companies or other companies use pricing both as a strategical tool and a tactical tool. As a strategical tool, the hotel companies have to assign due weightage to the development and expansion of hotels but as a tactical tool, they have to assign due weightage to the motivational strategy. The market is highly volatile and competitive and so, the decision-making practices are required to be based on an in-depth study of the market and the level of competition.

PRICING STRATEGY

Talking about pricing strategy is easier than the writing about. Pricing decisions are found vital as well as challenging. It requires an in-depth study of other elements of marketing mix, such as product, promotion and distribution. The futurologist, such as Henley Center suggests that as, discretionary income goes up, the symbolic and emotional values attached to the brand name also go up. We accept the fact that symbolic value occupies a place of significance even in the hotel industry. During the last few decades, the contours of development have undergone radical changes. We find multi-faceted developments — the trends in economy changing fantastically discretionary income has also shown an upward trend though the inflationary pressure has been found affecting the same adversely. However, we find a change in the lifestyles. This is found paving ways for the development of hotel culture. The new emerging trends in the economy world over have made customers much more price sensitive. The business environment is found more volatile in which fierce competition has reportedly complicated the task of decision-makers in almost all the areas — whether they produce goods or generate hospitality services.

A hotel fixes its own tariff but the patrons determine the price at which it will be actually sold. In a competitive environment, it is necessary that hotel companies as well as the customers have a feeling of trust. Here, the value and satisfaction are found to be a judgment motion which differs from person to person. The service providers look at the cost plus profit and the customers look at the satisfaction in return. The pricing strategies necessitate a fair blending of the two opposite interests. Of course, this requires professional excellence.

The pricing decisions are, however beset with diverse problems. No doubt, fixing the hotel tariffs is just like pricing other goods and services, the hoteliers however are expected to be more careful to the spending capacity of the prospects, and at the same time it is also ensured that the tariffs are remunerative to the hotels and hotel companies. In the hotel industry, the problem of price setting is more pronounced. This is mainly due to the fact that hotel services are perishable in nature. In addition, other aspects, such as seasonal growth in business, slag in demand and unadjustability of supply to demand in the short run are also found influencing the decision-making process. It is also right to mention here that no pricing decisions would be sensitive, unless the hoteliers consider the cost of construction, operating cost, location factors, the magnitude of competition etc. The experts also opine that room tariffs are not determined by the market forces of demand and supply. In the hotel industry, other factors are found to be more instrumental in making the pricing decisions. The important problem in the formulation of a sound pricing strategy is to make strategical and tactical decisions in such a way that hotel companies not only survive but also succeed in establishing themselves in the market.

The pricing decisions are made to fit the changing competitive conditions encountered by specific products and we call them pricing strategies. The pricing policies are general and are operative in long-run whereas pricing strategies are specific and short-run. In the formulation of pricing strategy, setting the price itself is a key element. The emerging trends in the competitive market conditions also influence the setting of prices. It is essential that pricing decisions are consistent with the desired image. Long-run pricing objective derived directly from company objectives provide guidance to decision-makers in determining pricing policies, formulating strategies and setting prices. Thus, it is right to say that like other companies, the hotel companies should also be more careful while making the pricing decisions. This would help them in many ways.

Managing relatively volatile demand around a relatively fixed capacity of highly perishable product supply is identified as one of the principle characteristics of the hotel business. The use of price as one of the four main levers in the marketing mix is found important in managing demand. It is not to be forgotten that its successful use involves reconciling customer interests and operational constraints within a strategic framework of business objectives. Pricing is a central concern in marketing all types of goods and services.

There are four main elements in the strategic marketing response which accommodation suppliers make to their external business environment, such as planning the most profitable business mix of segments and products, deciding the position or image which each accommodation unit or chain of units should occupy, encouraging and rewarding frequent users of the services and developing marketing integration between units in common ownership (chains) or units in individual ownership (voluntary cooperatives). Strategic decisions are expected to generate a profitable mix of bookings and room occupancy through the production and distribution of appropriately priced, distinctive products which match the needs and requirements of identified segments. In other words, for hotel operators, three of the four Ps of the marketing mix are of strategic importance and even, promotion, is planned within boundaries set by the positioning strategy.

The different stages in the product life-cycle are also to influence strategic decisions. While discussing pricing strategy, Kotler has pointed out nine possible price quality strategies.[12] This has been summarised in Figure 8.5. While discussing strategical and tactical planning, it is also said that strategies are concerned with the overall plans for the implementation of policy.[13] Thus, a strategy of discriminating pricing, involving the setting of different prices to different market groups, e.g., business travellers and holiday travellers may be introduced.

		Price	
	1 Premium Strategy	2 High value Strategy	3 Super value Strategy
Product Quality	4 Overcharging Strategy	5 Average Strategy	6 Good value Strategy
	7 Rip-off Strategy	8 False-economy Strategy	9 Economy Strategy

FIG. 8.5: STRATEGY ON PRICE/QUALITY

Here, an important problem is to decide whether to differentiate price to different geographic areas: should the price structure be common to all customers or it should vary to reflect different market demands in the various segments of the market. As for example, it is found more expensive to sell package tour arrangements in the USA than in France. Long haul holidays sold in Britain are found cheaper in Britain than the identical holidays sold in Germany. This is partially due to high marketing costs on the continent and partially because the market bears high prices. Alternatively, should the price be same in all markets but adjusted to take into account the changing condition like night flights vs. day flights, low season vs. high season? It is important here to mention that when Billy Butlin launched his first holiday camp, high pricing strategy was all — in pricing, a single price gave his customers access to every entertainment facilities in the camp. Here, it is clear that each decision must be made on its own merits and should reflect the market condition in the host and generating countries. Strategies must be designed to respond to the marketing initiatives.

Thomson Holidays is considered a market leader. It is the feeling of Thomson Holidays that not only competitors were waiting for them to launch their brochures before determining prices; some of them were even adjusting prices to undercut Thomson after the Thomson Brochure appeared in the market. Your strategy also answers to the questions that how should a company respond when challenged on prices?

Thus, we find pricing strategies critical as well as challenging. The hoteliers are required to show professionalism while formulating the pricing strategies. The motive behind the formulation of a strategy is to promote business and to excel competition. The hotels and hotel companies are found selling a number of items, such as bedrooms, function room, restaurant services, bar services. The market conditions cannot be uniform round the year. It is very natural that a change in the market condition necessitates a change in the pricing strategy. You have to identify sensitive time for adopting a particular strategy so that the competitors know about the same after its application.

We accept the fact that pricing menus and drinks in hotel food and beverage areas to obtain maximum sales and profits is a very complex subject and in many ways, even more complicated than preparing a strategy on rooms. While formulating a strategy, the hoteliers are supposed to take into account a number of factors, specially the diverse nature and character of dishes, involvement of costs and spending power of the customers. We need to consider carefully the economic criteria, target average spends, target covers per meal period, current menu and drink prices, estimated inflationary effects on costs, popularity indices for meal periods and average spending figures competition, customer segment profile and the total cost of staying in rooms.

The hoteliers are also required to formulate pricing strategy for room tariffs. The usual factors to be taken into consideration are current charges prior to a review, estimated inflationary pressure, general economic situation affecting markets, strategies for attracting foreign tourists to a hotel for the last five years, the currency exchange trends, the amount of composition and the rate of increase — we think competitors are going to change. Besides, it is also significant to get the answer of what tariff increase — if there is to be an increase wills the market bear? It is very natural that hotels and hotel companies in general are found neglecting this dimension, which carries a place of outstanding significance. Since the hotel industry is found different to other goods manufacturing industries, we find chances of disappearing from the market following the implementation of strategies in a stock manner. Of course, this is a real worry as an abnormal increase in room tariffs would affect the influx of tourists adversely *vis-a-vis* the demand of hotel rooms.

Of late, the business environment is found more volatile. This makes it essential that in addition to the aspects summarized earlier, we consider customer profiles which would tell us more about the markets we are obtaining now and would also provide clues to the markets we are missing. Added to this a much greater degree of segmentation with a pricing policy, taking into account the circumstances of the different segments would also help hoteliers. Besides, market research to ascertain whether the hotel is a first, second or third choice for the different facilities, e.g., rooms, restaurants, bars. This will help hotels in maintaining its popularity.

The above mentioned facts are important for formulating pricing strategy for the function of area since this would help to maximise the number of functions. Seeking an amount of profit on food and wines rather than a percentage can help an increase in sales. Here we find payroll an important aspect. If we want to stimulate an overall growth in the function market area, we should consider waiters as well as food cost as an important variable in the pricing strategy.

HOTEL PRICING STRATEGY IN INDIAN PERSPECTIVE

We find 21st century a landmark for the qualitative and quantitative transformation of hotel industry in the Indian perspective. The credibility for the same goes to the globalisation which made ways for a number of positive developments in the Indian economy. The mounting intensity of competition made it essential that the hotel industry assigns due weightage to pricing strategy. The professionals serving the hospitality industry required world class excellence for strategical and tactical decisions. Actually the pricing decisions become much more critical and challenging when we witnessed national as well as global biggies making professionalised efforts for excelling competition. The demand and supply factors play a decisive role in the making of pricing decisions. In India or in any part of the globe, we find pricing strategy depending upon the market mechanism. Seasonal fluctuation in demand keeps the hotel industry in a position, found a bit different to others.

The strategical decisions for pricing make it essential that hotel professionals keep themselves aware of the emerging trends in competition which during the yesteryears has been found moving upward. A good number of international brands have come up and many others are planning to enter. We cannot negate that positive attitude of global biggies is due to the prosperous future of Indian hospitality industry. It is amazing that despite market slump, the hospitality business in India is shining and there are no signs of burnout in the near future. It is forecast that Indian hospitality business would witness a rapid growth in demand position even in future. When we do not expect a fall in the demand side, the market would continue to remain competitive and for excelling competition, the hotel professionals would be required to consider the problems related to pricing. On the one hand, the hotels in general would be required to continually endeavour to upgrade their services and facilities while on the other hand they would also make their price structure much more competitive. Improving the quality and minimising the costs need due attention of hotel professionals. For minimising cost or practising cost economy, it is also significant that a number of incentives are provided by the central and state governments. The incentives like Tax holiday, rationalisation of luxury tax, special incentives for the hilly areas and rural areas would enable hotels to bring down the costs *vis-a-vis* the hotel tariff. It is significant to mention that keeping in view the Commonwealth Games, the Ministry of finance accorded Tax holiday for 5 years for 2-star, 3-star and 4-star categories. Such type of event needs to be organised frequently which would inject new life and strength to the Indian hospitality industry. The tax structure should not be based on the announced traffic but on the basis of actual payments made by the clients. The multi-faceted incentives thus would minimise the tax burden on the hotels which would minimise scope for bringing down the hotel tariffs and making the price structure competitive.

Increasing the occupancy ratio is an important decision-making area which creates a condition for minimising or rationalising the hotel tariffs. This makes it essential that hotel professionals take support of tactical decisions and offer the maximum possible discount to motivate the tourists. It is quite natural that aggressive promotional measures are activated to sensitise the potential tourists. The discounted or promotional price offered during off-season for the customers and the trade discounts for the tour operators and travel agents need priority attention of hotel professionals.

It is significant to mention that there has been a robust growth in the Indian economy specially during the yesteryears which has led to better purchasing power and has resulted into the influx of tourists both at domestic and global levels. The booming IT and ITES sectors have also contributed to the increasing demand. Besides, the Introduction of low-cost airlines in the country has given a major thrust to air travel in the country. Thus the surge in demand has also resulted into the price escalation. The Average Room Rate (ARR) and Occupancy Rate have witnessed more than 20% increase since 2004-05. In different towns and cities, we find variation in average room rate. Of course, the root cause for such a variation is non-optimal supply. In Bangalore, we find increase of about 50% and in Gurgaon, it is 30%.[11]

In view of the above mentioned facts, it is right to mention that in the Indian hospitality sector, we have witnessed positive trends and such a scenario will continue even in the coming years provided we do not find something abnormal in the national economy. To keep on moving the process of development, it is also essential that hotel companies activate innovative efforts for getting a success in making profits. The strategical decisions thus focus on the fact that hotel professionals will succeed in capitalising on the opportunities if the tools of marketing are used in a right way. If you continue to deliver the best and promote your services in a creative fashion; you succeed in increasing both the tools, viz., average room rate and the occupancy rate. In this context, it is also pertinent that you make the process cost-effective and succeed in maximising the profits.

With the entry of international biggies, the Indian hotels will face a number of challenges and threats. This makes a strong advocacy in favour of an overhauling of strategical and tactical decisions. It is much more pragmatic that the domestic players in lieu of excelling competition with Hyatt, Hilton, Starwood and Marriott concentrate on budget hotels. It is significant to mention that amongst the Indian players, the IHCL has been found promoting budget hotels with "Ginger" brand in Ahmedabad. The IRCTC too has been planning to develop budget hotels. We cannot deny that the growth in budget hotels will prove to be a major saviour for the hotel industry in Indian perspective. The hotel companies will have to make it sure that budget hotels are sincere to the basic needs of the tourists such as central air conditioning, hot and cold water, TV and cable, direct dial phone, mini fridge, tea/coffee maker, writing desk, electronic locks and WIFI. They would be required to make the price structure affordable. Integrating budget hotels with shopping malls would also have the advantage of retail outlets. Since we find a big increase in the number of middle class; the demand for such hotels will be amongst both the domestic as well as the global customers.

Upgrading the services and rationalising the hotel tariffs are the two strategical decisions for the hospitality industry which will make the way for their existence and prosperity. We cannot negate that the hotel industry is reeling under the euphoria of the room boom.[12] With titans foraying into the hospitality sector, the small players have been facing multi-faceted difficulties and constraints in keeping up with the benchmarks in terms of stiff remuneration, quality standards, and business opportunities. The results like high staff turnover, dearth of real estate, limited resources and lack of business confidence may topple the small players. The entry of the giant brands may lead to mergers, acquisitions and consolidation. Such a prescription will be helpful in excelling competition. The hotels have to reduce the tariff rates and in addition have also to focus on some of the areas such as de-risky by looking at new market segments for business, involvement of local committees for delivering quality hospitality services, professionalism and reduction in attrition rates.

To improve the financial health of hotels, it is also pertinent that they are allowed higher Floor Area Ratio/Floor Space Index (FAR/FSI) so that more rooms and commercial spaces are created out of the same space which helps in generating sustainable revenues.[13] The allotment of land to the hotels should be on a long-term lease basis or under the PPP mode through joint venture, revenue sharing etc. They can also focus on large revenue projects such as setting up of convention centers, golf courses, tourist trains etc. having substantial gestation periods. These facilities may be created by the private initiative with the government acting as a facilitator and catalyst.

In view of the above mentioned facts, it is right to observe that hotel professionals will be required to play a meaningful role in the formulation of strategical and tactical decisions. Exploring avenues for new emerging markets, innovating service quality, increasing the average room rate and the occupancy rate, practising creative promotional measures for sensitising the prospects as and when the discounts are offered and expanding avenues for minimising the hotel tariffs are some of the measures for making hotels financially sound.

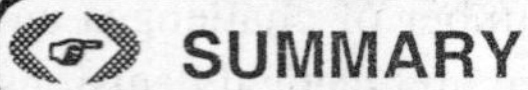

SUMMARY

You have studied in this chapter hotel pricing strategy. Before turning your eyes on other problems, be sure that the following facts are well versed:

- **Pricing Decision: Influencing Factors:** There are a number of factors influencing the hotel pricing decisions, such as internal and external. In the internal factors, we study problems related to product, promotion, distribution and in the external problems, we go through competition, economic health, governmental regulations, and psychology of users, ethical influence and code of conduct.
- **Strategic and Tactical Role of Pricing:** Strategic role of pricing reflects objectives of hotel companies such as maximum growth or maximum profit and therefore price is used here as a management tool to achieve strategic business objectives. Here, the pricing corresponds broadly with marketing strategy. The regular and published prices are found in this category. For hotels, this strategic price is the so called *'rack rate'*.

  The tactical role of pricing is related to promotion. This corresponds to marketing operations or tactics at which an operator is prepared to do business on a weekly, daily or hourly basis.
- **Pricing for Room Tariffs:** This is an important dimension of the hotel pricing strategy. Here, we go through the guidelines for room tariffs. While fixing room tariffs, it is essential that we adopt such a structure which the market would bear. The common factors to be taken into consideration are current charges prior to a review, estimated inflationary pressure, general economic situations; emerging trends in economic situations and the intensity of competition.
- **Pricing for Food and Beverages:** Here, the hoteliers are required to consider economic criteria, target average spends, target covers per meal period, current menu and drink prices, estimated inflationary effects on all costs, popularity indices for meal, average spending figures, competition and emerging trends, customer segment profile and total cost of staying in rooms plus average meal.
- **Pricing for Function:** While formulating pricing strategy for the function area, the hoteliers should consider all the factors while fixing pricing for room tariffs and food and beverages. In addition, the payroll is also an important factor.
- **Packaging up Pricing:** In an abnormal condition, the hotels and hotel companies have no option but to offer tactical pricing but it should not be a regular feature of the pricing strategy. Here, the hoteliers should explore opportunities for packaging up rather than pricing down.
- **Hubbert Formula for Hotel Pricing:** This is an important base for fixing hotel tariffs in the Indian context. There are a number of shortcomings in the formula which necessitate an amendment.
- **Types of Room Tariffs:** There are three types of room tariffs, e.g., American Plan, Modified American Plan and European Plan. The American Plan includes three full meals and room. The modified American Plan includes the price of the room, breakfast, lunch or dinner. The European Plan is found without any meal.
- **Pricing Objectives:** There are two types of objectives, such as general or business objectives and marketing objectives. In the business objectives, we find profit optimization, revenue

optimization, revenue on investment, achieving growth, minimizing risk, long-term survival, limiting indebtedness, industrial innovation. In the marketing objectives, we find maintaining market share, increasing market share, market penetration and cash recovery. The general or business objectives of pricing help in developing the hotel companies whereas the marketing objectives make possible qualitative improvements in the hotel business.

- **Pricing Strategy:** We find pricing strategies critical as well as challenging. The hoteliers are required to show professionalism while formulating the pricing strategies. The motive behind the formulation of a strategy is to promote business and excel competition. In a competitive and volatile business environment, it is significant that hotel companies as well as the customers show a positive. Our pricing strategies need a fair blending, of two opposite considerations found between the hotel companies and guests. The important problem in the formulation of a sound pricing strategy is to make strategical and tactical use of pricing in such a way that hotel companies not only survive but also succeed in establishing a leadership in the market. Managing relatively volatile demand around a relatively fixed capacity of highly perishable product is identified as one of the main features of hotel business. The hoteliers are here required to formulate pricing strategies for-room, restaurant and bar. The motive is to raise the contribution of restaurant to the total profit of the business. Pricing strategy for food and beverages also occupies a place of outstanding significance. The diverse nature and character of food and drink involvement of costs and spending power of customers are equally important. With the passage of time, we find multi-faceted developments which are likely to affect the strategic decisions for pricing. Frequent discussions with front-line staff would help hoteliers in formulating a sound pricing strategy and generate large revenues. The strategical and tactical decisions make it essential that hotel professionals need to make use of the different tools of marketing in the face of emerging trends in the demand and supply. On the hand they need to offer innovative services while on the other hand also to explore avenues for using discount as a motivational tool.

- **Hotel Pricing Strategy in Indian Perspective:** In the Indian hospitality industry, we find positive signs of development. The occupancy ratio is found increasing and the average room rate is also moving upward. The demand position makes a call in favour of improving the supply position. Since we find a number of international brands coming, it is pertinent that the domestic players focus their attention on budget hotels. With Titans foraying into the hospitality sector, the small players need to bring down their hotel tariffs. The hotel professionals would be required to play an outstanding role while managing costs and increasing the occupancy ratio, particularly during the off-season. We find Indian hotel industry reeling under the euphoria of the room boom which necessitates professionalised approach for strategical and tactical decisions. It is also essential that government offers tax incentives and creates a suitable nexus for the development of hotel industry under PPP mode. For improving the demand position, it is significant that marketers focus on the new areas of tourism for which we find the upcoming youths developing a craze. The demand may be generated with the promotion of medical tourism where we find ourselves potentially sound. Minimising the costs, reducing the tariffs, due focus on budget hotels, innovating the service quality, creativity in the sensitization process are some of the measures to bring demand and supply position at an optimal point. The pricing strategy for the coming years makes it essential that hotel professionals make use of pricing as a motivational tool.

KEY TERMS

- Strategical Pricing
- Tactical Pricing
- Average Room Rate
- Occupancy Rate
- Seasonal Fluctuation
- Quiet Period
- Controllable Factors
- Fixed Cost
- Variable Cost
- Service Tax
- Rack Rate
- Seasonal Discount
- Trade Discount
- League Tables
- Beverage
- Cocktail Party
- Package Up
- Hubbert Formula
- American Plan
- European Plan
- Niche Marketing
- Market Penetration
- Futurologist
- Premium Strategy
- Ripe-off Strategy
- Tax Holiday
- Luxury Tax
- Market Slump
- WiFi
- Floor Area Ratio
- Floor Space Index
- Titans
- Euphoria
- Room boom
- Foray
- Hotel Tariff

REVIEW QUESTIONS

1. Focus on the strategical and tactical role of pricing in the hospitality industry.
2. Explain the economic criteria while fixing the room tariffs.
3. Discuss the factors which you would take into consideration while fixing room tariffs together with league tables.
4. Throw light on the different variables which guide the pricing decisions in a hotel.
5. Explain some of the important points to be taken into consideration while pricing food and beverages.
6. Write a short note on pricing for function.
7. Focus on the Packaging up in pricing in the context of hotel industry.
8. Explain the computation of hotel rates according to the modified Hubbert Formula.
9. Explain the relative merits and demerits of different types of room tariffs.
10. Write a note on the pricing strategy of hotels.
11. What do you mean by Pricing Objectives? Explain the pricing objectives in relation to hotel industry.
12. Comment on the pricing strategy of hotel in the Indian perspective.

APPLICATION EXERCISES

1. "The internal and external variables draw your prime attention while making pricing decisions in the hotel industry." Comment on this statement as a hotel marketer.
2. In the capacity of a hotel professional focus on the conditions where you will make use of tactical pricing for increasing the occupancy rate.
3. You are working as a hotel manager and in that capacity you have to fix room tariffs. Will you prefer to make use of league tables for this purpose? Justify your opinion.
4. "In a majority of the hotels, we find three or four types of bedrooms but in almost all the hotels restaurants, we find dozens of dishes." In the light of this statement throw light on some of the important points which you would take into consideration while pricing food and beverages.
5. "Profitability by area and economic aspects of food areas are important points to be taken into consideration by the hotel managers while pricing food and beverages." Comment on this statement.
6. "You should prefer to package up rather than pricing down." Throw light on this statement in respect of packaging up in pricing.
7. "The general objectives of hotel pricing help in developing the hotel companies whereas the marketing objectives make possible qualitative improvements in the hotel services." Discuss this statement in the capacity of a hotel marketer.

End Notes:

1. J. Dean: *Managerial Economics*; Englewood Cliffs, NJ., p. 402.
2. Hollowway, JC & Plant, RV: *Marketing for Tourism*; Pitnan, London, 1992, p. 86.
3. Victor TC Middleton: *Marketing in Travel and Tourism*; Heineman Professional Publishing; Oxford, 1988, pp. 88-89.
4. *Hindusthan Times*, New Delhi, August 3, 1969.
5. Anand, MM: *Tourism and Hotel Industry in India*; Prentice Hall of India, New Delhi, 1976. The Hubbert Formula owes its name to Mr. J.R. Hubbert, Ex-Chairman, Residential Hotel Committee USA. He was authorized by the Hotel Association of America in 1947 to evolve a standard formula for computing hotel rates with the help of the reputed hotel consultants firm, Harwath and Harris Kerr Foster and Co. In 1957; the Hotel Rate and Structure Committee recommended the adoption of the above formula with slight modifications, pp. 119-20.
6. Jha, S.M.: *Services Marketing*; Himalaya Publishing House, Bombay, 1994, Chapter 6 *Hotel Marketing*, pp. 243-45.
7. Lynn, R.A.: *Price Policies and Marketing Management*; Homewood III, Richard D. Irwin Inc., 1967, p. 99.
8. Michael Deakin: *Pricing for Return on Investment; Management Accounting*, December, 1975, pp. 43-44.
9. Holloway, JC & Plant, RV: *Op. cit.*, p. 87.
10. Richard H. Buskrik: *Principles of Marketing*, p. 361.
11. Discovering India; *The Analyst;* Nov. 2006, p. 23.
12. Interview with Jaisree Anand; *The Analyst*; Nov. 2006, p. 21.
13. Eleventh Five Year Plan: Vol. III p. 345-51.

CHAPTER - 9

HOTEL PLACEMENT STRATEGY

The increasing heat of competition requires an attitudinal transformation so that the intermediaries with the help of e-channel succeed in activating the process of distribution. With the application of E-CRM strategy, the hotel professionals find it easier to satisfy and retain the customers.

CHAPTER OBJECTIVES

Introduction – Channel: The Concept – Distributions Policy: Influencing Factors – Distribution Chain: The Term – Tour Operators Travel Agents – Importance of Travel Agents to The Hotel Industry – Functions of Travel Agents – In-house Selling and Front-line Staff – Telephone Selling or Tele-marketing – E-CRM Strategy – Strategy for Restaurant Sales – Sales Action Plans – Balancing Inside and Outside Selling in a Hotel – Sales Letters and Mailing Shots – Other forms of Distribution of Hotels – Cost of Distribution – Improving Sales Techniques – Distribution Strategy for Hotel – Summary – Key Terms – Review Questions – Application Exercises – End Notes.

LEARNING OBJECTVES

This chapter aims at studying the different dimensions of distribution strategy to be practised in the hospitality industry. There are a number of options before the hotel professionals such as zero level, one-level and double level channels. Currently, the e-channel has been found beating all the traditional channels. The global biggies have been found promoting and penetrating e-channel. It is pertinent that hotel professionals penetrate e-channel for service distribution which would make the service deliverly process cost-effective. The hotel professionals need to promote E-CRM strategy for understanding the customers.

INTRODUCTION

A widespread myth persists even till now that because services cannot be put on shelves and stored in warehouses as inventory, the distribution system or channels are found less impact-generating in the service generating organisations in general and the hospitality industry in particular. But they need to change their perception because the service delivery processes, the channelisation of services and the location points for the service delivery process play a meaningful role even in the services sector. A sound distribution system is found significant to the development of organisation; either producing goods or generating services. We cannot deny that offering of services has a far reaching impact on the making of marketing decisions. Of course, the hotel services are found at the point of production known as in-house sale; however the channels play here an outstanding role. In the hospitality industry, the services are sold at three points through different channels, e.g., in-house sales where the front-line staff sell the services directly to the customers or guests or clients; by the tour operators who buy the services in bulk from the hotel companies and then sell them to the travel agents and third one the travel agents who act as a retailer and sell the services directly to the customers. This makes it essential that hotel professionals formulate a sound placement strategy so that the promised quality of services are delivered to the ultimate customers on time and in a decent way.

In the hotel Industry, the distribution of services is mainly related to the transmission of information by the providers to the users or agencies. The enquiries, bookings, confirmations and cancellations are the areas where the new generation of Information and communicate technology *vis-a-vis* the communication excellence of front line staff and hotel professionals play a decisive role. It is in this context that we find information management playing a commanding role in the hospitality sector. A number of factors are found influencing the distribution process such as points of sale, costs on distribution, managerial excellence, image of hotel companies and strategical and tactical decisions.

The responsibility of managing the distribution system is found on the shoulders of marketing professionals and in this context it is essential that the system is efficacious of purchasing the hotel bedrooms, function rooms, restaurants so that the rate of occupancy is found at its peak. The hotel professionals are here required to take a decision regarding a strong and efficient chain which can bring momentum in the service distribution process. With the infusion of new generation of information and communication technology, the hotels, offices of travel agents and tour operators are found well connected through internet which considerably increases the operational flow for time-honoured and promised quality of services to the customers. The location of points of sale, cost of distribution and professional excellence of marketers sizeably influence the distribution process. For the accomplishment of organisational goals or for bridging the gap between service-generation and service-delivery to the ultimate users, the distribution system must be efficient, positive and dynamic. The system requires to be efficacious of purchasing the bedrooms, function rooms and restaurants through the chain of distribution and at the same time should also be successful in projecting a fair image of hotel companies. The hotels and hotel professionals are here required to take a decision in favour of a strong and efficient chain which can successfully sell the business to the ultimate customers. They are also required to take a decision regarding the levels that the selling would be direct or through the tour operators and travel agents.

The choice of location is, of course, an important decision-making area specially for proprietor-oriented restaurants, guest houses and small tourist attractions. This is due to the fact that a well located small business can often be sure of an adequate flow of customers to its area. In this case, we find customers directly coming to the hotels and therefore the distribution channel becomes insignificant. However, the fundamental attraction of a well located site cannot be devalued. The researches undertaken during 1980s by international hotel companies seeking suitable hotel sites in major European cities provide some illustrations and testify the power of location.

The selection of tour operators and travel agents is an important decision-making area for hotel professionals. If the tour operators and travel agents work together with the hotel management, the occupancy rate may significantly be increased. Soliciting the s of tour operators and travel agents is an important functional responsibility of hotel professionals. If the hotel professionals have an innovative plan for motivating them, the task is found easier. The tour operators buy a range of products in bulk. This also includes accommodation facilities, function rooms, specially for organising conferences and seminars. After buying the different services, they develop an ideal package and sell them to the travel agents which we term as single product known as "package holiday". This makes it clear that tour operators play a decisive role in promoting the hotel business.

With the new generation of ICT, we find a radical change in the system of distribution because we witness the concept of total automation gaining popularity and almost all the services are now found well supported by computer governance. The customers *vis-a-vis* the hotel companies have immensely been benefited with the use of computers specially with the support of internet services.

The hotel professionals need to formulate a sound strategy at all the three stages. The front-line staff need to play multi-faceted roles such as interacting with the customers, answering to their queries, transforming the enquiries into bookings, showing empathy and providing to the customers an opportunity to enjoy and gain new experiences. Satisfying and retaining the customers considerably rest on the role and behaviour of front-line staff. Managing front-line staff is an important functional responsibility of hotel professionals. The tour operators evince interests in bulk selling. They play an incremental role in generating the hotel business in the capacity of wholesaler. The hotel professionals need to develop business relationships with them so that bulk selling improves their financial position. The tour operators need to develop business relationships with the travel agents who acting as a retailer sells hotel products to the ultimate users. At all the three stages, the hotel professionals need personalised efforts. The marketing tools need due attention of professionals so that they succeed in increasing the occupancy ratio.

In managing distribution services, the hotel professionals need to have an in-depth analysis of markets so that they take a decision regarding the channel to be preferred for selling the hotel products. The hotels have a basic choice whether to sell directly to the ultimate customers or to achieve sales through one or more third parties; we call them intermediaries. It is quite natural that size of hotel and the available rooms and function rooms will be a determining factor for exercising options. The location points for hotels, tour operators and travel agents are also an important decision-making area. It is significant that principal and intermediaries make it sure that ultimate users of services do not have any problem in locating the service or distribution points. Adequate flow of customers to the points of sale is significant. In this context, It is also important to mention that new generation of information and communication technology has been found redefining the concept of distribution. With the online booking, we find the channels becoming insignificant, however the hotels cannot devalue the distribution system.

In addition to other aspects, the hotel professionals also need to make the distribution process cost-effective. The cost of installing reservation systems, computers, staff capable of dealing with enquiries and bookings, the costs of brochure production, costs of sales promotion, incentives aimed at motivating the retailers and other points of sale, costs of support visits to intermediaries, costs on maintaining and motivating the sales people, costs of developing and brushing up the people need due attention of hotel professionals. The motive is to minimise the distribution costs.

Strategical decisions for the distribution of hotel service make it essential that hotel professionals ensure quality services which are to be delivered by intermediaries to the customers in different forms such as enquiries, bookings, cancellations, information regarding the destination, excursion, legal formalities, visa etc. They also need attention on tactical decisions so that the customers and intermediaries develop their awareness of the discounts and packages as an incentive for business promotion. The increasing heat of competition requires an attitudinal transformation so that the intermediaries with the help of techno-driven personalised services succeed in activating the process of distribution. From traditional channel to e-channel, we find the concept of distribution witnessing multi-dimensional transformation.

CHANNEL: THE CONCEPT

Marketing channels are the distribution network through which products flow to the market.[1] The middlemen constitute the building blocks the producers seek to link together into marketing channel to bridge the existing gap between themselves and the target market. We cannot deny the fact that distribution is a major decision-making area, in which the marketing channel is found important. More formally defined, '*a marketing channel or channel of distribution is a path traced in the direct and indirect transfer of ownership to a product moving from producers to ultimate consumers*'. In the hotel industry, the marketing channel describes the methods by which a service is distributed from its manufacturing source to its customers.[2] The customers get the services directly from hotels (in-house), from travel agents or tour operators. The tour operator works here as a wholesaler and the travel agent works as a retailer. The producers are the hotels and the hotel companies. The distribution channel simplifies the task of hoteliers by selling in bulk or in small number. Against this background, we call channel a path to move the services. If the path is clear, the movement is fast. Like this, if the distribution channel is sound, the distribution is found effective.

The concept of the distribution channel is not found confined to the distribution of physical goods as most of us believe. Like the producers of goods, the of service providers also face the problem of making their output available and accessible to target population. A distribution channel is any organised and serviced system created or utilised to provide convenient points of sale and/or access to consumers, away from the location of production and consumption, and paid for out of the marketing budgets. Thus channels are in no way left to chance, but carefully planned by producers and serviced regularly by them with sales visits, literature computer links and in many other ways.

Key Words in Services Distribution

Because of the special nature of distribution that we find in the hotel industry, we find many people getting confused over the way in which different terms are used. This necessitates a clarification of different terms used in the distribution process. Rathmell (1974) suggested that, *"To facilitate integration with conventional thought, location and distribution, channel and delivery are used interchangeably.*[3] If we use these terms interchangeably, the confusion is very natural. A brief explanation of different terms used would remove confusion.

Distribution	:	The process of creating access for the consumers in one or more process places Process convenient for him but away form the place and time of delivery or products being bought
Location	:	The geographical location of a site or sites.
Delivery	:	The physical process of producing or performing the services product simultaneously with consumption
Distribution	:	Any organised and serviced system, created or utilised to provide convenient points channel or of sale/or access to consumers, away from the location of delivery pipeline
Intermediary	:	Any third party or organisation between producer and consumer which facilitates purchases, the transfer of title to the buyer and sales revenue to the producer.

DISTRIBUTION POLICY: INFLUENCING FACTORS

The fact exists as a trend in today's market that the flow of distribution is an important consideration for making possible a time honoured movement of products to the customers. This movement requires a sound distribution policy. There are a number of factors influencing the distribution policy of hotels and it is essential that the marketers are well aware of these factors — such as location of point- of-sale, cost of distribution, effectiveness of the marketing efforts, image of the hotel companies and customers' motivations regarding the hotel products.

1. Points-of-sale: The potential points of sale are found instrumental in attracting customers. Here, it is essential that we have an idea of a particular point where they would collect in a very good number. The function room, restaurant or a bar in a hotel have emerged as potential points of business today. In addition, the important tourist attractions are also found sensitive points where potential guests collect in a good number. The front-line personnel in the hotel, the tour operators and travel agents working for hotels are supposed to have an idea of these points so that they reach successfully to the target audience. This would be more effective through oral communication.

2. Cost of distribution: The distribution policy not only in hotel companies but in almost all the goods or service generating organisations are found significant. Here, it is important that these organisations are particular to the distribution cost. It is not a commercially viable proposition, specially for small hotels to distribute through the tour operators and the travel agents as the cost will be increased and the pricing strategy would be high. But so far as the big hotel companies are concerned, they have to seek the cooperation of tour operators and travel agents both. Hence, it is to be particularly finalised with the viewpoint of a pricing strategy as to what would be responsible, or commercially viable; to prefer in-house selling or to make possible a fair blending of inside and outside selling.

3. Image of the hotel company: For the formulation of a sound placement strategy, it is also found to be an important point. Here, it is significant that products are purchased (forwarded) strongly through the distribution chain and create a right image for the product and the company, otherwise the creation of business is found doubtful. The image problem is found to be an obstacle in projecting the image.

4. Effectiveness of the marketing efforts: An evaluation of the marketing efforts is found significant to formulate a sound distribution policy. It is meant that the hotel companies have assigned due weightage to the effective incorporation of marketing resources. The distribution decisions should be viewed in the face of changing stages of the product life cycle.

5. Customers' motivation: In addition to other aspects, it is also pertinent that we think about the motivation of customers regarding the hotel services. If the products are found efficacious in fulfilling the motives behind visiting a hotel or a restaurant or if the products are in tune with the taste preferences of the customers, and if the products are found internationally competitive, the task of formulating a sound distribution policy is simplified in an appreciating manner.

THE DISTRIBUTION CHAIN

The term *'distribution chain'* denotes the methods by which a product or service is distributed from producers to the consumers. The middlemen are the link and if the link is strong, the producers find it convenient to increase the occupancy ratio of rooms in a hotel. The middlemen are wholesalers, buying hotel rooms in bulk and then selling the same to the retailers, i.e., the travel agents. In the hotel industry, the tour operators are found acting as a wholesaler — they package the service products and then sell either to the travel agents or even directly to the tourists. The tour operators are called 'products of services' by some of the experts a definition based on the logic that they buy financially potential services from different organisations and then combine the same which takes the shape of a new product. The travel agents buy the services at the request of their clients and provide a convenient network of sales outlets thus, catering to the needs of a local catchment area. In Figure 9.1, Figure 9.2, and 9.3 the middlemen and the distribution chain for the hotel industry have been shown.

A detailed study of the chain of distribution is found essential to make sensitive decisions. The hotel companies are to be made available a sound distribution chain or network. If the link is strong, the chain is strong. If the chain is strong, the movement is time honoured. If the movement is time honoured, the time leadership is possible. If we succeed in establishing the time leadership, success at the marketplace paves ways for long-term benefits. Consumption is considered to be the beginning and end of all

FIG. 9.1: TWO-LEVEL DISTRIBUTION CHANNEL

marketing activities. By managing the distribution system, we succeed in utilising the efficiency of middlemen. They are professionally competent to implement distribution strategies cost-effectively, paving ways for the satisfaction and appreciation of the hotel customers.

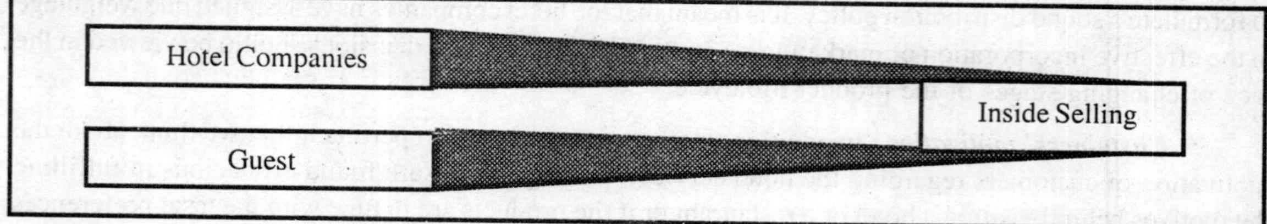

FIG. 9.2: ZERO-LEVEL DISTRIBUTION CHANNEL

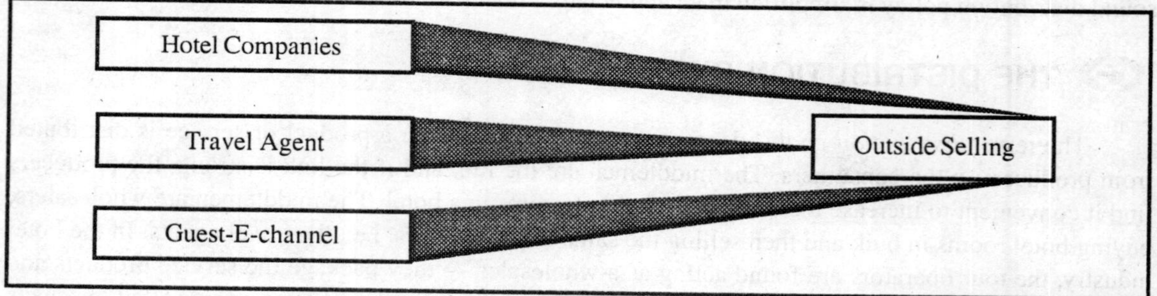

FIG. 9.3 ONE-LEVEL DISTRIBUTION CHANNEL

In Figures, 9.1, 9.2, and 9.3, we find three different systems for the distribution of services. In Figure 9.1, both the wholesaler and the retailer are bridging the gap between hotel companies and the customers. In Figure 9.2, we find .direct distribution where, the guests avail in-house services directly from the hotels. In Figure 9.3, we find one chain distribution, where travel agents buy from the hotels and the guests buy from the travel agents. In this system, we do not find any wholesaler.

Middlemen in The Hotel Industry for Outside Selling

Tour Operator

A tour operator (wholesaler) buys the services from the hotels in bulk. He invests in the individual elements in the travel product and combines them in such a way that he is selling a package of travel to his clients.[4] In common parlance, he is also referred to as a travel agent. He bears the responsibility of delivering the services. He reserves hotel rooms and function rooms for his clients. The tour operators buy a range of tourists products in bulk such as airline seats, assured hotel accommodation and coach transfers and package them for subsequent sale to travel agents or even directly to the customers. The tour operators, acting as ground operators normally provide services at the destination only and do not package or market transportation to and from the destination. These operators provide services like overnight accommodation, sight seeing, guides and transfers. The hotel companies sell rooms and even function rooms to the tour operators to maintain their business and ensure continuous cash flow.

A number of salient features of tour operators are improved profit margin, sales volume, good repeat business, acceptable rates of return, low cost of distribution, maximum care by travel agents, supply reliability, motivating retailers minimising risks and strategically thinking before applying novelty to accepted products. In view of the outstanding features of tour operators, we find instrumentality of this chain in selling and promoting hotel business. We find almost all leading hotel companies taking the support of tour operators for selling their source products. To a certain extent, big hotels find it difficult to work without tour operators.

Historically, the tour operator has mostly emerged from the retail travel agency. However, today we find an apparent difference between the tour operator and the travel agent. So far as the organisation of the tour operator and travel agent is concerned, we find some similarities as both are headed by the managing director. As summarised in Figure 9.4, we find four divisions, e.g., sales division, research and planning division, finance and control division. In the sales division, we find advertising, sales promotion, public relations and branch offices. In the research and planning division, we find market research, reservation, contact programmes and cost and pricing. In the destination and service division, we find contact with agents, tourist promotion and technical help. In the finance and control division, we do not find any specific division.

It is significant here to mention that small hotels do not need to take the support of tour operators as they sell directly to the customers. The medium and large hotels have to seek the co-operation of tour operators since this helps them in maximising the occupancy ratio. Here an important decision-making area is to select a leading tour operator who only not helps hotels in selling but also helps in promoting the business.

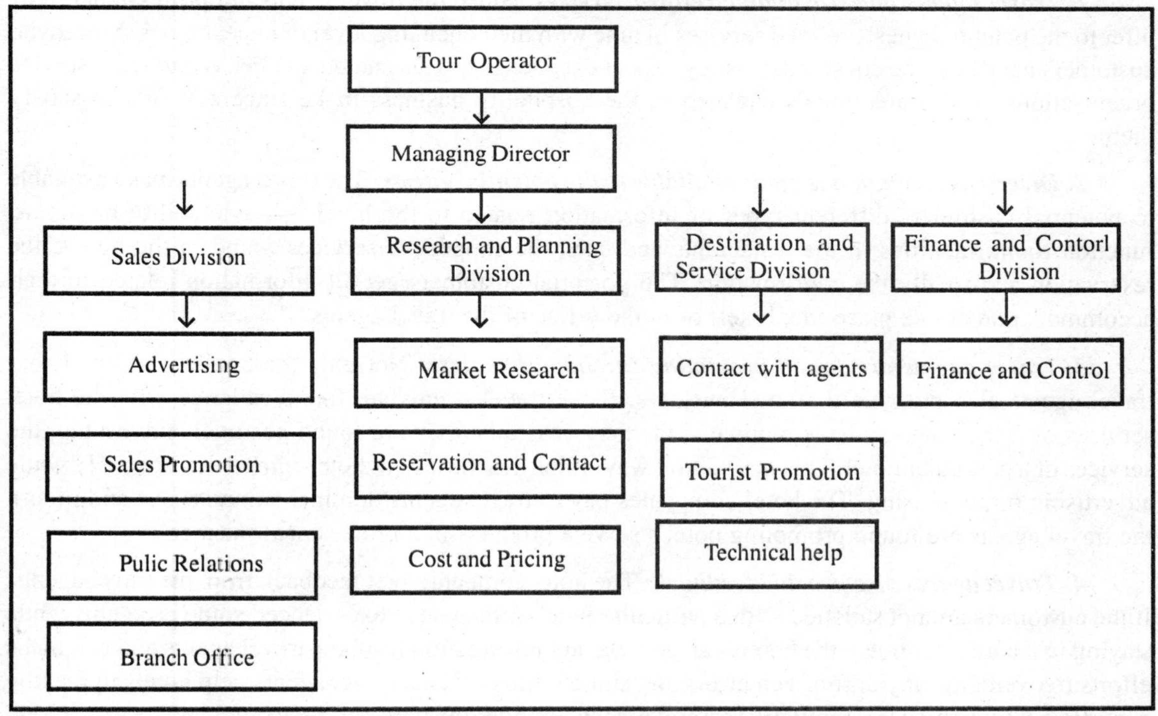

FIG 9.4: ORGANISATIONAL SET UP FOR TOUR OPERATOR

Travel Agents

The travel industry is one potential sector trying to achieve a co-ordinated results. The development of the hotel industry is substantially influenced by the development of the travel industry. The travel agents are found playing a commanding role in both the industries. A travel agent is one who acts on behalf of a principal, i.e., the original provider of tourism services, such as a hotel company, an airline, a tour operator or a shipping company. Travel agents form the retail sector of the distribution chain, buying services from the tour operators or from the hotels directly and selling the same to the clients. They buy the services at the request of their clients and provide a convenient network of sales outlets catering to the need of the local catchment area. In a few cases, we find travel agents also working as wholesalers. When they act as a retailer, we find direct dealings with the clients. A retail travel agent sells directly to clients and acts as a business agent for the hotel. Some of the travel agents operate both as wholesaler and retailer. The hotel business is vigorously influenced by the cooperation of travel agents. Not only for selling but even for promoting the business, the travel agents are found playing a significant role. Almost all the hotels are found linked to the travel agents who make available to their clients the necessary information regarding booking, reservation and confirmation.

IMPORTANCE OF TRAVEL AGENTS TO THE HOTEL INDUSTRY

Whenever we talk about hotel or travel and tourism, we find travel agents playing an outstanding role. The following points testify it:

1. Travel agents make available refined services: Since the travel agents are professional, they offer to the potential guests refined services in tune with their changing level of expectations. Moreover, customers have become conscious — they expect excellent services and decent behaviour from service organisations. The professionals engaged in the hospitality business make sincere efforts to satisfy them.

2. Diverse information is made available to the potential guests: The travel agents make available to potential customers different types of information related to the hotels — availability of rooms, function room, facilities in the restaurants and bars, the supportive services found in the hotels, the reservation and finally the confirmation. The potential customers get all information related to their accommodation at one place (the hotel) or in the office of the travel agents.

3. Travel agents are found promoting the hotel business: Not only the booking of hotels but travel agents also promote the hotel business. If the travel agents are found satisfied with the hotel services of it the hoteliers have motivated them successfully, they are found positively advocating the services of a particular hotel. This in a natural way simplifies the task of hotel companies, specially while advertising or publicising. The hotel companies pay to travel agents nominal commissions and in turn the travel agents are found promoting hotel's service products in a professional manner.

4. Travel agents also provide feedback: The hotel companies get feedback from the travel agents. If the customers are not satisfied with a particular hotel or they have experienced some problems while staying in a particular hotel, the hotels can get relevant information from the travel agents and can make efforts to overcome any unforeseen errors and shortcomings. Thus, travel agents help hotels in making possible qualitative-cum-quantitative improvements. In both the core and peripheral services.

5. Travel agents help in planning the services: If the hotel companies know in advance the realities about the demand side, it is easier for them to take efforts for strategic hotel planning. The travel agents inform hotels and hotel companies about the emerging trends in demand and pave ways for the formulation of a sound and rational business promotion plan.

In view of the above, it is right to appreciate that travel agents play a commanding role in the development of the hotel industry! *'A travel agent here, a hotelier there'* — we find this slogan true in the present day world. In the Indian context, the travel agents are found doing 70% of business of airlines and hotels.

FUNCTIONS OF TRAVEL AGENTS

Regarding the functions of travel agents, one expert says, *'to give advice to the potential tourists /customers on the merits of alternative destination and to make necessary arrangements for a chosen holiday which may involve the booking of accommodation, transport or other relevant services'.*[6] This speaks of the fact that travel agents perform diverse functions as noted below:

1. Providing accommodation information: We find different categories of hotels and all customers are not found in a position to afford the services of expensive five star hotels. This makes it essential that travel agents be well aware of the different categories of hotels and the services offered in these hotels. The availability of accommodation, the room rates, the payment mode etc. are some of the important information found useful to the potential customers. And the travel agents make available to them these information in detail.

2. Preparing itineraries: The travel agents also prepare itineraries, i.e., a composition of services of operation or record of a journey. The potential tourists need detailed information regarding the connecting links to enjoy the maximum part of their tours. From the point of origin of journey to the destination, excursion, transportation, connecting links, etc. and again from the destination to the point of origin, the potential customers get all information from the travel agents which make their tour economic, pleasant, safe and memorable.

3. Link with the provider of service: The travel agents are found connected with different hotels on computers and so they can inform any dislocation, if found in the services of hotel. We find travel agents well connected with the principal or hotel company, which has been possible through a computer link programme.

4. Planning and costing: The travel agents are also found helping potential customers while planning and costing their travel schedule. No doubt, it is a challenging task which calls for a great deal of initiative and drive. It requires considerable training and skills. The travel agents are supposed to be professionally excellent and therefore, they can make available to their clients the services in planning and costing.

5. Arranging hotel rooms, function room: In addition to the functions detailed earlier, the travel agents also book rooms and function room for their clients. They book and again confirm the same. In case of abnormal conditions or unexpected situations, they also inform their clients the cancellation of booking.

In view of the above, it is right to say that travel agents multi-faceted functions help smooth functioning of hotels and offer required information to the customers which make their stay in a particular hotel pleasant and comfortable. A leading American Journal finds the following functions of modern travel agents:

- Preparation of individual pre-planned itineraries, personally escorted tours and group tours and sale of prepared package tours.
- Making arrangements for hotel, motels, resort accommodation, meals, car rentals, sight-seeing, transfer of passengers and luggage between terminals and hotels and special features such as music festivals and theatre tickets.
- Handling of and advising on the details involved in modern travel, e.g., travel and baggage insurance, language study material, traveller's cheques, foreign currency, documentary requirements (Immunisation and inoculations),
- Possession of professional knowledge and experience as for instance, schedule of train connection, rate of hotel, quality of services.
- Arrangements of reservation for special interest activities such as religious pilgrimages, conventions, business meetings and special events.

In-house Selling

No doubt, we find problem with the average occupancy ratio in almost all the hotels as a number of hotels are found not even achieving their minimum target, there are still many nights in a year when a hotel is full and business is being turned away. When we find 100 per cent occupancy nights, the hotelier can increase sales by selling more to the existing guests. When a hotel or a restaurant is not fully booked, it is possible to increase sales by selling outside, and selling within the hotel or in-house selling. Hence, there are two important aspects of selling, e.g., selling inside and selling outside. Hence, we concentrate on inside selling or in-house selling.

Increasing in-house selling is, of course, one of the easiest methods to get very quick results. Paradoxically, if we say to a hotel owner or hotel general manager that he could improve sales within the hotel, he may react in a different manner, or perhaps ignore it. The higher we climb in the organisation, the more we find this attitude. A number of hotel managers and owners feel that they get special service even if they do not ask for it. It happens that when they eat in the restaurant and use room service. A number of hotels have a plan for selling outside the hotel. But we find least efforts for selling inside. This necessitates a considerable concentration of time, thought, energy and action on in-house selling.

If we turn our eyes to the multi-dimensional problems inside a hotel, it will be almost all clear that internal selling on priority basis is the need of the hour. Why do we find so many customers eating outside the hotel? How often a waiter comes up to you and asks: Would you like desert? Why do many of visitors to a hotel for the first time find it difficult to find their way around? Why are the sales on anything displayed visually in the restaurant higher than other very exciting dishes written as words on a menu?

Of course, the answers to these questions are lack of substantial efforts towards systematic in-house selling. This makes it essential that our in-house selling plans are formulated scientifically. In-house selling is defined as *promoting a sale by informing the consumer of the variety of products and services available and the benefits and advantages of using these products and services.*[8] It is very unfortunate that the front-line personnel find it difficult to work on effective strategies to increase in-house selling. We find it more logical to plan in-house selling by looking at it from the customer's point of view. This is related to empathy. For promoting in-house selling, it is significant that the front-line staff have an in-depth knowledge of customers. But in majority of the cases, we do not find it. Of course, they have complete knowledge of services made available by their hotels but so far as their understanding about the customer is concerned, we do not find it adequate. Traditionally, we find in-house selling fixed on an area basis, such as bars, restaurants, rooms etc. But it is significant here to mention that the customer is not fixed on the basis of preference in any one area as a bar customer may also become a restaurant customer. This makes it essential that we look at the unit as a whole and ask the questions to whom can the services be sold, what and where, i.e., the three 'W's — Whom, What and Where. When we complete identifying sales opportunities, the sales methods can be devised.

Whom : Potential customers, inside/outside the hotel, residents, bar customers etc.

What : Various products/services offered.

Where : Location of the maximum sales opportunities, such as reception, rooms, car parks, etc.

Here, it is essential to have an idea of action checklists for each department or area under the heading:

Informative signs : The products and services available (including photographs and other visual aids).

Directional sign : To where the various products and services are located in the area and where other facilities in the unit are located.

Displays : Menus, tariffs, brochures, physical displays like food, drinks, etc.

Here, we can use posters and other temporary promotional material, tent cards and other small promotional material, give-aways, hotel information packs and service directories, guest bills, advance reservations etc.

IN-HOUSE SELLING AND FRONT-LINE STAFF

We accept the fact that hotels in general tend to concentrate less on in-house selling, which is found easier and economic with the standpoint of minimising the selling expenses. This necessitates due emphasis on promoting in-house selling which is possible with the involvement and co-operation of the front-line staff. The restaurants, bar, accommodation and function rooms are the services to be sold and the receptionists, waiters, barmen and the sales executives are the personnel meant for this purpose. We are not making any advocacy against outside selling but are making a strong plea in favour of in-house selling. Are our personnel meant for inside selling competent enough to motivate the customers for a repeat visit? Are our personnel found showing empathy to the guests at the reception, in the restaurant and bar? We assign due weightage to these aspects as only front-line personnel can touch the impulse of customers for visiting hotels frequently. Here, we find two things important. First, our personnel are really professionals who are found committed to their job. Second, our motivational plans are lucrative and the front-line personnel are found satisfied with the same. It is linked to inside selling and the related personnel are getting their due on time.

If we feel that the personnel need a special training or are required to undergo a course in human resource development, we have to make it possible. Earlier we have talked about empathy, that plays a vital role in getting potential repeat business. This necessitates the study of psychology or knowledge of psychology. While recruiting, we have to be careful and further have to make provision for a special training programme. The waiters are performing well in the restaurant, the barmen are found serving well, the sales executives are managing everything in the face of changing conditions at potential points and more so that receptionists are showing empathy to business executives coming after a tired day to the reception counter for collecting their room keys. The sales executives are giving a special treatment to the clients coming to book a function room and are successfully closing the conversation with a final booking.

Another dimension related here is the motivational plan which induces personnel for inside selling. It is important that in outside selling, we are supposed to pay commission to the tour operators and the travel agents. Here, if we rationalise our motivational plan, no doubt, we will have to pay just a part of that commission but in proportion to our payment to the personnel the repeat business that we get with their support and co-operation would be helpful to raise the share of inside selling to the total selling.

If the front-line personnel understand customers well, the task is not so difficult. This makes it essential that internal selling strategies be promoted with the help of the front line staff. In preparing a simple but systematic action plan on in-house selling, it is pertinent to obtain ideas and suggestions from the staff and to involve them from the initial stages of drafting the action plan. The imparting of training facilities to them in this very context is found essential to follow the action plan. It is also significant that our staff are not overburdened. If the waiters and receptionists are in a true sense professional, they can remember a series of sales promotion points. We are also required to be careful while recruiting the staff and should tend to employ more and more people in hotels who are keen and motivated, but not necessarily highly skilled. It is better to motivate and train staff to cover the limited sales points. Thus, a receptionist may just try to sell a seat in the restaurant as a guest is checking in, or just as whether they can reserve a room as the guest is checking out. It is far better to stick to one point, specially to check deviation. Similarly for waiters, it is far more effective, if they are responsible to sell one thing at the start of a meal and one nearer the end.

We accept the fact that bad signposting annoys people and creates an additional threshold barrier. We know our way round the hotel and therefore cannot notice if the signposting is confusing. Bad signposting is found complicating the problem of a new customer. Suppose the new customer is entering your hotel for the first time. Of course, he is found confident on the exterior but deep down he finds himself in a strange territory where he is going to eat and sleep. It becomes essential to study and analyse the behaviour of new customers. Here, it is also significant that the signposts should be at a place where they are clearly accessible and visible.

Many of hotels are also found using attractive signs, tent cards and posters. Sometimes, we find them wrongly placed. All we need is empathy. We are supposed to watch our customers and to help them as and when they need. Where do they wait, stand and what do they look at? If we are watching this carefully, even a new customer will not experience difficulties. We also find a number of hotels in which the sales literature, restaurant menu etc. are placed out of sight in the rooms. Where should we place the key message? There are a number of sensitive points where we should put the message, such as over the telephone dial, on the television top, and on the bathroom mirror. These are considered to be sensitive points where your guests will look. We have to be careful while displaying the message and to the extent it is possible we have to make the message simple, like 'We have lobster on the menu tonight, dial 108 to reserve a table.' Thus, the instrumentality and approach of the front-line staff influences in-house selling substantially, provided the staff is efficient to do so.

TELEPHONE SELLING OR TELE-MARKETING

If we consider hotel industry a people's industry, if we accept the instrumentality of telephone calls for enquiries received in the hotels; we find justifications for using telephone even for selling. We cannot deny the fact that the telephone can be a very effective tool for selling to a new customer. Generally, we use it for incoming enquiries. Why not use the telephone to stimulaste business in a larger perspective? Of course, we find it a most cost effective method for achieving a sales objective. No doubt, in some of the countries telephone calls are expensive but compared with involvement of time on personal visits, a well-planned telephone call is found to be the most effective method of reaching out to customers and achieving a specific sales objective. Often, a number of people are found using a telephone to close a sale deal and make a firm booking. But a well-planned telephone sales call may be effective even while initiating the business, or activating the research calls.

The main thing here is to plan the content of the call strategically. Whatever the inhibition we find against telephone selling can be overcome with practice. If the call is to be polite and short with a limited rational objective, it will not last for more than a minute or two. We should not feel tense in making a telephone sales call While starting a call, our voice and message should have a natural flow. We find a number of persons who just before starting call, light up a cigarette. When you are smoking, it is very natural that everytime you breathe in smoke, your voice will have a pause. You will lose the thread of your message and may give the customer a chance to interrupt. The communication will be ineffective and your sales objective will not be fulfilled.

In view of the above, it is right to say that we can use telephone for sales call but the main thing here is to plan the call effectively and to train the person/persons as efficient telemarketing executives. There are a number of points to be taken into active consideration, before we make a call. If we are using telephone for research calls, it is better to involve different members of the hotel staff. If we practice this, we may cut corners. But if we divide the responsibility for research calls to some of our staff who are found well trained, the purpose 'will be fulfilled. It is important to mention here that research calls pertain to motto of finding out certain companies above a certain size to locate the name and position of the persons who book hotel rooms for overnight workers to their factory/office. In addition to other aspects, it is also impact-generating that we have been successful in creating a team spirit, motivating them rationally and planning the calls in tune with our requirements. In Exhibit 9.1, we find certain points[9] for effective telemarking.

EXHIBIT. 9.1: KEY POINTS FOR TELEPHONIC SELLING

- Before you make a call, keep by your side the indexed card and file of the prospects. If it is a first call, prepare a new card.
- Make up your mind beforehand what message you want to put across. Introduce yourself, and invite him for a drink and to view your service product range.
- Find out the name of the person to whom you are speaking before getting through to him and address him with his name.
- Be sure that you are not going to be interrupted by anyone.
- Instruct your receptionist/telephone operator to put you through to the hotel company not the man. Dial direct yourself.
- Introduce yourself by your surname and state the name of hotel or hotel company.

- If he/she is engaged in a meeting or he/she is in a totally unreceptive mood, say you will ring back but still try to get a short message across.
- Keep the conversation short and sharp. Do not go on for too long.
- Do not forget to detail the menus or a letter confirming the date of your meeting

Telephone marketing, also known as tele-marketing in the USA, has gained popularity the world over not for hotel selling but for the selling of the services provided by hotels. We find this method of selling reactive to enquiries and proactive to target customers. Its use for selling to the general public has undergone radical changes in the last decade. It may play a much larger role in the hotel marketing in future. It is also found cost effective and can be used successfully for selling these services and generating substantial revenues.

The key to success is to set up an achievable objective, a message that can be put across in a short-time and to let the person receiving the call know that you are not going to take up much of his time. Telephone selling saves a lot of time and can be remarkably effective. In one group of hotels, the problem was low food and beverage sales in the group's hotel restaurants at lunch time and mid-week. Most of the hotels were 4 star with excellent restaurants. Covers have steadily declined for about a year, but only on lunch time. In addition to other action points, it was also an important point to make a low-key telephone call, to past regulars. It was found that the majority of them just slipped out of the habit. The result of that call was wonderful. Across the range of forty hotels in this group, there was an immediate increase in covers of an average of thirty per day. This is the success story of telephone selling. This speaks of the fact that it can be used successfully even for reminding our old customers.

E-CRM STRATEGY

In the hospitality industry, we find internet emerging as the largest distribution, channel. We can not deny that internet has been beating all other traditional channels. Of late, we find a good number of hotel customers preferring website as their first choice for developing contact. With the help of E-CRM strategy, the hotel professionals find it easier to develop interactive relationship with their customers. It is pertinent to mention that in the hotel business, the hoteliers need to understand their customers in a right fashion and when we focus on E-CRM strategy, it throws light on developing online relationships with the customers. The professionals bear the responsibility of satisfying customers, increasing the repeat business and minimising the costs on creating new customers. The Customer Relationship Management occupies here an important place and with the help of online relationships, they find themselves in a position to sense and sensitise the customers, narrating them the promotional offers as well as features such as online booking, pre-arrival and post-stay communication with the customers. Presently we also find scope for enhancing the FAQ sand sensing the newsletters. The new generation of information and communication technology has virtually been found redefining the concept of customer relationship management.

Creating new customers and retaining the old customers are the two different dimensions. And the hotel professionals need to prefer retention which is found proactive and cost effective. The marketers with the help of their professional excellence may be successful in retention which may pave avenues for profit maximisation. Preparing stronger top-line and healthier bottom-line both are to be possible if we find hotel professionals evincing keen interests in broadening and deepening customer relationships.

Actually we find a large database of knowledge about existing hotel customers but the hotel professionals seldom use the same. With the help of effective data mining, the marketers can have greater insights into the food habits, spending habits, drink habits etc. By leveraging the new CRM technologies, the professionals get it easier to enrich the potentials of customer service workforce regarding the experiences of previous customers.

In the formulation of E-CRM strategy, the hotels may use the services of CRM analysts which may help professionals in developing peripheral services. Improving the customer experience and developing stronger customer relationships are to be possible with the help of CRM. The root cause of customer problems can be identified, the behavioural studies can be made possible, the customers can be retained and the profits can be maximised. The internet has virtually established an edge over the traditional channels. Earlier, the customers were required to visit a hotel or to the offices of travel agents but now we find a number of channels for developing contacts. Apart from the traditional channels like phone, white mail and visits; the customers now e-mail, web chat and fax they send requests through internet-based forms. The marketing and sales campaigns are now TV pint media, internet, e-mail marketing, telemarketing and door-to-door marketing.

These significant developments have virtually redefined the concept of service distribution specially in the hospitality sector.

We cannot deny that E-CRM strategy is a great way with endless possibilities to bring qualitative transformation and to improve customer satisfaction, retention and profitability. Using a combination of traditional and modern channels is found to be of prime importance particularly in the hospitality sector where the hotel professionals need an in-depth idea of the changing behavioural profile of customers. The customers and potential customers have been found developing their temptation to the hotel website. For a majority of the hotel customers, the first choice is hotel website which provides to them multi-faceted facilities and multi-dimensional information. It is the responsibility of hotel professionals to enrich the website for building mutually beneficial interactive relationships with the customers. Conversion or transformation needs due attention of almost all the marketing people engaged in the process. The hoteliers need priority attention on building online relationships with customers which would help them in conversion, retention and profit maximisation. The leading hotels have been found budgeting for the overhaul of the customer support facilities on the website. The web pages are now used also for promoting the business. Online booking information related to the pre-arrival and post-stay communication with the customers are some of the outstanding merits of new generation of new ICT which are now used by the modern hotels. We cannot deny that international biggies have an edge over the domestic players, specially in respect of penetration of e-commerce. Of course, they have been fulfilling their requirements with the human resources and innovative marketing but they should also make possible high level e-commerce penetration.

We are well aware of the fact that web technology is an universal access tool to acknowledge information and opinions. Interactive websites can be developed by using the new generation of technology such as Java Script Shockwave, CGI, DHTML etc. The hotel professionals need due attention while developing web pages. They should use the services of site designers for this purpose. In the high end e-commerce sites, the business is found gaining rapid momentum particularly with the help of database. There are a number of considerations for developing web pages and the hotel professionals need to ensure that the legal aspects have been given due weightage to avoid complications.

In view of the above mentioned facts, it is right to mention that in the hospitality industry, the internet has proved to be an important distribution channel making the task convenient both for the providers and the users. Conversion and retention are the two important aspects necessitating priority attention of hotel professionals while making use of internet. They need to understand the customers and their experiences and for that purpose, they can promote the use of online relationships. In addition to the CRM, the transmission of newsletters, pre-arrival and post-stay communication, developing awareness of promotional measures and offers may help hotel professionals in many ways.

STRATEGY FOR RESTAURANT SALES

A restaurant is considered to be an important part of hotel. While formulating a sound distribution strategy, it is pertinent that we increase restaurant sales. There are a few commandments for increasing restaurant sales shown in Exhibit 9.2.

EXHIBIT 9.2: TEN COMMANDMENTS FOR INCREASING RESTAURANT SALES

- Define catchment areas or different meal periods, such as lunch, dinner, midweek and weekend.
- Mention quiet, medium and busy periods.
- Increase in-house selling.
- Prepare mailing lists within catchment area.
- For a repeat business, remind your past customers that you are still in the business and expect their visit.
- Produce newsletter/mailing shot.
- Prepare action plan for quieter periods.
- Pay maximum possible attention to first time visitors and regular visitors.
- Use names/surnames.
- Say something appreciating to customers when they leave.

In Exhibit 9.2, we have summarised different commandments for increasing restaurant sales. Let's explain these commandments:

Catchment Area

There are some critical factors in this very context. It is essential that we know in detail about the catchment area, such as how far customers have come, how they come, the time consumed to get there etc. Paradoxically, very few restaurants sufficiently know about the catchment area where their customers come from and this can vary considerably between the different periods, such as lunch, dinner, weekend and midweek. Here, it is also significant that we meet periodically and think about the profile of our guests who spend money in our restaurant such as age group, sex, position, etc. A restaurant manager bears the responsibility of understanding the new customers. Every time a new customer arrives in the restaurant, if we attempt to find much more about them, the task of understanding them in the right perspective is simplified.

Quiet, medium and busy periods: It is important to discuss different periods of activity. In some of the restaurants, we find a pattern in each meal period which has a plateau effect. We find some restaurants busy for all periods, while others are found quiet till a peak time.

It is significant here to define busy periods. We should not neglect busy periods but we find less scope for promoting busy periods which would, of course, be a waste of time. We consider medium periods potential and easy to promote.

Increasing in-house selling: This is also an important aspect for increasing restaurant sales. Generally, we do not find a rational plan for increasing in-house selling. In the restaurant of a hotel, we do not find profits generated in a restaurant contributing substantially to the total profit. This does not indicate in anyway that in-house selling should not be encouraged. In a completely separate restaurant divorced from a hotel the profits achieved are found important and the in-house selling can literally double or treble the bottom line profits.

Preparing mailing list: In the different strategies for increasing restaurant/selling, this is an important dimension. Here, emphasis is laid on preparing mailing lists of past and potential customers. It should be within the defined catchment area. The mailing list can be produced from existing city and sales ledger accounts and from people and companies who have a credit facility. Here, we should also pinpoint the names of important potential customers, their companies and organisations. While listing, it is pertinent that we include two categories of persons, first-person actually making the booking and second-person using the services. Putting tent cards on the tables and in the cocktail bar area is also an important device to prepare mailing lists. Here, we find a sense of competition as visitors are suggested that if they want to be included and appreciated by services like future news, special evenings etc., they would simply drop their visiting cards into the box near the exit. The mailing list should not be extensive or sizeable. This is likely to generate numerous problems. If we include 50 to 100 names in the mailing list, it is to be an ideal mailing list. For a long-priced restaurant, it can be increased to 1000.

Reminding customers for repeat business: Another commandment is related to remind the customers regarding your existence in the market. It is very natural that customers in general want to be remembered and apprised of the services provided by a hotel they have patronised. Customers do not look upon the right kind of mailing shot. They expect a reminder, specially on a festival or a festive occasion. However, it is impact-generating that we apprise them on this front implying that you are interested in their visits.

Producing a newsletter or a mailing shot: This is another important commandment for increasing restaurant sales. Here, our emphasis is on the way of strategy requirements by hotel or reminding the customers of services given by hotel companies. In a few cases, we can send them a straightforward letter. If it is so, the letter should be personalised otherwise, it is not going to generate any positive impact. We find two important forms of mailing. First, your mailing list is giving advance knowledge of some change in menu or activities for a special week. Secondly, a detailed newsletter, consisting of news regarding food and wine.

***Preparing action plan for a quieter period*:** The strategy is related to the preparation of an action plan for quieter business periods. Restaurants have some very busy times of the year and at the same we also find some lean business periods. Often, we find certain days in the week when visitors are found visiting restaurants in small number. Here, it is significant that we prepare effective sales action plant to make the most of the quiet and busy periods in a restaurant. The quieter periods are also known as 'shoulder periods'. Generally, the restaurants offer a number of promotional schemes to increase their sales during the lean period. Reduction in price and special kinds of offer are found effective in increasing sales in the restaurants. But experiences show that in the quiet period, even the promotional measures provided by restaurants are also found ineffective if people fail to appreciate and accept the reduction in prices of services. Of course, people prefer to visit a restaurant when they prefer to celebrate a special occasion but pricing policy is not found here effective as a motivational tool to increase business during lean periods.

Attention to visitor: In this approach, intended for increasing restaurant sales, we find special attention to visitors in general, e.g., occasional or habitual. It is very natural that the restaurant staff should be friendly and pay particular attention to their customers. We find the staff showing special treatment to the guests or customers paying them tips. Anyway, the staff should pay more attention to regular guests as they are supposed to be the major buyers of the regular products or services.

Use names: Some of the hotels make people feel more comfortable, more at home. We do not find it in all hotels and restaurants. We select a hotel also on the basis of price or location. We also find persons selecting a hotel purely on status basis. This speaks of the fact that many people return to a hotel not because the facilities are superior but because of one overriding factor. This is not related to the physical advantages of the hotel property itself but because of people and recognition. If you show special treatment to your guests, recognise their personalities and appreciate their visit they would visit your hotel restaurants again and again. There is nothing nicer than walking into a hotel and seeing a well-known face. Of course, there is one thing nicer than this, i.e., your level of recognition in the hotel.

Say something when your guests leave: In addition to other commandments discussed earlier, we also find an important aspect for increasing restaurant sales. When a guest arrives, we find a verbal communication. The opening conversation is found impact-generating. When a customer leaves, someone from the restaurant staff should say good-bye to them properly at the door or exist. This is a small point which makes people appreciate the services of the restaurant again.

SALES ACTION PLANS

Sales action plans for hotels cover every source of business, e.g., business visitors, local tourists, foreign tourists, overnight conventions, day meetings, exhibitions, management seminars etc. In a large hotel company, we find a special executive time and energy to devote to selling. This necessitates concentration on the sources of business which are found vulnerable to decline in sales. Preparing a plan of action on how selling activities gain a rapid momentum is an important aspect. A well thought action plan is found, helpful in maximising sale. How to prepare a suitable action plan is a burning problem. In Exhibit 9.3, we find a broad strategy for preparing action plan.

EXHIBIT 9.3: BROAD STRATEGY FOR SALES ACTION PLAN

1. An overall strategy and policy for the whole hotel business and the different income producing areas. This strategy should cover the following:
   - Marketing Policy
   - Busy and quite periods and areas
   - Profit forecasts
   - Marketing cost
   - Capital expenditure plans, if needed

2. Analysis of local market strategy into a plan for each different area which produces or could produce sales by following sources:
   - Rooms
   - Restaurant(s)
   - Bars
   - Function areas
   - Meeting rooms
3. Strategy should define which aspects are going to be tackled in the *future and which* will not be tackled. We call it *management by exception.*
4. Targets of increase sales and increased profits should prepared
5. Preparation of a budget to analyse the amount of money to be spent
6. Time budget must be prepared, such as who is going to spend time on gathering information, key names research etc. who is going to sell and how much time is likely to be spent on outside selling. Who would organise and sustain in-house selling.

In Exhibit 9.3, the first deals with overall strategy, targets, defining busy and quiet periods. The second covers how to reach potential customers. Here we find, various methods for getting information as shown in Exhibit 9.4.

EXHIBIT 9.4: REACHING THE POTENTIAL CUSTOMERS

1. Explaining the action plan to staff
2. Outside selling:
   - Letters
   - Mailing shot/promotional literature
   - Telephone selling
   - Direct selling
   - Paid advertising
   - Unpaid publicity
   - Word-of-mouth publicity
3. In-house selling
4. Subdivision of action plans:
   - Past
   - Present
   - Potential customers
5. Periodic checking of expenditure in the face of budget
6. Monitoring sales results
7. Revision of plan

Making the Plan simple: Here, it is significant that we make a simple plan which may cover the following:

- Increasing the percentage of sales.
- Increasing covers in the restaurant.
- Increasing occupancy at weekends.

Here, the hoteliers are supposed to know the busy and lean periods of business so that the marketing and sales strategies are formulated accordingly. All sales action plans should be aimed at two objectives, e.g., getting people face-to-face and getting the prospects to visit the hotel, view and appreciate the facilities available. Though we accept the fact that a well-thought action plan may help hotels in many ways, it is also right to opine that the majority of the hotels find it difficult to prepare an ideal sales action plan. The key to success is not to overwhelm potential customers with saturation bombing. A successful approach is a '*steady approach*' to remind customers of the improved services, which would ensure in generating repeat business.

BALANCING INSIDE AND OUTSIDE SELLING IN A HOTEL

In-house selling is an important dimension, specially when we talk about the hotel industry. However, outside selling is found essential, specifically for large hotel companies. The tour operators and the travel agents have emerged as important channels working as wholesaler and retailer. It is an important problem before the hotel companies as to how to ensure and balance the two important dimensions for satisfactory sales results and effective promotional activities. Here, one thing is clear that hotels and hotel companies find it difficult to sell satisfactorily unless the channels extend to them the best possible cooperation. This necessitates a fine fusion of the two so that lean business period is minimised substantially the occupancy ratio is increased considerably and the restaurant business is maximised in an appreciating way.

Small hotels are, of course, in a position to survive even without taking any support from the distribution channel but so far as the large hotel companies are concerned, they have no option but to seek the best possible co-operation of tour operators and travel agents. The trend usually followed by one of hotel groups the world over has been competing strenuously to retain their potential through customers a wide variety of memberships or club schemes, frequent traveller awards and special arrangements for their key accounts. This has succeeded in paving ways for inside selling and repeat business. Holiday Inns have claimed that over a million members joined their 'Priority Club' within months of it being introduced in the USA in 1983. The operation of the club, only possible on the basis of Holiday Inns fully automated international reservation system, has since changed its basis of operation but it is an interesting example of modern direct response marketing, which is still in its early stages of development.[10] At the same time, it is also right to say that travel agents play an important role in getting the business and accomplishing the organisational goals. They also help hotel companies in promoting the business and projecting a fair image.

In view of the aforesaid facts, we need such a strategy which will help hotel companies in striking a balance between the two. So far as the restaurant and bar are concerned, internal selling would be found more effective but the function room business and room occupancy ratio cannot be impressive unless the hotel companies take the external support. The tour operators and travel agents can help them in boosting sale and raising the contribution of rooms and function room's profits to the total profit of hotel companies. Hence, a strategy in which we find a fair blending of both categories of selling would bring multi-dimensional positive results. Here, it is also pertinent to mention the strategic decisions regarding fixing a proportion between internal and external selling which would vary from hotel to hotel.

Don't Sell the Whole Hotel

To the extent it is possible, you should avoid selling the whole hotel. It is more rational that we concentrate the available resources and energy on the business sources expected to produce positive results, specially in terms of increasing sales and profits. It is not profitable to waste our energy and promote every aspect of the business area. In one hotel, the management team was working hard and trying to increase the sales of hotel. Of course, the results were positive but not very attractive. Even without getting satisfactory results, the management team continued their tempo. When they were asked to list the areas and aspects of the hotel that they were trying to sell in their brochures, advertising and sales approach generally, it was found that virtually they were trying to sell everything, such as:

- Overnight business visitors to local factories.
- Business users of major communication point.
- Tourist users of major communication point.
- Weekend breaks
- Overnight smaller conferences
- Smaller and larger day conferences
- The Restaurant
- Facilities available for weddings
- Functions

It was found that there were a number of competitive hotels near the major communication point. In addition, it was also found that the related hotel had far more competition for some of these sources than others. The remedy was to concentrate on some of the aspects, such as overnight visitors to local factories, weekend breaks, overnight smaller conferences and weddings. Earlier, the hotel company concentrated on nine heads and now they concentrated on four heads for the coming year and then to review the results. This was not done with the motto of ignoring or neglecting the other five heads but to concentrate on those heads where it was possible to face competitors. The result was very satisfactory.

It is pertinent to mention here that we need different advantages for the different sources of business compared with key competitors and more specific sales literature rather than just a brochure. Often, the market attending functions are totally different to the overnight convention/market and weddings. The market segments vary considerably. The motto is to increase sale and profit. If we attempt to tap all, it is unlikely to get the required success. This makes it essential that we understand the market segment and then make efforts to concentrate on those areas where our performance can be more efficient and effective. The aforesaid facts are a mute testimony to the proposition that we should avoid selling the whole hotel.

SALES LETTERS AND MAILING SHOTS

Writing sales letters has proved its instrumentality both for answering to an incoming enquiry and stimulating new business. Many are found using mailing shots to stimulate new enquiries and sales letters to deal with incoming enquiries. We accept that like every form of selling, writing a successful letter also needs empathy. The very negative point that we find with this form of selling is unavailability of time to the sales executives to go through these letters. This makes it essential that any sales letter and mailing shot is to grab the attention so that a busy executive starts to read it. An opening point in the form of a question can be helpful in attracting attention. The objective is to increase the future success rate and this makes it significant that the sales letters are drafted in a manner to attract customers and generate more revenues. You should rewrite the series of past letters and then ask someone to see that the important points or essentials as summarised in Exhibit 9.5 are found in these letters. Do not be afraid of criticism. Many times you will realise the faults while going through the letters. Once you are successful in grabbing the attention of recipients, they go through the same. The opening sentences should be interesting to make them read on. Keep the message to one aspect per letter, such as a conference, annual office party or special event in the restaurant. Of course, a good sales letter requires pre-planning and research.

EXHIBIT 9.5: ESSENTIALS FOR SELLING LETTERS AND MAILING SHOTS

- Write a headline or first paragraph to grab attention.
- Add an inspirational value.
- Define the product, such as conference, weekend attraction, festive activities.
- Tell a success story.
- Endorsements of satisfied customers and testimonials should be included.
- Point out the outstanding merits of your products.
- Devise such action conclusion which stimulates immediate response.
- Add short postscript.

Your letters should have the capacity to create an immediate reaction. Adding a handwritten short post script with one of the phrases linked to the lead in headline is found more impact-generating. Try to keep your letters short. Use 'You' in place of 'I'. Interspace each paragraph with some very short paragraphs. Try to start the letter with' You' in the opening three words of your letter.

Though majority of us fail to distinguish between the sales letters and mailing shots the major advantage that we find with a sales letter is that we can start it with the name of the prospects. So far as the mailing shots are concerned, we do not find the same. It is very natural as when we have the name of our customers we find it better to start it with his/her personal name and the letters tend to become more personalised. Here, it is also right to mention that a series of letters addressed to the managing director as **'Dear Sir'** are the same as mailing shots.

Besides, face-to-face selling has established its edge over the mailing shots. The hoteliers now realise that face-to-face selling, telephone calls and personalised selling are more potential strategies. The use of word processors has made it possible to type series of original letters to the prospects. We find it more effective if we cover a specific promotion, special event, opening of a new conference room or change in the menu of our restaurant. If we send the actual new menu through the post to our past customers, the mailing shots can be more effective. It is also possible to send the miniaturised exact copy of the menu.

In view of the above, it is right to observe that a steady and gradual impact on a major user of hotel services is found more impact-generating than a hard sell. Of course, it will take more time even one or two years to convert a major potential customer out of his inertia to visit your hotel. Contacting customers an the phone frequently, or writing a sales letter every quarter would, of course prove troublesome to your customers, and therefore you have to arrange sales letter, telephone call, mailing shot, face-to-face visit and a letter in a right fashion. It is recommended:[11]

a sales letter followed by

a telephone call followed by

a mailing shot

then a face-to-face visit followed by a letter,

Where you find it difficult to get the actual name of your customer, the mailing shots would be the most cost-effective in terms of time of launching a new hotel or after revamping of a restaurant, you will find it suitable. Where we find a large number of people spending a lower amount per person, the mailing shots would be effective but where a company is in a position to spend a large amount, the face-to-face (direct) selling would be effective.

OTHER FORMS OF DISTRIBUTION OF HOTELS

In the distribution strategies for the hotel industry, we also find some new forms. We also call them the third group of pipelines. Hotels, car rentals, restaurants and airlines are found using the same strategy for distribution. The channels reflected below are not normally referred to as pipelines, yet they can be used to perform all the distribution functions. Each of the pipeline below is relevant to specific users or segment group and is not found accessible to customers as a whole. In an era of increasing market segmentation these types of pipelines are increasingly used by most of the hotel companies. Refer to the exhibit shown below:

EXHIBIT 9.6: PIPELINES USED FOR DISTRIBUTION

- VIP/Privileged User Cards and membership clubs for frequent customers or habitual customers. (The hotel provides the same).
- Secretaries' Clubs (maintained by hotels).
- Special links with other bodies such as schools, clubs, societies (maintained by hotels).
- Allocations of product capacity to credit card companies acting for this purpose as tour operators.

In the non-physical nature of products, we find flexibility and this makes it essential that we have a third group of pipelines. Of late, hotels, airlines, car rentals, restaurants and some attractions have been found using these pipelines for distribution. Here, it is important to mention that the pipelines shown in Exhibit 9.6 are strongly associated with sales promotion, and some forms of direct response marketing. This association with other marketing functions is significant and requires a careful co-ordination in planning marketing campaigns. Unless a system is structured in advance to generate a targeted but unknown volume of business over a campaign period, each of the pipeline is found significant to the specific users.

Thus, while formulating the distribution strategy for hotels, it is significant that we also think of other alternatives. In the modern age of increasing market segmentation, this decision is found to be important.

COST OF DISTRIBUTION

In the formulation of distribution strategy for hotel companies, in addition to other aspects, the costs of distribution also occupy a place of significance. Here, emphasis is laid on fixed and variable costs. Some of the costs of maintaining and supporting distribution systems or pipelines are fixed for the duration of any marketing campaign. We except the organisation of outlets and servicing in advance of any business which is expected to flow. In this sense, the fixed costs include the following:

- The cost of installing reservation systems, computers and programmes and staff capable of dealing with enquiries and booking through each pipeline.
- The cost of production of brochure, distribution and maintaining supplies to the points of sale.
- Costs of sale promotion incentives with the motto of motivating retailers and other points of sale.
- Costs of support visits to intermediaries, merchandising efforts and display materials to be used at points of sale.
- Costs of maintaining and motivating salesforce to negotiate agreements with intermediaries to secure literature distribution and display.
- Costs of any educational seminars and workshops organised in support of distribution systems and staff training.

The aforesaid costs are fixed. In the hotel industry, it is significant that the aforesaid costs are fixed for the duration of any marketing campaign.

The variable costs are measured in terms of commission which is typically paid after achieving sales and any phone calls connected with bookings or enquiries and paid for by the principals. It is not essential to mention here that hotels or hotel companies are found here playing the role of principal. The commission paid to the tour operators and the travel agents or payment of commission to others are found active in boosting sale revenues.

Calculating the Costs of Distribution

The hotels and hotel companies tend to balance and monitor the costs of distribution. Since no physical transfer of goods is involved in the process of distribution, the distribution or access channels are found relatively flexible and may be increased at relatively low cost in tune with the availability of opportunities. The limit to creating additional channels is the marginal point at which unit costs of access exceed unit profits. Of course, up to that limit, we find generation of more profit by creating more access. It is very natural that hotels and hotel companies tend to monitor the costs of distribution.

An example is given here. Suppose a small hotel group with 3 hotels and 500-double occupancy rooms for which it targets 25 per cent nights to be distributed over twelve months through three channels other than referral between units and direct bookings arising from locations and repeat customers. For the sake of simplicity, it is assumed that all bookings have same unit value, e.g., ₹ 1,000 per person per night.

- 500 rooms × 2 persons × 365 nights × 25 % distribution via channels = 91,250 nights of occupancy.
- Channel A costs ₹ 2,50,000 to service and generates 50,000 nights of occupancy
  The average unit cost of distribution per night = ₹ 500

- Channel B costs ₹ 1,00,000 to service and generates 25,000 nights of occupancy
  The average unit cost of distribution per night = ₹ 500
- Channel C costs ₹ 1,95,000 to service and generates 16,250 nights of occupancy
  The average unit cost of distribution per night = ₹ 120

Here, the cost of service is the calculated cost of staff and equipment overheads which have to be spent to sustain a channel at the targeted level of the business turnover plus the brochure costs and expenditure on incentives to get the support of distributors. The cost of commission is not included here on sales which is assumed to be equal for all the three channels. If the level of commission is found different, it will be included in the cost of service as it would alter the average unit cost of distribution. The value of bookings may be greater in one channel or more useful in creating low season bookings in another but these complications are not to obscure the basic need to assess and compare the unit costs of providing access to customers in each pipeline. Such calculations are inputs to decisions with which existing channels to develop and valuable in assessing the potential value of any new channels might be opened up. The cost of creating pipelines for customers' access can be budgeted with precision, provided that a hotel group or the other principal is willing to apportion the costs of servicing and commission for each channel.

We find that in distributing the hotel services, multiple pipelines are commonly used. There are a number of significant costs in providing access to customers and a need to balance the costs of different channels used. It is not possible that large hotel companies concentrate only on inside or in-house selling. This necessitates zero-level channel (where we find direct selling), one level channel (where we find travel agents) and two-level channel (where we find both tour operators and travel agents).

IMPROVING SALES TECHNIQUES

The whole aim of the placement strategy is to persuade the prospects or customers to try you once. Of course, it is difficult to persuade the new customers but not so difficult to get repeat business. Getting a new customer to try and avail of service once often takes much time and a well-thought placement strategy. If you ask potential buyers of hotel facilities whether they are happy with hotels where they visit and stay. They will invariably say 'Yes.' This could pave the way for better performance by the hotel management in terms of services.

The response, shown by the customer should, however, be genuine. Of course, a number of customers are really satisfied with the hotels where they stay but not all. Maybe that hotels tend to take them far granted. When you ask them whether they are happy, they will not say 'Yes' in an instant. The reason maybe that they remember poor servicing by the housekeepers, waiters or others.

There are a number of critical aspects which any salesman must avoid and at the same there are certain points on which a salesman should concentrate to get the desired results. Here, one thing is found important as summarised below:[11]

- Avoid selling a mile wide and an inch deep.
- Non-verbal communication (NVC)
- Be knowledge,

- Be consumer-oriented rather than product-oriented,
- Be Jack (or Jill) to the problem solver rather than a problem generator.

Selling a mile wide and an inch deep It is an important reason for a decline in sales. Usually this stems from a very enthusiastic, dedicated management and sales team. Too often the management saturates a market with telephone calls, personal visits and mailing shots in the belief that a massive effort is bound to get results. Sometimes it does. But only when it is carefully planned. Very often, we find a very exhausted sales team working to generate substantial.

Non-verbal communication is already discussed earlier while business explaining face-to-face selling.

Regarding knowledge, a good hotelier needs the following:

Knowledge of the product.

Knowledge of the client.

Knowledge of how to sell the product.

Knowledge of the benefits of the product to the client.

A hotelier should sell:

A good accommodation,

Ensure relaxation,

Escape from pressure,

A feeling of contentment,

Impress your customers,

Put your customer in a more receptive mood,

Atmosphere and ambiance,

The customer should feel better when he returns to work.

In addition, some important points which improve your selling are: Where the person selling is firstly "Jack", the problem solver rather than "Jill" the problem generator and secondly consumer-oriented rather than product-oriented. We find both inter related. If you are consumer oriented, it helps you in becoming Jack, the problem solver. All your customers visiting hotels have some personal problems. If you succeed in finding out what the problem is and help in solving the same, you get a new customer. You can become Jack by having empathy allied to experience of hotel business and selling. If your client is likely to organise a conference and wants a function room for fifty persons and you are in a position to make him available the room, you are successful in this business venture. If he wants a U or V shaped table for a seminar so that delegates are in a position to talk to each other, if you make it possible, his problem is solved. The image of the hotel is largely enhanced.

Another example here is regarding a clean room for your client. You promise him that when you are having lunch, the whole room will be cleaned, you will put in fresh water jugs with lemon slices, and open all the windows for half an hour so that delegates feel good after lunch. You have solved his problem. Again, you are making a new customer and possibly expecting him to appreciate your hotel in future.

In the Indian hotels, we find a provision of taking a special care of the guests, specially early morning when they find it difficult to venture out on major business agendas. We have two early morning calls. The wake up call will prepare you for your plane, tour or conference.

These facts clearly indicate that hotels and hotel companies be consumer-oriented. This would help you in many ways. You will get repeat business and the occupancy ratio will go up. Cost-effectiveness would also be major avenues open up for oral publicity. Thus, you get both new business and repeat business and are in a position to sell more without spending much on advertisement. While selling, it is not only significant that you are selling for the present, it is more impact generating that you are selling for the future. If we find the consumer-orientation in taking favourable decisions, it is possible. You should contract ways for generating the problems. Always try to be a problem solver, never try to be a problem generator.

DISTRIBUTION STRATEGY FOR HOTEL

Product innovation cannot be the lone solution for demand penetration. Innovations in distribution are also found instrumental in the process.[12] The positive contribution of distribution decisions on business expansion cannot be neglected. Ensuring substantial business revenues necessitates a sound strategy for distribution almost in all the organisations — either producing goods or generating services. Like other service generating organisations, the hotel companies also realise the significance of a sound and well-thought distribution strategy. This helps them in raising the occupancy ratio and in increasing business in a big way. Of course, the small hotels can promote and sell even with zero level distribution but so far as the big hotel companies are concerned, they cannot survive and thrive in this competitive market unless they get external support. Hence, they need one-level or two level distribution channels for selling and promoting their services. Only inside or in-house selling would not serve their purpose. In this case willingly or unwillingly, they have to pave ways for tour operators and travel agents.

Building and maintaining middlemen's co-operation is a critical decision-making area. When a producer determines marketing channels and obtains the co-operation of middlemen in the distribution process, he gets a success. If the distribution strategy is found successful, the producer succeeds; if it fails, the distributor fails. This strengthens the hypothesis that middlemen or the tour operators and travel agents are customers for the product but they are not the ultimate users. This calls for a harmonious working relationship with the middlemen so that the hotel companies are not going to face the image problem. Whether the middlemen simply promote, actively recommend or just handle the products, depends substantially on their attitudes towards the hotel companies. It is right to mention here that forcing middlemen to handle a product involves high marketing costs, specially on promotion. Hence, it is upon the hotels and hotel companies to think about the extent of support to be taken from the tour operator and travel agents.

For the hotel companies working on a large-scale, it is important to select the best channel alternative. Of course, the most profitable channel is considered to be the best channel. But only the profitability element cannot be a base for judging the soundness of a distribution decision. Here, we need to assign due weightage to cost and satisfaction elements. It is an important consideration that the distribution cost is optimal and the channels have been making concerted efforts to satisfy the customers. They are playing a significant role in getting a new and repeat business. Thus, we can say that decisions taken for improved economic situation and satisfaction are to be considered sound.

A widespread myth still persists that because services cannot be inventoried on shelves and in warehouses, the distribution systems or channels are less important in service industries than in others. In the marketing practices, creating and manipulating access for consumers is one of the principal ways to manage demand for highly perishable products. Producers are willing to pay relatively high costs for the advantages of extending their points of sale. Here, it is important to mention that big hotel companies show commitment in the case to retain consumers since only inside selling cannot ensure increased accessibility. For most small businesses with only one production unit, such as proprietor-owned restaurants, guest houses, taxi firms, small tourist attractions etc., the choice of location is the most important business decision. A well located small business can be sure of getting an adequate flow of consumers. In these cases, we find zero-level channel since the customers come to the hotels directly and the concept of distribution channel has little relevance. Thus for small hotels, the important decision-making areas are product, pricing and promotion but not distribution. This forms the location-place of production-point of sale-front office.[13] But so far as the big hotel companies are concerned, the zero level distribution system cannot serve their purpose.

In view of the above, the big hotel companies have to think about one-level or two-level distribution system. This is due mainly to the fact that they need to provide substantial information to their prospects, such as convenient customer access, providing brochure and leaflets focussing on their service products, display and merchandising opportunities, itinerary planning, ancillary services, such as insurance, advice on other peripheral issues, passport assistance, serving as marketing intelligence for hotel companies, supplementing hotel's promotional activities and receiving complaints from customers. This information is meaningful and works out plans to solve them for the prospects and hotels as well and only well established travel agents and tour operators can be helpful in generating profits for hotels.

The main problem however, before big hotels is to face the challenges and threats from the competitive hotel groups. This is not only related to the quality and way of offering services but in addition other aspects are also found impact-generating in the very context, such as informing the prospects of their services and getting repeat business. Of course, the front-line staff also plays an important role in this context but their area of activity is limited. This necessitates the services of the distribution channel. The hotel companies have to take a decision regarding the one or two level distribution system. They need more care while selecting a travel agent with sophisticated communicative (information) technologies and efficient personnel to handle, operate and maintain major business revenues.

In the hotel industry, the distribution strategy is related to the transmission of information to the prospects — i.e., information related to availability of services, hotel tariffs, the booking, confirmation, cancellation etc. The motive to ensure that their stay proves comfortable. The hotels and hotel companies while selecting the distribution systems are supposed to make different decisions as per the demands of customers.

- Will hotels prefer to sell directly to the customer?
- Will they sell through clubs?
- Will they involve tour operators?

- Will they involve both tour operators and travel agents?
- Will they involve only travel agents?

Of course, while taking a decision, they would assign due weightage to the cost factor.

The representatives of the hotel industry have to make the channel decisions effective so that the guests get the services promised by them. How to reach the target market is an important problem which requires an in-depth study of the changing market conditions. The main thing is to push successfully the hotel products. If we are taking the support of channel, the fact remains that our decisions are favourably biased to such travel agents or tour operators who can help us in selling and promoting the business effectively. The image projection is also an important dimension as only professionally sound channels can help us in getting the desired results. Here, it is also significant that we are offering reasonable incentives to the channel so that they evince special interest in selling the services and projecting the hotel image.

Because of the choice and flexibility of distribution channels in service products in general and hotel products in particular, the strategic choice between internal and external selling programmes has always been found much more important. New computerised database technology, available for more than a decade, for identifying individual customers by their addresses, profiles and purchasing behaviour, is altering strategic choices being faced by many operators since the end of 1980s. This new technology looks likely to shift the emphasis in marketing toward direct response strategies for all types of products, either physical goods or perishable services. It is against this background that hotel companies are now concentrating on in-house selling. Hence, it is also an important strategic decision to maintain a balance between both categories of selling, depending upon their requirements.

Moreover, technological advances have paved the ways for a change in the distribution system. However, the in-house selling cannot be the only option. For hotel companies, it is significant that tour operators and travel agents are involved in the process because this would help them in many ways.

Zero level pipeline is of course, essential for all hotels as the front-line personnel working in hotels are professionals bearing an attitude of concern towards customers. They are found competent enough to motivate clients and to transform the sales dialogues into booking. The housekeepers, waiters, receptionists, barmen and sales executives are found responsible for selling and promoting service packages of hotels. They are also found helpful in generating the repeat business or transforming the light customers into the habitual customers. For the hotel business, this aspect bears an outstanding significance. It is the responsibility of the hotel management to prepare a good team of efficient sales personnel and give them different incentives so that they show personal-touch-in-service. In-house selling is found cost effective as it is going to minimise the selling expenses. The ultimate responsibility before the sales personnel is to see that the gap between services-promised and services-delivered is filled. This is directly related to the image problems. If we are not in a position to offer more at cost-effective prices, our promises should not be exaggerated.

With the increasing use of new generation of ICT, we find the hospitality industry considerably depending on internet services. In a true sense, we find internet establishing an edge over the traditional channels. The customers now have developed a temptation for making use of internet services and are considering website as their first choice. The high level penetration of e-commerce[14] has been found useful for providers as well as the users. Online booking has virtually brought a rapid momentum in the hotel business. The hotel professionals make use of internet services for diverse purposes. They find themselves in a position to interact with the customers, provide to them the necessary information personally or through web pages, obtain their pre and post-stay experiences, promote the hotel business, transmit the newsletters, take support of (FAQs) frequently asked questions, *et. al.* The international brands have been found taking support of internet and penetrating e-commerce and practicing E-CRM strategy[15] for getting the desired results. The domestic players need to momentise the same. Since the international brands have been found aggravating the magnitude of competition, it is pertinent that the domestic players also penetrate e-commerce for understanding the customers, fulfilling their needs, satisfying them by touching the desired level of their expectations, retaining them and increasing the repeat business and maximizing profitability.

It is high time that the domestic players assign due weightage to both the top and bottom lines and make them stronger and healthier. Broadening and deepening customer relationships are considered essential for satisfying and retaining the customers. It is in this context that we make a strong advocacy in favour of E-CRM strategy which would simplify; the task of hotel professionals. The database of knowledge about the customers may help hotel professionals in understanding the customers' past experiences.

In view of the above mentioned facts, we find distribution an important decision-making area for the hotel professionals. Increasing volatility in markets and sensitivity in customers make it essential that hotel professionals formulate a sound strategy by synchronising the traditional and modern electronic-based technology. All the levels and sub-levels of distribution are found relevant. The tour operators acting as bulk supplier, the travel agents working as retailer, the electronic channels focusing on e-commerce and promoting online booking, the telemarketers developing contacts and converting the enquiries into bookings, the marketing professionals maximising retention and repeat business are the key areas in the formulation of hotel distribution strategy. The marketers need to assign due weightage to cost economy and this focuses on promoting new generation of ICT. The high level penetration of e-commerce would help marketing professionals in different ways.

SUMMARY

You have studied in this chapter hotel placement strategy. After reading this chapter, be sure that the following facts are well versed:

- **Channel: The Concept:** Marketing channels are the distribution network through which the products flow in the market. The concept of distribution channel is found applicable to both goods and services.
- **Distribution Policy: Influencing Factors:** A number of factors influence the formulation of a distribution policy, such as points-of-sale, cost of distribution, image of the hotel company, effectiveness of the marketing efforts and customers' motivation.
- **Distribution Chain: The Term:** The term 'Distribution Chain' denotes the methods by which a product or service is distributed from producers to the consumers. We find three levels, e.g., zero level (directly from producers to customers), one level (travel agent between producers and ultimate customers), two level (tour operators and travel agents working as wholesalers and retailers).

- **Tour Operators:** A tour operator buys the services from hotels in bulk and therefore, we call them wholesalers. They are also found acting as ground operators. Historically, they have emerged from the retail travel agency.
- **Travel Agents:** A travel agent is one who acts on behalf of a principal. In the hotel industry, the hotels or hotel companies are found acting as a principal. The agents work on behalf of principal.
- **Importance of Travel Agents:** Making available refined services to the clients, divert information to them, promoting the hotel business, providing feedback to the hotels and hotel companies and helping customers in planning the services are some of the important contributions of travel agents.
- **Functions of Travel Agents:** Travel agents provide accommodation information, prepare itineraries for the customers, establish link with the provider of services, plan the journey schedule and expenditure involved, arrange bedrooms and function room for their clients.
- **In-house Selling:** In such a distribution system, we do not find any middlemen. The hotels and hotel companies sell the services directly to the ultimate users. In a few cases, the front-line-personnel or sales executives in particular organise sales events. In-house selling is one of the easiest methods to get very quick results.
- **In-house Selling and Front-line-staff:** In maximising and promoting in-house selling, the front-line-staff play a commanding role. The housekeeper, waiters, barman, sales executives, receptionists are found working as front-line-staff. If the front-line-staff is professional, the in-house selling is found more effective in the hotel industry.
- **Telephone Selling:** Telephone call is found to be the most effective method of reaching a key person without wasting much time.

  The call should be well planned. It is found effective even for market research calls. The personnel receiving and transmitting the messages should be trained.
- **E-CRM Stratetegy:** Apart from the traditional channels like phone, white mail and visits; the customers now e-mail, web chat and fax. They send requests through internet-based forms. The marketing and sales campaigns are now on TV, print media, internet, e-mail marketing, SMS marketing and door-to-door-marketing. The concept *of* distribution is now found redefined.
- **Strategy for Restaurant Sale:** Restaurant is an important part of a hotel. No doubt its contribution to the total profit of hotels is not so impressive still it occupies a place of significance. The hoteliers are supposed to keep in mind the ten commandments for increasing restaurant sales, e.g., defining the catchment area, quiet, medium and busy periods, in-house selling, preparing mailing lists, getting repeat business, producing a newsletter, preparing action plan, attention to visitor, using names and saying something when your guests leave.
- **Sales Action Plan:** Strategic decisions for preparing sales action plans are an overall strategy for the whole hotel, analysis of local market strategy, defining the aspects to be touched, preparing target, preparing of monetary budget and time budget.

- **Balancing Inside and Outside Selling:** For hotels and hotel companies it is found significant to strike a balance between the inside and outside selling, keeping in view the cost, profitability and satisfaction of the customers.
- **Selling of whole Hotel:** In formulating the distribution strategy for hotels, it is also pertinent that to the extent it is possible, we should avoid selling the whole hotel. Concentrate on a few areas of internal business and get improved results is considered to be a sound strategy.
- **Sales Letters and Mailing Shots:** Writing sales letters has proved its instrumentality both for incoming enquiries and stimulating new businesses. Mailing shots help in stimulating new business whereas the sales letters are found helpful in answering incoming enquiries.
- **Other Forms of Distribution in Hotels:** In addition to the different channels, we find a different type of distribution system in the hotel industry. W also call them the third group of pipelines. Cards and clubs are found to play an important role in the strategy.
- **Cost of Distribution:** In the formulation of distribution strategy, in addition to other aspects, the cost of distribution is also found to be important. Here, we compute both fixed and variable costs.
- **Improving Sales Technique:** Avoid selling a mile wide and an inch deep, non-verbal communication, knowledge about the customers, consumer orientation, acting as Jack are some of the important aspects for improving sales technique.
- **Distribution Strategy:** A widespread myth still persists that because services cannot be inventoried, the distribution system or channels are found less effective for the hotel industry. It is a wrong notion. It is found important even to the hotel industry. Of course, the small hotels and restaurants can prefer zero level distribution. While formulating distribution strategies, the important aspects to be taken into consideration are cost, competition and satisfaction.

While formulating a strategy for sound distribution of hotel services, the professionals need due attention on E-CRM strategy.

KEY TERMS

Tour Operators
Travel Agents
Top-line
Bottom-line
Brochure
E-CRM
Intermediary
Itineraries
Give-aways
E-channel
FAQs
One-level
Web chat
Plethora
Leveraging
Data Mining
E-mail marketing
SMS Marketing
Quiet Period
Website
Online Booking
Data Base
Zero-level
Two-level

REVIEW QUESTIONS

1. What do you mean by Marketing Channels? Focus on the key words used in service distribution.
2. Explain the factors influencing the distribution policy of hotels.
3. Throw light on the following:
   (a) Distribution Chain
   (b) Zero-level Distribution System
   (c) One-level Distribution System
   (d) Two-level Distribution system
4. What do you mean, by Tour Operator? Explain the importance of tour operator to the hotel industry.
5. What do you mean by Travel Agent? Explain the different functions of travel agents in selling and promoting the hotel products.
6. Discuss the importance of Travel Agents to the hospitality industry.
7. What do you mean by In-house selling?
8. Explain the role of e-commerce in the hotel industry.
9. What do you mean by telephone selling in the hospitality industry? Focus on its importance to customers and hotels.
10. Discuss the different commandments for increasing restaurant sale.
11. Explain the distribution strategy to be adopted by the hospitality industry in an age of new generation of information and communication technology.

APPLICATION EXERCISES

1. "Marketing channels are the distribution network through which the products flow to the market." Comment on this statement in the capacity of a hotel professional.
2. Throw light on the factors you will like to consider while formulating the distribution policy for your hotel in the capacity of a senior hotel marketer.
3. You are working as a hotel manager. Focus on the role you will be required to play for developing rapport with the travel agents for getting the business.
4. In the capacity of a hotel professional, explain the role of inside selling.
5. To improve the functioning of your restaurants, you need to keep in your mind some of the commandments. In the capacity of a hotel manager, explain those commandments.
6. Do you find E-CRM strategy essential for understanding the hotel customers? Justify your opinion.
7. In the capacity of a hotel professional, strike a balance between inside and outside selling so that you succeed in satisfying the customers, minimising the costs and maximising the profits.

8. "Avoid selling a mile wide and an inch deep." Do you agree with the statement? Justify your opinion.

End Notes:

1. Cundiff, Still and Govoni: *Fundamentals of Modern Marketing*; Prentice Hall of India, New Delhi, p. 268.
2. Holloway J. Christopher: *The Business of Tourism;* Pitman, London 1986, p. 77.
3. Rathmell J.M.: *Marketing in the Services Sector;* Winthrop, Cambridge, 1974, p. 104.
4. Burkart A.J. and Medlik S.: *Tourism – Past, Present and Future;* Heinemann Professional Publishing; London, 1974, p. 163.
5. Holloway J. Christopher: *Op. cit.,* p. 79.
6. Bhatia A.K.: *Tourism Development;* Sterline Publication, New Delhi, 1989, p. 260.
7. *Ibid.,* p. 264.
8. Melvyn Greene: *Marketing Hotels and Restaurants into the 90s;* Heinemann Professional Publishing, London, 1989, pp. 160-62, p. 264.
9. *Ibid.,* p. 264.
10. Victor T.C. Middleton: *Marketing in Travel and Tourism;* London, 1988, p. 203.
11. Melvyn Greene: *Op. cit.,* p. 229.
12. Jha, S.M.: *Services Marketing;* Himalaya Publishing House, Mumbai, 1994, p. 202.
13. Victor T.C. Middleton: *Op. cit.,* p. 184.
14. Interview with Jaisree Anand, Dean, NITHM, Hyderabad The Analyst; Nov. 2006.
15. Ray & Teckchandani: Indian Hotel Industry: Strategy for Utilising Unparalleled Growth Potential; The ICFAIAN Journal of Management Research, Vol. VII/5, May 2008.

CHAPTER - 10

STRATEGIES FOR EXPANDED MARKETING MIX IN HOTEL

The hotel professionals need to increase the operational flow which focuses on techno-driven service processing. They need to improve the quality of service ambience which focuses on physical evidence and attractions. They cannot do anything, if they do not have a team of dedicated, personally-committed and value-based people. Practising expanded marketing mix with a professional touch needs due attention of hotel marketers.

CHAPTER OBJECTIVES

Introduction – Expanded Marketing Mix: An Overview – Process – The Front and Back Offices in Service Processing – Physical Evidence and Attractions – Corporate Image – Corporate Identity –Essential Considerations for Physical Evidence – People – Role of Front-line Staff in Hotel – Strategical Decisions for Processing Hotel Services – Strategical Decisions for Physical Evidence and Attractions – Strategical Decisions for People Serving Hotels – Summary – Key Terms – Review Questions – Application Exercises – End Notes.

LEARNING OBJECTIVES

This chapter aims at studying the different dimensions of expanded marketing mix in the hospitality industry. The motive is to sensitise the readers to the process, physical evidence and attractions and people so that formulation of a sound marketing mix helps hotel professionals in improving the quality of managerial decisions. The increasing heat of competition due to entry of a number of international brands makes a strong advocacy in favour of strategic decisions related to the three submixes of marketing.

INTRODUCTION

Formulation of strategy requires professional excellence of world class. Particularly when we find the heat of competition increasing very fast, it is pertinent that hotel professionals not only concentrate on the strategical and tactical decisions related to product, promotion, price and place but in addition also keep into consideration the expanded marketing mix for services helping them in improving the quality and satisfying and retaining the customers. Of course, we find new generation of information and communication technology making ways for qualitative improvements in the services but the hotel professionals not getting a success in increasing the operational flow through techno-driven processing; not attracting working people and customers by creating service ambience instrumental in increasing the operational efficiency and creating a positive opinion of customers; not ensuring that hotels have satisfied group of quality people often fail in getting the technological advantage. It is against this background that we find expanded marketing mix drawing priority attention of hotel marketers while formulating the managerial and strategical decisions.

We find modern hotels considerably depending on the performance of e-channel. For a majority of the hotel operations, we find ICT playing an outstanding role. The hotel professionals promise delivery of quality services to the ultimate customers. Since we find techno-driven services playing a commanding role in the service generation and delivery processes; the hotel marketers need to make it sure that quality technology is used for quality service delivery. In this context, it is also significant that people managing, maintaining, handling and operating technology are tech-savvy. The promised quality of services are to be made available to ultimate customers on time and in a decent way.

The marketing experts feel that in the hospitality industry; the ambient conditions play a positive role. The servicescapes or service ambience focus our attention on the physical surroundings, amenities and facilities for the working people and customers helping them in working, performing, enjoying and gaining new experiences. The hotel professionals need to make use of the services of experts for this purpose. The interiors and exteriors, lighting, furnishing, ventilation, sanitation, music, equipments, aesthetic management, curtains, artistic favour, parking, etc. are some of the aspects found instrumental in generating service fragrance. In addition, the dresses and uniforms of people working in different capacities also play an incremental role. Adding additional attractions to the service ambience is found essential for which we find the hotel professionals to be innovative so that customers and working people gain unique experiences and form a positive opinion regarding the hotels. The professionals need to make service ambience efficacious of generating service fragrance and instrumental in nurturing service culture.

For increasing the efficiency flow, it is not only pertinent that we make use of new generation of information and communication technology. It is much more impact-generating that we provide a conducive environment in which the people and technology perform and get the desired results. In the modern hospitality industry, we find e-channel playing a decisive role and virtually it has established an edge over the traditional channels. This makes it essential that hotels develop such a service ambience in which people while processing succeed in increasing the operational flow and make it sure that possibilities of distortion, delay and indecency are ruled out. Sophisticated technology requires sophisticated ambience and each one of us feel comfortable while performing in the ambient conditions where we find no scope for stress or situational barriers.

The marketing people working in different capacities considerably influence the hotel business. The dimensions of direct selling where we find hotel managers, telemarketers and directly customers involved in the process make it essential that hotel companies recruit quality people and keep on moving the process of developing their potentials by imparting to them the required training facilities. There are a number of institutes educating and training people for the different specialised areas and well educated people are required to be recruited and at the same time, it is also significant that hotel professionals organise short-term training programmes to brush up' their knowledge. The people need to be behaviourally sound and personally committed. They need personal-touch-in-service *vis-a-vis* empathy. It is also significant that they are value-based and show human touch in behaviour. They need an attractive personality with high communicative ability. Thus the hotel managers need to play here an important role so that they succeed in increasing the number of star performers. Particularly in the Indian perspective where we find a good number of hotels not in a position to make the process much more sophisticated the availability of quality people needs priority attention of hotel managers.

Thus, the expanded submixes of marketing focus on three important dimensions, *viz.*, Process, Physical Evidence and Attractions and People. The three additional Ps of marketing would make possible qualitative improvements in the functional properties of hotels. Since the hospitality industry has been facing a number of challenges and threats, it is imperative that both the large and small players assign due weightage to the formulation of additional three submixes of marketing so that with the help of seven mixes, they find it easier to offer innovative services to the customers at an affordable price. The marketing mix would also help them in making possible creativity in the promotional measures for informing, sensing, sensitising, persuading and transforming the potential customers into actual and habitual customers. The customers would feel satisfied by using the quality services which would make ways for satisfaction and retention. An increase in the average room rate and occupancy ratio would help hotels in generating profits and excelling competition.

EXPANDED MARKETING MIX: AN OVERVIEW

Synchronisation based on professional excellence makes the ways for getting the desired results. The transformation of marketing inputs into marketing outputs makes it essential that hotel professionals have managerial proficiency. The strategic decisions related to Process, Physical Evidence and Attractions and People are the three submixes of the expanded marketing mix necessitating due attention of hoteliers for improving the quality of managerial decisions which may help them in satisfying and retaining customers found essential for increasing profits.

PROCESS

This submix of marketing focuses our attention on the elements helping in increasing the operational flow which may be standardised and customized. The standardisation is found concerned with the quality promised by the providers and the customisation is found related to the processing of services in tune with the changing lifestyles and taste preferences of customers. The processing may be simple and complex. With the increasing use of new generation of ICT in the hospitality industry, we find the processing becoming easier. But when the services are found manually operated, the processing becomes a bit complex. It is significant for the hotel professionals to develop their awareness of the customers preferences and this focuses on face to face communication or interaction. The development of package tour makes it essential that hotel professionals have an in-depth idea of the changing food habits, drinking habits, spending behaviour, lifestyles, temptation to tourism etc. In Figure 10.1, we find the different dimensions of processing.

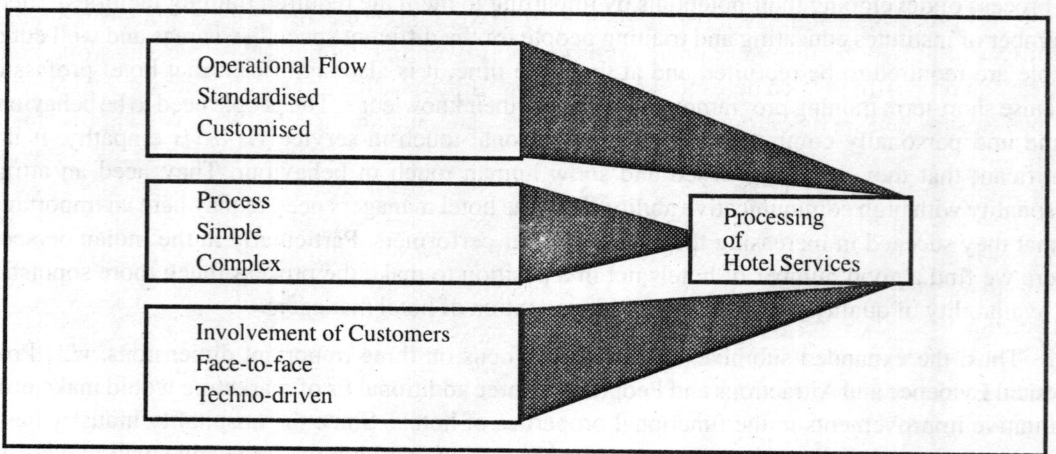

FIG. 10.1: PROCESSING OF HOTEL SERVICES

In the hospitality industry, we find different categories of hotels. The global biggies have been found promoting techno-driven services because a majority of the hotel operations are governed by new generation of technology. Even the small players are found showing their fascination to the ICT. The concept of e-channel has been found beating the traditional channels. Internet has been found governing the hotel business. The E-CRM strategy helps professionals in studying and understanding the customers. The hoteliers find it easier to innovate the services in tune with the results received from electronically -driven Customer Relationship Management.

The hotel professionals need to make it sure that services are processed in a right way. The front-line staff in particular are required to play a meaningful role in the service delivery process. In the hotels where we find manual operations having a domination, it is pertinent that the different levels of staff show their excellence while performing. The marketers have to play here a dominating role. We also find hotels where new generation of technology govern the operational flow. The receptionists and telemarketers play an incremental role in converting the enquiries into bookings. On the basis of their communication excellence, they are found successful even in getting the repeat business. The increasing domination of internet has been found redefining the concept of service processing. The customers and potential customers get the detailed information on the website and the telemarketers and hotel managers transform their enquiries into bookings.

The processing is found significant even with the view points of getting the feedback, studying and understanding the customers, knowing their taste preferences and lifestyles, receiving their reactions and complaints, answering to the queries of customers and based on multi-dimensional results innovating the services having much more uniqueness. Though, we find E-CRM strategy simplifying the task of managing the customers relationships, we cannot negate that face to face communication or interactions have an edge over the techno-driven interactions. It is in this context that the hotel professionals need to make use of direct processing of service with the help of different categories of staff which would not only activate the service delivery process but would also enrich the knowledge bank of hotel professionals regarding the taste preferences and levels of expectations of customers. It is against this background that we consider traditional channel for service processing the most effective prescription for studying and understanding the changing behavioural profile of customers.

The processing thus as an important submix of marketing occupies a place of outstanding significance. It may be manually operated or techno-driven but the motive is to ensure time honoured and decent processing which helps in satisfying the customers. The hotel professionals need to minimise scope for any gap in the service delivery process. The standardisation becomes significant in the hospitality industry because the global biggies have been making the best possible efforts to deliver the best. They are found innovative while creating the services and decent and punctual while delivering. They keep on moving the research and development activities and minimise the frequency in the service innovation process. They prove to be much more creative while informing, sensing, sensitising, persuading and transforming the potential customers into actual customers and get a success even in getting the repeat business. The domestic players need to take a lesson from the global brands which would considerably help them in having speedy processing, right processing, time honoured processing and decent processing. They need to assign due weightage to cost effectiveness which would help them in using pricing as a motivational tool.

THE FRONT AND BACK OFFICES IN SERVICE PROCESSING

In the hospitality industry, we find both the front and back offices instrumental in the processing of services. In both the areas we find the concerned hotel personnel engaged in creating and getting the services ready for delivery.

The Front Office

In this context, we find the concerned staff instrumental in performing and providing to the customers an opportunity to witness the services to be delivered. The services are directly experienced by the customers. In the hotel, we find dining room an example where customers assemble, the food and drink items are served to them which the customers directly experience and witness.

The Back Office

We cannot deny the role of back office in creating the service. In hotel, we find kitchen as the back office where the food items are cooked but the customers are not allowed to witness the same. In the front office, they witness food items served to them but they fail in witnessing that how these items are processed, managed and finally are made ready for delivering. Of course, we find some of the service generating organisations where customers get an opportunity even to witness the back office such as bank and insurance where we find visibility of the back office where the services are processed. The process of keeping the front office separate from the back office is known as "decoupling". In the hotel the dining room, the restaurants are allowed to work independently without any interference. The motive is to bring momentum in the functioning of the back office.

Striking a Balance

Though we find front office and the front-line staff playing an important role in the service delivery process, it is due to the sincerity and operational flow of the back office and the back line staff that the front office succeeds in delivering the services to the customers. The front office is found to be a centre for complex interactive session where the front line staff find the customers unpredictable. They cannot predict that when, why and to what extent the customers may react. The customers may be aggressive and even violent just for the minor faults because the attitudes and temperament of all the customers at all the times cannot remain static and identical. This makes it essential that the hotel professionals depute quality people as the front-line staff who must have the potentials to diffuse the tension of customers.

We find the working front-line staff as the important source for getting the feedback and reactions on the basis of interactions which may provide to the back office and back-line staff an effective prescription to minimise scope for reactions. In the hotel business, we find customer-contact or face-to-face communication with the customers significant but it is an unvarnished fact that the business of a hotel considerably rests on cooperation between the two.

PHYSICAL EVIDENCE AND ATTRACTIONS

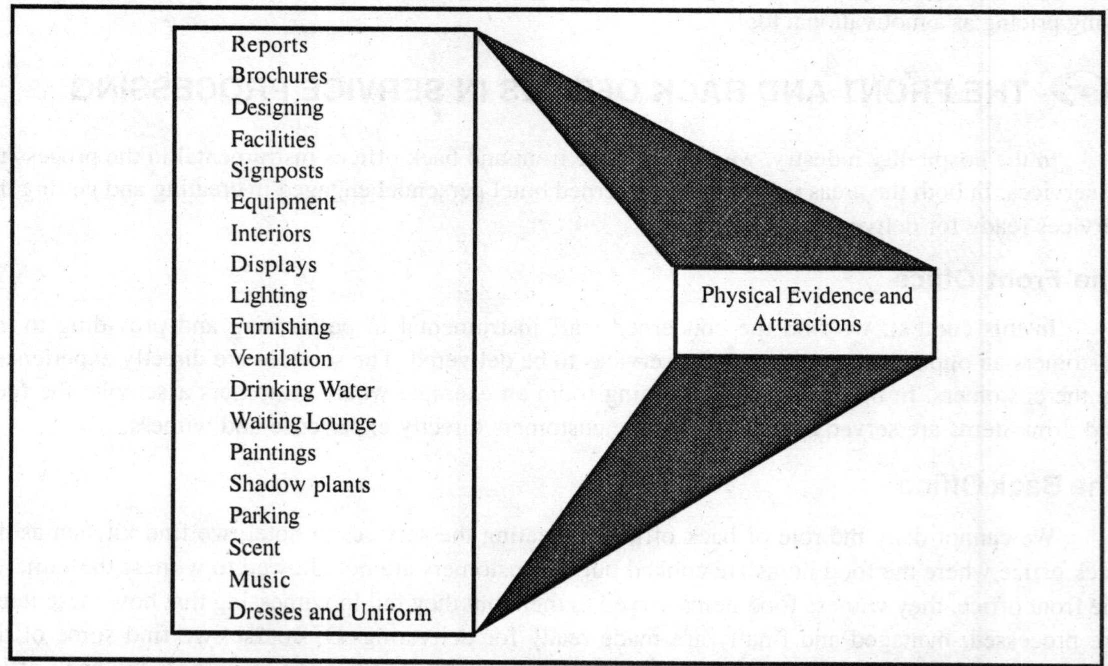

FIG 10.2: DIMENSIONS OF PHYSICAL EVIDENCE AND ATTRACTIONS

In the group of expanded marketing mix, this is the second submix which focuses our attention on physical surroundings for facilities helpful in increasing the performance of people and instrumental in providing an opportunity to the customers for gaining pleasure and new experiences in using the services. Comforts, conveniences and attractions are found to be significant in the hospitality industry where guests stay for enjoying and relaxing. The physical amenities and facilities have a big list. It is upon the hotel professionals to keep into consideration the taste preferences of customers so that they succeed in creating the service ambience adding additional attractions. We find tangibilisation process an important dimension. The customers often rely on tangible cues or physical evidence. The designing of servicescapes is found significant with the viewpoint of differentiating a hotel from others. The servicescapes facilitate performance or communication of services. The exterior and interior attributes are the areas where hotel professionals need due attention. Currently, we find web pages and virtual servicescapes conveyed over the internet also becoming a part of physical evidence. All the interior attributes communicate something to the service users or potential users. The online booking has been found redefining the concept of servicescapes where with the help of self-service environment, the customers witness on web pages the service ambience and with the help of internet succeed in booking, scheduling and planning. In Fig. 10.2, we find the different dimensions of services ambience.

Of course, we have witnessed significant developments in the field of online booking and E-CRM strategy through e-channel; however the hotel professionals cannot underestimate the concept of face-to-face marketing where they get an opportunity to study and understand the customers. The studies related to behavioural profile become easier when we find one-to-one communication. The dimensions of physical evidence and attractions as shown in Fig. 10.2 focus on a number of aspects instrumental in the creation of service ambience. The quality of reports and brochures or information materials need due care of hotel professionals. The designing requires architectural fragrance and in addition safety and protection elements so that the guests staying in the hotels feel secured. Since we find additional attractions to ambience playing an effective role, the hotel professional require to take the support of experts while managing interiors and exteriors. The lighting facility is found significant and the professionals here need to consider colour, intensity and positioning. The furnishing must be artistic specially in the waiting lounges where we find customers waiting for long duration. The artistic photographs, paintings need to be displayed at right places. The signposts must be at appropriate place so that even new customers do not have any problem in identifying a particular point. The ventilation and air conditioning also need due care. The selection of music should be in tune with the taste preferences of customers. The quality of music, volume, positioning cannot be undermined. The ambience must be in a position to generate service fragrance which would help in developing and nurturing service culture. The modern hotels considerably depend on the functioning of new generation of information and communication technology. A number of instruments and equipments are used in the service delivery process. The hotel professionals need to display them so that the customers witness and form a positive opinion.

The dresses and uniforms used by the different categories of staff also play an incremental role in the formation of opinion. The hotel managers need to ensure that working staff look smart, neat and clean and impress upon the customers and visitors. The most important thing in the look of working people is elegance which projects the image of hotel. The aesthetic sense is considered to be an important dimension in the hospitality industry for which the hotel professionals need to assign due weightage to aesthetic management. Positioning of indoor plants, artistic paintings and photographs, decorative items, neat and clean surroundings add additional attractions to the service ambience.

This submix of marketing occupies a place of outstanding significance in the hospitality industry. The hotel professionals need to remember that by developing world class servicescapes, the performance level of working back and front-line staff would considerably be increased. If we talk about service culture, it is not only the contribution of quality staff but in addition, it is also due to the quality of environment in which they perform. Thus service environment plays a contributory role in the development of service culture. If we talk about service fragrance, it is also the result of service environment. If employees feel pleasure in processing and delivering, if customers and visitors feel pleasure in witnessing;

the productivity level of working staff and assets used would be found high. Since customers feel pleasure in gaining new experiences, the satisfaction and retention levels would also be high.

The physical evidence thus plays a significant role while tangibilising the intangible properties or features of the services offered by the concerned organisation. The hotel professionals also make use of this submix of the marketing for providing a conducive and friendly working environment to their employees and fragrance generating ambience to their customers so that both of them find uniqueness and feel something different. We cannot deny the outstanding role of physical evidence for enhancing corporate image and establishing corporate identity. The two terms Corporate image and Corporate identity need due focus.

CORPORATE IMAGE

We find corporate image a picture framed in the eyes and minds of employees, customers, shareholders, media and donors about the corporation or organisation which accumulates in due course and takes the shape of opinion. It is the result of overall contribution of organisation to the different segments. It is quite natural that all the concerned segments have some variation in opinion and therefore creation of image and projection of image are the two different considerations. The marketing professionals help hotels in both the areas.

CORPORATE IDENTITY

The corporate identity focuses our attention on the accumulation of a company's history and strategies. The formation of identity is found over a period of time. The history of an organisation contributes to the process of formation of organisational identity. In addition, the beliefs and philosophy, nature of technology, ownership and people, personality of its leaders, ethical and cultural values and strategies also add to the formation of identity.

For the projection of corporate image and identity, we find logos, uniforms of staff, brand name and promotional corporate apparel or attire found instrumental in reinforcing corporate identity after corporate image. Communicating with the audience of the company such as employees, customers, shareholders is found significant which is found with the help of corporate mark or logo. The designing process has an important role in creating the visual statement which signifies what a company stands for. It communicates a consistent message to corporate customers, financial analysis and others regarding the identity of an organisation. The development of a corporate mark or logo thus requires services of experts.

The physical evidence thus proves to be an important submix even in the hospitality industry where ambient conditions help in the projection of a positive image. The employees servicing hotels as back or front-line staff or belonging to any cadre find it convenient to work in a conducive environment. On the other hand, the customers or visitors attending the hotels witness an opportunity of gaining new experiences. This helps in enhancing corporate image and establishing corporate identity. The service ambience in the hotels of international brands and the same in the domestic hotels or budget hotels are found different. The marketing professionals also get an opportunity to tangibilise the intangible properties of their hotels in a well designed service ambience where we find service environment and where we expect service culture. It is against this backdrop that development of service ambience occupies an important place in the strategic decisions.

ESSENTIAL CONSIDERATIONS FOR PHYSICAL EVIDENCE

Like other professionals, the marketing professionals also need a positive attitude and creative efforts to make the ways for Organisational prosperity. It is in this context that the hotel professionals bear the responsibility of developing service ambience found different to the rivals. Communication of promises and creation of expectations are the two important contributions of physical evidence, the hotel marketers need to remember the same so that their strategical decisions are found instrumental in developing servicescapes to be efficacious of generating service fragrance. The professional excellence of a hotel manager is coiled in the essence of taking the advantages of this submix of marketing which would benefit them in many ways. The following considerations are found significant in the very context:

- ***Link Physical Evidence Strategy with Organisational Goals:*** While formulating a strategy for physical evidence and attractions, the hotel marketers need to keep into consideration the organisational goals so that it plays an effective role or we can say a supportive role in the accomplishment of organisational goals. When our focus is on hotel companies, it is quite natural that they work with the motto of making profits and for that they need to protect and promote the interests of customers as well as their employees. Providing a conducive environment for working and developing a fragrance-generating environment for the customers, serve and promote the interests of both.
- ***Mapping the Evidence:*** In the process of designing a suitable strategy for the development of physical evidence, the hotel professionals also need a suitable map. Here our focus is on service blueprint. The important considerations while mapping are action involved in the service delivery, complexity of the process, points of human interaction providing opportunities to evidence and the tangibilisation at each and every stage.
- ***Clarifying the Role of Servicescapes:*** In this context, it is also pertinent that the hotel marketers clarify the role of servicescapes. The setting of services on marketing, organisational behaviour and customer satisfaction are found important in the process. It is but natural that in all the organisations we find some variations in the role of servicescapes and therefore we need to go through the fact that setting would be elaborate or lean.
- ***Assessing and Identifying the Opportunities for Physical Evidence:*** The marketing professionals while formulating a strategy for the development of servicescapes also need to assess and identify the opportunities for the development of physical evidence, of course in the face-of-identified variations. They also need to consider periodic updating and modernizing.
- ***Working in an Integrated Way:*** Since the professionals bear the responsibility of protecting corporate image, it is pertinent that all the functions of the organization must work towards the goal. The hotel employees need a different uniform for different areas, the designing process would also be different and advertising or promotional decision in general would vary.

PEOPLE

Of course, we find new generation of information and communication technology playing a commanding role in improving the operational efficiency of an organisation; still its existence and prosperity considerably rest on the availability of quality people. It is against this background that hospitality industry requires quality people commensurate with the changing global requirements. With globalisation, we find emergence of a cross-cultural society with changed food habits, drink culture and spending behaviour. Both in qualitative and quantitative terms, the hotel industry requires sound management of human resources. The hotel professionals while formulating people mix for the hotels need to think about capacity building so that the gap between demand and supply is bridged. We cannot negate that hospitality industry while building capacity needs to take into consideration the multi-faceted changes found in the demand side. The hospitality industry had been witnessing a boom which would bring an exponential demand for the workforce at managerial, supervisory, skilled and semi-skilled levels. This focuses on FCIs, IHMs and even other institutes for developing people in tune with the changing requirements. Since we find international brands making the Indian hospitality industry much more competitive, it is pertinent that world class institutions develop people commensurate with their requirements. Recently, we find Lavasa first and largest hill city of free India having Ecole Hoteliers de Lausanne of Switzerland which is the oldest and most renowned hotel school in the world. In addition, we find world class brands like SBC, Oxford University, GDST School UK starting hotel schools in India[4] which would bridge the gap between demand and supply of quality people for the hospitality industry. Because we find the concept of budget hotel gaining rapid popularity, it is essential that a large number of hotel schools are established even by the domestic players.

The hotel professionals need quality people bearing the potentials of increasing the number of satisfied group of customers because satisfaction paves the ways for retention. With the increasing number of almost all categories of hotels, there would be a significant increase in the number of hotel personnel of almost all the echelons which could not be fulfilled by a limited number of institutions. It is significant that the hospitality industry attracts, develops and retains potentially sound people. The young aspirants in this profession need right foundation of education and training so that they choose the tracks in tune with their potentials. Both the government and private sectors need to increase the number of quality people who are capable of growing, developing and maturing both in their chosen field and as individuals. They have tremendous opportunities to capitalise on either in India or abroad. They need to make it sure that their potentials and credentials are in tune with the changing global requirements. While educating and training, the hotel schools have to focus on their excellence making them distinct to others.

ROLE OF FRONT-LINE STAFF IN HOTEL

The hospitality business carries much more sensitivity. The customers expect quality services from the providers. In rooms where they stay; in restaurants where they take lunch or dinner; in bars where they drink; in lounges where they wait and at reception where they interact with receptionists for different purposes, we find much more scope both for satisfaction or dissatisfaction. At each and every stage, the customers find front-line staff delivering services, interacting with them and even ready for service recovery. Actually we find them acting as a link between the external customer and the internal operations of the organisation. They play a critical role in understanding, filtering and interpreting information and resources to and from the organisation and its external customers. They need communication excellence of high level and extraordinary levels of emotions in addition to the potentials of making an invasion on interpersonal and inter-organisational conflicts.

In the hospitality industry, we find front-line staff playing an incremental role. The receptionists, waiters, housekeepers, staff working on different windows act as front-line staff. The supportive staff or back-line staff play here a catalytic role. The success of front-line staff depends on the instrumentality of back-line staff. Thus both of them need to work with a common goal of satisfying the customers.

The following essentials need due attention of hotel professionals specially while developing quality front-line staff:

- Emotional Labour is considered essential for the successful front-line staff which focuses our attention on regulating the emotional behaviour by not receiving or noticing the bad mood of customers. Friendliness, courtesy, empathy, responsiveness need emotional labour.
- We find front-line staff often witnessing interpersonal and inter-organisational conflicts on the job. With the increasing levels of expectations, we find customers asking for even those services which are not possible for the front-line staff or in tune with the job requirements. The conflict may also arise when the policies and regulations stand as a barrier while obliging the customers. The situations may become explosive when customers become aggressive. The front-line staff in that very case need to be tactful and submissive for diffusing the tension.
- With the changing global scenario and increasing terrorism, the front-line staff in hotels face a challenging task specially while ascertaining identity. Even this may irritate the customers but the front-line staff in general and the receptionists in particular need to handle the irritated customers gently.

The hotel professionals while training and developing front-line staff need to observe even the small things specially to develop their potentials of doing much more emotional labour so that they show their excellence even in rough weather.

STRATEGIC DECISIONS FOR PROCESSING HOTEL SERVICES

The hotel professionals bear the responsibility of formulating strategies so that the time honoured and decent processing of services make possible the delivery of promised quality. It is not only significant that we make provisions for delivery of quality services. It is much more impact-generating that we ensure delivery of promised quality and rule out the possibilities of any gap at any stage. In the modern hospitality industry, we find new generation of information and communication technology simplifying the process of service delivery. A number of instruments and equipments are used at different stages which help increasing the operational flow. This makes it essential that the hotel personnel managing, maintaining, operating, handling and diversifying the usage of technology are well aware of their application. The hoteliers need not to forget that sophistication makes the ways for complications. A minor mistake may affect the service quality which would not only create a gap but would also tarnish the image of hotels. Particularly when we find international brands very much instrumental in the processing of techno-based world class services, the domestic players need to make it sure that their hotels have also been availing the technological advantage. Do we find any sense in infusing technology moreover when we find the operational flow not up to the desired level. The hoteliers need to formulate such a strategy which is to diversify the benefits of technology. The e-channel carries no meaning, if we find delay in processing. The employees managing technology, the customers operating technology and the hotel professionals monitoring technology are required to follow the norms. The hotel professionals as strategists need to make it sure that real benefits of technology are made available to the users. The processing of services cross different stages and at each every stage, there should be proper monitoring. The following strategic decisions are found significant in the very context:

- Make it sure that the new generation of technology instruments and equipments are handled, maintained and operated properly and are very much instrumental in the value-addition process. The situational barriers need to be regulated.
- Since the services are to be standardised, it is to be made sure that promised quality of services reach to the ultimate users without any gap. The customers have a high level of expectations and the service delivery process requires to meet the same. Mounting intensity of competition makes it essential that you define service quality and ensure punctuality and decency in delivery
- Customisation is considered essential because this is to provide competitive advantages. This makes it essential that hotel professionals are well aware of the changing taste preferences, food habits, drink habits and spending behaviour of customers. While developing a package, it is to simplify the task of hotel professionals.
- The customisation is found not only with the motto of generating profits but also with the stand point of meeting social obligations. The professionals need to keep their eyes open and minds active so that they move forward one stage ahead of their rivals. With the help of E-CRM strategy, it is easier for the hoteliers to enrich their knowledge bank specially related to the changing taste preferences. The interactions help them in identifying the changing behavioural profile of customers.
- It is also pertinent that the hoteliers make professionalised efforts to make the process much more simple. If quality technology is managed, maintained and operated by the quality people, the process of service delivery is simplified. The simplicity focuses our attention on simple generation and simple delivery. Since we find service delivery a joint effort of people and technology, it is significant that both of them work properly. The customers using new generation of technology and using online bookings are to be encouraged.
- The interruptions at any stage are to be removed. There are a number of reasons for interruptions and gap, such as technology may develop a fault, technology may be mishandled, technology may not be maintained properly, power breakdown may be frequent etc. Even in the context of face-to-face communications or interactions, we find scope for a gap mainly due to indecent behaviour of front-line staff. The hoteliers are required to ensure that working staff have communication excellence, patience, empathy and a sense of judgement.
- In the direct marketing, we find two different conditions. In the first condition the customers have a face-to-face communication and in another condition, we find virtual communication. Both the conditions are found different specially with the view point of understanding their behavioural profile. We cannot negate that face-to-face communication has an edge over the virtual communication. The hoteliers need to prefer face-to-face communication for studying and understanding customers.

The service delivery and the operating systems are the two different dimensions of processing the services. The customers judge the services also on the basis of operational flow and speed which rest on the quality of technology used. The international brands make use of high quality of technology and tech-savvy people manage and handle the same. This in a very natural way increases the value addition process and due to quality and speed, the customers are found satisfied. The domestic players also need to make it sure that techno-driven processing provides to the customers high level of satisfaction.

The hoteliers while formulating a strategy for sound processing of services need to take into consideration the above mentioned facts which would help them in getting the real benefits of technology. The value addition process would gain a rapid momentum and the levels of satisfaction and retention would be high.

STRATEGIC DECISIONS FOR PHYSICAL EVIDENCE AND ATTRACTIONS

Service environment plays an outstanding role in the development of service culture. This dimension of marketing mix focuses on the development of a sound service ambience in which hotel employees feel pleasure in performing and the customers and visitors gain new experiences before and after using. This draws our attention on the tangibilisation process which is found instrumental in facilitating performance or communication of the service. For improving the quality of service, it is important that customers are delivered the services in an ambient condition. The customers often rely on tangible cues or physical evidence. With the increasing heat of competition, it is pertinent that the hotel professionals assign due weightage to the development of a sound service ambience. We cannot negate that the international brands have an edge over the domestic players, specially in terms of servicescapes. Uniqueness makes the ways for attractions. By developing world class service ambience, you provide an environment to nurture service culture. It is against this background that the hoteliers need priority attention on the following strategic points. We need to remember that strategic decisions cover exterior as well as the interior attributes. In the modern hospitality industry, we find web pages and virtual servicescapes conveyed over the internet also becoming important. The hoteliers use them for communicating to the potential customers the outstanding features or uniqueness of service ambience. The designing of servicescapes also becomes significant to the hoteliers where they need to make use of the expertise of specialists.

- With the increasing heat of globalisation, we find corporate culture gaining a rapid momentum. The international brands keep on moving their search for getting a profitable market. It is an unvarnished fact that Indian hospitality industry has attracted the international brands or global biggies. This makes it essential that hotel professionals assign due weightage to the designing process so that the customers and potential customers get an additional attraction. When we talk about the servicescapes, our focus is not only on the interiors but also on exteriors which stimulate the sensitisation process. The potential customers in particular need to develop a temptation to go inside and witness the uniqueness.
- The designing of interiors is also found meaningful which draws our attention on a number of items such as signposts, lighting, furnishing, ventilation, sanitation, music, display of ornamental plants and artistic paintings etc. The motive is to activate the stimulants so that the customers and potential customers form a positive opinion regarding the quality of services to be delivered. It is very natural that hotel professionals make use of the services of experts because it is not only important that we post or place a particular thing at a particular point. In a true sense, it is positioning which if right provides to us the real benefits. This makes a strong advocacy in

favour of expertise. In each and every area the experts and the hoteliers need to make it sure that their services have been used.

- In the corporate culture, we find show-value playing an effective role. Particularly in the hospitality industry, this dimension carries an outstanding significance. The international brands are found very particular to even small things to be instrumental in adding additional attractions. The domestic players also need to follow the same. We find aesthetic sense adding fragrance in the service ambience and for that the hotel professionals are required to make place for ornamental indoor plants, artistic photographs and paintings, well designed carpets and curtains helpful in differentiating a hotel from others. Hence while developing service ambience, the hoteliers have to assign due weightage to show value.
- The dresses and uniforms of hotel employees also help in adding attractions. The hoteliers need to make it sure that the staff working in different capacities look neat and clean and smart. The quality of dresses and uniforms worn by employees virtually project the image of an organisation. It is quite natural that customers and visitors coming to the hotels minutely observe these things. Particularly the employees having one-to-one interaction with customers and visitors, should have something special in their personal score and something very special in their behavioural profile covering empathy and personal Philanthropy.
- The display of materials is also an important dimension of strategic decision. The customers and visitors while witnessing quality information and publicity materials form a positive opinion regarding the hotels. The business cards, brochures, visiting cards, posters and pamplets, newsletters, menu cards are some of the materials helpful in the creation of a positive impression. The materials must be of world class. The hotels having international brands are found very careful while displaying these materials.
- Today, we find new generation of information and communication technology paving copious avenues for virtual servicescapes. In this context, we find web pages used by hotels for tangibalising the evidence of the service offered by them. This medium offers to the hotels an opportunity to communicate to the customers the experiential aspects of the services. But here it is essential that the hotels have been making use of web pages. The hotel professionals may display the features and photographs of different tourist sites and in addition the speciality of hospitality to be made available to them in the hotels.
- The hotel professionals need to make use of new generation of ICT as a facilitator so that the hotel employees feel pleasure in performing. A well designed functional facility can make the service a pleasant experience specially with the viewpoint of customers.
- We cannot negate that human behaviour is influenced by the physical setting in which it occurs. The environmental psychologists believe that individuals react to places in which they have to perform or receive. Of course, we find human beings designing and creating environment but here it is pertinent that the environment created and developed by them must be conducive and positive.
- In the ambience for hotels, we find lighting playing an important role. The colour of light, intensity of light, positioning of light are found significant in the very context. We cannot deny that natural light has an edge over others but it is not possible to have natural day light at all places for most of the time and therefore hoteliers have to make provisions for artificial sources. The intensity of light depends on a particular condition which conveys something about

atmosphere. Low level of lighting is found associated with romantic setting. Some colours have a soothing feeling while some have disturbing. Greens and blues are cool colours whereas red, oranges and yellows are warm colours.

- Signs, symbols and artifacts are the various dimensions of decor. The signs are found effective in creating first impression which may be used for directional purposes such as parking, entrance and exit and rules of behaviour such as no smoking zone. The signs must be clear, visible and rightly positioned. The paintings and photographs on the wall create a good impression. The styles of the decor create an impression and service differentiation.
- In the context of socialisation process, it is pertinent that hotel professionals watch the expected roles, behaviour and relationships in the interaction process. The individuality is to be suppressed and uniformity in behavioural profile of staff is to be made possible. It is right to mention that in a majority of the cases when we find staff wearing uniforms, the possibilities for idiosyncrasies in behaviour and appearance are considerably minimised. Appearance and attitude of the service staff are minutely observed by the customers and therefore the hotel managers need to tangibilise the properties of their staff such as technical skill, interactive skill, personality and attitude towards work, consistency of quality performance and their appearance. By appearance of staff, our focus is on the friendly behaviour of employees, sense of confidence, professional excellence and empathy.
- The hotel professionals need to make it sure that physical evidence creates promises and customer expectations. The physical evidence strategy is to be linked with goals and objectives of hotels. This draws attention of professionals on service blueprinting which makes it easier to witness the action involved in the service delivery, complexity of the process, points of human interaction. We also call it *service mapping*. Tangibilisation of intangible nature of services need much more care and professional excellence. Projection of corporate image and identity are considered significant and the strategic decisions related to physical evidence may simplify the projection process.

Thus, the hotel professionals need to consider the physical facilities combining essential and peripheral evidence; physical setting containing appearance of the premises, design and decor and social setting covering appearance of staff.

STRATEGIC DECISIONS FOR PEOPLE SERVING HOTELS

The success of an organisation considerably depends on the availability of quality people. Though we cannot deny the instrumentality of new generation of technology in increasing the operational flow and efficiency still the existence of an organisation is found in danger failing the supply of thematically sound, personally committed and value-based people. It is in this context that hotel professionals need to develop back and front-line staff commensurate with the changing requirements. A mix of different categories of employees is to be prepared by the hotel professionals so that a team culture is to make the ways for service culture. The global biggies assign due weightage to the management of human resources and therefore we find their rate of productivity high. They recruit quality people, keep on moving the process of their development, motivate them in the face of their contributions and in return get the higher productivity, and profitability. They link incentives with performance and increase the number of star performers. Presently, we find a mismatch between demand and supply. With the increasing demand side, we need to improve the supply position which focuses on the number and quality of hotel schools. The government policy makers as well as the corporate sector need to open quality hotel institutes to be successful in educating and training hotel people in the face of changing requirements. The strategic decision-making areas are the followings:

- Increasing the number of hotel schools of world class is the urgent need of the hour. The international brands need to open hotel schools preparing quality people for the hospitality industry. In addition, the domestic players also need to take part in the process. The state and central governments independently or under the PPP mode have to assign due weightage to the opening of hotel institutes. To bridge the widening gap at skill-level, the existing Food Craft Institutes are required to be strengthened and new ones to be opened. To enlarge the scope, hospitality education needs to be imparted through the network of ITI, Polytechnics and at the +2 stage as a vocational stream of the school system IHMs which are processing bulk of manpower at managerial and skill levels need to be strengthened and capacity augmented with international linkages for quality human resources in a good number. New IHMs, in the states or regions which have not been covered as yet, need to be established for proper distribution of government resources . For the young untrained staff who continue to join the hospitality industry, the government should promote short-term training programmes. The existing scheme of "Train the Trainer" is required to be strengthened and practised countrywide for boosting availability of adequate trainers for training. The training programmes must cover the skill development including language courses for fresh as well as existing service providers, training of trainer programme and creating awareness programme in rural areas of the country.
- Since we expect a significant increase in the traffic, the creation of quality accommodation is found essential. It is estimated that more than 2,00,000 approved quality accommodation rooms would be required by 2011.[7] This in a natural way focuses our attention on increasing the number of quality human resources for the hospitality industry. The hotel industry requires people from different levels, specially skilled personnel in food crafts and other specialised areas. Particularly after globalisation, we have witnessed significant changes found in the lifestyles of customers staying in hotels. Due to the emergence of a cross-cultural society, the food habits, drinking habits and spending behaviour are also changing. This make it essential that the concerned schools or institutes develop hotel people in the face of changes found in customers and potential customers. Brushing up their knowledge by organising short term refresher courses is found significant. Institutes of Hotel Management and Food Craft institutions need to consider quality people for the hospitality Industry. We cannot negate that the international brands assign due weightage to the development of human resources for the hospitality industry and it is in this context that they not only focus on their thematical competence but also consider other dimensions of personal score such as developing aesthetic sense, etiquette management, event management and even disaster management, specially in the present condition when we find international terrorism aggravating the magnitude of problem.
- Personal commitment and value orientation are two important dimensions necessitating attention of professionals while developing people. The hotel professionals need to make it sure that while transforming human resources priority attention has been given to the personal-touch-in-service and humanised behaviour. In addition, we find sincerity, honesty and ethical dimensions also occupying a place of outstanding significance. We find hotel customers much more sensitive and therefore even minor things show major results. A minor case of menu

fatigue may considerably furnish the image of hotel. The hotel personnel also need to know about empathy because sharing of pains, by the front-line staff in particularly may help hotels in increasing the rate of retention.

- The motivational factors need priority attention of hotel professionals specially to get the best result from the human resources. The hoteliers need to ensure lucrative financial incentives to the hotel people and in addition, they should also think about the amenities and facilities to them so that quality people continue to serve the hotels. The professional may link their incentive plans to the occupancy rate of hotels. This will be helpful in increasing the hotel business.
- The above mentioned facts make it clear that the hotel professionals need to concentrate on the development of human resources in the face of changing customers. Consistent efforts for the development of human resources transform them into human capital. The hotel professionals need to develop and mobilise the human resources because they prove to be human capital.
- Developing people for your organisation is also an important strategic area. We find cases where world class hotels have engaged themselves in educating, training and developing quality people. The International Holiday Inn chain has its own Holiday Inn University. In India, the Oberois have their own training schools. When we talk about the development of people for the hospitality industry, not only the technical skills but interactive skills also become significant. This focuses on eye contact, smiling, tone of voice, standard of dresses *et. al.* The hoteliers need to develop people in both the areas.
- In the context of strategic decisions, it is also pertinent that hoteliers make best of their efforts to retain quality people. They need to treat employees as customers and may also include them in the company's vision. Appreciating the contributions of employees and rewarding them suitably are found significant. Involvement of employees in the deliberations may also be considered.
- The hotel professionals need to be careful while recruiting people. They should hire the right people. Selecting the best match or fit into the organisational setting is our motive. The hoteliers may view even customers as a potential employee. McDonald's views every customer as a potential employee. Once you identify a potential employee, the screening process may help you in getting the best. They should have competency to perform *vis-a-vis* the inclination to serve.

Of course, we find amenities and facilities provided by the hotels playing an important role in satisfying and retaining the customers but here it is also significant that they have world class people to deliver the World-class services. We cannot deny that what do we offer is found significant but how do we offer is found much more impact-generating. The world class services offered by a hotel prove to be ineffective, if we find customers not witnessing smile on the faces of employees serving them. This makes it essential that professionals are very much sincere and honest while developing and managing human resources. Humanised leadership has an edge over others. The hotel managers need human touch in behaviour. Developing employees sensitive to the interests of customers requires priority attention of hotel professionals. This is due to the fact; that satisfied group of employee evince keen interests in satisfying the customers. Bill Marriott of Marriott hotels asked to the job candidates that the hotel chain wants to satisfy three groups, viz., employees, customers and shareholders. While all the three groups are important, in which order the groups are to be satisfied requires due attention of professionals. A majority of the candidates said that the customers must be satisfied first. Bill Marriott was of the view that first the employees be satisfied because the satisfied group of employees would start loving their jobs and would feel a sense of pride in the hotel which would result into satisfaction of customers followed by retention and profit maximisation which would ultimately benefit the shareholders. It is against this backdrop that in the formulation of people mix, the interests of employees need to remain at top. The strategic decisions thus require priority attention on the interests of hotel employees.

SUMMARY

- **Expanded Marketing Mix:** In the expanded marketing mix, we find focus on three sub-mixes such as Process, Physical Evidence and Attractions and People.
- **Process:** This submix of marketing draws our attention on the elements helping an increase in the operational flow which may be standardised and customised.
- **Physical Evidence and Attractions:** This submix is found related with service ambience or servicescapes. The decision making draws our attention on designing; facilities, signposts, interiors, exteriors, displays, lighting, furnishing, ventilation, drinking water, waiting lounge, scent, music, reports, brochures, parking, dresses and uniforms helping an increase in the performance level of employees and providing to the customers an ambience to gain new experience and enjoy.
- **People:** This submix of marketing is related to people. The management of human resources is found important even in the hospitality industry. The hotel professionals need to recruit quality people and to impart proper training facilities to them so that they succeed in developing a team of thematically-sound, personally- committed and value based people.
- **Strategic Decisions for Expanded Marketing Mix:** The hotel professionals need to identify the strategic areas so that they succeed in making hotels competitive. The front-line as well as the back-line staff need proper training facilities. The managerial staff also need to be developed in the hotel school. A satisfied group of employees may help hotels in satisfying customers and maximising profits.

  The physical evidence and attractions focus on the service ambience. The hotel professionals need to make use of the services of experts for developing service environment successful in increasing the operational efficiency of employees and at the same time providing to the customers a place for gaining new experiences. It is also significant that hotel managers assign due weightage to the dresses and uniforms of employees working in different capacities. The environment needs to generate service fragrance for developing service culture.

  The people serving hotels in different capacities need to be recruited, developed and motivated with the motto of increasing the levels of satisfaction. A group of satisfied employees evince personal interests in satisfying the customers which makes ways for maximisation of profits. We need to increase the number of hotel schools for improving the supply position.

KEY TERMS

Servicescapes
Service Ambience
Physical Evidence
Customisation
E-CRM
Front Office
Back Office
Corporate Image
Corporate Identity
Blueprinting
Logo
Artifacts
Emotional Labour
Menu Fatigue
Aesthetic Management
Empathy
Catalytic
Tech-savvy

REVIEW QUESTIONS

1. What do you mean by Expanded Marketing Mix? Explain the different submixes of expanded marketing mix.
2. Focus on processing as a submix of hotel services.
3. Explain Physical Evidence and Attractions as a submix of the expanded marketing mix.
4. Discuss People as a submix of marketing the hotel services.
5. Throw light on Front and Back Office in the context of hotel industry.
6. Explain the essential conditions for physical evidence in respect of hotel industry..
7. Throw light on the role of frontline staff in the hospitality industry.
8. Focus on the strategic decisions for processing the hotel services.
9. Throw light on the strategic areas for physical evidence in the industry.
10. Discuss people of marketing and throw light on the strategic decisions for marketing people in the context of hospitality industry.

APPLICATION EXERCISES

1. In an age of technology, we find service processing in the hospitality industry considerably influenced by technology. Comment on this statement as a marketing professional.
2. You are working as a hotel professional and have been asked to develop service ambience for your hotel. Explain essentials for physical evidence in the context of hospitality industry.
3. For satisfying the customers, you need to satisfy the employees. Comment on this statement as a hotel professional.
4. As a marketing professional, throw light on the role of frontline staff in the hospitality industry.
5. In the capacity of a hotel professional, identify strategic areas for the development of service ambience.

6. You are working as a hotel manager and want to increase the levels of satisfaction of different categories of staff working with you. Focus on the strategic decision-making areas.
7. The international brands have been found assigning due weightage to the development of servicescapes. Suggest a strategic plan for the domestic players in the Indian perspective.
8. As a marketing professional, how would you manage frontline staff working in restaurants.

End Notes:

1 Zeithaml & Bitner: Services Marketing; Tata McGraw; New Delhi. 2003, pp. 24-27.

2. *Ibid.*

3. Ray & Teckchandani: Journal of Management Research; The ICFAI Business School; Vol. VII/5, May 2008, pp. 64-78.

4. Times of India: Ad. Materials, May, 2009.

5. Jha, S.M.: Services Marketing; Himalaya Publishing House; 2009, Mumbai, Chap. l2.

6. Eleventh Five Year Plan: Planning Commission; pp. 245-51; Government of India, New Delhi.

7. *Ibid.*

8. Bhasin J.: A Study of Educational Scenario in Hospitality and Tourism Industry; Vol. 2/1, Jan-June, 2006.

9. Greene M.: Marketing Hotels and Restaurants into the 90s; Heinemann Professional Publishing; England, 1989.

....ঌ৩ঌ৩....

CHAPTER - 11

OVERALL MARKETING STRATEGY FOR HOTEL

Hospitality business in India is shining and we do not find any sign of burnout in the immediate future. The marketers need an overall marketing strategy to counter the challenges and threats in the business environment, specially generated by global biggies.

CHAPTER OBJECTIVES

Introduction – Overall Marketing Strategy: Concept and Application – Formulation of an Overall Marketing Strategy – Selecting the Marketing Inputs – Factors in Selecting the Marketing Inputs – Implementation of Overall Marketing Strategy – Strategies for Marketing Inputs – An Optimal Product Mix – An Optimal Promotion Mix – An Optimal Price Mix – An Optimal Place Mix – Smooth, Decent and Time-honoured Processing – Employees and Customer-friendly Service Ambience – Satisfying and Retaining Quality People – Strategic Marketing Tasks – Planning the Business Mix – Deciding the Position or Image – Encouraging and Rewarding Frequent Customers – Integrating Marketing Across Several Units – Evaluation of Overall Marketing Strategy – Systematic Marketing Audit – Understanding the Marketing Mix in Hotel – Summary – Key Terms – Review Questions – Application Exercises – End Notes.

LEARNING OBJECTIVES

This chapter aims at studying the different dimensions of overall marketing strategy. The readers develop their awareness of the various marketing inputs for getting the desired marketing outputs. The role of a marketing professional is like a chef who with the help of quality recipes prepares a delicious dish. Synchronisation of different submixes in tune with the changing taste preferences of customers is significant. The marketers come to know the process of developing a sound marketing mix.

INTRODUCTION

We accept the fact that mission of an organisation is to manage the controllable in terms of uncontrollable in such a way that both the variables meet the needs of target market *vis-a-vis* facilitates the accomplishment of organisational goals. The controllables are the different submixes of marketing which can be tailored in tune with the changing markets. The orchestration of different submixes such as product, promotion, price, place, process, physical evidence and people need world class professional excellence. The hotel professionals need to formulate strategies related to the different submixes which must be in the face of changing taste preferences and lifestyles of customers. To put it another way, the hotel managers bear the responsibility of making possible a fair synchronisation of strategically decisions into a deliberately planned competitive posture. Here we find planning, action and control more instrumental in the formulation process. An organisation like hotel where we find intensity of competition increasing fast it is pertinent that marketers make use of their excellence while formulating and implementing overall marketing strategy and in the process, concentrate on the identification of opportunities to serve target markets and keep on moving the process which makes it difficult, for the competitors to take business away.

Overall marketing strategy is a composite build up which makes possible a fair blending of various inputs, marketing channels, advertising, personal selling, pricing and other devices to get the designed outputs also known as objectives, e.g., targeted return on investment, market share and brand image. We find an overall marketing strategy dynamic as the inputs and outputs are required to be changed with a change in the business environmental conditions. This makes it essential that hotel marketers continually monitor the overall marketing strategy. Like other industries, the hospitality industry also requires to study the problems related to the overall marketing strategy. The multi-dimensional problems studied in the very context are found helpful to the hoteliers and the hospitality industry on the whole. The professionals make use of their excellence while answering to the following questions:

- How to make possible a fair blending of inputs and outputs?
- How to pave the ways for excelling competition?
- How to incorporate the necessary changes in the marketing mix in the face of emerging trends in competition?
- How to reach to the target markets?
- How to accomplish the organisational goals?

With the increasing heat of globalisation, we find positive trends in the hospitality industry. The increasing demand position has been found increasing the intensity of competition because we find global biggies evincing keen interest in the Indian hotel industry.

With the entry of international brands like Amanda, Satinwoods, Banana Tree, Hampton Inns, Hilton, Mandarin Oriental, Golden Tulip, Marriott; we find the Indian markets becoming much more competitive. The global biggies have been found innovating their strategic decisions. The key Indian players such as ITC, EIH, Bharat Hotels, Viceroy, DLF, Unitech, Royal Palms, The Park Hotels, Leela, The Oberoi, Taj have been found independent benchmarks on their own in terms of world class services and amenities provided by them. Thus, the Indian hospitality industry is becoming much more competitive.

This focuses our attention on the formulation of an overall marketing strategy which would help the industry in many ways. We cannot deny that the Indian hospitality industry has been witnessing positive trends because we find demand outpacing supply, leading to a hike in the average room rate and the occupancy rate. The growth momentum that started in the second half of 2004 is found moving up ward. According to Abacus' statistics, the industry has shown tremendous growth with 24% YTD June 2006 and is expected to grow at the rate of 25% per annum during 2005-10. Going by the positive outlook by the World Travel and Tourism Council (WTTC) by 2020, Indian tourism is expected to contribute a hefty ₹ 8,50,000 cores to the country's GDP.

In view of the above, it is right to say that the Indian hospitality industry requires world class excellence of marketers who with their world class efforts, succeed in capitalizing on the opportunities existent in the markets. Innovative strategies would simplify the task of marketers. Since we find international players making the markets much more competitive, it is imperative that domestic players focus on budget hotels. This is due to the fact that we find a significant increase in the number of middle class. The increasing domination of corporate culture has been found changing the lifestyles of even middle class people and for them the budget hotels would be a priority choice. It is in this context that we find even reputed domestic players switching over to the budget hotels. We cannot deny that the budget hotels essay an integral role on the canvas of the hotel industry in India and the world over. When we find hospitality industry reeling under the euphoria of the room boom; the hotel professionals are likely to get an opportunity for increasing the average room rate and the occupancy rate which would significantly increase the hospitality business.

In the changing scenario, the hotel professionals are supposed to play a catalytic role. They need to intensify the research and development activities so that the process of innovation keeps on moving uninterrupted. If the marketing inputs are of quality and the overall marketing strategies are commensurate with the changing customers; the marketers are to get a positive response. Systematic, critical and unbiased appraisal of the basic market policies and objectives would help marketers in making the processes much more cost effective. But here it is significant that they develop their awareness of the changing taste preferences of customers and offer to them the services which are not within the reach of their competitors. Uniqueness makes the ways for attractions which opens new vistas for business promotion.

Hospitality business in India is shining and we do not find any sign of burnout in the immediate future. Of course, a number of factors are responsible for such a robust growth but the most important thing is globalisation which has strengthened corporatisation and has also activated the process of economic transformation. Though we find worldwide economic recession showing red, green and amber signals however, the Indian hospitality industry would continue to shine. The marketers need to show their world class excellence. We find brand loyalty a fragile idea in the cost transparent world and there fore the hotel professionals are required to promote India as a brand for creating new customers and retaining the old ones. Developing rapport with the media people needs due attention of marketers so that they continue to support the industry's efforts through a visible and perceivable projection of the new developments taking place in the hospitality industry and tourism sectors. They also need to correct the wrong perception of those who still feel that service facilities and hotel tariffs in India are not in tune with their preferences. They need to convince them that Indian hospitality industry is comparable and competitive with the hotels in competitive destination countries. Indeed, they are likely to get in India a package which is not to be available in other parts of the globe. By visiting India, they would be in a position to discover one of the oldest civilisations of the world to enjoy the plurality of cultural enjoyment offered by this country. The hotel professionals need to go to the right persons and their messages are to be transmitted to a few of the selected countries having a special temptation to visit the country of their origin and discover their roots. The diversification of principal source markets is needed which would focus on the countries like South Africa, Israel, Spain, China, Japan, South Korea, Australia, Brazil, Argentina etc. offering high growth potential and from those countries where the present level of inbound tourist is low. We need to concentrate on South Africa, Mauritius, Kenya, Malaysia, Fiji etc. with a large Indian diaspora for higher tourist arrivals from those countries. The hotel marketers need to create greater resonance in NRIs and persons of Indian origin. We need world class marketing professionals and innovative promotional measures to brush up the minds of those nurturing negative feelings about India.

In the formulation of overall marketing strategy, the hotel professionals need to synchronise different submixes of marketing in such a way that they succeed in making their services much more competitive. Since we find a number of international brands entering the Indian hospitality industry, it is pertinent that the services offered by them are of world class and at the same these are affordable. The domestic players may find it difficult to compete with global biggies and therefore mergers, acquisitions and consolidations will be the formula to stay competitive. The domestic players may also think in favor of budget hotels. A projection for the coming years shows an increase in the attrition rate *vis-a-vis* the wage bills. Hence, the hotel professionals also need to consider that how and in what way they would be successful in increasing the average room rate and the occupancy rate which would help them in profit maximisation.

OVERALL MARKETING STRATEGY: CONCEPT AND APPLICATION

The overall marketing strategy of an organisation is its competitive status in the market place. It is a competitive build-up. It is found dynamic; its nature both in specific inputs and the desired outputs must change with changes in the company, its competitive situations, its markets and economic climate.[1]

In the face of the aforesaid concept of overall marketing strategy, it is said that the overall marketing strategy is concerned with the identification of opportunities to serve the target markets profitably and to serve them so effectively that it becomes difficult for the competitors to take business away, on a profitable basis. We consider it a systematic approach which involves an evaluation of the possible inputs to the overall marketing strategy in terms of outputs. To make it possible, it is essential to make an analysis of all the dimensions of major inputs like product, promotion, pricing and distribution. In addition, it is also significant to evaluate the impact on the desired outputs related to the achievements of the objectives of hoteliers. Here, we select the inputs with the notion that the overall marketing strategy is the best for getting the desired outputs.

In the hotel industry, when we talk about the formulation of an overall marketing strategy, our emphasis is on making possible a fair blending of inputs and outputs. Here, the inputs are hotel products, promotion, pricing and placement and the outputs are the objectives, such as the target return on investment, market share, brand image and leadership as summarized in Figure 11.1. The hoteliers, while formulating the overall marketing strategy for the hotel industry, are required to select the best product, e.g., well managed rooms, restaurants, bars and function rooms. In addition, the peripheral or supportive services made available by hotels are also important. The hotels and hotel companies are here also required to select efficient professionally sound travel agents so that the products information reach to the target markets in a decent way. Here, it is also significant that promotional strategies are based on latest development, the pricing strategies are sound and the front-line staff engaged in inside selling are doing well. After managing the inputs, they have to manage the outputs where the hotels and hotel companies feel ensured that their investments in no way are to be unproductive or unprofitable and the brand image created is found helpful in establishing a leadership in the market.

In Figure 11.1, we find a sound combination of inputs and outputs which makes it clear that overall marketing strategy is a fair blending of strategies related to the different submixes of marketing, with the motto of accomplishing the organisational goals. In the formulation of an overall marketing strategy, the professional excellence of hoteliers constitutes a place of outstanding significance.

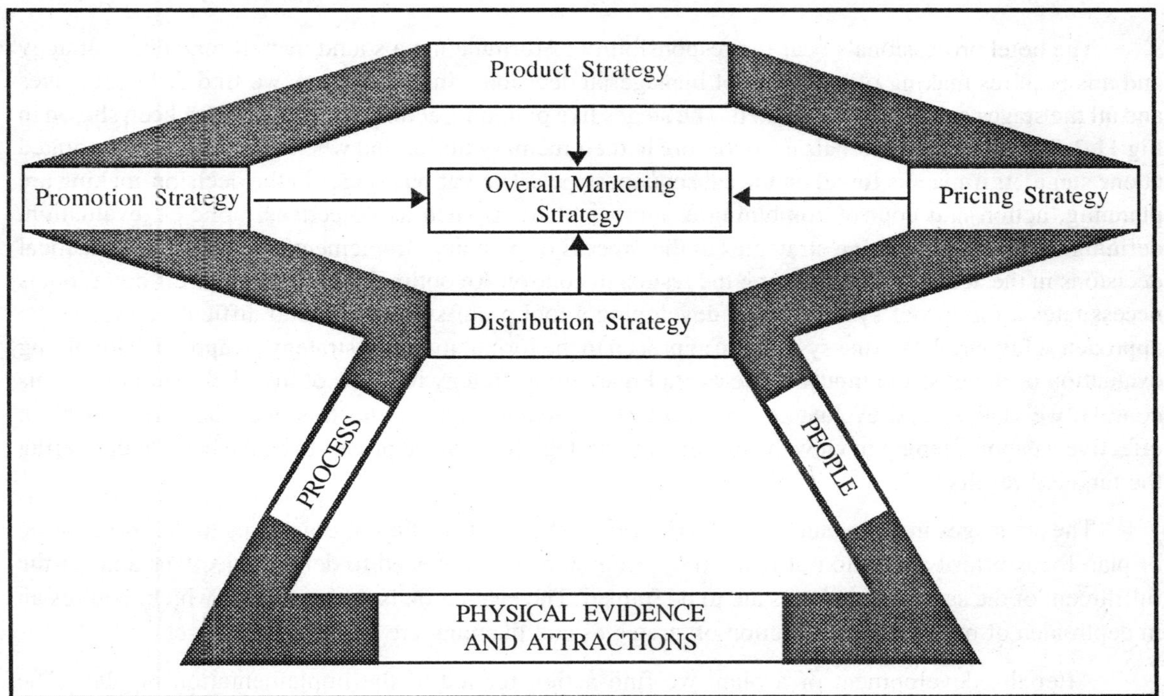

FIG. 11.1: OVERALL MARKETING STRATEGY

In the formulation of overall marketing strategy, the hotel professionals also need to make strategic decisions related to process, physical evidence and attractions and people. The process as a submix makes it essential that services are generated in a right way and ultimately are delivered to the service users on time and in a decent way. In the techno-driven processing, we find scope for high level of operational flow and service quality. The strategic decisions related to physical evidence and attractions make it significant that hotel professionals are sincere to the creation of service ambiance to be instrumental in the generation of service fragrance and efficacious of maintaining service culture. This helps back and front-line staff in showing their excellence. The strategic decisions related to people make it essential that hotel professionals recruit develop and retain quality people. The hotel managers need to satisfy and retain quality people.

In view of the above, the following facts emerge:

- Overall marketing strategy is an optimal combination of inputs and outputs
- It is a composite build up.
- It is an integration of all dimensions of marketing efforts.
- The inputs are product, promotion, price, place, process, physical evidence and attractions and people.
- The outputs are objectives such as return on investment, market share, brand image and leadership.

FORMULATION OF AN OVERALL MARKETING STRATEGY

The hotel professionals bear the responsibility of formulating a sound overall marketing strategy and this requires making of a number of managerial decisions. In this context, we find different stages and all the stages are found interrelated. The stages like planning, action and control have been shown in Fig 11.2. The hotel professionals need to store in their memory that as and when a change is incorporated at one stage, its impact is found on the subsequent stages. The various stages in the decision-making are planning, action and control combining a number of items such as objectives, policies, evaluation, defining of area and selecting strategies in the process of planning; implementation of plan and tactical decisions in the action and monitoring the results in control. An optimal combination of different inputs necessitates a fool proof system. Since developing a fool proof system is found difficult, a systematic approach is favoured. We fine systematic approach to the formulation of a strategy an approach involving evaluation of the possible inputs to the overall marketing strategy in terms of the likely outputs. In this context, we analyse and evaluate each aspect of the major inputs. After this, we find selection of an effective weapon keeping in view the fact that the strategy formulated proves to be the best for delivering the targeted results.

The six stages in the planning group right from the identification of objectives to the formulation of plan focus priority attention of marketing professionals. They need to define objectives and for the fulfillment of the same, the policies are to be framed. The evaluation is the next stage which requires an in depth idea of markets. The selection of strategies and planning are the next two stages.

After the development of a plan, we find action related to the implementation of plan. The professionals in the very context need to make tactical decisions. The motive is to implement the plan on time. The marketers need to make use of their excellence while implementing the plan.

The last stage is control which focuses our attention on monitoring the result. We cannot deny that control makes the ways for the formulation of a new plan.

With the development of a techno-driven information system, the task of a marketer is considerably simplified. The various inputs need to be analysed in the face of defined objectives. The feedback received regarding the various inputs help professionals in identifying the wrongs in the plan formulation and implementation, processes.

With the increasing domination of globalisation, we find corporatisation gaining a rapid momentum which has been making ways for corporate culture based on a different lifestyle. It is in this context that professionals are required to be much more sensitive to the increasing heat of competition. The global biggies have already made the markets much more competitive. A number of internal brands have already entered and the strategical decisions need creativity.

In Figure 11.2, we summarise different stages or phases. We accept the fact that magnitude or intensity of competition is an important consideration in the formulation of an overall marketing strategy.

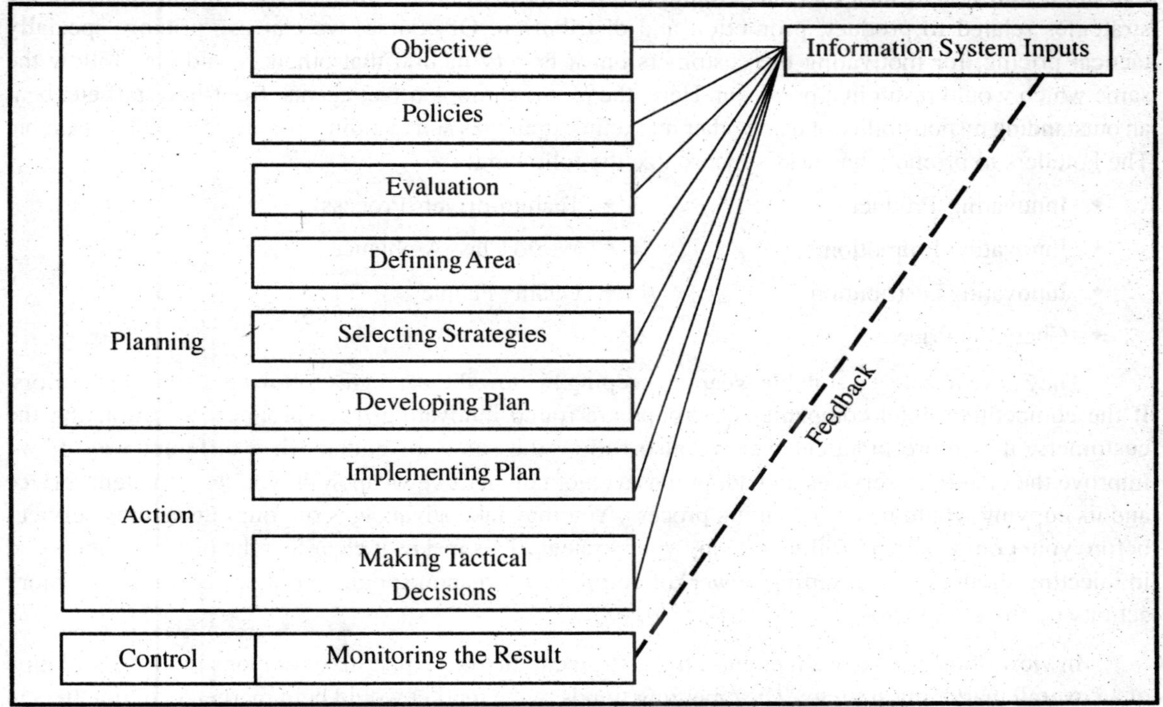

FIG. 11.2: STAGES IN MARKETING DECISIONS

Modified from: David J. Luck & O.C. Ferrell; Marketing Strategy and Plans, Prentice-Hall, NJ, 1979, p. 9.

In Figure 11.2, we find nine stages:

Stage 1 : Related to defining the objectives

Stage 2 : Related to the determination of policies

Stage 3 : Suggesting evaluation

Stage 4 : Defining the areas

Stage 5 : Selecting the strategy

Stage 6 : Developing the plan

Stage 7 : Implementing the plan

Stage 8 : Making of tactical decisions

Stage 9 : Monitoring the results

In the planning group, there are six stages.

In the action group, there are two stages.

In the control group there is one stage.

SELECTING THE MARKETING INPUTS

We are well aware of the fact that product, promotion, pricing and distribution are known as marketing inputs. The hoteliers are supposed to select such a strategy which is not to create a situation like price war. It is against this background that a number of hotel companies are found changing the strategies related to product, promotion and distribution. Of course, we can use pricing, specially tactical pricing, for motivating the customers but it is very natural that others would also follow the same which would result in a price war. Here, the tour operators, travel agents, front-line staff etc. bear an outstanding responsibility of using other marketing strategies and avoiding pricing as a tactical weapon. The hoteliers to promote business synchronize the following:

- Innovating Product
- Innovating Promotion
- Innovating Distribution
- Changing Price
- Techno-driven Process
- World Class Ambiance
- Quality People

They have to select a suitable weapon, keeping in view the strategies followed by the competitors. If the competitive hotel companies or groups are found innovating there products for attracting the customers, it is more practical that we also follow the same, of course, in a different way. If we improve the quality of services and adopt it as a chief competitive weapon, it would be a patent service and its copying would be a time taking process. You may take advantages of your outstanding services before your competitors to follow or copy your strategy. This makes it clear that the hoteliers interested in injecting strength to the 'hitting power' of competitive weapon should avoid or delay the retaliatory actions by the competitors.

In view of the above, we recognise the instrumentality of competitive weapons in the formulation of an overall marketing strategy. The emerging trends in the market would help marketers or hoteliers in selecting a suitable weapon found more sensitive in reaching to the target market. The hoteliers, tour operators, travel agents are supposed to study the emerging trends in the market. It is very natural that when hotels with some product mix are using tactical pricing, the other hotel groups would also have to follow the same. This makes it clear that while formulating a marketing strategy, we have no option but to turn our eyes on the strategies adopted by our competitors.

FACTORS IN SELECTING THE MARKETING INPUTS

We need a strategy for marketing the perishable services. It is important here to mention that some of the marketing inputs have synergistic potential. To put it another way, some of the marketing inputs are capable of being mutually reinforceable. The hoteliers are required to consider this while formulating the strategy.

An investment in point-of-sale displays, integrated with a national advertising campaign increases the effectiveness of promotional efforts far more than equal investment in additional advertising. The displays and advertisements are found mutually reinforcing since the display repeats the advertising messages when the customers are found in an outlet (office of travel agents) where the products are sold. In the same way, we find product inputs and channel inputs mutually reinforcing. If the customers buy from the tour operators or travel agents, they are found in a position to identify the product from its brand image. Intensity of substitution is also an important consideration for the selection of marketing inputs. Here, the hoteliers are supposed to know the extent to which one input can substitute another. The following questions would suitably answer the problems related to the formulation of marketing strategies.

- Do we find quality of product higher in competitive brands substituted for a promotional budget smaller than those of competitors?
- Will a large promotional budget substitute for shortcomings in travel agents' co-operation?
- Will a price lower than competitive substitute spare distribution?

Here, we find decisions regarding substitutes important which would help in determining the inclusion of suitable inputs in the formulation of an overall marketing strategy.

IMPLEMENTATION OF OVERALL MARKETING STRATEGY

The marketing strategies set the parameters for a number of activities. The strategies involve decision on almost all aspects of the marketing mix. What product can be offered profitably to specific markets or market segments. The policies are found based on strategies. For the long-term survival and growth of hotel companies, there must be a continuous search for new markets, product, promotion, pricing and distribution methods.[3] In the marketing strategy, the implementation process is found significant. The marketing inputs used need a planned approach. This simplifies the implementation process for the inputs used. If in the hotel companies, the sales personnel are to be increased, it is significant that the hoteliers are well aware of the requirements in advance so that the recruitment processes are managed properly, the training facilities, if needed, are imparted on time and the concerned people are deployed at the points where their services are to be more productive. Suppose an important hotel group is interested in opening a hotel in India. It is natural that sufficient time is needed to materialise the process for opening. In implementing advertising strategy or innovating promotional efforts, in formulating or innovating distribution strategy, in innovating product; they need more time and professionalised co-ordinated efforts.

	Marketing Inputs	January	February	March	April	May
1.	Product Launching of a new package holiday					
2.	Distribution Tour operators Travel Agents					
3.	Price Commission to Whole-salers Commission to Travel Agents					
4.	Advertising Planning and Programming Contracts with media					
5.	Selling Tour Operators Travel Agents					

FIG. 11.3: INPUTS PROGRAMMING FOR NEW PACKAGE HOLIDAY

It is important to mention here that all inputs to the overall marketing strategy do not retain equal effects for the same duration and for all the time to come. If the hotels and hotel companies produce new brochures, folders, publish new literature, prepare or develop a new package, these are found more impact-generating till the competitors produce or introduce another new package of improved quality. If the hotel companies package up pricing, the competitors have to wait and watch. We call them 'competitive innovation' which can occur any time. It is very natural that an advertisement is found effective for the long time where another is found ineffective just after its launching. This makes it clear that the hoteliers consider the relative rate of decay in effectiveness in planning the inputs targeted to the overall marketing strategy. The availability of lead time for scheduling of marketing inputs is found significant here. In Figure 11.3 and Exhibit 11.1, we find inputs programming for holiday packages. This clarifies as to how the hoteliers develop a sequence for the introduction and application of each input in its overall marketing strategy.

EXHIBIT 11.1: INPUTS PROGRAMMING FOR NEW PACKAGE HOLIDAY

1. Product	Launching of a new package holiday	
		= February to April
2. Distribution	Tour Operators	= March
	Travel Agents	= April
3. Price	Commission to wholesalers	= March
	Commission to Travel Agents	= April
4. Advertising	January	= Programming
	January mid to May mid	= Contact with media
5. Selling	Tour Operator	= February
	Travel Agents	= March to April

The main thing in the programming is to make provision for the lead time. Figure 11.3 clarifies that how a sequence for the introduction and application of each input in its overall marketing strategy can be developed. We find sufficient lead time for the scheduling of each input, mainly to avoid delay in the level of effectiveness of marketing inputs.

STRATEGIES FOR MARKETING INPUTS

The strategies related to product, promotion, pricing and distribution or the marketing inputs become important for the formulation of an overall marketing strategy. The hoteliers are here expected to see that an optimal combination of marketing inputs is made possible. We accept the fact that the desired outputs cannot be possible unless the inputs strategies are sound and are blended and formulated in the face of multi-dimensional changes in the environmental conditions. The hotel companies and hotels should be particular regarding the lead time for programming the inputs which would help them in many ways. The strategies related to different marketing inputs are summarised below:

AN OPTIMAL PRODUCT MIX

Tailoring of a product to meet the market needs is, of course, the most significant aspect of the product development. A well-thought strategy makes it essential that hoteliers be aware of multi-dimensional changes in the environmental conditions. In addition, they are also supposed to have an in-depth knowledge of changing needs and lifestyles, found vigorously affecting the nature of demand. In view of the emerging new changes the world over, the need of the hour is to formulate a product package to suit the target market. While formulating the product mix, it is essential that room management, restaurant management, bar management and the management of function rooms are given due weightage.

In an institution of commercial hospitality, the development of a product has a far-reaching impact on the formulation of a sound product strategy. It is very natural that sensitive products of today are found insensitive for tomorrow. Scientific and technological advances, innovations and inventions in the field of communication, latest developments in the field of transportation, increasing efforts for developing global partnership, fast growing commercialisation and the positive impact of electronics revolution have made it essential that hotels innovate their products frequently.

Our strategies bear the efficacy of turning the negative into positive. In the formulation of a sound product strategy, the management of marketing information is found playing a significant role. The hoteliers need to make the system of information management sound. What to offer, what to modify, what to eliminate; these are found pertinent while formulating the product strategy for hotels. If we find that competitive hotels are innovating their products, we have no option but also to invest in the innovation programming. If we want to project our image as a market leader, it is essential that we declare our products obsolete much earlier than our competitors. We accept the fact that innovation is based on information. We need background information related to the local community and industry, communication, local events, attractions and catchment area. We have to collect information from both areas — producing revenue and not producing revenue. The information regarding the details of competition are also to be collected such as rooms and other peripheral services. The information regarding the profile of guest would play a vital role, as mentioned earlier. Besides, we also need information regarding hotel activities, such as occupancy statistics, turnover percentages, pattern of empty days, pattern of sales in the restaurant and bar. The information related to the selling ability of the staff also carries some meaning, e.g., analysis list of staff employed between those who have established a good contact with guests, some contact with guests and no contact with guests.

In the formulation of product strategy, it is also important to be careful regarding promises to the prospects. We should not promise to customer luxury services as it could be dangerous unless we are absolutely sure to deliver.

Ultimately, what to offer is also an important dimension of strategic decisions.

In the hotel industry, the innovative decisions are needed at almost all the stages. The services related to rooms and peripheral services, are also required to be innovated from time to time depending on the busy and team periods of business.

In view of the above, it is right to mention that hoteliers should frequently improve upon the innovation process of services. We need to work not only with the operative motive but also with the marketing motive. It is significant here to mention that the extent to which the hoteliers are successful in innovating the product line would have a telling impact on the net gains and customer satisfaction.[4] If the product mix is sound, it is natural that the prospects would get an incentive. To make an organisation internationally competitive we need due weightage not only to the socio-economic considerations of the customers but also to the governmental regulations. It is right to say strategically that the core service is the prime benefit that customers seek from the hotels. The core service often becomes a commodity as a service industry matures. Customers expect the hotel companies to be competitive in providing the core services. The result is that the peripheral services often become the way in which the customers' loyalty is won.[5] Thus, while formulating the product mix, it is significant that strategic decision-makers feel that the key dimensions to service quality thus become reliable which is the ability to perform as promised. It is also responsiveness which is meant the willingness to help customers and to provide prompt services.

AN OPTIMAL PROMOTION MIX

Creation of awareness has a far reaching impact on the formulation of a sound promotion mix. The scientifically designed promotion strategy simplify the task of informing, persuading, motivating and influencing the prospects. Of course, product innovation plays a commanding role in the hotel industry but we also find cases where even the world class services have failed in getting a positive response in the market. This necessitates an innovative promotion which succeeds in transforming the potential guests into habitual guests. To be more specific in the hotel industry, oral communication or word-of-mouth promotion plays a commanding role wherein the promoters work like a potential sales force and attempt to publicise the hotel products without charging any price. The satisfied group of customers make an advocacy in favour of your outstanding services to their friends and relatives and thus the impulse of potential guests significantly contribute to increased business revenues. This is due mainly to the fact that the sales force have credibility in the eyes of potential guests, which is judged as an objective assessment.

In the hotel industry, we find personal selling significant. Personal selling is the personal presentation of a tangible or intangible product or idea to the potential customers. The product, price and market in particular, determine the nature and form of personal selling required. The front-line staff also play an important role in promoting inside selling whereas tour operators and travel agents are found instrumental in promoting outside selling. Here, it is essential that we have a team of efficient front-line staff and we have selected the well established tour operators and travel agents having professional excellence and a positive image.

Advertising, a paid form of promotion, is also found to be impact-generating. Here it is significant that we take the support of a leading advertising agency who prepares creative advertisement copies and makes possible sensitive advertisement slogans. Cost-effectiveness is an important aspect of advertisement which focuses our priority attend on web pages. In addition, it is also pertinent that we select a suitable, sensitive, effective and economic vehicle for extending the messages to customers. Here, our emphasis is on media. Though some of the experts feel that relatively, we find advertisement least sensitive in promoting the hotel business but the leading hotel groups have no option but to advertise their product effectively.

Sales promotion is found to be another important component of promotion mix. The publication of brochures, folders, leaflets, menu, sales literature, offering of gifts, and incentives to staff, discount, concession and several trade promotion tools play an effective role in making light guests into habitual ones. The hotel companies and hotels are required to make a decision on the essence and duration of sales promotion so that the opportunities are capitalised timely and the market potentials are tapped successfully.

In the formulation of an overall marketing strategy, promotion input assumes an outstanding significance. The hoteliers are supposed to take a decision regarding the different promotional measures. When we talk about promotional strategies for hotels, all components are not found exceptionally effective. The only way of identifying a suitable component is to test various components in the face of predetermined criteria. The hoteliers should have a correct idea of the target market or audience. The market standing of hotels is also an important aspect to be taken into consideration while formulating the promotional strategies. In addition, the strategies related to develop product and market expansion or changes felt necessary for long-term development are found playing an important role.

The market is found more competitive and even the intensity of competition is found moving upward. To survive and thrive in the expanding competitive market, it is essential that promotional efforts are given priority for a high level of occupancy ratio. The creativity is an important dimension, specially when we talk about advertising the hotel product. As it is not possible for all hotels and hotel companies to have their own professionals for this purpose, they have no option but to take support of leading advertising agencies. Since we find new developments in printing technologies, there has emerged enough scope for making advertisements more and more attractive. In the early 1980s, Holiday Inns Inc. ran a series of advertisement in the USA with the headline 'Only one hotel chain guarantees your room will be right.' Subsequently extended to Europe, the advertising copy said 'Every thing in Your Holiday Inn room will be right'. Or we will make it right. Or we will refund the cost of your room'. The important aspect of theme of advertisement is 'guarantee'. Holiday Inn created the proposition, claimed it first and made it their own concept since no other hotel chain could say, 'we guarantee our rooms too' without appearing to copy the original; This makes it clear that creativity is an important dimension of an advertisement message. If the slogans, messages, campaigns are creative, the responses would, of course, be positive.

In view of the aforesaid facts, it is right to say that the success rate of a hotel is coiled in the essence of transforming the negative into positive and registering long-term customers in their records. This task is found easier when the promotional strategies are well designed. In making the promotional decisions, the hoteliers have to see that all possible merchandising aids are available. We find people often equating promotion almost exclusively with advertising, which is hardly surprising given that advertisement pervades every aspect of our lives, appearing not only on TV, video and posters and in newspapers and magazines, but also on every surface on the sides of buses to hot-air-balloons and of late, even on websites. Of course, advertising is instrumental but other components of promotion are found equally effective for the hotel industry.

AN OPTIMAL PRICE MIX

We find pricing decisions critical as well as challenging. The hoteliers are supposed to take into consideration a number of factors while formulating the pricing strategy. The internal and external factors are found governing the pricing decision. The product, promotion and distribution are the internal or controllable factors which can be adjusted or regulated by the hoteliers as and when the circumstances warrant so. In addition to internal factors, the external factors are also found instrumental while making these decisions. Competition, economic health of a country, changing government regulations, behavioural profile of hotel users, ethical consideration and code of conduct are the uncontrollable or external factors considerably influencing the pricing decisions. The hoteliers should have a correct idea of different variables influencing pricing decisions.

In making pricing decisions, hoteliers have to use and implement this strategy very carefully. When and how to use pricing as a tactical tool so that it is not going to create a situation like price war is equally important in the very context. The strategic role of pricing reflects objectives of companies such as maximum growth or profit. It communicates the expectations of product quality, status and value to prospects, reflects the stage in the product life cycle and determines the long-term revenue flows and return on investments. Here, pricing acts as a management tool to achieve strategic business objectives. The hotels and hotel companies use pricing so as to achieve their business objectives. The tactical role of pricing is also involved in the essence of using pricing as a tool to promote the business. This corresponds to marketing operations or tactics at which an operator works on a weekly, daily or hourly basis. The tactical pricing is well advertised. It provides a short-term tool for crisis management and determines short-run cash flows. Pricing decisions are found important in both the strategic and tactical sense.

In the formulation of a sound price mix, it is essential that hoteliers consider pricing of room tariffs, food and beverages and function in a financially feasible manner. In pricing for room tariffs, there are some common factors that everyone looks at — such as current charges prior to a review, estimated inflationary impact on cost, general economic situation, emerging trends in foreign exchange markets and the intensity of competition. In addition, it is also significant that you examine your own internal information management and take support of any information which you can gather on the emerging trends in the marketplace. Besides, you should also use your own experience and judgment to define more potential sources of business.

While pricing for food and beverages, the hoteliers face a number of difficulties. This is due mainly to the fact that we find different types of food preferences, dishes and drinks but not more than four or five types of rooms. The following aspects are found significant while making the pricing decisions for a hotel restaurant:

- Economic criteria, target average spends, target covers per meal period.
- Current menu and drink prices.
- Estimated inflationary pressure on all costs.
- Popularity indices for meal periods and by period.
- Average spends.
- Competition and emerging trends.
- Customer segment profile — outside visitors to hotel — guests eating in.
- Total cost of staying in rooms plus average meal.

The hoteliers have also to think about function pricing. It is natural that depending upon the commodity cost of the dishes served the prices may vary. Payroll does not enter into the calculations. A number of hotels are found fixing a staff standard for functions based on their style of a preference hotel or one waiter to a table of ten people or one waiter to two tables. In the hotel industry where we want to stimulate overall growth in the function market, it is essential that we consider waiters as well as consider food cost an important variable in the pricing strategy.

Packaging up in pricing is also an important decision-making area. Some of the hoteliers and sales executives feel that the only way to get a major deal is to offer discounts or to prefer tactical pricing. We find an opportune moment for offering discounts, specially during lean business periods. To the extent it is possible, hoteliers should avoid the high intensity of discounting. Professional excellence is involved in the essence of studying the market, customers and the competition and to take a decision in the face of changing market conditions. If you prefer to package up, you are not only to sell more but also in a position to project your fair image. Hence, you should prefer to package up rather than pricing down. Of course, it is unwise to pay too much and again it is also unwise to pay too little. This is due mainly to the fact that when we pay too much, we lose a little money but when we pay too little, we lose everything.

In view of the above, it is right to say that there are a number of important points to be taken into consideration while making pricing decisions for different categories of rooms and peripheral services. What strategic decisions would simplify your task of promoting your business and excelling competition are the important considerations which should be given due weightage while formulating a sound price mix. Over the next decade, we expect a number of changes which directly or indirectly affect the ways of fixing pricing strategies. We need a frequent change in our decisions, or course based on meaningful discussions and the changing environmental conditions.

AN OPTIMAL PLACE MIX

A widespread myth still persists that services cannot be inventoried on shelves and in warehouses, and therefore the distribution channels are found less significant in service generating organisations. However, this is not a true fact. We find distribution channels or placement strategies significant even in the service organisations. In the hotel industry, it is not possible that major hotel companies would be successful in promoting the business, if external selling is not promoted. The professional excellence of hoteliers is involved in the essence of making possible a fair blending of inside and outside selling. And for this, the hoteliers have to take the support of tour operators and travel agents who have been referred to as wholesalers and retailers earlier. In addition to an increase in sales, they are also found helping hotel companies in advertising and publicizing their products. Against this background, we find marketing inputs important for the development of hotel industry in terms of substantial revenues sales.

For accomplishing the organisational goals or for bridging the gap between production and distribution, it is essential that an organisation formulates a sound distribution strategy. The distribution system should be efficacious if promoting the business of hotel, its rooms and peripheral services through the chain of distribution including being successful in projecting a fair image of the hotel companies. This necessitates the selection of efficient tour operators and travel agents. In addition, it is also essential that hotel companies assign due importance to the development of front-line staff responsible for promoting internal selling.

With the introduction of computers, robots and new communicative technologies, we expect a radical change in the distribution system which is also going to influence the strategic decisions taken by the hotel management. Of late, we find a number of hotels, having become computerised to develop and expand their business and generate revenues. This has proven to be financially beneficial to the hotel industry.

The motive is to make available to the ultimate users, the services as desired and promised to them. We concentrate on innovating the placement strategy with the motto of time-honoured and cost-effective distribution. How to make it possible?

Building and maintaining middleman's co-operation is a critical decision-making area. If the distribution system is sound, the producers find it convenient to maintain cash flow. Contrary to it, faulty distribution strategies complicate the task of producers and distributors as well. In a true sense, the tour operators and travel agents are found acting as customers but not the ultimate users. This necessitates a harmonious relation with the middlemen so that the hotel companies find it convenient to project a fair image. Whether the middlemen simply promote, actively recommend or just handle the products, depend substantially on the working of the hotel industry and ensure good trade relations.

The hotels working on a small scale do not face problems as they can promote business even with zero level distribution in which they are found selling directly to users. But for big hotel companies, it is not possible to depend entirely on internal selling. In a few cases, they can work with one level distribution in which only travel agents are involved and in a few cases, they are found working with two-level distribution in which both the tour operators and travel agents are involved. Hence, the placement strategy constitutes a place of outstanding significance, especially for big hotels. While formulating the placement strategy, it is pertinent that we select a strategy which is cost-effective and convenient to the ultimate users.

The main problem before big hotel companies is to face challenges and threats from the competitive hotel groups. This is not only related to the cost and satisfaction but even other aspects, such as informing the prospects, earning their appreciation and getting repeat business. Of course, the front-line staff play here a significant role. Thus, to have the efficient front-line staff have been referred to being instrumental in meeting the demands of customers.

Because of the choice and flexibility of distribution channels in service products in general and hotel products in particular, the strategic choice between inside and outside selling has always been much more important. New computerised database technology available only in very recent years for identifying individual customers by mailing address. Profile and purchasing behaviour is found helpful to tour operators in altering the strategic choice. The new technology has considerably helped e-channel for diverse purposes. The E-CRM strategy helps professionals in knowing about the customers. Online booking, in-house selling has been gaining popularity.

SMOOTH, DECENT AND TIME-HONOURED PROCESSING

With the infusion of new generation of information and communication technology, we find the service processing taking a new shape albeit in the hospitality industry. Designing of a service delivery process is a creative process which begins with a service concept and concludes with the delivery of service to the customers. The processes are manually supported or techno-driven or a mix of the two. Of late, we find hotels making use of technology and physical aids for improving the quality of services. With the increasing importance of Internet, there has been a significant change in the to processing of hotel services. The computers have been found helping to both the providers and the users. The customers with the help of online booking, enquiries, confirmation, cancellation and complaints find it easier to process their requirements, whereas the hotel staff with the help of computers know everything about the hotels and their customers. In the function room, conference hall and even in restaurants, we find technology helping professionals in ensuring quality processing. The motive is to increase the operational flow and to maintain punctuality and decency. One of the secrets of McDonald' hamburger restaurants is the way the physical tools and the layout have been planned. The high-level penetration of e-channel and E-CRM strategy has been found adding new feathers in the service processing of hotel industry. The hard, soft and hybrid technologies have redefined the concept of service processing specially in the service generating organisations.

The hoteliers, of late, need to innovate their strategic decisions which make their services much more competitive. The international brands have been innovating the process of technological sophistication. A few of the selected national brands have also been making sincere efforts to speed up the process. The government policy makers as well as the hotel top management have to explore opportunities for enriching the technological strength but at the same time they have also to make it sure that scope is left albeit for manual based operation and interaction.

They need soft technology to generate high quality, to control costs to increase speed and flow, to ensure cleanliness and to have a sophisticated look. We find here designing of special hardware and routines significant. Kentucky Fried Chicken, McDonald, Pizza Hut *et. al.,* make use of the system for quality results. Cafeterias, restaurants, salad bars, prepackaged vacation tours etc. rest on soft technology. The hotels also, need to make use of hard technology specially to minimise the terrorism. The X-ray Surveillance equipment is now found essential for hotels particularly for replacing a personal body search and embarrassing personal search of luggage. Of late we find hotels considerably depending on hybrid technologies for greater efficiency and speed. The telemarketing, online booking, creation of web pages, personalised information etc. have been redefining the quality of hotel services.

In addition to the different types of technology, the hotel professionals need a team of dedicated and decent people. The front-line as well as the back-line staff play a significant role in service processing. Since the services are found standardised, the hotel professionals need to make it sure that promised quality of services reach to the service users in a decent way. The professionals with the help of E-CRM strategy would be successful in having an in-depth knowledge of the customers. The interruptions at any stage are to be removed. The service delivery and the operation systems are the two different dimensions of service processing. The customers judge the service quality also on the basis of operational flow which requires a mix of soft, hard and hybrid technologies for diverse purposes. Accelerating the pace of value addition is an important aspect which the hotel professionals need to take into consideration.

In the hotel services, we find different points for service delivery such as restaurants, bars, function room, conference hall and rooms. It is to be made sure that possibilities for mistakes have been minimised. A minor mistake committed by hotel employees may affect the service quality in a big way which may tarnish the image of hotel. The hotel professionals as strategists need to make it sure those real benefits of technology are made available to the customers *vis-a-vis* to the hotels. The processing of services cross different stages and at each and every stage, the professionals have to monitor the processes. Because we find hybrid technology redefining the concept of service delivery, it is pertinent that the professionals managing, maintaining and monitoring the same are tech-savvy. With the increasing heat of competition, we find customisation occupying a place of outstanding significance and the hotel marketers in the very context need to develop their awareness of the changing lifestyles, food habits, drinking habits, spending behaviour and likes and dislikes of customers.

With the increasing techniculture, we find new generation of technology governing the hospitality industry. The formulation of an overall marketing strategy also makes it essential that motto of infusing technology should be improving the quality and minimising the cost. When we find quality people working with the help of new generation of technology; the delivery of world class services cannot be negated. Synchronisation based on professional excellence makes the ways for getting the desired results but it is not essential that in all the conditions the hotel professionals depend on technology because we also find cases where technology complicated the task of professionals.

"When I was shown to my room I walked into the bathroom and found the washbasin blocked and full of dirty water. I telephoned the housekeeping department to have this attended to and was told that the computer said it was all right for letting and the telephone was put down. I then rang the deputy manager and after a pause, he repeated. "The computer says the room is all right for letting".

This speaks of the fact that we of course, need to promote techno driven services but not to depend on the same. We have to make it doubly sure that a tool used for value addition is not to make ways for value degradation.

EMPLOYEES AND CUSTOMER-FRIENDLY SERVICE AMBIENCE

In the hospitality industry show-value has a telling impact on the customers *vis-a-vis* on the employees. This focuses our attention on creation of a sound service environment instrumental in attracting the customers and efficacious of increasing the operational efficiency of employees as well as the technology. The customers often rely on the tangible cues or physical evidence. The tangibilisation process becomes here impact generating because the displays in different forms help professionals in exhibiting the features of intangible services. Uniqueness makes the ways for attractions. By developing world class service ambience, the hotel professionals get an opportunity to nurture service culture. In the modern hospitality industry, we find web pages and virtual servicescapes also playing a significant role. The hoteliers make use of the same for conveying to the customers the uniqueness of service ambience. It is against this background that the overall marketing strategy needs due attention of hotel professionals on the uniqueness of service ambience.

Making use of the services of experts in different areas appears significant to the development of servicescapes. The designing of interiors is found meaningful which draws our attention on lighting, furnishing, ventilation music, scent, aesthetic management, artistic decors etc. The motive is to activate the stimulants of customers and potential customers for bringing an attitudinal change. The color of light, intensity of light, positioning of light, positioning of signage, symbols, artifacts, music arrangement, volume of music, quality of music, positioning of music, scent and fragrance are found meaningful for attracting the customers. Attractions make the ways for service differentiation. The painting and photographs, display and positioning of ornamental shadow plants display aesthetic sense. The hotel professionals while developing service ambience need to concentrate their attention on physical surroundings and facilities made available by the competitors so they display something distinct.

The hoteliers need to make it sure that physical evidence creates promises and customer expectations. The physical evidence strategy is to be linked with the organisational goals and objectives. This focuses our attention on service blueprinting. We call it *service mapping*. This makes it easier to witness the action involved in the service delivery, complexity of the process and points of human interactions.

The dresses and uniforms of employees also need due attention of hotel professionals. They need to make it sure that the staff working in different capacities look neat and clean and smart. The quality of dresses and uniforms worn by the employees virtually project the image of hotel. The display of quality information materials, brochures, visiting cards, pamphlets, menu cards etc. are some of the materials helpful in the creation of a positive impression. The display of hybrid technology also conveys uniqueness of services to be delivered. The hotel professionals need to make use of new generation ICT as a facilitator.

We cannot deny that human behaviour is influenced by the physical setting in which it occurs. The environmental psychologists opine that individuals react to places in which they have to perform. The front-line as well as the back-line staff working in hotels need a sound service environment where they have to perform. To increase the operational flow, it is essential that in addition to employees, the technology has also been made available suitable environment.

An ambient condition enhances corporate image and establishes corporate identify. The employees serving hotels and the customers making use of the services delivered to them are considerably influenced by physical evidence. It is quite natural that framing of a picture in minds of employees and customers is also the result of service ambience. The professionals are required to watch the expected roles, behaviour and relationships in the interaction process. The individuality is required to be suppressed and uniformity in the behavioural profile of staff is to be made possible. When we find staff wearing uniforms, the possibilities for idiosyncrasies in behaviour and appearance are considerably maximised. The customers minutely observe the appearance and attitude of the service staff and there fore it is to be made sure that by communication, interaction, personality, technical skill, attitude towards work, consistency of quality performance and their appearance at the service points, they transmit a positive message in the minds of customers.

The above mentioned facts make it clear that exterior and interior attributes are the areas where the hotel professionals need due attention. All the interior and exterior attributes communicate something to the service users. We do not find any boundary for the same. Since the intensity of competition is found gaining a rapid momentum in the hospitality industry, it is pertinent that hotel professionals minutely study the attributes of competitors and then based on the expertise of designers and developers develop such a service ambience which add additional attractions and create uniqueness. It is in this context that we make a strong advocacy in favour of blueprinting.

With the changing business environment, we find international brands preferring India as a profitable market for the hospitality industry. It is quite natural that the servicescapes they design and develop establish an edge over the attributes developed by the domestic players. In a true sense, the domestic players lag behind in terms of expertise, finance, managerial proficiency and professional excellence. Hence, it is imperative that domestic players formulate a different strategy. They have two options, viz., first to take help of mergers, acquisitions and consolidations and second to become stronger to excel competition or second to develop budget hotels. The focal point is distinctness which focuses on uniqueness. Making servicescapes unique and establishing an edge over the rivals is found to be an effective prescription in the Indian business environment where globalisation has injected new life and strength to the hotel business. Since the corporate culture is to continue, the hotel culture will flourish.

SATISFYING AND RETAINING QUALITY PEOPLE

With the increasing demand for accommodation, it is but natural that the demand for quality people would also gain a rapid momentum in the Indian hospitality industry. Qualitative and quantitative improvements in the hotel people make it essential that a good number of quality hotel schools and institutes are opened. The public sector, corporate sector and PPP mode are to be tapped for this purpose. The global biggies have been found assigning due weightage to the development of quality people for the hospitality sector. There are a number of cases where they open their own institutions for educating and training hotel people. Presently in the Indian hotel industry, we find a mismatch between the demand and supply of quality people, and therefore the hotel companies in particular need to think about the development of world class institutions. To bridge the widening gap at skill level, the existing Food Craft Institutes are, required to be strengthened and further new ones are to be opened. New IHMs in the states or regions which have not been covered as yet need to established for proper distribution of resources.

While educating and training in addition to the subjective knowledge, we need to inculcate those properties which help them in the projection of a positive image. Personal commitment and value orientation are the two important dimensions essentially required for quality hotel people. Personal-touch-in-service or the personalised services play a significant role in satisfying and retaining customers. They need civic sense, aesthetic sense and awareness of etiquette management. Inculcating and cultivating the additional properties need due attention of hotel professionals.

The motivational factors are found essential for the number of satisfied group of hotel people. This also helps in retaining because satisfied employees are the real assets of an organisation. It is essential that quality people continue to serve the hotel industry. The lucrative financial incentives and quality amenities and facilities would increase the retention rate. The hotel professionals also need to ensure that behavioural dimensions of different echelons of people are sound.

Developing people for your organisation is also a strategic area where hotel companies need to explore opportunities. The leading brands have been found opening quality hotel schools or institutes for this purpose. The technical as well as the interactive skills are required to be enriched to develop their potentials of influencing the customers. The hotel professionals need to make it sure that while opening and developing hotel schools, they take into consideration the national as well as the international customers because globalisation has been found influencing the taste preferences and lifestyles of people. The food habits, drinking habits and spending behaviour are now found considerably changed. The hotel professionals need an in-depth idea of the changing behavioural profile. All the required properties are to be developed during the training programmer.

The two categories of staff such as front-line and back-line play an incremental role in the hotel industry. Creation of services and their delivery particularly in restaurants are found significant. Providing an opportunity to customers to witness the services to be delivered where customers directly experience the service quality requires skill. The dining room, restaurants are the points where the front-line staff performs. In addition, the receptionists also have a face-to-face communication with the customers. The front-line staff find the customers unpredictable. They do not know that how and in what way the customers are going to react and what would be the intensity of their reactions. The customers may be aggressive even due to a minor reason and the front-line staff in the very context is supposed to diffuse the tension. They need much more emotional labour for making the customers cool and calm. This makes it essential that it is a strategic point where the hotel professionals need to depute quality front-line staff. We consider that meeting point a center for interactive session where the feedback received from the customer simplifies the decision-making process. The hotel professionals need to monitor the interactions both for quality delivery and recovery.

The front-line staff cannot be successful in the service delivery when the back-line staffs do not play a significant role in the creation of services. In hotel, we find kitchen as the back where a number of skilled people work together. We cannot deny that it is due to the sincerity and skill of back staff that the front staff succeeds in making the delivery of quality services.

The hotel professionals need to play here a decisive role. Striking a balance between the front and back-line staff is found essential. Establishing a co-ordination and co-operation between both the categories of staff requires excellence. The hotel professionals need quality people so that a team culture helps in improving the service culture. The motive is to satisfy the customers. But the professionals also need to make it sure that all categories of staff working with them and instrumental in the service delivery process are satisfied. Increasing the number of satisfied group of employees is an important strategic decision for the formulation of an overall marketing strategy. If you satisfy your subordinates the avenues are paved for satisfying the customers because in that case we find personal involvement of the concerned staff. Since you bear the responsibility of satisfying and retaining the customers, it is pertinent that your prime attention is on satisfying the employees.

Thus in the formulation of an overall marketing strategy, the hotel professionals need to manage human resources in such a fashion that they prove to be an asset *vis-a-vis* a capital for the generation of assets and creation of profits. We cannot deny that the yawning gap between the demand and supply of quality is to be bridged and hotel professionals in the very context need to show their excellence.

STRATEGIC MARKETING TASKS

In the strategic marketing response, we find some important elements, such as planning the most profitable business mix of segments and products, deciding the position or image which each accommodation unit or chain of units should occupy, encouraging and rewarding frequent users of the services and developing marketing integration, between units in common ownership (chains) or units in individual ownership (voluntary co-operatives).

PLANNING THE BUSINESS MIX

Determining the optimum or most profitable mix of segments for whose needs specific products are to be created and promoted is found to be an important strategic decision for hotels. For example, a city center hotel obviously targets clients traveling for a range of business purposes, a resort draws different categories of leisure visitors and so on. The optimum customer mix for majority of the businesses comprises several segments which combine to maximise achievable revenue and maximise the effects of seasonal fluctuation and other normal business fluctuations. Hotels and other service sectors appear to have more scope to plan a co-ordinate consumer mix, exactly the same operators for self-catering operators in the non-service sector. For example, holiday park owners, marketing static units such as caravans, owners and chalets for holiday helps to plan a segmentation strategy which separately targets adults aged over 50 traveling in pairs, from families with children of school age who are largely tied to school holidays of their children.[6] Here, they can differentiate between visitors who go for the traditional one or two weeks stay and others who are interested in weekends and shorter stays. Of course, it involves some form of marketing research to analyse the volume and revenue potential of existing and potential customers in each location.

DECIDING THE POSITION OR IMAGE

This is the second aspect where we decide the position or image which each accommodation unit or chain of units should occupy. We also find cases where producers offer similar products to the same group of customers at very similar prices. Here, it is important for operators to differentiate and brand their products with particular identities. In marketing jargon, we call it identity positioning which is based on the strengths of a building and its location, the specification of products on offer, the quality of services made available, the design and quality of rooms offered and furnishing or any combination of these features. For example, in the developed countries around the globe, hoteliers for many years have recognized the value of their regular visitors. Yet, the systematic marketing battle for the favorable opinions of these important customers in Britain can be dated to around 1984.

In Britain in 1984, when a regular and syndicated survey of frequent business travelers was launched by NOP (National Opinion Pools) Market Research to contribute some two-thirds of all nights stayed in Britain hotels. Frequent Business Travelers were defined as people who stay at least twenty-one nights a year in hotels.[7] The survey concentrated on measuring awareness of advertising, ranking preferences for different hotel companies in terms of users and non-users and quantifying customer perceptions of the wide range of attributes on which such hotels were positioned. The survey provided a sophisticated measuring tool with which competing hotels could trace the success or failure of their positioning strategies over time.

ENCOURAGING AND REWARDING FREQUENT CUSTOMERS

The third element here is regarding frequent customers. The fact remains that it was against this strategic decision that most hotel groups and airlines created membership clubs and other schemes during the 1980s. The user cards were found biased to the regular customers. Here, a number of schemes offered credit facilities in addition to the normal benefits made available to them. Some of the hotels also offered awards through which frequent customers earned points for each stay, leading to attractive and expensive prizes based on the number of points credited. We do not find any confusion in the motive of rewarding the frequent visitors. This is to increase the occupancy ratio and to use the quiet periods. But most of these schemes could not deliver the expected results. Horwath and Horwath estimated the level of repeat customers in larger hotels in Britain in 1985 as between 30% and 40%. The small hotels, of course, were found doing well as in that case the repeat visit was up to 70%. It is right to say that frequent customers should be encouraged and rewarded as it is found helpful in many ways.

INTEGRATING MARKETING ACROSS SEVERAL UNITS

The fourth and last element to be discussed here is integrating marketing across several units. It focuses on the level of co-ordination which individual units can achieve in marketing their products. There are a number of positive effects of marketing co-ordination in the context of distribution-referrals of business between units, central reservation service and better access to distribution networks. In the context of promotion, the corporate positioning and branding, joint advertising opportunities, use of professional marketing teams, access to group brochures and leaflets, group representation at trade fairs and shows and product and price harmonisation in group quality assurance schemes to satisfy the customers are needed. Co-ordination is obviously secured through ownership and is part of the process whereby big or multi-task accommodation chains have emerged in the past few decades.

EVALUATION OF OVERALL MARKETING STRATEGY

Multi-dimensional changes in the environmental conditions make it essential that the hotel companies evaluate their marketing strategies so that the lapses or errors if any are identified and suitable corrective measures are taken. The hoteliers are supposed to monitor the overall marketing strategy continually. This makes possible effectiveness in our strategic decisions. We are well aware of the fact that the main task before an organisation is to achieve the target of achieving substantial revenues. If the marketing inputs are blended optimally, we find enough scope for qualitative improvements. It is against this background that marketing experts suggest marketing audits for evaluating the overall marketing strategy. The marketing audit is a systematic, critical and unbiased appraisal of the based marketing objectives and policies of the organisation, methods, procedures and personnel employed to achieve those objectives and implement these policies.[8] It is also said that a true marketing audit is a systematic and comprehensive appraisal of a company's total marketing operation.[9]

In view of the above, it is right to mention that each evaluation of the marketing personnel, organisation or individual inputs of marketing strategy cannot be a marketing audit since most of the evaluations are only parts of an audit. Though we do not find a standardised format for designing marketing audits, there are some general guidelines for designing the same, as shown in Exhibit 11.2. The main purpose of a marketing audit is to uncover opportunities to improve the effectiveness of the total marketing operation. It is important here to mention that this evaluation process is in addition to the normal procedures for controlling the progress of the annual marketing plan designed to reveal in part, the long-run opportunity of the company's total marketing programme.[10] While undertaking an audit, the hoteliers, are supposed to identify strengths and weaknesses as well. In a true sense, the marketing audit is found helpful not only to evaluate the past performance but also to formulate the same for future. The term 'audit' refers to evaluating the performance, identifying errors and suggesting corrective measures to eliminate these errors. In marketing audit, it is found essential to examine both market and the product. The auditors meant for this purpose are supposed to answer the following questions:

- Who are visiting hotels?
- Why are they visiting hotels?
- Who are selling?
- How are they selling?
- Which are the strong competing hotels?
- How are the competitors promoting their business?
- How are we doing?
- Does our product meet the demand of the target market?
- Does our product have the required stability and acceptance level and breath?

EXHIBIT 11.2: INPUTS PROGRAMMING FOR NEW PACKAGE HOLIDAY

Objectives	: Each market input should have clear objectives in terms of desired output.
Policies	: Consistency in achieving the marketing objectives. The explicit and implicit policies should be appraised.
Organisation	: Capacity of hotel companies should be evaluated.
Strategies	: Strategies adopted by a hotel for carrying out the stated policies. Available opportunity for improvement.
Procedure	: Implementation of individual strategy for carrying out the stated policies. Suitability of strategies in the situational area.
Personnel	: Evaluating the role of executives in planning and marketing operations.

Here, in Exhibit 11.2, we find six stages. The hoteliers are here required to assign due weightage to them for undertaking the marketing audit. If they undertake the auditing programme scientifically, we find possibilities for identifying the possible weaknesses and subsequent errors. In addition, the marketing audit would also simplify the task of hoteliers, specially while exploring opportunities and identifying suitable strategies to capitalise them. The first stage concentrates on defining the different marketing inputs so that we know about the services to be offered, the promotional efforts to be made, the pricing strategies to be adopted and the distribution system to be followed. The second stage is related to consistency in marketing objectives. If we do not find consistency, the task would be difficult. The third stage is to evaluate the organisational competence to face the challenges and threats in the market. The fourth stage focuses on the formulation of strategies. The fifth stage is regarding procedure for the implementation of strategy and the sixth and last stage is related to the evaluation of personnel meant for the marketing programme specially the sales executives responsible for promoting the business.

SYSTEMATIC MARKETING AUDIT

Evaluation of an overall marketing strategy is found essential to ensure substantial qualitative improvements and identify errors and weaknesses in the strategic decisions. Like other industries, the hotel industry also needs a well-thought strategy to meet the objectives. We find three important elements of systematic marketing audit, e.g., marketing environment review, marketing system review and marketing activity review.

The first element, i.e., the marketing environment review, is found in different areas like markets, customers, competitors and the socio-cultural environment. We identify here the major markets and segments and know about the size and characteristics of each market. Regarding customers, we know their level of appreciation towards a particular hotel group, their behavioural profile, lifestyles and satisfaction. In the socio-cultural environment, we know about demography, economy, technology and strategies of the government.

The second element is the marketing system review. The long-term and short-term objectives, statement of objectives in the hierarchical order, reasonability of the objectives in the face of competition and opportunity are equally important. In the context of the market programme, the core strategy of the organisation, the adequacy of resources to targeted market territories, product, personal contacts, promotion and distribution are also impact-generating. In respect of implementation, the development of an annual marketing plan and the effectiveness of planning procedures need to be periodically reviewed. The marketing information system is also found important. In the context of an organisation, the availability of high level marketing executives, training, incentives, supervision and evaluation of various strategies are important.

EXHIBIT 11.3: ELEMENTS OF SYSTEMATIC MARKETING AUDIT

Marketing Environment Review	*Marketing System Review*	*Marketing Activity Review*
Hotelier: Identifying major market and segments. Size and characteristics of each market or segment.	*Objective:* Long-run and short-run objectives. Statement of objectives in the hierarchical order. Reasonability of the objectives for the organisation, its competitive position and opportunity.	*Product:* Extent of price setting on cost, demand and competition. Response to demand, Customers' psychology to interpret the price level. Temporary price promotion.
Customers: Feelings of customers towards the organisation. Buying decision of customers. Present and expected future state of customer needs and satisfaction.	*Programme:* Organisational core strategy. Adequacy of resources allocated to markets, territories and product. Adequacy of the marketing resources to product, personal contact, promotion and distribution.	*Distribution:* Alternative methods of distributing the services.
Competitors: Major competitors of the organisation. Emerging trends in competition.	*Implementation:* Development of an annual marketing plan and effectiveness of planning procedure. undertaking periodic studies. Adequacy of marketing information system.	*Personal selling:* Adequacy of sales force to accomplish the organisational objectives. Organisation of sales force to the best line of specialisation. Adequacy of procedures for setting quota and evaluating performance.
Macro Environment: Relevant development related to demography, economy, technology, government and culture.	*Organisation:* Availability of high level marketing executives. Training incentives, supervision and evaluation. Optimal structure of marketing	*Advertising:* Organisational advertising objectives. Theme and copy. Media chosen. Publicity: A careful programme of publicity

	responsibility. Ability of organisation personnel to understand and practice the marketing concept.	Sales Promotion: Well conceived sales promotion used by the organisation.

The third element is marketing activity review. Here, the extent of price setting, the response to demand and customer psychology are found important while studying the product. In distribution, the alternative methods of distributing the product are significant. In personal selling, the adequacy of sales force, organisation of sales force and the adequacy of procedures are studied. In this context of advertising, the objectives and effectiveness of advertising themes and copy and chosen media are studied to generate sales revenues. In respect of sales promotion, the affluent tools used are reviewed.

In Exhibit 11.3, we find details about the different elements of systematic marketing audit. It is important to mention that systematic marketing audit helps hoteliers in evaluating the sensitivity of marketing strategies. Based on different studies, they are found in a position to evaluate the effectiveness of strategic decisions, identifying the lapses and testing the corrective measures to be adopted to retain their earlier performance.

EXHIBIT 11.4: MARKETING MIX FOR HOTELS

Product:	Location/building size/grounds/design/room size/facilities in hotel furnishing/decor/lighting/catering styles. (Related to designed characteristics, packaging) Staff numbers/uniforms/attitudes, e.g. (Related to service component) Branding, positioning, Holiday Inn, rest, Savoy Image, reputation. Up market down-market.
Promotion:	Advertising (TV/Radio/Press/Journals) Sales Promotion/merchandising Public Relations Brochure Production and distribution Sales force
Price:	Rack Rates Normal or Regular Price (corporate rates) Promotional Prices for each product offered Privileged user rates, tour operator discount rate.
Place:	Channels of distribution including reservation system Central Reservation System Other hotels in group Tour Operators Travel Agents Airlines 800 telephone lines
Process:	Operational Flow - Standardized, Customized Process - Simple, Complex Involvement of Customers Face- to-face and Techno-driven

Physical Evidence and Attractions:	Designing Facilities, Signposts, Equipment, Interiors, Exteriors, Furnishing, Lighting, Ventilation, Waiting Lounges, Music, Scent, Reports, Brochures, Dresses and Uniforms.
People:	Skilled, Supervisory, Professional, Clerical, Manual

UNDERSTANDING THE MARKETING MIX IN HOTEL

The term Marketing Mix was firstly coined by McCarthy in 1960. The four submixes begin with letter. P. Kotler defined it as the mixture of controllable marketing variables that a firm uses to pursue the targeted level of sales in the targeted market. The central concept of adjusting and synchronising the controllable variables in the face of changing market conditions is the important point to be received about the marketing mix decisions.

The emerging changes and challenges made it essential that the service marketers make an in-depth study of the situational reprimands due to heterogeneity, perishability, intangibility which would improve the quality of managerial decisions particularly for the marketing of services. This made ways for additional three Ps, viz., Process, Physical Evidence and People.

In Exhibit 11.4, we find Marketing Mix for the services sector in general and the hotel sector in particular. The outstanding features at different submixes of marketing in the context of hospitality industry make it essential that the service marketers develop their awareness of the changes in the market conditions and tailor the different submixes in the face of emerging trends. The role of a marketing professional is like a chef who has professional excellence in the field of cooking. He knows about the recipes to make the dish delicious and therefore the marketing professionals are supposed to know about the real proportion of different submixes for the formulation of a sound marketing mix. Tailoring the different submixes in tune with the changing requirements of markets with the motto of satisfying customers depends on the professional excellence of a hotel manager.

In the Indian hospitality industry, we find intensity of competition gaining a rapid momentum. This has been possible due to the entry of a large number of international brands. The corporatisation has injected new life and strength to the national economy and we find its impact on the taste preferences and lifestyles of people. The corporate culture has made the ways for the development of hotel culture. This has made possible a significant increase in the demand for accommodation which makes a strong advocacy in favour of increasing the supply side. The public sector, corporate sector, PPP mode have been found improving the supply position but still we find a big gap between demand and supply.

When the markets become competitive, the professional excellence of a marketer determines the magnitude of success. It is in this context that we need to develop world class professionals to be efficacious of taking the benefits of competition. The hotel professional need to market the services in such a way that helps them in capitalising on the opportunities, increasing the average room rate and maximising the occupancy ratio. The innovative services, at an affordable price, would open new vistas for excelling competition. A sound marketing mix is necessitated which focuses on enriching the excellence of tailoring the marketing inputs.

 SUMMARY

You have Studied in this chapter overall marketing strategy for hotels. A glimpse of facts are summarised below:

- **Overall Marketing Strategy: Concept:** The overall marketing strategy of an organisation is its competitive position in the market place. It is a composite built-up. It is found dynamic in nature both in specific inputs and desired outputs which must change with emerging new trends in company ethos, its competitive situations, its markets and the economic climate. In the hotel industry when we talk about the overall marketing strategy, our emphasis is on a fair blending of inputs and outputs. The inputs are hotel products, promotion, price and place strategies. The outputs are the objectives, such as the target returns on investments, market share, brand image.
- **Formulation of Overall Marketing Strategy:** The hoteliers while formulating an overall marketing strategy, are supposed to make diverse marketing decisions. Planning, action and control strategies are the different stages and all of them are interrelated.
- **Selecting the Marketing Inputs:** The marketing inputs are product, promotion, price and place. The hoteliers are supposed to make possible innovation in selecting appropriate marketing inputs. The emerging trends in the market help hoteliers in doing so.
- **Factors in Selecting the Marketing Inputs:** It is important to mention that some of the marketing inputs have synergistic potential and they are mutually reinforceable to a large extent. The hoteliers are supposed to know that product inputs are mutually reinforcing.
- **Strategies for Marketing Inputs:** The strategies related to product, promotion, pricing and place are found important for the formulation of an overall marketing strategy. The hoteliers have to see that an optimal combination of marketing inputs is made possible.
- **An Optimal Product Mix:** This is termed as the tailoring of products to meet the changing market needs. We should have a package to suit the target market. Room management, restaurant and bar management, function room management are the important dimensions of a hotel's product.
- **An Optimal Promotion Mix:** In this promotion mix, the hoteliers have to see that personal and non-personal promotional strategies are sound. Strategies related to personal selling, advertisement, public relations and sales promotion are found important in this case.
- **An Optimal Price Mix:** In the price mix, the hoteliers have to see that strategic and tactical decisions are taken carefully.
- **An Optimal Place Mix:** In the place mix, the decisions are taken regarding a balance between internal and external selling. To promote selling with the support of the front-line staff or to take the support of tour operators and travel agents would prove this strategy beneficial.
- **Process Mix:** This submix of the marketing mix draws our attention on service processing. The hotel professionals are supposed to make possible smooth, decent and time-honored service delivery which may be a mix of manual and techno-based operations.

- **Physical Evidence:** For increasing the operational efficiency of different categories of hotel personnel and the technology used in the process, it is pertinent that a suitable service environment is developed. Quality service ambience creates uniqueness and attractions. This helps in the formation of a positive opinion of customers coming to the hotels for availing the services. The differential aspects are interiors, exteriors, furnishing, lighting, music, scent, ventilation, aesthetic management, equipment, parking etc. The hotel professionals also need to make use of the services of experts so that an internationally competitive service ambience helps in developing service culture. The professionals also need to care the quality and maintenance of the dresses and uniforms of employees working in different, capacities.
- **People:** This submix of marketing focuses our attention on the quality of hotel people. The leading institutes or schools are supposed to develop quality people. We need qualitative and quantitative improvements in the supply side. The hotel personnel need to be professionally-sound, personally-committed and value-based. The hotel professionals need to develop them and to keep them satisfied by offering to them lucrative incentives and amenities and facilities.
- **Strategic Marketing Tasks:** Planning the most profitable business mix of segments and products, deciding the position or image which each accommodation unit or chain needs to occupy, encourage, and reward frequent hotel users and develope marketing integration between units in common ownership(chains) or units in individual ownership (voluntary co-operatives) are the important elements of strategic marketing.
- **Evaluation of Overall Marketing Strategy:** It is also known as marketing audit where the hotel professionals evaluate their efforts for managing the inputs and getting the outputs. The key areas for marketing audit are objectives, policies, organisation, strategies, procedure and personnel. The elements of systematic audit are review of marketing environment, marketing system and marketing activity.
- **Marketing Mix for Hotels:** In this context, the hotel professionals concentrate on the formulation of a sound marketing mix by synchronizing the different summits of marketing such as product, promotion, price, place, process, physical evidence and attractions and people. Like a chef in a hotel, the professionals need to set the proportion so that the marketing decisions are found result-oriented. Right recipes result into a delicious dish and right proportion of submixes result into proactive marketing decisions found successful in satisfying the hotel employees and getting them personally involved in the business so that the task of satisfying the customers is considerably simplified.

KEY TERMS

Mission
Marketing Inputs
Marketing Outputs
Attrition
Brand Image
Service Ambience
Packaging up
E-CRM
X-ray Surveillance
Hybrid Technology
Idiosyncrasies
Attributes
Servicescapes
Front-line
Back-line
Systematic Marketing Audit
Recipes
Chef
Savoy
Customized
Upmarket
Downmarket
Brochure
Hoteliers
Information System Inputs
Package Holiday
Catchment Area
Target Audience
Physical Tools
Soft Technology

REVIEW QUESTIONS

1. What do you mean by Overall Marketing Strategy? Explain the process of its formulation.
2. Explain the importance of overall marketing strategy to the hospitality industry in the Indian perspective.
3. Focus on the different phases in the formulation of an overall marketing strategy.
4. State and explain the various marketing inputs used in the hotel industry.
5. Explain the instrumentality of optimal marketing mix for the smooth functioning of hotels.
6. Explain the key elements of systematic marketing audit.
7. Discuss the key elements of strategic marketing in relation to the hospitality industry.
8. Explain the relevance of service ambience in the strategic decisions for marketing.
9. Focus on the strategies for marketing inputs for the hospitality industry.
10. Throw light on the factors to be considered while selecting the marketing inputs for the marketing of hotel services in the Indian perspective.
11. Explain the process, physical evidence and attractions and people in the context of hospitality industry.

APPLICATION EXERCISES

1. "Overall Marketing strategy is a composite buildup." In the capacity of a hotel professional comment on this statement.
2. You are working as a hotel manager. Focus on the different phases you need to go through for the formulation of an overall marketing strategy.
3. Strategies related to marketing inputs are found important to get the desired outputs. In the capacity of a hotel professional throw light on this statement.
4. Planning the business mix, deciding the position or image of a hotel encouraging and rewarding the habitual customers and integrating marketing across several units are the important elements of strategic marketing. As a marketing professional comment on this statement.
5. Multi-dimensional changes in the environmental condition make it essential that the hoteliers evaluate their marketing strategies so that the lapses or errors are identified and suitable corrective measures are taken to make the strategic decisions proactive to the changing needs. Focus on this statement as a marketer.
6. The main purpose of the marketing audit is to uncover the opportunities to improve the effectiveness of the total marketing operation. Discuss this statement as a hotelier.

End Notes:

1. Cundiff, Still Govoni: *Fundamentals of Modern Marketing;* Prentice Hall of India, New Delhi, 1982, pp. 428-29.
2. David J. Luch and O.C. Ferrel: *Marketing Strategy and Plans;* Prentice Hall, NJ, 1989, p. 9.
3. Foster Douglas: *Travel and Tourism Management;* Macmillan, London, 1986, pp. 215-16.
4. Jha, S.M.: *Services Marketing;* Himalaya Publishing House, Bombay, 1994, p. 195
5. Mason J. Bary: Foreword to the Book, *Services Marketing* by S.M. Jha.
6. Victor T.C. Middleton: *Marketing in Travel and Tourism;* Heinemann Professional Publishing; Oxford, 1989, pp. 260-61.
7. *Ibid.*, p. 291.
8. Cundiff, Still and Govoni: *Op. cit.*, p. 429.
9. Kellerge E.J.: *Marketing Planning and Competitive Strategy;* Prentice Hall, NJ, 1972, p. 121.
10. Kotler Philip and Richard S. Lopata; *The Marketing Audit: The Marketing Manager's Handbook,* Steuart H. Britt, The Dartnell Corp., Chicago, 1973, p. 1074.
11. Mccarthy, E.J.: *Basic Marketing: A Managerial Approach;* 7th Edn, Irwin, Homewood, Illinois, 1981, p. 42.

....ഌഌഌ....

CHAPTER - 12

EMERGING CHALLENGES BEFORE HOSPITALITY INDUSTRY

Optimism paves the ways for development. Conversely, pessimism seals all the possible avenues for transformation. The outlook for the Indian hospitality business is bright and extremely positive. We need to identify the long-term optimism so that the corporatisation process is activated with titans foraying into the hospitality sector, the professionals need to be creative and innovative.

CHAPTER OBJECTIVES

Introduction – Demand Penetration: A Clarion Call – Law and Order Problem: A Challenging Task – Information Technology: Channelizing its Uses – Increasing Volatility in the Business Environment – Inadequate Supply – Long-term Optimism in the Indian Hospitality Industry – Summary – Key Terms – Review Questions – Application Exercises – End Notes.

LEARNING OBJECTIVES

This chapter aims at studying the different dimensions of emerging challenges and threats in the Indian hospitality industry. The motive of this chapter is to sensitise the readers to the optimisation process so that mismatch between demand and supply of hotel accommodation is removed. The hotel professionals need to know about the potentials that we find in the Indian Tourism Industry. They also require to develop their awareness of avenues where hotel accommodation can be increased. On the one hand we need luxury hotels while on the other hand we also realise the significance of budget hotels.

INTRODUCTION

The hospitality industry in India has witnessed a robust growth during the yesteryears. According to a CRISIL's report, Indian hospitality sector observed an increase in both leisure and business travel. The outlook for the Indian hospitality business is extremely positive and bright because we have tremendous opportunities to capitalise on. It is against this background that we find a number of international brands like Amanda, Satinwoods, Banana Tree, Hampton Inns, Hilton, Mandarin Oriental, and many others evincing keen interests in the Indian hospitality industry. Of course, we find positive signs of development and the demand also has also been outpacing supply but at the same, there are a number of threats and challenges before the hotel sector which need priority attention of government policy makers so that process of development keeps on moving without any break.

The intensity of competition is to gain a rapid momentum in the years to come due to the entry of global biggies. Hence the domestic players have either to strengthen their strength or to shift to the budget hotels or to welcome mergers, acquisitions and consolidation to stay competitive. The focus should be on looking new market segments for business, involvement of local committees for delivering quality hospitality services, professionalism and a reduction in the attrition rates which create a condition for staying in competition. We cannot deny that excelling competition in any field makes it essential that both the large or small players endeavor to upgrade their services and facilities. Though we find domestic players like Oberoi, Taj, ITC, Palla Hotels, Leela and Bharat offering world services however they still need to make their services internationally competitive.

The Indian hospitality industry also requires to improve the quality of supporting infrastructural facilities because in comparison with the global standards, we find our infrastructure poor which is also an impediment necessitating due attention of hotel policy makers and the government. The world class infrastructural facilities simplify the task of hotel professionals. The government has to make sincere efforts and has also to motivate PPP mode for enriching the quality of infrastructure. We cannot deny that the development of quality infrastructure would also benefit the tourism industry *vis-a-vis* the national economy. One of the major bottlenecks in creation of hotel infrastructure is non-availability of land for hotel. This focuses our attention on preparing a Master Plan of major cities and identifying commercial sites. The hotel sites need to be allocated on a long-term lease basis or under PPP through joint venture, revenue sharing etc.

It is also right to mention in the Indian hospitality industry we find low level penetration of hybrid technology. Today when we find international brands promoting e-commerce for the development of hotel business and taking support of new generation of information and communication technology for defining and redefining service quality, it is pertinent that even domestic players practice the same strategy. Till now we find that shortfalls on that account are compensated through quality human resources and innovative marketing, but it is not to serve our purpose specially when the customers cultivate a habit of using techno-driven services. For excelling competition, it is essential that the Indian hospitality industry develops a mix of manual and techno-driven operations. We cannot deny that of late the internet has become the largest distribution channel in the hospitality industry which has established an edge over all the traditional channels. This is supported by the fact that in a majority of the leading hotels, we find website becoming the first point of contact. The international brands have been found making use of webpages for advertising and influencing the customers. The Indian hospitality industry requires to be creative while promoting and tech-friendly while distributing. The hoteliers need to focus on developing online relationships with customers. They have to budget to overhaul the customer support features. Enhancing the FAQs and establishing pre-arrival and post-communication with customers are significant to enrich customer feedback features. Studying and understanding the customers in a right fashion is found significant and the domestic players would have to do something special with the help of electronically-driven channels.

The travel and tourism industry considerably influences the hospitality industry. If we find international brands coming, it is but natural that they would be successful in increasing the number of high spending foreign tourists. We find a number of features in the Indian T&T industry. The innovative areas of tourism are found to be the first choice of foreign tourists. The cultural tourism, heritage tourism, rural tourism, adventure tourism, sports tourism, eco-tourism, health tourism, medical tourism are the areas preferred by the foreign tourists. We have a mix of all but we fail to be creative while promoting.

The deteriorating law and order situations and increasing fear psychosis due to terrorism have been found aggravating the image problem. Not only the foreign tourists but even the domestic tourists would stop visiting a place if they feel themselves insecured. This makes it essential that the MoT, tour operators, travel agents and hotel companies remove the wrong perception of masses specially related to safety and insecurity. In addition to other aspects, the hotel planners also need to assign due weightage to the safety and security elements while designing hotels. The media would play here an effective role by transmitting the message that everything is fine and normal or nothing is to harm them.

With the increasing economic activities, it is natural that tourism industry would gain popularity which would increase the gap between demand and supply. Since we find a significant increase in the number of middle class and development of low-cost airlines, the influx of tourists would gain a rapid momentum. To meet their requirements, the concept of budget hotels needs priority attention of government as well as the private sector. It is right to opine that budget hotels may play an incremental role on the canvas of the hotel industry. The PPP mode may be to bridge the gap between demand and supply. The surplus railway land at strategic points may be preferred for constructing budget hotels. The possibility of constructing hotels on surplus land with Airport Authority of India near international airports may also be considered.

The hospitality industry has been facing the problem of inadequacy of quality human resources. If we find an increase in the number of hotels to meet the demand, it is pertinent that quality human resources are developed and for that the international brands or global biggies need to open their own hotel schools for developing people in tune with the changing requirements. In addition, the Food Craft Institutes, IHMs under PPP mode are to be encouraged. The training programmes need to cover the skill development in general for fresh candidates, specialised skill development including language courses and training of trainers programmes. The motive is to increase the supply of quality human resources.

Due to threshold barrier, we find hospitality industry facing a number of problems. The concerned institutions need to educate and train people in such a way that threshold barrier found specially amongst the people coming from rural background is removed. The civic sense, aesthetic management, etiquette management are the key areas where we need due care. Behaving with the customers, communicating with them, showing empathy are the areas where the hotel professionals have to be careful. We also find threshold barrier amongst the people visiting hotels for the first time. People who have already crossed the threshold barriers at least once or say, who have eaten in the hotels main expensive restaurant at least once or twice or who have eaten at the hotels medium priced coffee shop are likely to be less inhibited in trying out the restaurant or bringing their close relations to the hotel on a special occasion.

The threats on account of vulnerability to geopolitical events also need due care of hotel professionals. Any undesirable development on the geopolitical scenario is likely to have tremendous impact on the flow of global tourists. The 9/11 attacks, 26/11 attacks and Iraq and Afghanistan wars have sizeably affected the tourism *vis-a-vis* the hospitality industry.

Thus, the Indian hospitality industry has been facing numerous challenges and threats but in the face of existent strengths, the threats can be countered if we find hotel professionals showing special interests in the qualitative transformation of hotel services. The most important thing in this context is removing the psychophobia convincing masses that strengths are optimally used for capitalising on the opportunities.

DEMAND PENETRATION: A CLARION CALL

Hospitality in India is shining and the shine is to continue even in the coming years. We cannot deny that the outlook for the Indian hospitality industry is extremely positive and it is mainly due to the fact that the potential and the reach of Indian tourism is enormous. Opportunities if not capitalised on carry no meaning and the corporatisation process specially in a highly competitive environment, requires world class professional excellence. The Abacus' statistics make it clear that the tourism industry has shown tremendous growth with 24 % YTD June 2006 and is expected to grow at the rate of 25% per annum at least till 2010. The growth would continue to remain steady even after 2010 and would continue at least till 2016. However, the Indian tourism industry makes a strong advocacy in favour of professionalised efforts. The worldwide economic recession has been found affecting almost all the development sectors and if we are not sincere to the emerging problems; the shine, the brightness that we find today would not remain the same. It is against this backdrop that we consider penetrating the demand position, Clarion Call or a strongly expressed demand of the emerging corporate world.

There are a number of factors to be instrumental in penetrating the demand position but the most important factor is development of industry for which we have globally competitive potentials. We go through some of the dimensions to be helpful in demand penetration:

1. Development of Tourism Industry: Promoting domestic and world tourism is an effective prescription to increase demand for hotel occupancy. With the increasing influx of tourists, we may also expect a significant increase in the number of hotels, restaurants, bars because all of them would get a sound milieu for their development. In India, a number of efforts have been taken to promote tourism but still our share to tourism is just around 0.50 per cent.[1] Of course, we have not been successful in maintaining tourism as a national priority. Showcasing India's vast heritage requires priority attention of MoT. We have a mix of both tangible and intangible heritages but we lag far behind while promoting. Almost all the new areas of tourism in which we find high spending tourists showing special interests, we have additional attractions. The adventure tourism can be promoted in an effective way because India offers the best mountain based adventure tourism in the world in the Himalayas. The medical tourism can be promoted because we are in a position to provide world-class medical aid at an affordable price or the First World Services at the third world price. The heritage tourism can be promoted because we have a mix of both tangible and intangible-cultural heritages. Like this, we have potentials for developing convention tourism, beach tourism, rural tourism, eco-tourism, pilgrimage tourism, sport tourism and what not.

Potentials remain unproductive if we do not tap them in an optimal fashion. Since the development of tourism industry is to affect a host of industries, it is pertinent that MoT assigns due weightage to the development of Indian tourism industry. This makes it essential that we develop such a package which is in tune with the taste preferences of domestic as well as the global tourists. The government, corporate sector and PPP mode need to develop world class supporting infrastructural facilities. It is significant to mention that creation of tourism infrastructure has a positive impact on over all economic growth because we find high intensity of multiplier effects influencing almost all sectors of the economy.

We find safety and security considerations significant and therefore the central as well as the state governments need to make it sure that tourists visit, enjoy and safely go back to their destinations. The incidents like 9/11 and 26/11 have worldwide negative effects which may obstruct the influx of tourists *vis-a-vis* the tourism industry. The management of destinations must be of world class. We need to regulate the problem of atmospheric pollution.

2. Strengthening the Convention Industry: We find convention industry as the backbone of hospitality industry. With the increasing heat of globalisation, we find enough scope for organising conventions, conferences or seminars. The increasing business activities, global partnership, socio-cultural exchange programmes, political activities, academic activities pave avenues for organising conventions. In France, Japan, Singapore, USA, we find convention industry sizeably supporting the hotel industry. This makes it essential even in Indian context, the government, corporations, educational institutions, social and political organisations organise national and international conferences and make use of hotel rooms, restaurants, function rooms etc. The delegates visiting or participating in the conferences benefit tourism as well as the hospitality industry.

3. Festivals, Fairs and Sports: Penetrating demand for the hospitality industry makes it essential that we promote our festivals and fairs and attract domestic as well the foreign tourists to visit the same. Besides, the organisation of national and international sports would also increase the demand position for the hotel sector. The music concerts at national and international levels Olympic Games, Commonwealth Games, Film Fare and Festivals significantly contribute to almost all sectors of the economy. Frequent organisation of these events benefit tourism *vis-a-vis* the hospitality sector.

4. Tax Concessions: For the penetration of demand, it is also imperative that government offers tax incentives to both sectors of the economy. Provision of Travel and Tourism industry may be considered to encourage investments from non-tourism sectors to the tourism sector. The Ministry of Finance requires to consider Tax holiday at least for five years to the new hotels. Special incentives may be considered for the hilly areas, rural areas and places of pilgrimage. Rationalisation of luxury tax in different states is found essential. The tax structure should not be based on the announced traffic rather it should be on the basis of actual payment made by the clients.[2] The rules and regulations for Visa are to be made liberal and the airport tax is also to be rationalised. The travel agents, tour operators and transport operators are required to be given tax incentives.

5. Introduction of Low Cost Airlines: The burgeoning middle class particularly in the Indian context makes it essential that low cost airlines are introduced. Though we find worldwide economic recession adversely affecting the airways and airlines around the globe however, for promoting domestic as well as the world tourists we cannot deny the instrumentality of low cost airlines. Since this is to make the tour economic, we find its positive impact both on domestic and world tourism. A number of airlines have been found offering low-cost services such as Air Deccan, Go Air, Paramount Airways, Spice jet, Indigo Omega Air, Magic Air, East West, Indus[3] etc. some of the airlines have been found benefiting the tourism industry.

6. Open Sky Schemes: With the increasing impact of globalisation, we find benefits of open sky scheme to be very much instrumental in increasing the tourist traffic. Recently, India and US has agreed to allow unlimited flights between the two nations. India has also entered into similar agreement with Europe. The additional services have been launched to different routes by British Airways, Virgin Atlantic, Air France and Lufthansa. We cannot deny that open sky policy has been successful in boosting international travel to India. To inject life to the tourism sector, the policy of open sky is required to be promoted.

7. Development of Budget Hotels: With the entry of international brands, we find intensity of competition on a rapid momentum. This focuses our attention on the concept of budget hotels. We cannot deny that small players find it difficult to compete with the global biggies and the middle class would not find the luxury hotels affordable. This makes essential that particularly the Indian Railways and Airport Authority of India promote budget hotels at strategic points. The reasonably priced quality hotel accommodation for budget travelers would be help developing tourism as well as the hospitality industry.

The above facts make it clear that by promoting travel and tourism industry and also by initiating and activating other motivational measures, the avenues would be paved for increased rate of demand for hotel accommodation. This would enable hoteliers or hotel professionals in increasing the occupancy rate and average room rate. Promoting India as an Incredible destination would considerably benefit the tourism and hotel sectors. The huge growth potential of Indian tourism industry has been attracting international brands like Hyatt, Hilton, Starwood and Marriott who have set themselves in the Indian markets and are found increasing the intensity of competition.

Penetrating demand focuses our attention on increasing the influx of tourists and in addition offering to them other incentives so that domestic as well as the world tourists are lured to visit India. A significant increase in the tourist arrivals would open doors for the hospitality industry which would require an analogous increase in the supply position by increasing hotel accommodation of different types and for all the segments.

LAW AND ORDER PROBLEM: A CHALLENGING TASK

In the West, the image of India till 1940s was found as an exotic country which at the early stage was projected by the English, of course in their own interests. The Western world for the long period perceived India as the land of snake charmers and elephants. With the surge of Indian IT firms on the global map, and now traditional forms of therapy and yoga in addition to the world class modern medicare the popularity of medical tourism has been moving upward and we find the hospitality sector getting the biggest rub-off effect. Since the attainment of independence in 1947 till present, we have witnessed a number of development avenues on the socio-economic fronts but at the same time, the law and order problems have aggravated which has tarnished our image. The increasing cases of snatching, robbery, misbehaviour, sexual harassment, murder specially of foreign tourists would tarnish our image which would considerably affect the influx of tourists both in the domestic and world tourist areas.

We cannot deny that image problem due to deteriorating law and problems and particularly on account of terrorists attacks need due care of central and state governments. If we find social unrest, tension and domination of terrorists on the government administration continuing with the same pace; all our measures would turn into a fiasco. If we are really interested in the development of tourism and hospitality, we have to prepare a strong base and in doing so, the government administration would be required to intensify stringent measures.

The image of a place or a country plays a significant role in promoting tourism and hotel sectors. The economy of New York was in a bad shape because the deteriorating law and order situations had compelled tourists to avoid travelling to this place. The hotel industry was found badly affected because the occupancy ratio in the hotels of New York came dow The fear psychosis was the real factor because the tourists did not like to visit New York even th ugh the derailed law and order problems came-back on the track. At this juncture, a Slogan, "I LOVE NEW YORK" was found effective which attracted the tourists *vis-a-vis* an increase in the occupancy ratio of hotels. This was a short-term problem and therefore creative promotion was found effective. But when we find the law and order becoming a permanent problem, it becomes difficult for a hotel professional to bring an attitudinal change.

We need here two-fold measures. Firstly, the government administration regulates the deteriorating law and order problems and secondly, the hotel professionals intensify creative promotional measures. Since this is not the problem of an industry but of the nation on the whole, the policy planners and government administration need priority attention. The social environment thus substantially contributes to the development of tourism and hospitality sectors.

INFORMATION TECHNOLOGY: CHANNELIZING ITS USES

The new generation of information technology has virtually revolutionised the hotel operations. During the yesteryears, we have witnessed significant developments in the field of information and communication technology. The techno-driven services have been found establishing an edge over the manual-based operations. The new dimensions like online booking, E-CRM and e-channel have redefined the concept of service quality. The global biggies have been found promoting the use of technology for multi-dimensional purposes. The small players find it difficult to compete. On the one hand, we find technology simplifying the process of service generation while on the other hand, we also find it inviting multi-faceted complications .The following facts clarify the emerging changes and challenges mainly on account of the increasing domination of new generation of information technology:

1. Inventory Management: In the reservation and booking processes, we find use of new generation of information technology. A majority of hotels, of late, have been making use of computers and internet services. Computerisation has served to increase customer convenience specially by accelerating operational productivity by increasing the access to products and reducing the number of hotel personnel involved including minimising the unit costs of making individual bookings. Air transport is found linked with hotel inventories and car rental capacity to make possible international bookings in seconds. The consumer credit developments get automatic credit transform transaction. The online booking has virtually changed the concept of hotel booking.[4]

2. Distribution Channel: The data based marketing is now found commonly used in the hospitality business. The e-channel has virtually been found promoting direct-response marketing. The increasing internet services has redefined the concept of hotel booking. The computer linkages in the hotel, industry make possible flexibility resulting into fierce struggle between principal and retailers. A shift from the traditional channel of distribution to the e-channel has been inviting numerous problems before the hospitality industry. The situational barriers have been found obstructing the operational flow.

3. E-CRM: In the hospitality industry, we find internet emerging as the largest distribution channel. In a true sense, the internet has been beating all other traditional channels. Of late, we find a large number of customers opting internet as their first choice. With the help of internet, the hotel professionals find it easier to develop interactive relationships with customers.[5] With the help of data mining, the marketers may have greater insights into the food habits, drinking habits, spending behaviour of customers. Presently we also find scope for enhancing the FAQs and sensing the newsletters. However, the CRM studies based on technology cannot make available the hotel professionals a clear picture as found in the face-to-face communication. We cannot deny that the studies related to customers relations are found much more effective, if we find personal involvement and interactions.

4. Management Control: We find much more frequency in the change of technology. A recent review of Air Transport in Europe suggested that what happened to date (in the application of information technology) is only the start of revolutionary development which will transform the way airlines operate in the future. Pricing and inventory management, the automation of marketing and alternative distribution systems today have become vital components of airlines profitability and survival. We find tour operators, travel agents today considerably depending on the new generation of information technology. Since the inventions and innovations keep on moving; we expect much more sophistication in the technology of tomorrow. The management and control of hospitality industry would be slowed down and the task of professionals would be found much more complicated in absence of new generation of ICT. Peter and Austin opined.[6] Excellence is a game of inches or millimeters. No one act is per se, clinching. But a thousand things...each done a tiny bit better, do add up to memorable responsiveness and distinction loyalty and slightly higher margins. Marketing the margins thus would help hoteliers to face the challenges generated by international brands.

5. Management Accounting: We are well aware of the application of Management Accounting Techniques in the hospitality industry. Computerisation of the hotel operations is an important area where we lag behind. It is not only sufficient that hotels make use of the computers. In addition, it is also significant that hotels fully exploit the computer technology. Confining ourselves to word processing would not serve our purpose. The hotels need to reap the benefits of technology by diversifying their uses. Such other uses may include using the computer with the relevant accounting packages in processing the financial and accounting transactions up to the production of financial statements, Cost quality reporting, use of computer for Activity Based Budgeting (ABB), Activity Based Costing (ABC), Activity Based Management (ABM) and Benchmarking are the new areas where professionals need to show their excellence.[7] We cannot deny the fact that a good number of hotels are not aware of Management Accounting in Hospitality. Hence the hotel professionals while developing human resources need to enrich their knowledge bank specially in the field of accounting and finance with the help of short and long-term training courses. We cannot deny that a majority of the hotels make use of computer but fail in diversifying their uses. Hence, it is essential that in addition to the infusion of technology, the diversification also gets priority attention.

The above mentioned facts make it clear that hospitality industry would be required to reap the benefits of technology which make the process of service generation and delivery cost-effective *vis-a-vis* activate the process of value addition. The international brands have been found channelizing the uses of new generation of information technology but the domestic players need to take a lesson from them. In the coming days, we would find much more sophistication in technology which would make the ways for complications because sophistication paves avenues for complications provided the professionals fail in making use of their world class excellence.

INCREASING VOLATILITY IN BUSINESS ENVIRONMENT

The task of a professional is found much more complicated when we find a market becoming much more volatile. The emerging trends in the Indian hospitality industry indicate that the intensity of competition is moving upward. We agree that such a market condition never remains static and therefore volatility complicates the task of professionals. The worldwide economic recession has been found injecting new life and strength to volatility. Competition in any field and especially in the hospitality sector stimulates and spurs all participants in the industry large or small to continually endeavour to upgrade their services and facilities. In the Indian hospitality industry, we find a number of international brands entering to capitalise on the opportunities.

The launch of the campaign "Incredible India" and emerging positive trends in the national economy of India are the key factors attracting global biggies in the hospitality sector. More than 142 luxury hotel projects are coming to India where more than ₹ 8,000 crores are to be invested. The increasing business activities have been found increasing the number of middle class. The corporatisation has been successful in strengthening and deepening the roots of corporate culture where we find much more scope for the development of techniculture considerably influenced by hotel culture. The international brands like Amanda, Satinwood, Banana Tree, Hampton Inns, Hilton and Mandarin Oriental, Golden Tulip, Kingdom Hotel Accor, Marriott, Starwood and many others have been enticed which would make the task much more difficult for the domestic players. They have no option but to prefer mergers, acquisitions and consolidation for excelling competition.

On the one hand, we find the entire globe facing a number of uncertainties and odds and on the other hand, we find Indian economy struggling hard to survive and thrive. Such an uncertainty makes the ways for volatility. The only prescription to remain effective in the present changing scenario is offering quality services to the customers at an affordable price. We cannot deny that acid test of a professional is found in a rough weather. Of course, during the yesteryears, the hospitality industry in India has found a condition like room-boom but how long this is to continue looks uncertain. According to a survey by the global consultancy firm, Deloitte, the hospitality in India has seen an impressive growth in recent years with an increase of 30.3% in Revenue Per Available Room[8] but we cannot be sure that worldwide economic recession would not affect the hospitality sector. Hence, the hotel professionals have to be much more innovative so that based on uniqueness and additional attractions, they succeed in attracting those tourists who have a temptation for a package tour that we can offer. This focuses our attention on the creative role of media and enormous co-operation of government.

The strategic decisions thus make it essential that hotel marketers with the help of their innovative efforts succeed in countering the challenges and threats aggravated by volatility.

INADEQUATE SUPPLY

We cannot deny that during yesteryears, there has been a significant increase in the demand side. We have found cases where tourists have outnumbered the hotel rooms and demand has been rising far ahead of supply. Such an imbalance in demand and supply makes a strong advocacy in favour of improving the supply position by increasing the accommodation facilities. It is quite natural that hotel professionals find their tasks difficult as long as they fail in getting the real data. The hotel planners face a number of constraints specially while procuring land for the construction of hotels. The non-availability of land for this purpose is a major bottleneck. The hotel professionals need to identify the strategic points for the construction of budget hotels and in this connection, the Airport Authority of India and Indian Railways may be approached for land on lease.

The professionals need to identify commercial sites for construction of hotels, convention and exhibition centers. In addition to the lease, the PPP mode may also be preferred. The land should also be allocated for building of guest houses in all major cities and tourist destinations. While developing the sites for the construction of hotels, the expertise of specialised persons may be obtained so that land-scaping adds additional attraction to the sites. The architects or landscaping experts are considered specialists of the related area.

We expect that in the coming years, the demand for accommodation would increase further. The arrival of international tourists is expected to increase in larger number. Since we find a good number of international brands evincing keen interests in the Indian hospitality industry, the possibility of constructing hotels on surplus land with Airport Authority of India near international airports needs to be considered on a priority basis. Besides, the surplus land at strategic railway stations may also be utilised for the construction of budget hotels. Roughly, we need to double the accommodation facilities by 2012 against the current level of about 1,00,000 rooms.[9]

The hotel professionals also need to consider the problem of sites for new hotels. In almost all the metropolitan towns and cities, we find the problem of inadequacy of land. This has been found bringing an increase in the Average Room Rate which will deprive the Indian hospitality industry of getting the competitive advantage of India as a business and tourism destination. The hotel professionals need to identify the changing taste preferences of tourists and to prefer the sites helping tourists in staying and enjoying. The concept of rural tourism, adventure tourism, health or medical tourism have been found getting priority attention of tourists in general and the high spending tourists in particular. The sites for construction of apartments, cottages may be possible in those areas where we find abundant land available at cheaper prices. The government encouraging PPP mode may be successful in making available to the hotel companies the required land on a long term lease. They need to identify the strengths and weaknesses of their customers so that whatsoever the strategic decisions they make are found result oriented. It is pertinent that the hotel companies keep on moving the process of identifying the new markets, new segments or niche markets where we find tremendous opportunities to capitalise on. The service innovation process needs priority attention of hotel professionals.

In a majority of the countries of globe where the hotel industry has got strong roots, it is mainly due to their service quality. With the efforts, they succeed in establishing their domination in the competitive markets. They offer short products, packaged tours, stay in hotels or other forms of accommodation for leisure purposes. They also focus on shopping, entertainment, visit of heritage towns for short stay, cultural attractions, visits to farm houses and high quality self catering cottages to make their services distinct to others. In addition, we also find them offering trips for the regions where they can enjoy nature. In a true sense, they add attractions and uniqueness in their services and try to keep and prove themselves distinct to their rivals. Since we find economy of countries very much liberal to the security schemes; the senior citizens emerge as productive market for the hospitality industry.

The professional excellence coils in the essence of identifying the opportunities, searching the niche markets, innovating the services, minimising the frequency of developing new packages and keeping themselves ahead of the competitors. Of course, they have strategical and tactical options and managerial excellence helps them in selecting the most effective prescription or option. Excelling competition is the motive for which the hotel professionals need to make use of strategical and tactical decisions. Studying the changing markets and understanding the customers in a right fashion need due attention of professionals for servicing and thriving in a competitive market. The global biggies and domestic players need a sound strategy for establishing a respectable position in the Indian hospitality industry.

An in-depth study of markets is found essential to formulate a result-oriented strategy. The hotel professionals need to intensity the research and development activities so that the process of innovation gains a rapid momentum. With the increasing heat of corporatisation, we find a significant change in the lifestyles of almost all the segments. The marketing professionals need to develop their awareness the incoming changes and the emerging trends.

For making the strategical and tactical decisions much more pro-active, it is essential that hotel professionals identify and list the competitors in which we find a majority of them committing mistakes in the process of preparing a comparative list of advantages and limitations (A/L) of competitors, the hotel professionals need to be positive because negative attitude makes ways for development of bias where you cannot be right in the identification process. At the same time, it is also right to say that no hotel does business with only advantages for the different sources of business.

It is pragmatic as well as judicious that professionals are honest to the process of identifying advantages and limitations with a free mind. In this context, a little industrial espionage is presented.[10]

Stay the night in competition;
drive, walk, get a taxi to them;
eat there;
examine all other facilities;
find out their rates for a typical function,
day, conference, overnight conference etc.;
assess their standards.

We can not claim the process "spying with horror" because as and when you need to formulate a strategy and design a tact to excel competition, you have no option but to know in details about the strengths of your competitors and it is against this background that we find car manufacturing companies buying a new model launched by the competitors. This helps them in assessing, identifying and learning something new from the products of their competitors. The hotel professionals are well aware of the limitations, volatility existent in the Indian hospitality industry and therefore it is essential that they are much more honest and professional while formulating a strategy and designing a tact. Based on a techno-driven information system they design a list for advantages and limitations (A/L). The researchers are to be assigned the responsibility of reaching to their competitor taking a close, hard and objective look at their available facilities, standards and pricing strategy; identifying uniqueness in their services and promotional measures; witnessing their service ambience and the service delivery and recovery processes and based on the identified properties, designing an innovative strategy simplifying our task of excelling competition.

The hotel professionals cannot undermine the emerging trends in the global economy because the primary cause for the increasing demand in the Indian hospitality sector is the acceleration in the transformation of global economy *vis-a-vis* the national economy. The direct positive effect on the industry is due to the high GDP rate resulting into rapid transformation in the national economy. The better purchasing power has increased the demand position which resulted into influx of domestic as well as the international tourists. But the existing worldwide economic recession has started reversing the cycle of development all over the world and therefore even the national economy of India can not keep itself isolated. The domestic players need to be much more selective specially to protect their existence. In no case, they can compete with the global biggies and therefore we find it much more pragmatic that they shift to the budget hotels and make pricing as a tool for motivating the customers. We cannot deny that the demand for budget hotels would increase in future because the current economic recession is to affect the purchasing power in an adverse way *vis-a-vis* to make the customers much more sensitive to price.

The hotel professionals need to formulate an innovative strategy to survive and thrive in a volatile market.

LONG-TERM OPTIMISM IN THE INDIAN HOSPITALITY INDUSTRY

Optimism paves the ways for development. Conversely, pessimism seals all the avenues far transformation. If we have potentials and we nurture optimism; the pace of development will witness acceleration. We cannot negate that the outlook for the Indian hospitality business is extremely positive and bright. It is substantiated by the fact that the scope, the potentials and the properties of Indian tourism are enormous. It is right to mention that the Indian hospitality industry is reeling under the euphoria of room boom. Of course, the global biggies have been capitalising on the opportunities but the small domestic players have been experiencing multi-faceted difficulties because the titans have been found foraying into the sector. If we keep on moving the process of innovating our services and make use of creative promotional measures, the hospitality business in India will continue to shine.

Challenges, threats, barriers and constraints are only for those who are pessimists; and who are potentially deficient. The Indian tourism industry is potentially sound which can make the hospitality business much more sound provided the world class professionals make use of their excellence while tapping the opportunities. If we offer the package in tune with the taste preferences of tourists; the process of demand generation gains a rapid momentum. The innovative areas of tourism such as health tourism or medical tourism, culture tourism, heritage tourism, adventure tourism, rural tourism, convention tourism are a few of the selected areas where we can be globally competitive. The high spending tourists of globe have developed a special attraction for these destinations. We need to be innovative and creative while promoting and this requires services of world class marketing professionals.

The increasing heat of corporatisation has made possible an emergence of corporate culture which has opened new vistas for the development of hotel culture. The lifestyles are changing; the food habits and drinking habits are changing and even the spending habits are found changing. The development of a cross-cultural society, the globalisation of fashion, culture and civilisation; the mix of east and west make it essential that hotel professionals develop their awareness of the changing taste preferences of customers and offer to them the service quality fulfilling their expectations and satisfying them to the desired level. The hotel menus need a mix preferred by the guests. A mix of Chinese, Mexican and Indian foods would lure customers and the restaurant business will flourish.

The corporatisation has also cultivated new habits and new hotel culture. The budding or upcoming generations today are more outgoing than their parents. They have virtually crossed the threshold barrier which their parents could not. Since the process of development will keep on moving; the socio-cultural dimensions would be considerably influenced by the west. The direction will remain the same but the pace will be accelerated. The live-in culture will gain popularity. There would be a significant increase in the number of working women and these developments would be instrumental in the development of hotel culture.

A generation gap particularly between the age group 20 to 45 which we find today was not found earlier. This is due to the fact they enjoy the benefits of electronic cottage which their parents could not. They earn more and want to enjoy in a different way which their parents even did not imagine. They view television on an average for more than six hours. They have proved themselves the "me" generation of spenders. This has created and will continue to expand incredible opportunities for the hotel industry.

A new trend is found emerging in the age bracket of 45 plus. Since they find their children earning and spending lavishly; they also believe in enjoying because they are care free. Globally, we find those customers continuing to add to the hotel users. Of course, they have started to appreciate enjoyment and even spend on it. Earlier, they have worked hard and now they wish to relax and enjoy. In this age bracket, we also find people taking more than one holiday each year and this is considered to be a positive development for the hotel industry.

An increase in the standard of living, nutritional awareness, significant developments in the field of medical sciences, increasing health consciousness are some of the factors bringing a significant increase in the life expectancy even in the Indian condition. We find a good number of people even into their 70s, more active than their earlier generations and they evince keen interests in travelling more to make the most of their holidays. This is also a positive development for the hospitality industry.

With the increasing heat of corporatisation, we find an attitudinal change in the parents and then naturally in their children. Women have developed their temptation to the professional and technical education. And it is also right to mention that women business executives have established an edge over men in the same position. They need to travel and stay in hotels and it is also an addition. Free economy, free society, free sexual behaviour in the free market based economy are found positive to the development of hotel culture.

Corporatisation has made ways for the organisation of convention. The organisation of business conferences, conventions and seminars by the educational institutions and the political social organisations have also been creating a new market for the hotel industry. Almost all the hotels have now conference halls. Since the process of economic transformation is to continue, the convention would also inject new life to the hospitality business. Business incentive holidays and business study tours are found to be the potential growth markets.

Globalisation of economy has made ways for globalisation of fashion, culture and civilisation. A majority of us have now started believing material culture. The customs, traditions are now becoming non-existent.

The burgeoning middle class specially due to development of corporate sector and emergence of corporate culture would play a dominating role in the development of hospitality industry even if the worldwide economic recession is to continue. In a country where we find about one third of the population as middle class we expect a significant increase in the demand for hotel accommodation. A significant increase in the discretionary income of the middle class would inject new life and strength to the hospitality industry because the travel and tourism industry is to flourish. But here it is pertinent that we assign due weightage to the development of budget hotels. Increasing sensitivity amongst a majority of the population also makes a call in favour of budget hotels. The strategic points are to be identified for the construction of budget hotels and the surplus land with Indian Railways may be the first choice. The increasing domination of global biggies in the Indian hospitality industry also favours development of budget hotels. The domestic players would find it difficult to compete with them and they would have only two options; either to prefer mergers, consolidations or acquisitions or to shift to the budget hotels where we find tremendous opportunities to capitalise on. Amongst the Indian players promoting budget hotels along with premium hotels, we find IHCL an important name developing budget hotels with Ginger in Ahmedabad. The Indian Railway Catering and Tourism Corporation (IRCTC) too has been setting up budget hotels. In addition, ITC, Taj, Accor Hotel, Nikko Metropolitan and Crone Plaza found to be a few of the important names to favour the budget hotels.[11] It is right to mention that the focus on budget hotels would benefit the tourism and hospitality sectors in many ways.

Generating the demand and improving the supply position are the two important problems before the hotel planners. Quality accommodation at an affordable price would help Indian hospitality industry in getting the competitive advantages. The most important problem before them is to promote the travel and tourism industry so that the process of demand generation keeps on moving. We are well aware of our potentials in the field of tourism industry. We need to identify the tourists developing a temptation to the properties that we have. We need to make use of innovative marketing strategy so that we succeed in sensing and persuading them. During yesteryears, hospitality industry had the party time and even in the years come, we would not find any sign of burnout. But we should continue to support efforts of hospitality industry through a visible and perceivable projection. The innovative developments taking place in the tourism and hospitality sectors are to be transmitted to the potential customers in a creative way. Retaining customers is considered to be the vital task before the hotel professionals and this makes it essential that we offer to them services with distinction and uniqueness not even imagined by the competitors. Not only this, we also need to offer them the best at the lowest price. If we find Indian hospitality industry developing with this strategy even the economic recession would not harm them. With titans foraying into the sector, we have to be innovative and creative.

The emergence of a free market, free economy, free culture and free sexual behaviour are the new developments of material culture virtually derailing the social orders and garboiling the cultural norms. The changes that we find in the socio-cultural orders carry both the positive as well as the negative effects. We may consider it negative with the view point of Indian culture but it is very positive with the viewpoint of hotel culture. This is a new development in the Indian society which would pave avenues for the development of hospitality industry.

We are well aware of the fact that significant developments in the field of national economy and enormous potentials in the Indian tourism industry have activated the process of demand generation but on the flip side, the impressive growth in demand has not met with adequate supply This is also a long-term optimism that we find for the development of Indian hospitality industry. It is quite natural that with the increasing participation of international brands, domestic players, Airport Authority of India and Indian Railways, the supply position would significantly be increased and the mismatch that we find right now would not continue.

Hospitality business in India is shining and will continue to shine even in the days and years to come. The projection of tourist inflows by WTTC TSA report 2006 is very promising specially for India hospitality industry. The projection clarifies that from 2006 to 2011, the hospitality industry would see rapid growth; 2011 to 2016 would see steady growth and 2016 onwards would witness nominal growth. Hence, we find the second decade of 21st century to be very much productive particularly for the development of hospitality industry *vis-a-vis* the Indian tourism industry.

The most important thing that we find significant to the development of Indian hospitality industry is the positive mindset of government policymakers. We cannot negate that government has been found making professionalised effort. In addition, the PPP mode is also found to be an important aspect for engineering a scientific plan for the development of hotel industry.

If we make a microscopic audit of strengths and weaknesses in the Indian hospitality industry with the viewpoint of formulating a sound strategy, the strengths are coiled in the essence of enormous potentials that we find in the Indian tourism industry and weaknesses are found in our promotional measures which fail in sensitising and persuading the potential customers. Opportunities carry no meaning, if we fail in capitalising on the same. Weaknesses obstruct the process of development, if we delay their resolutions.

With the increasing intensity of competition, it is but natural that challenges would emerge in diverse ways and forms. It is upon the hotel professionals to develop their awareness of the emerging trends and to formulate a strategy that helps in countering the challenges and threats. In the process, they may also be required to make tactical decisions to be instrumental in luring the customers for excelling competition. We cannot deny that acid test of a professional is found in the rough weather when market conditions are found adverse.

SUMMARY

You have studied in this chapter the new challenges before the Indian hospitality industry. Before starting another chapter, be sure that the following facts are well versed:

- **Demand Penetration: A Clarion Call:** The most important task before hotel professionals is to penetrate demand which focuses due attention on development of tourism industry, strengthening the convention industry, organising fairs, festivals and sports, offering tax concessions, introduction of low cost airlines, promoting open sky schemes and development of budget hotels.

- **Law and Order: A Challenging Task:** The most important thing for penetrating demand is to regulate the law and order problems. The government administration and hotel professionals both of them need to make it sure that the customers or tourists visiting destinations or staying in hotels are safe.
- **Information Technology Channelising its Uses:** The new generation of information and communication technology has virtually revolutionised the hospitality industry. The hotel professionals need to diversify the uses of technology to reap the benefits. Inventory management, distribution channel, E-CRM, management control and management accountancy are the areas where we can make use of new generation of technology. This will help improving the service quality and minimizing the service costs.
- **Increasing Volatility in the Business Environment:** With the increasing heat of globalization, we find volatility in the business environment moving upward. The hotel marketers by making use of their professional excellence need to make innovative efforts for countering the challenges and threats aggravated by volatility.
- **Inadequate Supply:** With the increasing demand of hotel accommodation, we find a mismatch between the demand and supply. The international brands, domestic players, Airport Authority of India, Indian Railways and PPP mode may be helpful in improving the supply position. On the one hand we luxury hotels while on the other hand also the budget hotels which would meet the requirements of those segments who can not afford the expensive hotels. We need to double the hotel accommodation. A mix of modern and traditional accommodation would be helpful in improving the supply position.
- **Long-term Optimism in Indian Hospitality Industry:** We find positive of development in the Indian hospitality industry. The enormous potentials of Indian tourism industry may be successful in penetrating the demand even if we find the worldwide economic recession attempting to reverse the development cycle. We find multi-cornered efforts for improving the hotel accommodation which would meet the requirements of almost all the segments. The outlook for the Indian hospitality business is very positive. We need professionals having world class excellence to capitalise on the opportunities.

Global biggies
Threshold barrier
Euphoria
Psychophobia
Fear psychosis
Milieu
Clarion Call
Visa
E-CRM
e-channel
FAQs
Management Accounting
Inventory Management
Activity Based Budgeting
Activity Based Costing
Activity Based Management
Acid Test
Titan
Advantages and Limitations (A/L)
Demand generation

REVIEW QUESTIONS

1. Focus on the different steps to be effective in the process of generating demand for the hospitality industry.
2. Discuss the different threshold barriers hampering the development of hotel industry not only in India but all over the world.
3. "The deteriorating law and order situations are to affect the tourism as well as the hospitality industry." Comment on this statement.
4. Explain the role of information technology in the hospitality industry.
5. Throw light on the multi-faceted challenges found before the hospitality industry in the Indian perspective.
6. Do you find the business environment for the hospitality industry volatile? Justify your opinion.
7. Write an essay on the long-term optimism that you witness in the hospitality industry in India.
8. Focus on the measures helping you in increasing the supply of accommodation in the Indian perspective.
9. Throw light on the challenges and threats before the hospitality industry in India.
10. Focus on the diversified uses of information technology in the hospitality industry.

APPLICATION EXERCISES

1. You have been working as a hotel manager and bear the responsibility of penetrating demand for increasing the occupancy rate. Focus on the measures you would adopt to achieve the target.
2. In the Indian context, the deteriorating law and order conditions creates an image problem. Do you agree with this view? Justify your opinion.
3. Do you find threshold barriers hampering the development of hospitality industry in the Indian perspective? Defend your opinion as a hotel manager.
4. As a marketing professional, you need to diversify the uses of information technology in a hotel where you work as a manager. Focus on the areas where the information technology is to be helpful.
5. In the Indian hospitality industry, we find long-term optimism which can be helpful in improving the hotel business. Do you agree with this view? Throw light on the areas where you need to make use of your professional excellence.
6. "With the increasing heat of globalisation we find much more volatility in the business environment." Comment on this statement as a hotel professional.
7. "For increasing the supply position, the hotel professionals need to promote the budget hotels." Throw light on this statement in the capacity of a hotel manager.

End Notes:

1. Jha, S.M.: *Tourism Marketing*, Himalaya Publishing House, Mumbai, 2009.
2. Eleventh Five Year Plan: Planning Commission Government of India, New Delhi, Vol. III, pp. 245-51.
3. Ray & Teckchandani: Indian Hotel Industry – Strategy Building for Utilizing Unparalleled Growth Potential; The ICFAIAN Journal of Management & Research; Vol. VII/5, May 2008, pp. 64-78.
4. Jha, S.M.: *Op. cit.*
5. Ray & Teckchandani: *Op. cit.*
6. Peters & Austin: A for Excellence; Fontana, London, 1986 (Follow up of Peters & Waterman) In Search of Excellence, 1982, p. 46.
7. Subdat N.S.: Application of Management Accounting Techniques in the Hospitality Industry; Journal of IMS Group, Vol. 5/2, 2008, pp. 47-60.
8. Sisodiya & Putta: Discovering India; The Analyst, Vol. 12/11, 2006.
9. Eleventh Five Year Plan: *Op. cit.*
10. Melvyn Greene: *Marketing Hotels Restaurants into the 90s*; Heinemann Professional Publishing; Oxford, 1989, pp. 130-31.
11. Interview with Priya Paul & Jaisree Anand; The Analyst 12/11, 2006.

....ಐಐಐಐ....

CHAPTER - 13

HOTEL PLANNING FOR 21ST CENTURY

The outlook for the Indian hospitality business is extremely positive. We have incredible opportunities to satisfy almost all the segments. To bridge the yawning gap between demand and supply, the hotel planners and professionals need to formulate a realistic plan.

CHAPTER OBJECTIVES

Introduction – Hotel Location – Hotel Building – Hotel Bedrooms – Hotel Function Rooms – Hotel Restaurants and Bars – Hotel Peripheral Services – Focus on Personal Care Services – Planning for Hotel People – Strategical and Tactical Marketing Planning – Summary – Key Terms – Review Questions – Application Exercises – End Notes.

LEARNING OBJECTIVES

The motive of this chapter is to sensitise the readers to the various dimensions of hotel planning in the Indian Perspective. The dimensions like location, building, bedrooms, function rooms, restaurants and bars, peripheral services, people, strategical and tactical marketing plan need due attention of hotel planners and professionals. A mismatch between the demand and supply is required to be bridged both in qualitative and quantitative terms.

INTRODUCTION

The development of hospitality industry is the result of social industrialisation process. Coiling more dynamism in its nature, hotel planning is considered to be an uphill task. Unplanned development of an industry paves the ways for multi-faceted complications. Hotel planning must be regarded as an integral part of the country's overall socio-economic development planning. For the formulation of a realistic plan, it is essential that we forecast. And for right forecasting, it is imperative that we have support of a techno-driven information system helping hotel professionals in enriching their knowledge bank for making sound managerial decisions. The emerging trends in competition, changing levels of expectations, increasing flow of information domination of corporate culture, emergence of hotel culture are some of the key areas influencing the plan formulation process.

The business rule about a new hotel clarifies that in the first year of its operation, it loses money; in the second year, it breaks even and in the third year, it shows profits. If we find hotel planners systematic, intelligent, and pragmatic; the established business rule may also change. It we talk about hotel planning, it is important that we also consider designing of the hotel building, furnishing, decor, development of service ambience, landscaping etc. If we realise role of aesthetic management in the development of hotel, the servicescapes or ambience cannot be undermined. The hotel planners need to keep into consideration the changing taste preferences of customers so they are found satisfied.

With the increasing heat of globalisation, we find contours of development undergoing radical transformation almost in all the areas. We find a sea of change in the attitudes of customers after corporatisation. The emergence of corporate culture has virtually changed their lifestyles. We find a good number of tourists preferring to stay in the hotels, apartments, cottages located in suburbs or the rural and hilly areas. They now prefer to stay in hotels away from the hustle and bustle of city life specially in the context of leisure tour. They now prefer adventure tourism, culture tourism, heritage tourism, health or medical tourism, eco-tourism, rural tourism and this makes a strong advocacy in favor of location and ambience. We also find a change in the working hours, with more shift work to operate and supervise expensive capital equipment. We also find people working at home if not at all the time, at least part of the time, communicating with a central head office by the potential information technology gadgets. The tradition of visiting offices frequently by the executives has also been found changing due to personal computers (PCs) from most countries in the world directly to their major computers, they get all the information with the support of hightech business operations.

With the emergence of material culture followed by techniculture; we find patterns of governance changing both in official and personal transactions. A change in the composition of business offices and Like this a change in the composition of a family unit are the results of deeply rooted corporate culture, techniculture and material culture. Our social commitments and family commitments have now no meaning. We are moving forward "live-in" culture and making an invasion on our heritage. It is not to be refuted that the materialistic gains have trapped our cultural patterns and behavioural profile. We predict the transformation processes becoming much more volatile. An in-depth study of future markets is found essential to have an intelligent plan.

During the yesteryears, we have witnessed multi-dimensional transformation in socio-cultural and economic streams. The budding or up-coming generations are found much more crazy. They have developed magnitude of temptation to the modern westernized culture and we find none to regulate or guide their behaviour. We find these developments negative to the Indian socio-cultural norms but very positive to the development of hotel culture. Outings are likely to be the way of our lifestyles. In the coming years, we predict the existence of only one culture, i.e., the material culture.

The hotel professionals have to realise gravity of the emerging trends and to formulate a plan in the face of multi-dimensional changes in the socio-cultural and economic tracks. There are a number of areas where the hotel planners have to focus such as hotel location, hotel building, bedrooms, function hall, wedding hall, restaurants and bars, service ambience or servicescapes, landscaping, premises and surroundings, personal care services etc. The policy makers as well as the hotel professionals have to know about the changing requirements of new generation *vis-a-vis* the details about the emerging organisations and institutions so that the formulation of an idea hotel plan is made possible. This makes it essential that hotel professionals assign due weightage to the techno-driven marketing information system which may help them in different ways.

We find different categories of customers staying in hotels with diverse motives. The corporate executives for business transactions, the domestic and foreign tourists for traveling and enjoying, the patients and attendants for getting medicare, the athletes for sports activities, cine stars for shootings etc. require a change in the sites for locating a particular hotel. The tourists preferring leisure travel, the marriage parties for wedding and enjoying, the business executives for organising events need location of their own preferences. The function halls, exclusively designed wedding halls, specially designed event management hall, restaurants and bars need due attention of hotel planners and designers and architects and landscaping experts. The designing of servicescapes and development of service environment must be commensurate with the changing taste preferences of customers. The hotel planners need to consider the likes and dislikes of customers belonging to different segments.

HOTEL LOCATION

Location implies accessibility and conveniences to the customers. The selection of a suitable place is found important, specially with the viewpoint of attracting the prospects. The centrally located hotel is found easily accessible and it is against this background that a number of hotels are found located in the cities and specially in their precincts. While locating a hotel, it is also pertinent that the place selected should be free from all health hazards. To be more specific in a big industrial town, we find environmental problems. The hotel professionals and particularly the hotel planners need to prefer a central place as this implies convenient accessibility for working people and the visiting guests. The hotel planners also need to consider the interests of active leisure segments found to be much or more conscious of their health or more conscious of ill health. A large section of people of both the sexes have developed into physical fitness fanatics, playing tennis or squash, jogging etc. A majority of them do not feel right if they cannot have a regular workout or an opportunity to jog when they are away from home. The modern hotels have started realising the significance of leisure travel and they assign due weightage to their interests. Commonwealth Holiday Inns of Canada provide a Gym and Tonic area near their swimming pools with a circuit of exercise machines suitably supervised. They have a color code so that users can start with the easy circuit and build up. The hotels have now also started recognising the increasing craze for jogging and include a series of maps in the bedrooms for the necessary directions and instructions. They also supply track suits and shoes. Thus, we find a change in the perception of hotel in the minds of modern customers and therefore the hotel planners while locating and designing need to assign due weightage to their interests.

Of late, we find tourists preferring to stay at a place with a clean and eco-friendly environment, beautiful surroundings and landscape and calm atmosphere. This is the attitudinal change that we witness in the modern tourists therefore they avoid living or staying in the hotels located centrally and prefer apartments and cottages located in the hilly areas, suburbs or rural areas. Adding additional attractions to the destinations needs due attention or hotel planners and designers where the services of a number of experts may be used. Planned afforestation, beautification of surroundings, lighting, signposts need due attention of planners while locating hotels. Particularly in the western countries, we find hotel planners assigning due weightage to the development and beautification of surroundings and premises and therefore they motivate customers for long duration who stay as a part of their leisure travel.

Making a decision for location is thus found an important area where hotel planners and designers may transform tourist destination as a potential growth asset for the hotel companies. In a true sense, hotel tends to dominate all hotel operations.

We find hotel an immovable fixture and therefore once located and established it cannot be shifted. An airline can move its fleet around the world to serve alternative destinations but the hotel is required to make use of its skills in marketing to overcome the difficulties emerging after its initial location. During pre-location, the hotel planners and designers play an important role and after location the marketers govern the magnitude of success. The seaside resort hotels in Britain relied on the traditional summer holiday market and they were found facing difficulties during 1980s because their location were no longer able to attract the volume of holiday demand for which they were originally located and built. Hotels in Singapore also faced very difficult times in the late 1980s because the influx of tourists considerably increased and this created accommodation problems as the supply of hotel accommodation was non-optimal to the demand anticipated in the feasibility studies. These facts are a mute testimony to this proposition that an appropriate location decision holds a place of outstanding significance because it substantially determines the profitability of hotel operations.

In the Indian hospitality industry, we find so many turning points. After globalisation, we find a significant increase in the hospitality industry. Particularly in the 21st century, we have witnessed good auguries due to high rate of national economic transformation. To be more specific after 2005, we find robust growth in the hospitality industry. We cannot deny that Indian tourism and hospitality sectors continue to remain highly competitive and attractive specially to foreign tourists. It is certainly party time for the hospitality industry in the country.

The hotel planners also have to strengthen their realization that medical or health tourism has played a commanding role in the development of tourism and hospitality. In the global map, India is now regarded as Health Tourist Destination. A study by McKinsey and Confederation of Indian Industries (CII) reveals that at its current pace of growth, healthcare tourism alone can earn over US $ 2 billion additional revenue by 2012. There are certain places in India such as New Delhi and Bangalore evolved as key destinations for cardiac care; Chennai is recognized as a place for superior eye care while Kerala and Karnataka have emerged as hubs for state of the art Ayurveda healing. Now, it is upon the hotel planners to locate budget hotels close to the medical centers. They have to develop surroundings and premises and develop ambience which may help patients and attendants in enjoying the destinations. Health tourism is now over $ 300 mm industry attracting about 1,50,000 patients every year. The demand may increase in future and therefore the hotel planners have to assign due weightage to the development of budget hotels.

Planning for the hospitality industry is, of course, a challenging task. And decisions regarding a suitable location is equally critical. We need to consider the present, we need to turn our eyes to future and in the face of present and future, we can make our location decisions for future much more result-oriented.

HOTEL BUILDING

Construction of building is an important component of hotel planning and development. It is related to the planning of bedrooms, function rooms, restaurant and equipped bar. It is also related to the development of ambience, surroundings and premises. The task of designing is found on the shoulders of architects. They need to keep into consideration the taste and temperament of visiting customers or guests. Of late, we find a significant change in the taste preferences of customers because they now prefer apartments, cottages, old palaces and havelis having historic value. When the architects plan for hotel buildings, it is pertinent that they keep into consideration the likes and dislikes of potential customers.

During yester decades, we have witnessed numerous changes in the lifestyles of people who have developed appreciation for modern amenities and facilities in their houses. Their financial status or spending power has considerably increased. Till 1970s, majority of the people did not install central heating, double glazing, showers, extra bathrooms, extensions, playrooms, wet bars, wall-to-wall carpeting, tiled bathrooms and kitchens. Since the beginning of 1980s, we find a change in the lifestyles which after 1990s gained a rapid momentum and with the beginning of 21st century, we find much more sophistication in the living conditions. Hotel planners must be aware of the emerging trends so that they provide in their hotels even much more sophisticated living conditions.

In the hospitality industry, 'nostalgia'[2] has been found playing an important role and even in future this will continue to play a dominating role. Since long, the sentimental feeling has been found influencing the hotel industry. It is in this context that even today the unusual, nostalgic or historic hotels are getting positive response and even in future, it is likely to continue. The buildings and facilities are not only important but in a true sense it is nostalgia which is prevailing. The hotel planners can develop old palaces or havelis as hotels. The high spending foreign tourists are found fascinated to these types of hotels.

While designing the hotel buildings, a number of factors are to be taken into consideration. The architects are required to be creative and to the extent it is possible they should make space for adding additional attractions and fragrance. Since it is a permanent investment in which we find least scope for alteration and modification, it is essential that the hotel designers keep in their minds cost effectiveness and good returns. They should also make provisions for commercial spaces which would help in generating sustainable revenues. They should make it sure that the hotels are allowed higher Floor Area Ratio Floor Space Index (FAR/FST) so that more rooms are created out for commercial purpose.[3] The safety considerations also need due attention specially in the face of increasing terrorism. Making ways for ensuring crisis management cannot be undermined in the very context.

HOTEL BEDROOMS

While planning for hotel bedrooms, it is significant that the designers keep into consideration all the required amenities and facilities to the guests staying in the bedrooms. The sanitation services, water supply, power supply are some of the sensitive areas where designers need due priority attention. The furnishing, curtains, bedsheets, entertainment services, positioning of light, communication services also become significant. They need to take into consideration the requirements of both the genders. With women participating as business executives, we find them at par with their male counterparts. This is due to the emergence of corporate culture which has been found influencing, the hospitality sector. Women want to avail hotel services like their male counterparts. The taste preferences of women are found different to men. Women often read different publications, magazines and prefer different TV channels. While planning for hotel bedrooms, the planners and designers have to consider the needs and requirements of all the expected guests. The classification and grading of hotel would be an important consideration for the amenities and facilities provided in the hotel bedrooms. In an age of new generation of information and communication technology, the governance and reporting of the functioning and status of bedrooms or other rooms must be foolproof. Wrong reporting may tarnish the image of hotel. The hotel professionals need to make it manually secured that everything is in order and all the systems are working satisfactorily. In a majority of the hotels, we find cleanliness and poor maintenance of water supply creating a major problem.

The hotel planners and designers need to consider the taste preferences of coming generations. In addition, they also need to consider the safety and security provisions. Currently, we find fear psychosis due to terrorism and this makes it essential that while planning and designing, there is enough scope for protecting the guests. Besides, we also find cases of natural calamities and therefore the planners and designers cannot undermine the safety to the guests as and when we find a case like this. The cases of fire may also complicate the problem and therefore while designing, they should make scope for protection of guests and assets of hotel. It is not only significant that we consider just the amenities and facilities because accidents and causalities may occur any day, at any time. We also find cases where faulty supply of power in the bedrooms creates numerous problems. The internet fails in transmitting right information regarding the status of bedrooms and the complaints are not taken seriously because the computers show everything in order. The hotel planners need to make place for ornamental indoor shadow plants, paintings and photographs on wall, the positioning, colour and intensity of light, the quality and volume of music, the colour and quality of bedsheets pillow covers, the colour of wall etc. The bedrooms play an important role in the formation of attitude because we find guests staying their for long duration.

HOTEL FUNCTION ROOMS

With the development of corporate culture, we find a significant increase in the economic activities. The political and social organisations often organise conferences and seminars. The educational institutions also need function rooms on special occasions. The changing social system has promoted organisation of wedding functions in hotels. Thus, all these developments make it essential that hotel companies plan for a function room equipped with all the modern amenities and facilities in addition to the public address system. It is in this context that planning for hotel convention room or hall makes it an essential dimension of hotel planning.

There are a number of aspects for developing a modern convention hall. The hotel planners and designers need to assign due weightage to the installation of communication and information technology of new generation. It is said that the convention business is the back-bone of hotel industry.[4] It benefits a number of segments such as travel and tourist agencies, social and political organisations, business organisations, individuals and above all hotels in the form of profitable business. It is right to mention that in the organisation of conferences and seminars, more than 40 % of the total expenses are found on hotel accommodation for the delegates coming from different places. Thus it proves to be a profit earning head for the hotel business. It is against this background that find we find a number of countries very much instrumental in developing convention as an industry which benefits hospitality sector *vis-a-vis* the tourism industry. The countries like Japan, Singapore, Hawaii, France, Switzerland have been found promoting convention as an industry. This focuses on the marketing of convention business. Currently, we find Americans spending billion of dollars annually for attending conventions. The convention industry has been found significantly contributing to the American economy. Even in the Indian context, we find a positive trend particularly after globalisation when economic activities started gaining a rapid momentum. This draws attention of hotel planners on the development of convention hall or function room.

In the Indian perspective, we find a number of international brands coming to India for business purposes. In Japanese hotels, the hotel convention halls are prepared keeping in view the requirements of business houses. In the Indian context, we find the demand side showing a positive trend and therefore the hotel sector needs to assign due weightage to the development of convention hall. This necessitates a well thought plan for the development of function rooms. Particularly in the Indian perspective, we find even marriage and other social functions organised in hotels. Hence, it is imperative that hospitality industry assigns due weightage to the same. The governmental regulations need to encourage the hotel sector for the development of conference hall.

Thus, the hotel professionals need to plan out strategies for the development of conventional facilities. The hotel planners are required to play here an important role.

HOTEL RESTAURANTS AND BARS

With the changing lifestyles and cultural patterns, we find a change in our food habits and drinking habits. This makes it essential that hotel planners develop their awareness of the multi-dimensional attitudinal transformation in prospects and make available to them the food, drinks and ambience they like. It is in this context that we find management of restaurants and bars essential, specially in terms of food and drink preferences. The corporate culture has made junk foods much more popular. Besides, we find guests also developing temptation for Indian, Chinese and Mexican dishes. If we make an analysis of the pre and post-globalisation period, specially in terms of taste preferences, it is found that a majority of the customers prefer to eat outside as this simplifies their professional commitments. With the increasing participation of working women in the corporate sector, there has been a significant increase in the number of women visiting hotels. In the coming years, we expect this trend becoming much more matured both in terms of schedule and menus. If the hotel professionals are not aware of the incoming changes they would find it difficult to make the restaurants and bars a center for making profits. We expect that normal menus for lunch and dinner would be replaced by light meals and the schedule would also be changed. The corporate people are becoming more conscious to their health and physique which would bring a change in their menus. The multi-dimensional social and technological changes affect the normal meal schedule of lunch between 1 p.m. to 2 p.m. or dinner between 6 p.m. to 7 p.m in America; between 7 p.m to 8 p.m. in Britain; 9 p.m. to 10 p.m. in Spain and 8 p.m. to 9 p.m.

in India. We find a number of people going to work for flexible hours and a large number of them are found going to work in shifts. It is expected that in the coming years, not less than 25% of people would work at home if not at all time, at least part of the time. They may be called home workers comprising of a natural market where they would buy a weekend break meal out in a restaurant. Since we find people working during odd hours, they have no option to eat outside. Hence, the restaurants and bars would have a profitable business.

In view of the above, it is pertinent that restaurants would be required to be much more flexible in design and a varied menu mix is to be popular to benefit people working during odd hours. It is essential that hotel planners keep into consideration designing with flexibility to change the lighting for the different business hours or to cover a self-help buffet on Sundays. The working hours of restaurants and bars would also need a change in tune with the working hours. While managing restaurants, the management of menu is an important decision making area for the hotel professionals. We find a good number of people now preferring spicy food items and therefore a mix of Indian, Chinese and Mexican food may get a positive response. The hotel professionals need an in-depth study of the customers visiting restaurants so that they find themselves in a position to plan for the diverse group of customers. It is to be made sure that in any case the possibilities for menu fatigue are to be sealed. The corporate culture has also influenced our drinking habits. Not only the soft drinks but quality beverages and liquors have become a common choice of corporate youths in general and the software youths in particular. The working girls and women have also been found developing temptation to the drinking culture. We find it an important consideration for the hotel planners and professionals so that restaurants and bars prove to be a point for profit generation. The impact of western culture is found considerably influencing our lifestyles. We find Japanese emerging as heavy consumers of whiskey. In traditional beer drinking countries, we find an enormous swing from traditional beers to lager and real ale. It is important to mention that in Britain in 1981, the proportion of lager sold out of the total beer increased from 9.9 per cent to 30.8 per cent.[5] It was against this background that some of the top managers in Glasgow (Europe) felt that green beer would be a drink of choice in future. A few years back, the young Britons preferred drinking beer standing in the pub. Today, we find a change and they are now found drinking green cocktails in modern restaurants. In America, we find a galloping increase in the sale of wine. The type of wine is now changed as Americans prefer white wine in place of red wine. In addition, we also find a change in the style of drinking. In restaurants, we find a majority of the guests drinking beer like water. Thus, a change in the type and quantity of drinks would affect the investment planning strategies of restaurants and bars. This makes it essential that barmen develop their awareness of the emerging taste preferences. This would help them in preparing quality people and developing bar business.

We consider restaurants and bars most sensitive places in hotels and therefore the barmen, hotel professionals and hotel planners need to keep into consideration the changing taste preferences of customers *vis-a-vis* their health and cases of menu fatigue. A minor mistake may tarnish the image of hotels because this is to result into irreparable losses. They attend restaurants and bars to enjoy, not to invite health problems. We also find cases of food poisoning and associate health hazards. The emergence of a cross cultural society and multi-dimensional imprints of westernized culture on our taste preferences would increase the responsibility of hotel professionals.

In view of the aforesaid facts, it is right to mention that hotel planners have to assign due weightage to the designing and management of restaurants and bars, management of food and drinks management of service ambience, the dresses and uniforms of employees working there in different capacities, maintenance and cleanliness of places where the food items are cooked and served, quality of water served etc.

 HOTEL PERIPHERAL SERVICES

If we wart to make the hospitality industry nationally and globally competitive; if we want to protect and promote the interests of domestic players; if we want to increase the contribution of hotel to the development of national economy, the hotel planners would have to enrich the quality of peripheral services because this helps in adding additional attractions to the hotel product. The hotel professionals need to remember that the core services are the primary benefits that customers seek from the hotel companies. The core services often become a commodity as a service industry matures. The customers expect the firm to be efficacious of providing the same. The result is that the peripheral services often become the way in which the customer heart is won. Hence, it is significant that peripheral services are made innovative which would make the ways for customer satisfaction and retention.

If the customers get supporting services like the availability of transportation facilities to and from the hotels, well developed shopping complex malls, well developed personal care services, adequate space for jogging, co-operation in getting the air tickets, visa and foreign exchange etc., it is natural that the customers would patronize a particular hotel by which these services and facilities are offered. The hotel industry is becoming much more competitive. The global biggies with well established brands have made the Indian hotel markets much more competitive. The intensity of competition will move upward with the entry of new international brands. If hotel planners make professionalised efforts to increase and retain the market share and innovate the peripheral services which are yet to be introduced by the competitor, there will be a significant increase in the number potential customers and creative promotional measures would transform them into actual and habitual customers.

The corporate culture makes ways for personal care and hotels need to offer the same so that the hotel customers make use of the services as a part the aesthetic sense to add additional attractions to their physique. It is essential to look smart and attractive. The hotel planners need to develop different devices for health care. The services like beauty parlours both for men and women, hair dressing and dyeing, facial etc. would lure customers. Besides, they can also make provisions for shopping malls and multiplexes.

The corporatisation has been found gaining a rapid momentum which would inject new life and strength to hotel culture. The hotels innovating peripheral services would be preferred by customers and the possibilities for repeat business would also be increased. Actually, hotel planners and professionals have to be innovative so that the peripheral services prove to be a point of attraction. It is not enough that we make available a room to sleep. It is much more significant that we develop mini-suites with an attractive partition which would be much more useful to the business executives.

FOCUS ON PERSONAL CARE SERVICES

Hotel planners formulating a plan need priority attention on personal care services. The very foundation of corporate culture is found based on attraction. A number of customers coming from different segments stay in hotels. Making hotel a point for additional attraction makes a strong advocacy in favour of different dimensions of personal care services. The hotel planners may think over providing sufficient space for the customers having a temptation for the same. The personal care services include beauty parlour, barber shop, dry cleaners, laundry, garment making and shoe making and polishing and in addition the healthcare services.[6] The hotel complexes may also think in favour of hair dressing, nail trimming, personal hygiene, skin care, aerobics, gym and jogging which would provide additional attractions to the guests staying in hotels.

There is nothing more appealing than a man with a sense of fit and fun. There is nothing more paying than an aesthete.[7] With the growing influence of corporate culture in the process of socio-economic emancipation, we find a basic change in the perception of personalty development. The corporate decision-makers need a look that is different to others. A look that generates a positive image, a look that magnifies optimism, a look that bears the efficacy of coiling the communication excellence and a look that visualises elegance. The potential customers staying in hotels are cine artists, technocrats, bureaucrats, corporate executives, academics requiring personal care services in different ways. Our focus here is on a sound physique with a make up that suits the position that we hold.

The emerging trends in society make it clear that prospects in general are now developing a craze for sophisticated living. If we find an attitudinal change in the potential customers, the hotel planners and professionals need to develop a special wing for such services to lure customers. The constraints related to space and finance can be removed if the hotel planners and professionals think over the issue on a priority basis. Mobilising the financial resources and renovating the hotel buildings are the two important aspects to translate the plans into action. The hotel planners and designers need to formulate a plan for that.

The motive is to make hotel a point of attraction. Hence the planners and professionals may also consider Dental care, Body-weight care, Nutrition, and Yoga. The high spending tourists prefer these services on a regular basis whereas we find occasional demand for such services by selected segments of the society on a special occasion. The services of beauty parlours and beauty clinics are now becoming common and required by even those segments who make use of function hall for engagements or marriages.

The above mentioned facts make it clear that hotel planners while formulating a plan for the development and expansion of hotels should make provisions for personal care services which would be helpful in increasing the occupancy rate. We should not forget that the craze for looking attractive will continue even in the years to come and therefore the personal care services developed in hotels would remain in demand.

PLANNING FOR HOTEL PEOPLE

Of course, we find technology of new generation very much instrumental in developing techni-culture and influencing, our lifestyles however, we cannot devalue the significance of quality human resources in the modern hospitality industry. The hotel professionals need to accelerate the pace of human capital formation. This focuses our attention on the development of quality human resources for the hotel industry. The role of education in hospitality industry is widely recognised as it is one of the top three employers worldwide and its employment base is the largest of any in the private sector. The hospitality industry in India is experiencing party time and the stage of room boom requires quality people in a very large number. We find an exponential demand for the workforce at managerial, supervisory, skilled and semi-skilled levels. The increase in growth will have a direct impact on the demand and supply mismatch that the hospitality industry is already passing through. To bridge the yawning gap particularly at skill-level, the existing Food Craft Institutes are required to be strengthened and new ones opened. To enlarge the scope, the hospitality education needs to be imparted through the network of ITIs, Polytechnics and at the +2 stage as a vocational system. IHMs which have been processing the bulk of manpower managerial skill level need to be strengthened and capacities augmented with international linkages for quality and quantity output of human resources. New IHMs in the states and regions not covered as yet are to be established for proper distribution of government resources. The States, IHMs and PPP mode are to be encouraged.

We need quality human resources for different areas such as general operation, front office, sales and marketing, housekeeping and catering. The Kitchen Executive, Sous Chef, Senior Sous Chef, Executive Sous Chef, Regional Chef, Executive Chef, Waiters, Housekeepers are some of the areas where we need world class human resources. The National Council for Hotel Management and Catering Technology New Delhi, Indian Institute Hotel Management, Aurangabad, Welcome Group Graduate School of Hotel Management, Manipal, Taj Group Hotel, Oberoi Center of Learning and Management and Institute of Hotel Management Catering Technology and Applied Nutrition etc. are some of the institutions offering educational aid and training facilities. We also find foreign hotels evincing keen interests in opening hotel schools.

The motive is to develop quality human resources efficacious of offering quality services to the customers. World class communication excellence and an attractive personality are essential considerations on which the institutions need due focus. With the development of a cross cultural society, it is imperative that we educate and train people in such a fashion that they prove to be an asset and play an incremental role in making the hospitality business profitable.

STRATEGICAL AND TACTICAL MARKETING PLANNING

The more volatile a market in terms of fluctuations in demand, the more important it is to work within a framework of agreed objectives. We cannot deny that increasing scope for development makes ways for volatility. With the increasing heat of globalisation and corporatisation, we find a significant increase in the intensity of competition because a number of International brands have entered the Indian hotel markets to take the competitive advantage. In order to provide an orderly and agreed business on which to conduct its business in an ever changing competitive market environment, any business has to plan its activities. The larger the business, greater the importance of effective planning; the hotel professionals need to strengthen their realisation. They need to focus here on two important aspects, viz., strategical planning and tactical planning for marketing.

Strategical Marketing Planning

For marketing purposes, the marketing planning may be defined as the process whereby an organisation makes an anatomy of its strengths and weaknesses of its current market, devises the position it seeks to attain and defines strategies and cost-effective programme to accomplish the objectives. Strategic decisions are always focused on the long-term consideration because we usually define them three or more years ahead. In the marketing process, we include goals and objectives, image and positioning and budgeting and programming. Larger organisations with multiple products in the multiple markets such as hotel chain requires strategic planning to achieve relationships and allocation of resources between the parts of business. Strategy is essentially proactive as it defines and designs the future shape of an organisation responding to market conditions and perceived needs of customers.

In the set objectives and goals, we know about the place in its market which an organisation seeks to occupy in future in the face of defined target segments, volume of sales product range, market share and profitability. In the context of images and positioning, it is found where an organisation seeks to be in terms of perceptions of retailers and customers about the product and corporate image. In the context of budgeting, we study that what resources are needed to achieve its goals. In the programming, we know in depth the actions required to achieve the goals and objectives expressed in terms of buildings, equipment or plant, people administration, organisational structure and marketing.

In planning for hotel marketing, we find programming an important dimension. Since after the beginning of 21st century, we find an increase in the intensity of competition. The hoteliers are required to take a decision regarding the size of hotel buildings, installation, maintenance and operation of information and communication technology, imparting of training facilities to the hotel staff in the face of changing markets and customers, structuring the organisation, exploring avenues for mergers, acquisitions and consolidations, promoting budget hotels etc. The future shape of hotel is to be defined with the help of strategic marketing planning. Effective relationship and an optimal allocation of resources between the different components are also to be made possible.

Tactical Marketing Planning

We are aware of the fact that tactics are found associated with the decisions focused on the short-run to plan, implement and evaluate specific marketing campaigns. Inevitably, tactics are responsive to market circumstances and competitors actions. The tactical or operating marketing plans include objectives and budget, action, programmes, evaluation and control. The main contribution of marketing is to secure additional marginal sales from targeted buyers at times when rooms are likely to be operating at less than optimum occupancy, reflecting seasonal fluctuations. The tactical decisions of hotel professionals help in achieving or exceeding the target to cope with sudden or dramatic losses of anticipated business due to unpredictable economic or political events. Increasing the occupancy rate is the motive which is influenced by a number of factors. As and when we find an increase in the occupancy rate, the hotel professional get an opportunity to increase the average room rate. This focuses our attention on making tools of sales promotion much more innovative and effective to be instrumental in influencing the short-run purchasing decisions.

In the hotel business, the hotel professionals witness a number of odds due mainly to the high intensity of competition. This may affect the occupancy rate. The sale promotion tactics for accommodation businesses include short-term price discounting used to sell the unsold capacity in an unanticipated condition. The value addition is also a process for promoting the sale which helps marketers in attracting targeted customer segments used to attract business at times of predicted seasonal troughs or a point where we do find low activity. We also find commission as an incentive motivating a retail distribution system and in the hospitality business, the travel agents in particular play an effective role to bridge the gap between demand and supply specially during the off-season. The hotel professionals may take the support of deep price discount to motivate and conclude deals with the third parties such as tour operators and other agents making bulk contracts for the supply of hotel accommodation. The professionals acting as marketers also use the services of sales people for generating additional sales volume. It is not only significant that you offer. It is equally important that you promote or advertise, inform, sensitise, persuade and transform the customers where the tools of sales promotion act as a stimulant.

The hotel professionals need to make an in-depth study of markets that they find themselves in a position to make their tactical decisions result oriented. Tactical use of advertising is also significant with the view point of achieving better communication of promotional offers. How and in what way the hoteliers may be in a position to make the tactical decisions competitive would determine the magnitude of their success. In the Indian perspective, we find a significant increase in the intensity of competition and this makes it essential that hotel professionals plan for tactical marketing which would bring an increase in the occupancy rate.

SUMMARY

You have studied in this chapter, the strategies to be effective while planning for the hotel business. After reading this chapter, be sure that the following facts are well versed:

- **Hotel Planning:** The is related to strategic planning for hotels. Since we expect a number of changes in the marketing environment, it that we have a plan for the future development of hospitality industry. Here we go hotel location, hotel building, hotel bedroom, function room, restaurant and bar and the peripheral services.
- **Hotel Location:** The hotel planners at the very outset would be required to select a suitable place for hotels which is free from all the health hazards. The prospects in general now prefer a place which is calm and quiet.
- **Hotel Building:** The hotel planners would also have to think about the nature, style and type of building for hotels. The prospects have been found tempted to historic and artistic building. Architectural flavour requires due attention of planners.
- **Hotel Bedrooms:** White designing bedrooms, it is essential that the hotel planners keep in mind the needs of the prospects belonging to both the genders because we find a major change in their taste preferences.
- **Hotel Function Room:** The function room or convention hall requires to be well designed and equipped with the sophisticated information and communication technology. The benefits of hybrid technology should be made available to the function room.
- **Hotel Restaurants and Bars:** The hotel planners have to take into consideration a numbers of factors related to the designing and management of restaurant and bar. Since we find a change in the lifestyles, food and drinking habits of customers, it is significant that hotel planners manage them in tune with the emerging changes.
- **Hotel Peripheral Services:** The hotel planners have also to make possible a fair blending of core and peripheral services. They need to remember that the peripheral services often become the way in which the customer heart is won.
- **Hotel People:** The success rate of a hotel is considerably influenced by the quality of people working in different capacities. Waiters, House keepers, Executive, Kitchen executive, Sous chef, Executive Sous chef, Regional chef, Executive chef need proper education and training facilities.

- **Strategical and Tactical Marketing Planning:** The strategical planning for hotel would determine the future shape of a hotel whereas the tactical planning would be effective in luring the customers for the achievement of targeted occupancy rate. The hotel planners need to make it sure with the help of sound strategical and tactical marketing, the hoteliers succeed in increasing the average room rate. Since we find marketing environment becoming much more competitive, the hotel planners need to develop such type hotels which meet the requirements customers and further keep themselves ready use the tact which proves to be proactive.

KEY TERMS

Strategical Plan	Kitchen Executive
Tactical Plan	Sous Chef
Electronic Revolution	Senior Sous Chef
Gym	Executive Sous Chef
Tone-up Area	Regional Chef
Jogging	Executive Chef
Hub	Waiters
Service Ambience	Menu Fatigue
Floor Area Ratio	Gymnastics
Floor Space Index	Average Room Rate
Housekeepers	Occupancy Rate

REVIEW QUESTIONS

1. Explain different aspects to be taken into consideration while planning for the hotel services.
2. Do you find location of hotel an important area while planning for the development of hospitality industry? Justify your opinion.
3. Throw light on the important considerations while designing hotel building for the emerging customers.
4. Explain the development of hotel function room and the relevance of function room in improving the hotel business.
5. Do you find planning for restaurants and bars essential for the hospitality industry? Defend your opinion.
6. Focus on the different aspects to be taken into consideration while developing peripheral services for the hospitality industry.
7. Explain the relevance of strategic marketing planning for the future development of hospitality industry.
8. Do you find personal care services helping hotels in adding additional attractions to the hotel services? Justify your opinion.

9. Do you find strategic planning significant to the hotel chains? Defend your arguments.
10. Throw light on the planning for the development of human resources in the hospitality industry.
11. Explain role of tactical planning for touching the targeted occupancy rate in the hotel industry.

APPLICATION EXERCISES

1. "Location implies accessibility and convenience to customers." In the light of this statement how a location point is to be selected for the establishment of a hotel specially when the cities precincts are in the grip of health hazards. Comment in the capacity of a hotel professional.
2. While designing hotel buildings and hotel bedrooms, we do not consider the needs and requirements of women. Emerging trends show that women are likely to be a profitable segment for the hospitality industry. Focus as a hotelier, the important aspects to be considered while designing hotel buildings and bedrooms.
3. "Convention business is the backbone of the hotel industry." Comment on this statement as a professional and explain the development of function rooms for the hotel business in an age of corporate culture.
4. "With the emergence of a cross cultural society, we find numerous changes in the food and drinking habits of hotel customers." As a hotelier throw light on this statement.
5. "Peripheral services often become the way in which the customers' heart is won." Explain this statement and suggest the important aspects to be taken into consideration while developing the peripheral services by hotels.
6. A hotel chain requires to formulate strategic and tactical plans to increase the hotel business. Comment on this statement in the capacity of a hotelier.

End Notes:

1. Victor T.C. Middleton: *Marketing in Travel and Tourism*; Heinemann Professional Publishing Oxford, 1988, p. 257.
2. Jha, S.M.: *Services Marketing*; Himalaya Publishing House, Mumbai, 2011.
3. Eleventh Five Year Plan: Planning Commission; Government of Indian, New Delhi, pp. 245-51.
4. Anand, M.M.: *Tourism & Hotel Industry in India*; Prentice Hall of India, New Delhi, 1976, pp. 132-33.
5. Melvyn Greene: Marketing Hotels and Restaurants into the 90s; Heinemann Professional Publishing; Oxford, 1989, p. 106.
6. Jha, S.M.: Marketing of Personal Care Services; Planned Selling, Annual Volume, New Delhi, 1989.
7. Jha, S.M.: Looks Make a Man; The Hindustan Times, April 17, 2000.
8. Bhasin Jaya: A Study of Educational Scenario in Hospitality and Tourism Industry; BVMIR Management Edge; Vol. 2/1, January-June, 2006.
9. Eleventh Five Year Plan: Planning Commission; Government of India, New Delhi, p. 250.

....ꙮꙮꙮꙮ....

BIBLIOGRAPHY

American Hotel and Motel Association : Hospitality for Sale, 1980.

American Society of Travel Agents : The Dilemma in Developing Printed Materials for Travel Agents, ASTA, New York, 1974.

Anand, M.M. : Tourism and Hotel Industry in India; Prentice Hall of India, New Delhi, 1976.

Anderson, N. : Work and Leisure; International Library, Sociology, London, 1961.

Andea, R.H. and Diana K.P. : Economics for the Hotel and Catering Industry; B & J Ltd., London, 1977.

Bannett, K. : Consumer Behaviour; Prentice Hall International, 1972.

Brent, Ritchie J.R. and Goeldner, C.R. (Editors) : Travel,Tourism and Hospitality; A Handbook for Managers and Researchers; John Wiley and Sons, New York, 1986.

Burkart A.J. and Medlik S. : Tourism: Past, Present and Future; Heinemann Professional Publishing, Oxford, 1981.

Buttle, F. : Hotel and Food Service Marketing: A Managerial Approach; Holt, Rinehart and Winston, London, 1986.

Clayne R. Jensen : Leisure and Recreation — Introduction and Overview; Philadelphia, 1977.

Colin J. Coulson, Thomas, Collier : Service Management: Operating Decisions; Prentice Hall International, 1990.

Cooper, C.P. : Progress in Tourism Recreation and Hospitality Management; Belhaven, London.

Cowell D. : The Marketing of Services; Heinemann Professional Publishing,Oxford, 1984.

Daltos, A.J. : Protecting Service Markets with Consumer Feedback is Cornell Hotel and Restaurant Administration Quarterly, May 1977.

Davidoff, Davidoff : Sales and Marketing for Travel and Tourism; National Publication,1983.

Davies, A.H.T. : Business Planning in the Thomas Cook Group; *International Journal of Tourism Management*, Vol. 2, No. 2, June 1981.

Donald, E. : Tourism Marketing and Management Issues; Macmillan, Washington, 1980.

Donelly, J.H. : Marketing Intermediaries in Channels of Distribution for Services; *Journal of Marketing*, Vol. 40, January 1976.

Doswell, R. and Gamble, P.R. : Marketing and Planning Hotel and Tourism Projects; B&J London, 1979.

Douglas, Foster : Travel and Tourism Management; Macmillan, London, 1985.

Drucker, P.F. : Management Task and Responsibility, 1973.

Durant, H.W. and D. Thompson : The Problem of Leisure; Current Affairs Bureau,London, 1938.

Edward Anthony : International Tourism Development Forecasts to 1990; The Economic Intelligence Unit, London.

Eiglier P. and D. Langeard, E. : A New Approach to Service Marketing in Marketing Consumer Services, New Insights; Report 77-115, Marketing Science Institute, Boston, 1977.

Fieldman, S. and Thiebar, G.W. : Lifestyles: Diversity in American Society; Berkeley, California, Little B & Co., 1972.

Gerald, W. Lattin : The Moderm Hotel and Motel Management; W.H. Preeman, 1968.

Gray-Liguori : Hotel and Hotel Management; Prentice Hall International, 1990.

Greene, M. : Marketing Hotels and Restaurants into the 90s; Heinemann Professional Publishing, London, 1988.

Heape, R. : Tour Operating Planning Thomson Holidays UK, Tourism Management December, 1983.

Henry, Assael : Consumer Behaviour and Marketing Action, Boston, 1987.

Holloway, J.C. : The Business of Tourism; Pitman, London, 1986.

Housden, J. : Franchising and other Business Relationships in Hotel and Catering Services; Heinemann Professional Publishing, London, 1984.

Jeffries, D.J. : The Role of Marketing in Official Tourism Organisation; Paper to 23rd Congress of AIEST in Tourism etc. Marketing Vol.13,15, Bern, Switzerland, September, 1973.

Jha, S.M. and Singh L.P. : Marketing Management in Indian Perspective; Himalaya Publishing House, Bombay, 1988.

Jha, S.M. : Service Marketing; Himalaya Publishing House, Mumbai, 2009. Tourism Marketing; Himalaya Publishing House, Mumbai, 2009.

Kotas, R. (Ed) : Market Orientation in the Hotel and Catering Industry, Surrey University Press, London, 1975.

Kotas, R. : Management Accounting for Hotels and Restaurants; 2nd Edition; Surrey University Press, 1986.

Kotler, Bloom : Marketing Professional Services; Prentice Hall International, 1984.

Krippendorf, J. : The Holiday Makers; Heinemann Professional Publishing, London, 1987.

Lewis, R.C. : The Positioning Strategy for Hotels; Cornell Hotel Restaurant Administration, Quarterly, Vol. 22, No. 1, May 1981.

Levitt, T. : Marketing Intangible Products and Product Intangibles; H.B.R., May-June, 1981.

Lovelock, C.H. : Services Marketing; Prentice Hall International, 1984 Managing Services, 1988.

Lundberg, Donald, E. : The Hotel and Restaurant Business; Boston, CBI Publication, 1979.

Medlik, S. : The Business of Hotels; Heinemann Professional Publishing; London, 1980. The British Hotel and Catering Industry; London, 1961. Profile of the Hotel and Catering Industry; Heinemann Professional Publishing; London, 1972.

Middleton V.T.C. : Marketing in the Hospitality Industry; Cassee, E. and Reulad, R. (Ed) The Management of Hospitality; Pergaman, Oxford, 1983.

Product Marketing : Goods and Services Compared; Quarterly of Marketing; Vol. 8, No.4, July 1983. Profitability through Product Formulation Strategies in the Practice of Hospitality Management II, AVI Publishing, Conn., 1986.

Neulinger, J. : The Psychology of Leisure; Springfield, 1974.

Nykiel, R.A. : Marketing in the Hospitality Industry; C.B.I. Publishing, Boston, USA, 1983.

Patmore, J.A. : Land and Leisure; David and Charles, London, 1970.

Peters, R. and Austin, N.A. : A Passion for Excellence; Frontana, London, 1986.

Petersen, C. : Promotions Boom in Confusion Marketing; September 1978.

Pundey John : The Thomas Cook Story; Michael Joseph, London, 1933.

Rao, A.V.S. : Services Sector Management in India; Allied, Hyderabad, 1986.

Rathwell, J.M. : Marketing in the Services Sector; Winthrop, Cambridge, 1974.

Reneghan, L.N.: A New Marketing Mix for the Hospitality Industry; Cornell Hotel and Restaurant Administration,Quarterly, August, 1981.

Richard, K. : Recreation and Leisure in Modern Society; M. Corporation, New York.

Rogers, A. and Diana, K.P. : Economics for Hotel and Catering Industry; B&J London, 1977.

Sasser, W.E. and Olson, R.P.: Management of Services Operations; Allyon and Bacon Inc., 1978.

Schmidgall R.S. : Hospitality Industry Managerial Accounting, AHLA, 2002.

Shaffer and Revelshad : Tourism Planning and Development Issues; Washington DC, 1980.

Sharma A and Upneja A : Factors Influencing Performance of Small Hotels, 2005.

Shaw, S. : Air Transport: A Marketing Perspective; Pitman, London, 1979.

Sigaux, G. : History of Tourism, Leisure Arts; London, 1966.

Strong, E.X. : The Psychology of Selling McGraw-Hill (India), New Delhi, 1991.

Taylor, D. : How to sell banquets; Northwood, London, 1979.

Torkildsen, G. : Leisure and Recreation Management; 2nd Edition, London, 1979.

Wheatcroft, S. and Lipman, G. : Air Transport in a Competitive European Market; Economist Intelligence Unit; London, 1986.

Wheatley : Marketing Professional Services; Prentice Hall International, 1983.

Wood, M. (Ed.) : Tourism Marketing for the Small Business; English Tourist Board, London, 1980.

Yukie, T.S. : Fundamentals of Recreation; Harper Row; London, 1963.

Zehuder, L.E. : Florida's Disney World; Promises and Problems; Penninsular, Tallahassee, Florida, 1975.

Journals, Newspapers and Magazines:

The Economic Times, September 7, 2006 January 4, 2007.

The Financial Express, October 12, 2006.

Business Standard, March 2, 2007.

The Analyst, November, 2006.

The Icfaian Journal of Management Research, May, 2008.

Journal of IMS Group, July-December, 2008.

BVIMR Management Edge, January-June, 2006.

Journal of Marketing and Communication, January-April, 2008.

International Journal of Contemporary Hospitality, Vol. 7/7, 1995.

International Journal of Contemporary Hospitality, Vol. 12/1, 2002

Journal of Service Marketing, Vol. 20/1, 2006.

Journal of Marketing, Vol. 60/2, 1996.

Journal of Business Research, Vol. 52/1, 2001.

Journal of the Academy of Marketing Science, Vol. 30/3, 2002.

Websites:

http:www.chennaionline.com/nindex.asp

http:www.hotelbenchmark.com

http://www.ifac.org/Library/Speech Article

http:www.essex.ac.uk/AFM/research/working papers

http:///www.hospitalitynet.org/index.html

www.dominicantoday.com

www.tata.com

www.tajhotels.com

....ജ്ഞജ്ഞ....

SUBJECT INDEX

Words	*Pages*
[A]	
Active Leisure	53, 54
Activity Based Budgeting	309
Activity Based Costing	309
Advertising	144, 156,157, 282
Advertising Agency	158, 162
Advertising Campaign	167
Advertising Strategy	168
AIDA Model	145
AIL List	197
American Management	15
Analytical Marketing System	72
ARR	210
Attitudinal Change	35
Audit	293
[B]	
Behavioural Management	11
Brand Loyalty	173
Brand Stretching	130
Business Environment	310
Buyer Behaviour	39
[C]	
Capital Appreciation	193
Capital-intensive Equipment	51
Cash Recovery	206
Catchment Area	53, 232
Chalet Facility	5
Chance Trade	59
Channel	219
Circulation	159
Code of Conduct	191
Competitive Innovation	280
Conditioning	31
Consumer Orientation	150
Corporate Culture	16
Corporate Identity	258
Corporate Image	258
Corporatisation	49, 63, 297, 314
Cost-effectiveness	282
Creativity	142
Crisis Management	193
Cross-fertilised	189

Culture 130
Customer Psychology 296
Customer Satisfaction Analysis 99
Customisation 137, 262

........[D]........

Decoupling 255
Demand Generation 315
Desk Research 82
Differentiation 167
Direct Marketing 262
Direct-response Marketing 309
Direct Sales Technique 54
Discretionary Income 29, 41, 64, 190
Disposable Income 29
Distribution Chain 221
Distribution Strategy 240

........[E]........

E-CRM Strategy 109,308, 230, 246, 254
E-Commerce Portals 89
Economic Recession 313
Economic Transformation 41
Electronic Revolution 124, 189
Emotional Labour 261
Empathy 36, 100, 148
Envy 33
Etiquette Management 290
European Plan 202
Expression Techniques 152
Extended Product 127

........[F]........

FAR 4, 211
Fear Psychosis 20
Field Research 82
Fixed Cost 240
Floating Hotel 6
Focal Point 289
Forecasting 110
Forward Segmentation 61
Function Room 4
Futurologist 206

........[G]........

GDP 313
Generating attraction 35
Generation Gap 314
Global Biggies 255, 265
Globalisation 3, 50
Going Rate Policy 205

........[H]........

HOE Model 161
Hospitality 2
Hotel Product 118
Hubbert Formula 200
Hybrid Technology 287, 289

........[I]........

Indian Hospitality Sector 117
Industrial Transformation 10
In-house Selling 226
Innovative Services 18

Internal Gap 105
Internal Variables 189
Inventory Management 308
Itineraries 225

........[K]........

Knowledge Gap 105

........[L]........

League Tables 196
Learning 30
Liberalisation 3
Lifestyle 31, 32, 55
Logo 129

........[M]........

Managerial Proficiency 10
Market Information System 69
Market Penetration 205
Market Segmentation 49, 50
Market Slump 210
Marketing Activity Review 295
Marketing Audit 294
Marketing Environment 294,295
Marketing Information System 14
Marketing Intelligence System 71, 89
Marketing Research 72, 82, 85
Marketing Strategy 274
Market-oriented Approach 127
Media Decision 159
Media Planning 167
Media Selection 159
Mental Relaxation 33
Menu Fatigue 59
Merchandising 176
Microscopic Audit 316
Motel 5
Motivational Research 83

........[N]........

Non-customers 27
Non-verbal Communication 150, 241
NOP 292

........[O]........

Occupancy Ratio 19, 43, 64, 96, 127
Open Sky Schemes 307
Operational Flow 287
Optimal Inflationary Pressure 64
Optimism 3, 108,313
Oral Publicity 146

........[P]........

Package Holiday 218
Pareto Principle 145
Perception 37
Perception Gap 105, 107
Performance Evaluation 81
Peripheral Message 160
Perishability 119
Personal Selling 142,144, 147
Personal Skill 153
Points-of-sale 220
Potential Customers 27, 50, 54
PPP Mode 21, 94, 116
Premium Strategy 208

Price Deregulation 193
Price Escalation 210
Price Mix 284
Price-sensitive Customers 13
Price Sensitivity 56
Pricing Strategy 187
Priority Club 236
Product Innovation 116, 282
Product Life Cycle 123, 124
Product Line 133
Product Mix 133
Product Positioning 203
Product Strategy 120, 134
Product-Market Strategy 121
Profit Maximisation 204
Promotion 143,144
Promotional Budget 190
Prospects 10
Psychographic 55
Psycholocomotion 37, 38
Psychological Terms 26
Psychology 148
Psychopobia 89,305
Public Relations 170
Publicity 142, 144, 172

........[Q]........

Qualitative Transformation 87

........[R]........

Racial Tension 15
Rack Rate 192
Readership 159
Recall Test 166
Recognition Test 166
Reference Groups 28
Rejuvenating 125
Resort Hotel 6
Restructuring 125
Result Data 71
Result-oriented Strategy 312
Rip-off Strategy 208
Rub-off Effect 307

........[S]........

Sales Promotion 142,144,172,173
Sales Test 166
Screening Process 128
Selling 148
Sensitive Marketing Strategy 51
Service Ambience 43
Service Delivery 99
Service Differentiation 265
Service Environment 103, 263
Service Mapping 265, 288
Service Product 119
Service Quality 94
Servicescapes 259
SERVQUAL 101
Shelf Life 7
Short Break Market 53
Shoulder Periods 233
Signposting 228

old Required 2016 HPH 45843/

Simultaneous Analysis 61
Skimming the Cream 205
Social Skill 154
Social Transformation 53
Socio-economic Transformation 16
Socialisation Process 265
Sociologists 28
Soft Culture 130
Spin-off 79
Standard Gap 106
Steady Approach 236
Stimulus Response 39
Strategic Decisions 120, 190, 275
Supernatural Forces 2
Synchronisation 288

........[T]........

Tactical Price 193
Tangibalisation Process 43, 100, 256, 288
Tangible Heritage 130
Tangible Products 119
Tax Concessions 306
Technical Quality 95, 108
Techno-driven Process 278
Tech-savvy 252
Tele-marketing 177, 229
Test Marketing Strategy 129
Third Wave 15
Threshold Barrier 304
Tour Operator 222
TQM 108
Transcendental Priority 10
Transformation Process 34, 37
Travel Agents 224
Two-level Channel 241

........[U]........

Uniform Accounting System 198
Unpolished Customers 35

........[V]........

Value Orientation 290
Variable Cost 240

........[Z]........

Zero Level Channel 241, 244